whole Car catalog

By The Editors Of Consumer Guide®

A Fireside Book Published by Simon and Schuster

CONTENTS

Louis Weber, President
Publications International, Ltd.
3841 West Oakton Street
Skokie, Illinois 60076

Manufactured in the United States of America
1 2 3 4 5 6 7 8 9 10

Library of Congress Cataloging in Publication Data

Main entry under title:

Whole car catalog.

(A Fireside book)
Includes index.
1. Automobiles — Maintenance and repair.
I. Consumer guide.
T1152.W512   629.28'8'22   77-10991
ISBN 0-671-23022-0

A Fireside Book
Published by Simon and Schuster
A Division of Gulf & Western Corporation
New York, New York 10020

COVER DESIGN: Frank E. Peiler. COVER ILLUSTRATIONS: Bruce Hawkins. COVER PHOTO: Lincoln-Mercury Division, Ford Motor Company. TECHNICAL ILLUSTRATIONS: C. A. Moberg.

CONSULTANT: Robert R. Duncan, Acting Coordinator, Automotive Technology Apprenticeship Program, Oakton Community College, Morton Grove, Illinois.

ACKNOWLEDGEMENTS: Our thanks to Crawford Auto Parts, Chicago, Illinois, for allowing us to take photographs of various automotive products; to Champion Spark Plug Company for the photographs on spark plug conditions used in the section on Evaluating and Installing Spark Plugs in the Ignition System chapter; and to Cadillac Motor Car Division of General Motors Corporation for allowing us to reproduce the line drawing for the Parts Locater Guide.

Publications International, Ltd., has made every effort to ensure accuracy and reliability of the information, instructions and directions in this book; however, it is in no way to be construed as a guarantee, and Publications International, Ltd., is not liable in case of misinterpretations of the directions, human error or typographical mistakes.

EXHAUST SYSTEM 88

Ignoring your exhaust system can be hazardous to your health. A system that is operating properly keeps the car quiet and its passengers alive. A flashlight and a screwdriver are all you need to make an inspection of your exhaust components.

FUEL SYSTEM 96

Dirt is the biggest enemy of the fuel system. A clogged fuel filter could bring your car to a halt. The life of your engine could be shortened by a faulty PCV valve. Do you know how to keep your fuel system clean and obtain the maximum miles per gallon from your car?

IGNITION SYSTEM 125

Spark plugs are the business end of the ignition system. When they are worn out, your engine will misfire, be difficult to start, waste gas and lack the pep and performance that was designed into it.

TRANSMISSION, DIFFERENTIAL AND REAR AXLE 169

With reasonable care, an automatic transmission will remain in sound condition for the life of the car. Maintenance is simple — change the transmission fluid and filter at recommended intervals.

STEERING AND SUSPENSION 186

If your car bounces up and down several times after you apply the brakes, your shocks are probably in poor condition. When replacing one, it is a good practice to replace both shocks on an axle.

BRAKES 205

From a safety standpoint, the brake system is the most important system on your car. It is possible to have nearly worn out brakes and not know it until it is too late. Prevention is a simple inspection.

TIRES 230

The cost of keeping good quality tires on your car could as much as double if you fail to give them the attention they deserve. Twenty percent of every dollar spent on tire replacement is the direct result of overinflation or underinflation.

AUTO CARE...................240

A great deal of what you do in the care of your car will determine whether you will be preventing or correcting trouble. Preventive maintenance is cheaper!

BODY REPAIR 260

Most new cars need minor body repair the minute they leave the dealer's showroom. Chipped paint, small scratches and other minor defects can be the breeding ground for major corrosion.

TOOLS 280

Don't let do-it-yourself do you in. Give yourself every break by having the proper tools and safety gear on hand. Faulty tools are a hazard.

TROUBLE-SHOOTING CHARTS 284

Diagnosing car troubles is half the battle. Many automotive problems can be corrected by the do-it-yourselfer.

HOW TO BUY A BETTER USED CAR ..290

Put your new-found knowledge to work for you. The main thing to keep in mind when buying a used car is that "you are buying someone else's trouble." Here is how to find out what the trouble is.

AUTO REFERENCES AND INFORMATION 298

DIRECTORY OF MANUFACTURERS ...302

GLOSSARY 307

INDEX 316

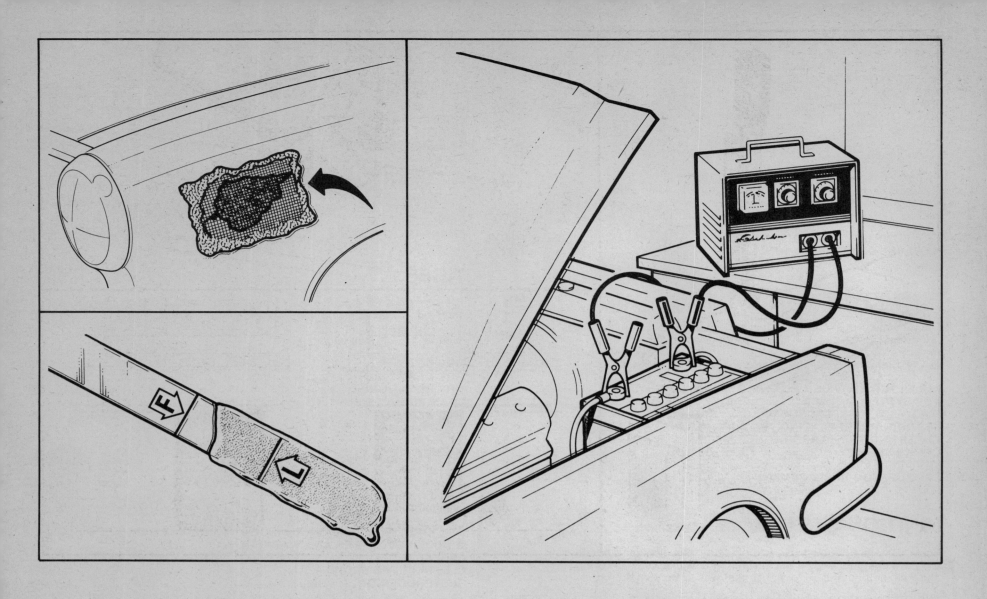

BE YOUR CAR'S BEST MECHANIC

THE BEST mechanic your car will ever have is probably staring back at you in your bathroom mirror each morning. Whether you are an accountant, secretary, banker or nurse and lack the touch of a neurosurgeon or the strength of a blacksmith, you are able to master more car repairs than you believe possible.

Overcoming fear and gaining confidence is a way car owners can save considerable cash. The thing that keeps most people from saving money by doing their own car maintenance and repairs is fear — fear that they will bungle the job and later will have to resort to a professional mechanic to repair the damage at an even stiffer price. Another fear is that the modern automobile is an inscrutable mechanical beast requiring the deft hands of an engineering genius to tame. Nothing could be further from the truth.

Once the world of nuts and bolts was considered "off limits" to women. Today, more and more women are finding that servicing a car is much easier than they believed and actually can be enjoyable. And, there is no denying the feeling of security when you know more about your car and how it functions.

Car owners — men or women — can learn how to save valuable time by doing their own repairs. You can eliminate the need to get on a service station's "waiting list." Instead, why not do the work at your convenience — not someone else's.

The WHOLE CAR CATALOG is NOT written for the master mechanic. It has been planned and designed by automotive experts for the average car owner, and a quick glance through the contents will prove that there is indeed plenty the average man or woman can do to save money.

By exercising talents you may never have suspected you have, you can save hundreds of dollars a year by performing many of your own auto repairs and maintenance chores. For example, an engine tune-up that may cost $70 or more at a professional garage can be self-performed for about $20. Even simple tasks like changing an air filter or windshield wiper blades will mean immediate cash savings for you.

Professional Car Care Is Costly

THE CAR repair industry is undergoing drastic changes. The cost of professional auto care is high and getting higher all the time. Even with elevated prices, obtaining quality service is becoming more and more difficult. Even routine maintenance such as an oil change or engine tune-up is disappearing from the list of services normally offered by many service stations. And, as a growing number of stations become places to purchase gasoline only, the average motorist must search out alternatives to keep his or her car running efficiently.

Today, the average American car owner spends about $350 a year on maintenance and repair. But as with all averages, it means that there are those who spend only a hundred dollars and those who splurge a thousand dollars on car care. How much YOU will spend depends on how much you care about your car and whether you are willing to get a little grease under your fingernails to keep money in your pocket.

Car owners who remain unaware of how their vehicles function

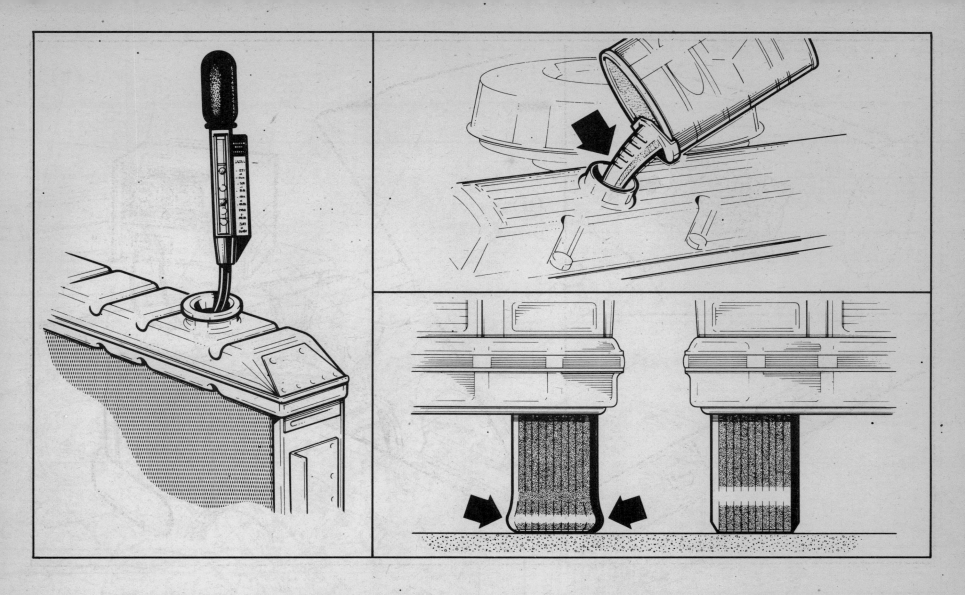

are at a serious disadvantage. They could be jeopardizing an investment of many thousands of dollars, plus their safety as well as that of their passengers. If an owner ignores regular oil changes, for example, the useful lifespan of a car can be reduced from 100,000 miles to as little as 50,000 miles due to excessive engine wear. Tire manufacturers' studies show that 20 percent of every dollar spent on replacement tires is the direct result of simple overinflation or underinflation.

Virtually any automobile mechanic you encounter began his career as a do-it-yourselfer. He tried it, liked it, and continued his automotive education. If you are still exploring career opportunities, the WHOLE CAR CATALOG may be one step in the right direction for you.

A Unique Publishing Achievement

THE WHOLE CAR CATALOG is a unique publishing achievement that includes the most common — and some not so common — problems that can afflict your car. It covers the gamut of automotive repair from fixing a flat to relining drum brakes in a simple, easy-to-understand, step-by-step format that will guide the most inexperienced car owner from start to finish.

The "how-to" of auto repair, however, is only part of the WHOLE CAR CATALOG story. What tools, parts and materials should you use to do a job right? The WHOLE CAR CATALOG not only tells you what to do and how to do it, it also is the ONLY auto repair book that presents the tools, parts and materials to do the job with.

Two graphic features — a Parts Locater Guide and a series of Trouble-Shooting Charts — take away the mystery and help pinpoint symptoms to specific components. A bonus section shows you how to use the valuable maintenance and repair information in the WHOLE CAR CATALOG to your advantage in buying a used car.

The WHOLE CAR CATALOG is arranged in an easy-to-follow format with chapters covering the major automotive systems: Battery and Starting; Charging; Accessories; Lubrication; Cooling and Heating; Exhaust; Fuel; Ignition; Transmission, Differential and Rear Axle; Steering and Suspension; Brakes; Tires; Auto Care; Body Repair; and Tools.

Each chapter explains and outlines specific projects that the average car owner can do for himself. Well-planned, easy-to-read directions, and outstanding line drawings and photographs clearly depict important steps. Not every car repair job, of course, should be performed by the home mechanic. Some require special, costly equipment or expertise. The WHOLE CAR CATALOG frankly lets you know which tasks are best left to professionals. Despite this, some of these complex repair jobs can still be inspected by the backyard mechanic to determine the exact nature of the problem so that when the car is brought to a mechanic, the car owner will be able to discuss the repairs intelligently. There is great satisfaction and a big advantage in being able to tell a mechanic precisely what is wrong and exactly what you expect him to do. It is one way to avoid having needless and often costly servicing performed.

Quick-Reference Maintenance Guide

IT IS highly unlikely that your car will require all of the repair projects covered in the WHOLE CAR CATALOG. And, many of the projects are purely preventive maintenance which should be done periodically. To this end, we strongly suggest that you program yourself into seasonal and monthly car care projects. Turn to the Quick-Reference Maintenance and Lubrication Guide on page 241. Here you will find a handy reminder as to when different projects should be performed to keep your car operating safely and efficiently.

Although there are many products in WHOLE CAR CATALOG, readers are advised that, in many cases, tools, parts and materials of equivalent quality are also available. If you cannot locate the specific product recommended, read the description and go shopping. You may well be able to find comparable products at your local retailer.

As you might expect, your nearby auto supply outlet is the most logical place to find and purchase most of the products recommended in the WHOLE CAR CATALOG. Manufacturers whose products are in wide distribution — and such distribution was one of the factors weighed in selecting products — generally will not sell direct to consumers. If you cannot track down a particular product or one of comparable quality, you can write to the manufacturer and ask where you can obtain the item in your area. The WHOLE CAR CATALOG provides a directory of manufacturers' addresses covering the makers of products recommended in this volume.

The first step in any auto servicing job is overcoming fear and gaining the confidence to do your own car maintenance and repairs. It is the key to saving considerable money. And, like the journey of 1000 miles, all it takes to begin is that first step.

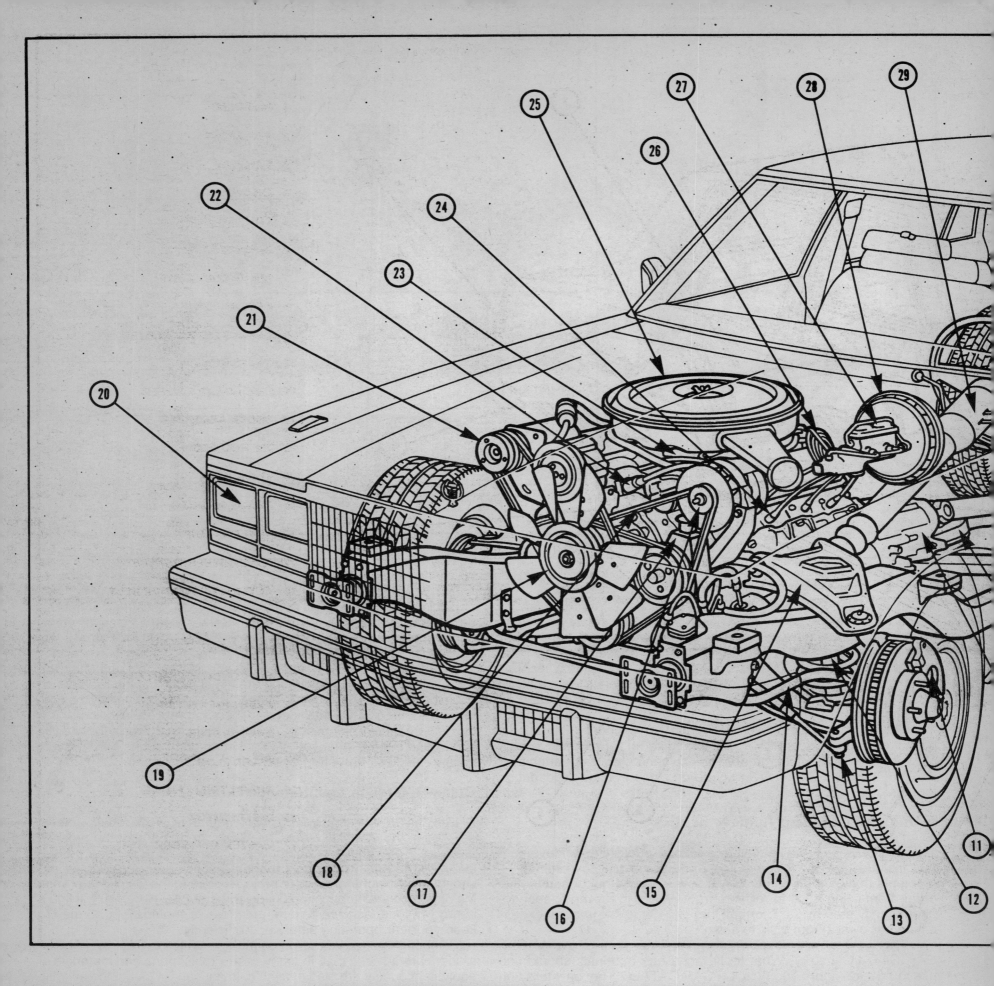

PARTS LOCATER GUIDE

THERE ARE more than 100 million cars on the road in America today. Over six million more are being built each year. For millions of people, hardly a day goes by when they do not see hundreds, if not thousands, of cars. Despite the fact that cars are so much a part of our everyday lives, they remain a mystery to most of us.

For some people, the engine compartment of the modern automobile is frustrating. It simply overwhelms them. Once they raise the hood, all they see is a jungle of wiring, a maze of belts and pulleys, and sinister-looking parts in between.

Which belt is the one that drives the car's water pump? Which one handles the air conditioner's compressor? Where is that carburetor? (It is supposed to be somewhere in the middle!) Which of those round things is the starter motor?

Most people probably have not taken a really good look at the underside of their car — or any car for that matter. Most likely they failed to take the opportunity to watch a mechanic lubricate their vehicle on a hydraulic lift or see which parts are concealed behind a brake drum or the dashboard, or hidden under the air filter.

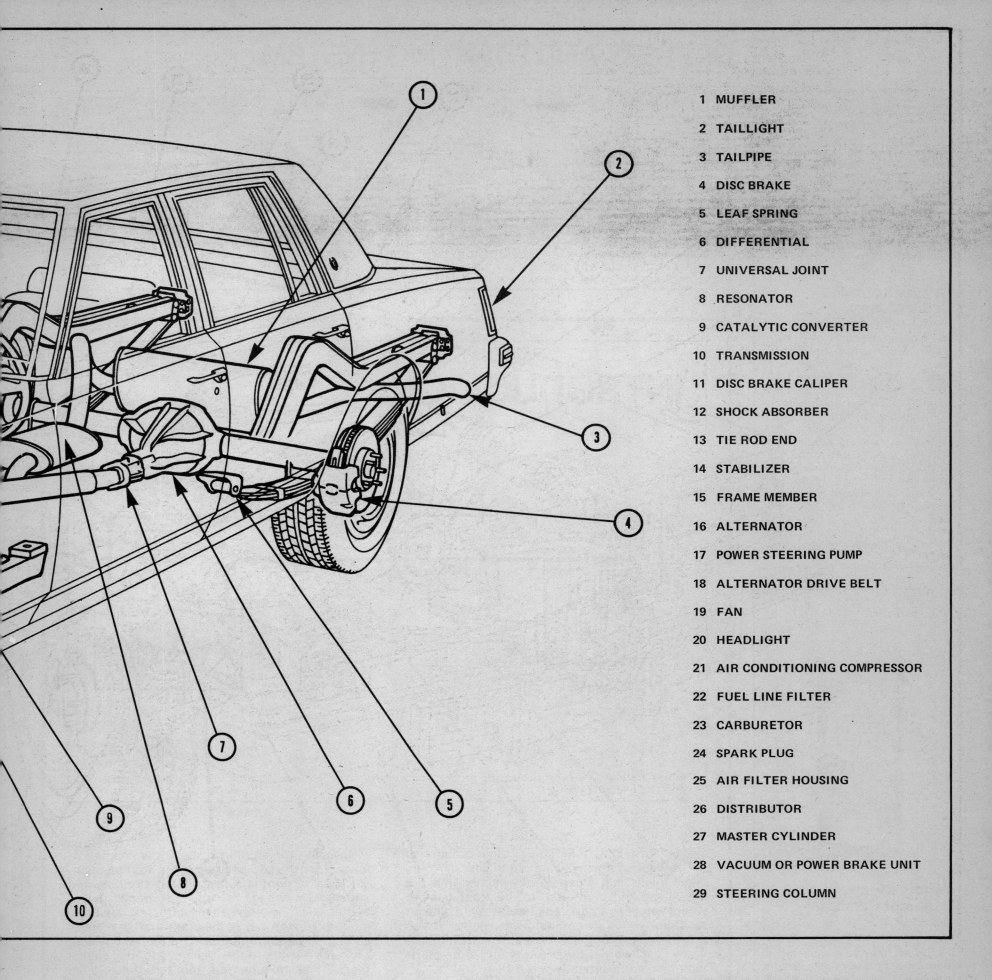

1 MUFFLER

2 TAILLIGHT

3 TAILPIPE

4 DISC BRAKE

5 LEAF SPRING

6 DIFFERENTIAL

7 UNIVERSAL JOINT

8 RESONATOR

9 CATALYTIC CONVERTER

10 TRANSMISSION

11 DISC BRAKE CALIPER

12 SHOCK ABSORBER

13 TIE ROD END

14 STABILIZER

15 FRAME MEMBER

16 ALTERNATOR

17 POWER STEERING PUMP

18 ALTERNATOR DRIVE BELT

19 FAN

20 HEADLIGHT

21 AIR CONDITIONING COMPRESSOR

22 FUEL LINE FILTER

23 CARBURETOR

24 SPARK PLUG

25 AIR FILTER HOUSING

26 DISTRIBUTOR

27 MASTER CYLINDER

28 VACUUM OR POWER BRAKE UNIT

29 STEERING COLUMN

Well, you now have an opportunity to get to know your car intimately. Across these pages is the WHOLE CAR CATALOG's Parts Locater Guide which pinpoints many of the components of the typical automobile's major systems. More detailed views will be found within the chapters dealing with these systems. In using this book, you will learn which systems are mainly confined to one area of your car, which are not, and which systems are interrelated.

The WHOLE CAR CATALOG will explain how each system functions and which systems the home mechanic can tackle. For some, such as the ignition system, you will be able to install a distributor, breaker points and condenser, ignition coil, spark plugs and spark plug wires. In addition, you will be able to adjust your engine dwell and timing, and test its vacuum and compression.

On other systems, such as the transmission, differential and rear axle, there is less repair work you can handle. Major repairs in this area of your car are better left to the professional mechanic who has the expertise and special equipment required for such work. So, projects in this particular chapter will primarily deal with inspections of components to help you determine the nature of the problem or to avoid one. But you will be able to trouble-shoot the drive shaft, universal joints and clutch.

The Parts Locater Guide, as well as detail drawings of various systems within each chapter, will save you considerable time and effort. Take the time to study them so you will be able to go right to the component for servicing. And, be sure to read the complete procedure for any project before actually beginning so that you understand what you will be doing.

Do not let the number of auto components and systems overwhelm you. It is hardly likely that your car will ever need repairs in all the areas covered within the scope of the WHOLE CAR CATALOG. Many of the projects are purely preventive maintenance and only require your confidence, a little time and some tools.

Pull Off Corroded Cable Clamps

Using the wrong tools to remove a battery terminal has resulted in a cracked battery case more times than we care to think about. K-D Manufacturing Company is one of several companies that offers the right tool for this job. K-D's battery terminal puller, Model 202, features extra-sharp points on its jaws for getting under the corroded clamp—including spring types—so that you can safely lift the clamp off without breaking or damaging the battery post. The teeth dig into the sides of the clamp in situations where getting under the clamp proves impossible.

Battery Cleaner And Protector Combats Corrosion

If you wish to avoid manual labor, there are battery terminal cleaners available in spray cans that can blast away corrosion. Unival Corporation makes one called Hi-Power Battery Terminal Cleaner and Protector. It is formulated to dissolve acid buildup, corrosives, grease and oil deposits on battery cases, terminals and hold-down assemblies. The spray also leaves a protective film to combat the buildup of those nasty substances that reduce electrical contact between the battery terminal and clamp. If you let your battery accumulate a great deal of corrosion, you may still have to do a bit of scrubbing, but regular use should help you avoid muscle work. The spray comes in both 5 and 15 ounce spray containers.

Electric Tester Locates Shorts In Electrical Circuits

Without a good electric tester, you could spend all day looking for a short in your electrical system and draw a blank. But by using a tester, such as the one offered by Blackhawk Hand Tools, finding electrical problems is a snap. This needle-point type circuit tester is easy to use. You attach its ground clip to the car and probe the suspected circuit with the needle point. If the circuit has power, a small bulb lights in the transparent handle. The instrument, Model ET-3000, can be used anywhere you are looking for electrical trouble: on batteries, ignition wires, lamp circuits, starter coils, switches, exterior and interior lights.

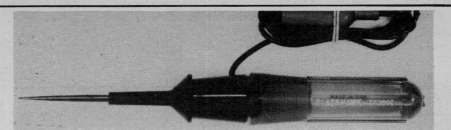

INTRODUCTION

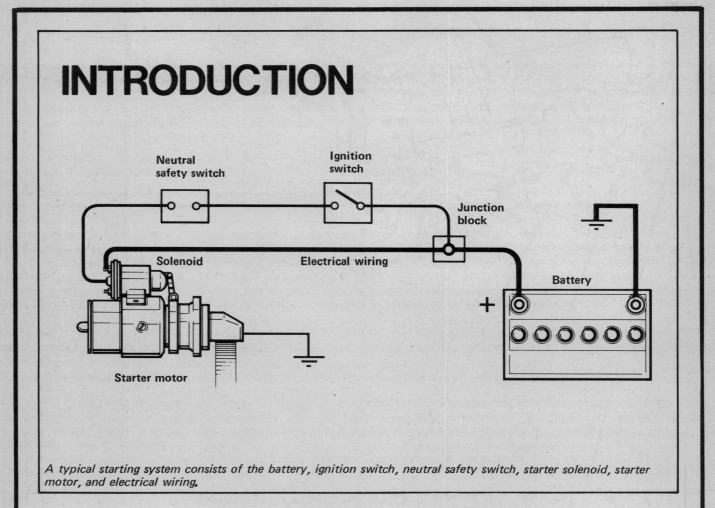

A typical starting system consists of the battery, ignition switch, neutral safety switch, starter solenoid, starter motor, and electrical wiring.

PICTURE YOURSELF on a cold morning half a century ago, walking out to your car. You climb inside, flip a couple of switches, move a few levers and then stroll to the front bumper where you grab a big crank handle. With all your strength, you start cranking the engine. If you are lucky, the engine—instead of kicking the crank backwards to break your arm—starts chugging and continues to run.

For most of us in this day and age, this is even hard to imagine. There is not even a hole through which to insert a crank handle. Even if there were, most engines are too big and have too much compression to turn over by hand. Thanks to a big starter motor plus a strong battery to power it, we get it all done with a twist of the key.

Indeed, the electric starter is credited with having put women (and many men, too, for that matter) behind the wheel.

The Starting System

THE COMPONENTS of the starting system are: battery, neutral safety switch, ignition switch, starter solenoid, starter motor, and electrical wiring.

Basically, the starting system operates as follows: when the key is turned to the start position, electrical current is sent to the starter solenoid and battery voltage is supplied directly to the starter. The starter then turns a flywheel mounted on the rear of the crankshaft that starts all engine parts in motion. The ignition system provides a spark to the spark plugs that ignites the air/fuel mixture from the carburetor. If all components are in good working condition, the engine should start right up. Here are the essential parts of the starting system:

1. THE BATTERY. The heart of the electrical system is the battery. If you were to narrow the functions of the battery down to one, it would be to provide the electrical energy to operate the starter motor and ignition system to start the car. Today it is also called upon to power a couple of dozen lamp bulbs, the windshield wipers, washers, taillight switch, heater, and defroster blower—and possibly radio, tape deck, CB, electric windows, electric seats, and electric door locks.

The battery does not store electricity; it stores chemicals and metals that interact

Get A Good Grip On Your Battery Work

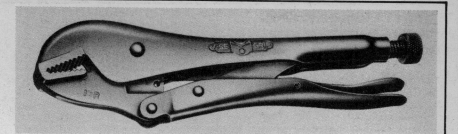

The Vise-Grip locking hand tool —in either the straight jaw (Model 10R) or curved jaw (Model 10CR) style—can make tough jobs a breeze. Just place the jaws around whatever you want to tighten or loosen and lock the Vise-Grip in place. Available from Petersen Manufacturing Company, the tool will not slip or let go until you press the release trigger. A special micro-adjustment screw, moreover, allows you to adjust the pliers' action or locking pressure to the exact degree required. Vise-Grip locking hand tools are made of high-grade alloy steels and finished with a bright nickel plating.

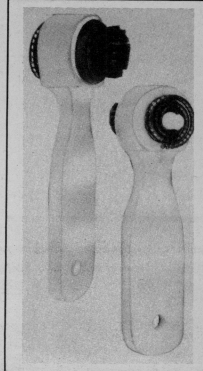

Cleaning Tool For Side Terminal Batteries

If your car has a side terminal battery, you may want to pick up a side terminal cleaner. These cleaners work better and faster than tools designed for conventional batteries with the terminals mounted on top. Lisle Corporation has a one-piece side terminal battery cleaner, Model 11400, with coil spring cutters that polishes the battery contact while stainless steel brushes clean corrosion off the cable terminals. Both the coil spring cutter and the stainless steel brushes are rust resistant and rinse clean under hot water. Since both parts are attached to the one-piece handle, there are no extra parts to lose.

---

to produce electricity upon demand. The colder the weather or the lower the charge of the battery, the less capability the battery will have to do its job. A fully charged battery at 80°F will deliver only about 65 percent of its power at 32°F and only 40 percent at 0°F. Unfortunately, the time when the battery is in its weakest condition, in extreme cold, is the time when it is confronted with its heaviest burden— cranking a stiff engine. For this reason, it is advisable to pay special attention to the battery during the cold weather.

When your battery lets you down, it is probably due to one of four reasons: you have problems in the charging system; it is getting old; it is not big enough to do the job on your car; or you have some bad connections. The battery should not always be blamed for starting system trouble, however. It could be that your terminal connections are corroded, you might have a bad ground, or your engine might need a tune-up. Be sure that the battery is the culprit before investing in a new one.

2. THE NEUTRAL SAFETY SWITCH. This switch allows the starting system to be operated only when the transmission gearshift lever is in the neutral or park position. This switch is also called a starting safety switch.

3. THE IGNITION SWITCH. The ignition switch generally has four positions: accessories, off, on, and start. On most cars, the Off position will also lock the steering wheel with the transmission in park. The first three positions of the ignition switch will automatically stay in position when the key is turned there. The start position, however, is like a momentary contact switch. It has to be held there to crank the engine.

4. THE STARTER SOLENOID. The solenoid connects the battery to the starter by principles of magnetism. Electrical windings are wrapped around a hollow core and an iron plunger is placed partially in the area. When the key is turned to Start, a magnetic field is created and pulls the plunger into the core. The plunger touches two contacts and connects the circuit between the battery and starter. Some solenoids, such as those used on General Motors, Chrysler,

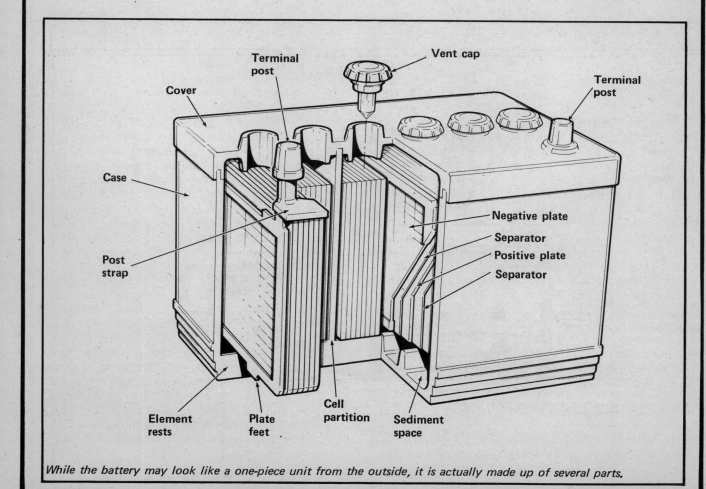

While the battery may look like a one-piece unit from the outside, it is actually made up of several parts.

Battery Filler Eliminates Messy Filling Jobs

Filling battery cells can be a messy job. If you are not careful, you can end up with more water on top of the battery than in it. J-Mark Quality Products, Inc. offers an automatic battery filler that helps prevent overfilling and water spillage. The battery filler pours only when the spring-loaded spout tip is pressed in, and shuts off automatically when the pressure is released. The company's battery filler is constructed of unbreakable polyethylene and will not scratch or mar auto finishes.

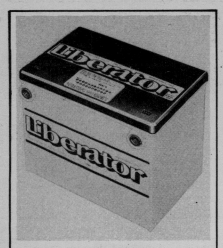

Battery Comes In Two Styles

Liberator batteries from The Prestolite Company are shipped with electrolyte inside; therefore, there is no need to add any acid. The Liberator's lead-calcium grid alloy is designed to reduce water loss and terminal corrosion. Available with either side or conventional terminals, the Liberator features a polypropylene container and cover for exceptional strength and impact resistance.

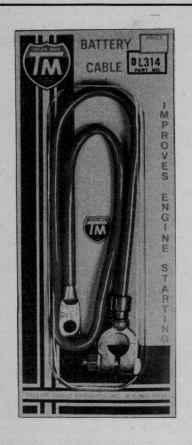

Cables Feature Tough Insulation

Duraflex is the name Taylor Cable Products, Inc. uses for its tough flexible PVC plastic insulation that helps resist acids, gasoline, oil, and abrasives. The terminal bites into this insulation in a process Taylor calls "Swedge/Bond" construction, insuring that the copper conductors are protected from acid fumes. The universal tapered hole assures that the cable terminal will make full surface contact with both positive and negative posts.

Highway Emergency Kit Includes Battery Jumper Cables

Breaking down on the highway can be frustrating, expensive, and sometimes dangerous. The Carter Hall Company sells a bag of goodies called the Executive Highway Emergency Kit that can be helpful when you find yourself in a tough spot. The contents, contained in a simulated leather case, include items that can save a tow (jumper cables), to products that can save your entire car if a fire becomes the problem. Besides the cables, which are eight-feet long and have copper-plated steel clamps, the kit includes: an aerosol tire inflator, a U/L approved 2 B:C fire extinguisher, a battery-operated emergency blinker, a spotlight that plugs into your cigarette lighter, a tire gauge, and a gas siphon-pump. It also includes a handy first-aid pouch, SOS pennant, a "Need Gas" banner, a first-aid book, and an instruction sheet that tells you how to use everything. Ask for Model 650.

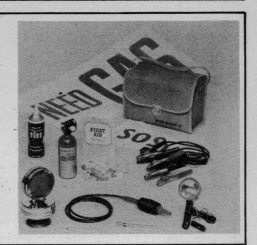

INTRODUCTION

and some late model Ford products are also used to engage the drive mechanism. The plunger is connected to a shift lever that engages the starter drive gear with the flywheel.

5. THE STARTER MOTOR. The starter motor is a direct-current motor that develops high torque for short periods of time. A starter may draw several hundred amperes of current when it is in operation. For this reason, the wiring in the starter must be of good quality and in good condition.

6. THE ELECTRICAL WIRING. The wiring in a car is of different types and gauges and is designed to do specific jobs. When replacing a piece of wire on your car, it should be replaced with wire of the same type, length and gauge. If the new wire is longer or of too thin a gauge, it will increase the resistance or give you poor conductivity, which can have a detrimental effect on some parts of your electrical system.

It is not unlike putting the wrong kind of replacement wire on a toaster. The manufacturer originally installed a particular length of heavy-duty gauge wire on the toaster in order to provide a given amount of current into the toaster to do its job. If you shorten it or if you connect it to a lightweight extension cord, you could run into problems ranging from untoasted bread to an electrical fire.

Your best bet when replacing a wire on your car is to take a piece of the wire you are replacing to your auto parts store and ask for an identical replacement. Be sure the insulation of the wire you are buying is at least as good as the wire you are replacing.

Good connections in your circuit are essential. Whenever possible, you should have soldered connections or good, secure solderless connections. When tightening a nut type connection, always use a lock washer or an internal tooth lock washer. A loose electrical connection in your car can cause hard starting and undue wear on the battery.

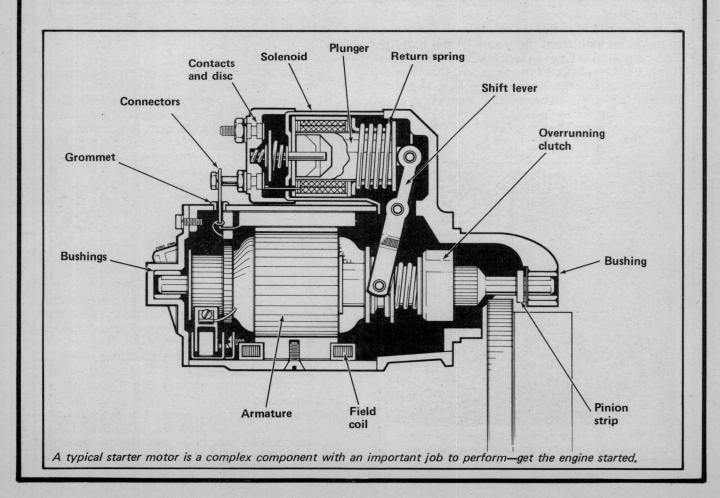

A typical starter motor is a complex component with an important job to perform—get the engine started.

Battery Janitor Cleans ST Batteries

While corrosion is more common on batteries with top mounted terminals, you cannot neglect those batteries with the terminals on the side. E-Z-Red manufactures a handy cleaner for ST/Side Terminal Batteries. Designed for convenient removal of corrosion from both female and male contact points, the company's Model 504

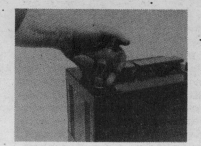

Battery Janitor has a durable steel brush that will survive many years of rugged use.

Check The Battery Hold-Down

Two of the more vulnerable components under the hood of your car are the battery hold-down and the battery support base. Subject to destructive corrosion (especially on older model cars), these components can virtually be eaten away over a period of time. As part of your seasonal clean-up maintenance, therefore, remove the hold-down bolts, the hold-down bracket, and the battery, and then scrape all the dirt and corrosion from the support until it is clean enough for you to apply a coat of rust-inhibiting primer. Following the primer, add a coat of paint or at least a coat of corrosion-resistant grease. Then do the same for the hold-down and hold-down bolts. A coating of corrosion-resistant grease for the battery cable connections is also a good idea.

BATTERY MAINTENANCE

KEEPING YOUR battery clean is one of the most essential services you can do on your car, and it is one of the easiest. Obviously, we are not talking about the aesthetic factor of a clean battery. We are concerned about cleanliness to prevent power loss.

On every battery, there is a positive and negative terminal (or connector). If a wire were to be placed across these two terminals, you would have a short circuit and plenty of sparks. A wire is a superb conductor of electricity.

Dust and dirt are conductors of electricity too, especially when they are damp. Without realizing it, you can have a fine, nearly invisible conductor of electricity on a dirty battery that slowly bleeds away your battery's power. It is not strong enough to create sparks, but nevertheless, the "leakage" is there.

Another, and more common, power loss is through poor connections to the battery terminals. We are all familiar with the buildup of whitish-green corrosion that accumulates on the battery terminals on the top of the battery. This material is the result of the chemical action due to gases coming from the inside of the battery. This corrosion is an excellent insulator and often forms between the battery cable and the terminal. The outside of the connection may look good, but inside there is just enough corrosion to prevent electricity from flowing.

A recent survey by the Car Care Council of

Here Is What You Will Need

Materials

- Masking Tape
- Baking Soda
- Water
- Penetrating Oil
- Steel Wool
- Sandpaper
- Petroleum Jelly
- Battery Terminal Nuts
- Battery Cable
- Battery Cable Clamps

Tools

- Stiff Wire Brush
- Wrenches
- Battery Terminal Puller
- Battery Pliers
- Penknife
- Battery Terminal Cleaner
- Battery Cable Cutter or Hacksaw

garage mechanics pointed to battery cables as the second most neglected part of their customers' cars. A similar survey was done five years ago when battery terminals took the number one spot for neglect. Here is how to clean your battery:

1. Wear old clothes. The stuff you are going to be cleaning off the battery contains strong acid. Do not let it touch your skin, and if it does, be sure to wash it off immediately. **CAUTION:** Do not smoke or tackle this job in the vicinity of an open flame. Batteries can be highly explosive due to hydrogen gas.

2. Be sure the vent caps are in place on the battery and cover the vent holes in the caps with masking tape to avoid getting your cleaning solution in the battery. You do not want to neutralize the acid that makes the battery work.

3. In about a pint of water, pour enough baking soda to get a strong solution . . . . it should fizz. Pour this on the battery top and wait until the foaming stops. Scrub the top of the battery with a stiff brush. Then rinse the battery off with plenty of water.

4. Remove the battery cable clamps. This is done by loosening a nut and bolt on most batteries with a wrench. But if your car is equipped with a spring type cable clamp, you will have to squeeze the prongs with pliers. Use a terminal puller to lift off the clamp. In either case, remove the ground cable first. This is the negative terminal on

Prevent Corrosion Buildup With Battery Terminal Protectors

Corrosion to a battery is like rust to a car body; either will cause problems if not taken care of in its early stages. East Penn Manufacturing Company makes a polyester pad impregnated with a chemical corrosion inhibitor that will corrosion-proof your battery and thereby extend its useful life. Bearing the brand name Deka, these terminal protectors, Models 640 and 641, prevent a loss of cranking power and a loss of charge due to electrical leakage. They also prevent increased water consumption due to overcharging and increased fuel consumption due to overcharging. East Penn also markets a protection spray, No. 647, for battery terminals, and a spray battery cleaner, No. 648.

Poor battery terminal connections can prevent the flow of current, resulting in a no-start condition.

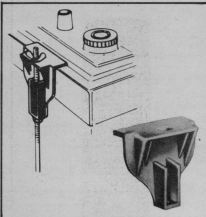

Replace Those Corroded Hold-Down Brackets

A wide range of replacement hold-down brackets designed specifically for particular car models and years is offered by Whitaker Cable Corp. If you cannot find the specific bracket for your car, however, the company also makes universal hold-down brackets that will work on most batteries. The manufacturer's universal hold-downs are unbreakable, non-corrosive, and strong, yet flexible, with nylon clamps that fit both long and standard batteries.

Battery Terminal And Clamp Brush

A battery terminal and cable clamp brush is a basic necessity for proper battery care. They are inexpensive and designed to do their cleaning chores thoroughly and efficiently. A typical model is made by Hastings Manufacturing Company. The tool has a cylinder-shaped plastic case with a circular brush inside. To clean a terminal, you just fit this case over it and twist to remove the corrosion. The other end of the case has a wire brush that fits inside the cable clamp. A cover fits over this brush when not in use, and the cover also gives you a good grip when you are using the tool as a battery terminal cleaner.

Remove Rusted Or Corroded Nuts With Battery Pliers

If they are rusted or corroded, the nuts on battery terminals are particularly stubborn to remove. This problem is so common that a special type of pliers has been designed to deal with it. Proto Tools offers such a tool, Model 3318. Its thin jaws, at a 30-degree angle, make working with side-terminal type batteries especially easy.

Red Camel Seldom Needs Water

Like other maintenance-free batteries, the Red Camel battery from ESB Brands Inc. seldom demands even a drop of water. What makes this maintenance-free battery a bit different from similar batteries, though, is that it comes with vent caps, allowing it to take water if necessary—i.e., the car's electrical system malfunctions.

BATTERY MAINTENANCE

most cars. If the positive cable is disconnected first, you could accidentally ground the wrench or pliers against the body or some other part of the car and create a spark. (On cars with positive ground systems, remove the positive cable first.) **CAUTION:** There is the possibility of exploding the battery, ruining the wrench or burning your hand with the heavy current flow. So always remember, follow the instructions to be safe.

Because of the highly corrosive nature of battery acid, you may find that the cable clamp nuts have been so eaten away that they are virtually impossible to remove. In this case, you may have to apply some penetrating oil for a while until whatever remains of the nut can be turned. This is a good case for owning a battery terminal puller; sometimes the cable clamp is too corroded for normal measures. If so, it is advisable to replace the cable when the job

Spring-type cable clamps have tabs that must be squeezed with a pliers for removal.

is finished or at least to replace the clamp if the wire in the cable is still good. Avoid putting a new clamp on a wire where the insulation is bad or where too many strands of wire have deteriorated. (See the instructions for replacing a cable and for replacing a cable clamp at the end of this section.) **NOTE:** Most late-model General Motors cars have side terminal batteries. These terminals are less likely to corrode but still should be checked periodically and cleaned if necessary.

5. When both cable clamps are removed, use a wire brush or steel wool to clean the battery terminals and clamps until they are shiny. The inside of the clamps can be cleaned with sandpaper or lightly scraped with a penknife. A good investment is a battery terminal cleaning tool. (This tool can be bought in kit combinations that include the terminal puller and battery pliers.) The terminal cleaner has a round "female" brush that is slipped over the battery terminal and twisted to remove all traces of corrosion. On the other side of the brush is a "male" end that slips inside the battery cable clamp. Instead of using a penknife, a few twists of this brush removes the corrosion.

6. Replace the clamps on the battery, making sure they fit well down onto the terminals. Do not hammer the clamp down or over-tighten the nut, as this could damage the battery case or the clamp. If the old nuts are in bad condition, they should be replaced with a special type that is obtainable at your auto parts store.

Part of the battery cleaning and checking process should be a close examination of the cables. Sometimes a cable looks okay at the

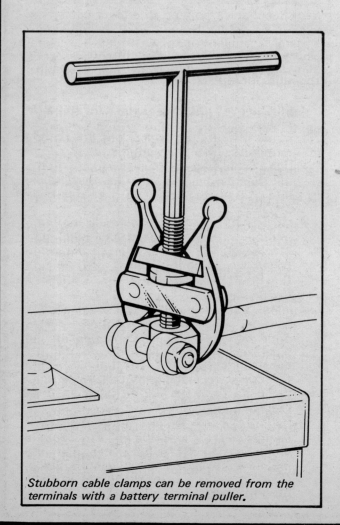

Stubborn cable clamps can be removed from the terminals with a battery terminal puller.

Combination Carrying Strap

Do you have one car with a con-. ventional battery and one with a side terminal battery? If so, you can purchase a combination carrying strap, Model K-D 2279, from K-D Manufacturing Company, that will let you carry either battery with the same carrier strap. This

two-in-one device is made of high-strength, acid-resistant plastic. The strap also offers knurled

screws that allow it to function as a charging adapter for batteries with side-mounted terminals.

Clean And Protect Battery Terminals

To remove the buildup of corrosion and grease from your battery terminals, Krylon Department, Borden Chemical Division of Borden, Inc., makes a battery cleaner that will get the job done. The company's battery cleaner, No. 1336, cuts through and dissolves power-robbing acid corrosion on the battery terminals, cable connections, and hold-down frames. Krylon also makes a battery protector, No. 1307, that, when sprayed on the terminals and hold-down bolts, leaves an airtight, waterproof, insulated seal to help prevent battery corrosion.

terminal, but closer to the engine you may find the insulation cracked, brittle, or even split open. Be sure to replace any cable that has defective insulation or frayed or broken strands of wire. And always replace the cable with one of the same conductor quality, at least the same gauge and the same length. Otherwise you are likely to have starting problems. An inadequate gauge or incorrect length of battery cable creates a resistance that prevents sufficient current from getting to the starter motor—the result, a slow turning starter and eventual damage to the starter motor. Play it safe by taking the old battery cable to your auto parts store to replace it with one of equivalent quality and capacity. Here is the correct procedure for replacing a battery cable.

1. Whether you are replacing a negative cable, a positive cable, or both, the negative cable must be removed first. (Positive cable must be removed first on a positive ground system.) Loosen the nut on the clamp with a wrench. Use a battery terminal puller to remove the clamp from the terminal. If your battery has the spring type clamp, use a battery pliers to squeeze the clamp.
2. Next, remove the other end of the cable or cables that you intend to replace. The negative cable can be loosened by removing a bolt with a wrench. It is connected to the engine block or some other good ground. The positive terminal is connected to the starter motor solenoid, which is mounted either on the starter motor or on the inside of the fender well, depending on the make and model of car. The positive terminal can be disconnected by removing a nut with a wrench at the starter motor solenoid. (Remember, if your vehicle has a positive ground system, the negative cable will be connected to the starter motor solenoid and the positive cable will go to ground. Remove the positive cable from the battery terminal first on this system.)

   On side terminal batteries, either cable can be removed by loosening a retaining bolt from the clamp. The cable and clamp will then come loose. The other ends of the negative and positive cables are connected and removed in the same way as the conventional battery cables.
3. Clean the cable clamps, battery terminals, and the top of the battery following the instructions given earlier in this section.
4. After having obtained the correct type and length of replacement cable from your local parts store, reverse steps one and two for proper replacement.
5. Coat the cable clamps and battery terminals with petroleum jelly to help protect them from corrosion.

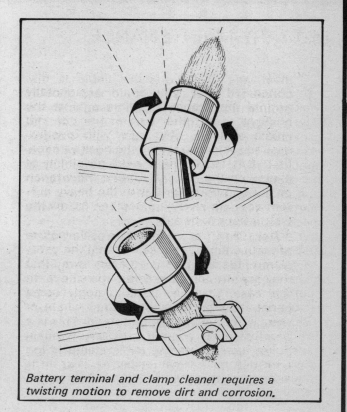

Battery terminal and clamp cleaner requires a twisting motion to remove dirt and corrosion.

If the battery cable is still good, but the cable clamp needs to be replaced, here is a quick procedure for replacing it.

1. Whether you intend to replace the negative clamp, positive clamp, or both, first remove the ground cable from the battery terminal as previously outlined.
2. Use a cable cutter or hacksaw to cut off the old clamp where it joins the thick cable and strip the insulation on the cable back one inch.
3. Make sure the cable will still be long enough to reach the battery terminal, otherwise you will have to replace the entire assembly—cable and clamp. Also be sure that the battery terminal is clean to insure a good connection.
4. Install a good quality replacement clamp, available at auto supply stores. This is done by loosening the two bolts on the clamp, placing the stripped end of the cable into the clamp, and tightening the two bolts. The insulation of the cable must be flush against the bottom of the clamp so that no uninsulated cable is exposed.
5. Regardless of which cable clamp or clamps you replaced, the positive clamp is connected to the battery first, then the negative clamp as previously outlined. (This procedure is reversed on positive ground systems.)

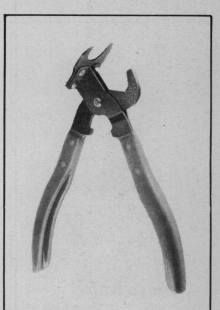

Pliers Pull Off Corroded Clamps

Removing corroded battery clamps from battery terminals can sometimes be a tough job. Having the right tool for the job, however, will make the task easier. K-D Manufacturing Company offers battery terminal pliers that quickly and easily remove corroded clamps—including spring types—from battery terminals. Just slip the bottom plier jaw under the clamp and squeeze. The firm pressure you exert through the pliers will lift the clamp; no twisting or prying is necessary. The handles of K-D's Model 2325 battery terminal pliers are insulated for safety.

Power Analyzer Tests Batteries, Charging System, And Starting System

Batteries are often blamed for trouble they never caused. When trying to pinpoint an electrical problem, the battery should be the starting point. However, the starter and charging system should also be checked. ESB Brands, Inc. has a power analyzer that checks all these components —the alternator, regulator, and starting system in addition to testing the condition of the battery. Battery tests include a state of charge test and a cranking amp test, the latter determining cranking performance in amperes. Model BT-300 also has a temperature compensation knob to adjust for variations in fluid temperature. The unit is designed only for 12-volt batteries with cold cranking ratings in excess of 600 amps.

Get A Five-Function Tester In One Rugged Unit

If you have an electrical problem with your car and you do not know where to begin to look for the trouble, take note. Solar, a division of Century Manufacturing Company, offers a battery tester that shows the battery's performance level, tests its percent charge, checks the vehicle's charging system, checks its starting system, and detects any short circuits in the electrical system. Model 142-001-002 will work on any 12-volt battery down to 40 percent of charge. The recessed, brushed aluminum instrument panel is surrounded by a well-constructed steel case to protect it from rugged use.

Follow the Floating Balls

Periodically checking your battery is the best way to prevent your battery from going dead when you least expect it. Thexton Manufacturing Company makes a battery tester, called the Hydro-Mite, that does the job of a full size hydrometer. It gives quick, accurate readings of four battery conditions, with the number of floating balls showing the state of charge. With no balls floating, the battery is completely discharged; one ball floating, poor charge; two floating, fair charge; and three floating, full charge. The leakproof vacuum tube is break-resistant.

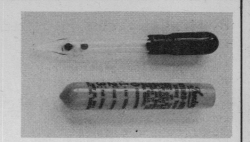

TESTING THE BATTERY

Here Is What You Will Need

Materials
- Water—Plain or Distilled
- Toothpick

Tools
- Hydrometer
- Voltmeter
- Clip-on Jumper Wire

BECAUSE THE starting system of a car is engineered to operate with a battery that is fully charged, a battery hydrometer is an indispensable tool for checking a battery's performance. The hydrometer compares the density (specific gravity or weight) of the battery fluid to that of water. The acid in your battery is heavier than plain water. Therefore, the more fully charged your battery, the heavier the fluid. This, of course, is the tip-off to the degree of charge in your battery. The "heavier" the fluid, the higher the degree of charge.

A hydrometer test of your battery should be made seasonally to avoid strain on the car's electrical system as well as to detect battery trouble before outright failure befalls it.

Before performing a hydrometer test, make sure your battery is in good condition. Visually inspect the case for cracks and other damage. Loose hold-down frames, freezing, or flying stones are the most likely causes of battery cracking. A bulging battery case can cause starting failure, too. This can be caused by overcharging or freezing. A bulged battery will probably have buckled plates and cracked partitions. Once you have judged your battery to be in good shape, you can perform the hydrometer test as follows:

1. Remove the vent caps and check the fluid level of the battery. If there is not enough fluid in the cells to allow you to take a good sampling of fluid with the hydrometer, you will have to add water. If this is the case, run your engine for approximately 20 minutes to let the fresh water mix thoroughly with the fluid already in the battery. Then let the car cool for 15 minutes before performing the hydrometer test.
2. Test each cell of the battery with the hydrometer, one at a time. Suck enough battery fluid into the hydrometer with the attached rubber bulb to float the indicator inside the tube and take a reading. On a bulb float type tester, you will get a false reading if the indicator touches the sides or the top of the instrument.

A reading from 1.260 to 1.300 in each cell means the battery is healthy. A consistent reading of approximately 1.225 probably means the battery is satisfactory but low on charge. Any cell that varies more than

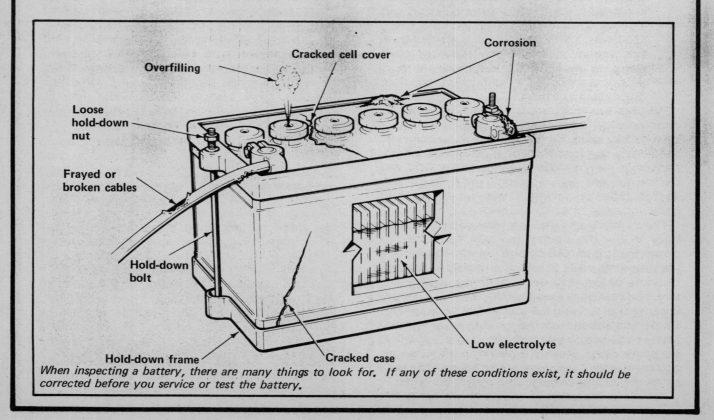

When inspecting a battery, there are many things to look for. If any of these conditions exist, it should be corrected before you service or test the battery.

BATTERY AND STARTING SYSTEM

Battery Cell Tester

You need a cell tester for testing cell voltage in hard case batteries where the connecting bars are not exposed. Model 1725 sold by Hastings Manufacturing Company includes a meter, which is enclosed in a rubber case, and two corrosion-resistant probes with wire leads. To test a cell in the battery, you merely remove the cell cap and insert the probes into the cell for a fast reading. This cell tester also includes a handy bracket for hanging when not in use, and the rubber case will not scratch the car finish if you place it on a fender.

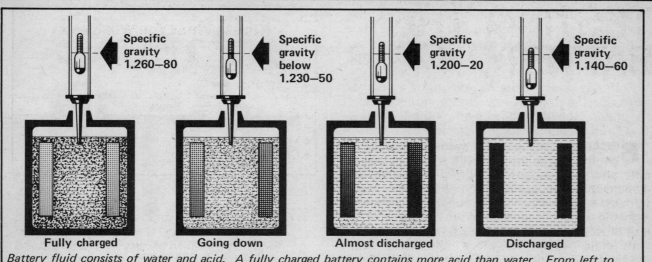

Battery fluid consists of water and acid. A fully charged battery contains more acid than water. From left to right, you can see how a battery becomes less efficient as it loses its charge.

Specific gravity 1.260—80	Specific gravity below 1.230—50	Specific gravity 1.200—20	Specific gravity 1.140—60
Fully charged	Going down	Almost discharged	Discharged

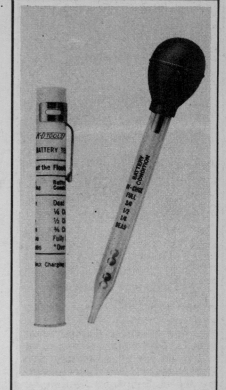

Spot Check Your Battery's Condition

There are several types of battery testers on the market, most of which do a good job of determining your battery's condition. K-D Manufacturing Company sells a "Spot Check" battery tester with floating balls inside that allows you to determine at a glance precisely the condition your battery is in. In addition to checking car and truck batteries, the company's unit can test the condition of batteries in boats, farm machinery, etc.

0.050 point from the others indicates a defective cell, and the battery should be replaced.

If you have a battery tester that uses floating balls to indicate the battery's state of charge, draw in some battery fluid and observe the floating action. If all three balls are floating, the battery is fully charged; with two balls floating, the battery condition is fair; one floating ball means a poor state of charge; and no floating balls indicates a discharged battery.

3. Now check the battery vent caps and clean any plugged or dirty holes with a toothpick. This will help prevent acid fumes from building up dangerously in the battery. **NOTE:** Under normal driving conditions and weather conditions, a battery will lose up to two ounces of its fluid every 1000 miles. If the fluid loss is greater than this amount, check other parts of the car's charging system. Maintenance-free batteries are designed in such a way that they do not lose any fluid.

Beyond this basic test, more elaborate instrumentation is needed. Your next check would be a battery capacity test to determine how well the battery can function under heavy load. If you happen to own a battery-starter tester, or if you decide to rent one, you can go through this sophisticated procedure. If not, a best bet is to have a qualified mechanic check it out for you.

The capacity test indicates the battery's capability to run the starter and still have enough power left in it to take care of the ignition system requirements while the engine is getting started. Because of the very heavy draining on the battery, you could have a situation where the battery is capable of turning the starter but because of a borderline situation in the ignition system there just is not enough electricity to cause a spark at the spark plugs. Were the battery a bit stronger, or if the starter itself were not draining excessive power from the battery, you might be okay.

In lieu of investing in a battery-starter tester, we suggest you try the following procedure with a voltmeter. In effect, you will be using the starter motor itself as a loading test device. However, you will need a voltmeter.

1. Lift the "high tension" (center) lead from the center tower of the distributor cap (See Parts Location Guide) and ground it to some part of the body or frame with a clip-on jumper wire.
2. Connect the terminals of your voltmeter to the battery. Be sure you are putting positive to positive and negative to negative.
3. Turn the ignition key to crank the engine for 15 seconds while observing the reading of the voltmeter. If you cannot position the voltmeter where you can see it while you crank the engine, have someone crank it for you. At the end of the continuous 15 second test, the voltmeter still should read 9.6 volts or more on a 12-volt system and 4.8 volts or more on a six-volt system. If the voltage drops below 9.6 or 4.8 volts, you have a bad battery. **NOTE:** Never operate the starter for more than 30 seconds without stopping for a while to cool it off.

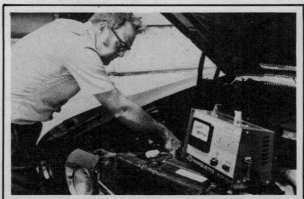

To determine how well your battery can stand up under a heavy load requires more elaborate testing.

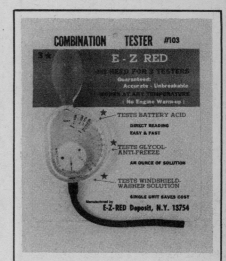

E-Z-Red Makes Battery Testing Easy

Having one tester that checks the battery, cooling system and windshield washer fluid is convenient and less expensive than buying three separate tools. The E-Z-Red Company makes such a tool. The Combination Tester is a handy syringe-type device for checking battery acid (range: 1.125, 1.175, 1.200, 1.265), glycol antifreeze (range: +10°F to -60°F) and windshield washer solution (range: 0°F to -30°F). The easy-to-use, easy-to-store tester can handle either hot or cold solutions.

ESB Offers A Choice In Quality Chargers

Getting your car to a repair shop with a dead battery usually requires an expensive service call. That money could be better spent on a battery charger that would get you started time and time again, paying for itself after just one or two uses. ESB Brands, Inc. markets three battery chargers designed for economy-minded do-it-yourselfers. Model BE-4 is a four-amp unit and Model BE-6 is a six-amp unit; both are capable of charging six- and 12-volt batteries. Model BE-6A is also a six-amp charger, but it differs from the other two in that it is an all solid-state unit for 12-volt charging only. It can be left on for an extended period and shuts off automatically when the battery is properly charged.

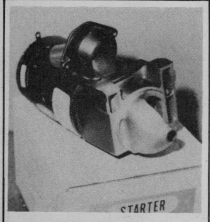

Buy A Rebuilt Starter Motor And Save

Progressive Armature Company manufactures a line of rebuilt starter motors available for most cars through auto supply stores. Rebuilt starter motors are less expensive than new ones, but offer the same quality and durability. According to the Automotive Parts Rebuilders Association, rebuilt parts are as good, and in some cases better, than new ones because the newest engineering changes have been incorporated to improve the old part. Quality rebuilt parts will also last as long as new ones, but the biggest advantage is the 20 to 25 percent savings in buying the rebuilt part.

BATTERY CHARGING

THERE IS probably nothing more aggravating than hurrying out to your car on a cold morning and, upon attempting to start it, hearing a clicking sound or nothing at all. This no-start condition does not necessarily mean that your battery is completely dead. It may just be a little tired.

Batteries can become run-down for a number of reasons: a defective alternator, faulty voltage regulator, too much corrosion on the terminals, bad cables, etc. In addition, studies have shown that batteries are often blamed for trouble that can be traced to other areas of the car. For example, you may call the Auto Club for a battery boost, explaining that your battery has failed, when actually your problem is a faulty choke on the carburetor, or your car is in desperate need of a tune-up.

Another way to run down a battery is through carelessness. If you accidently leave your lights on for several hours, you will most assuredly end up with a dead battery. In this case, you will need to recharge your battery. Battery chargers are designed to bring life back to the chemicals in your battery. These chemicals in turn provide the electrical current necessary to start your engine time and time again.

Whatever the reason, if your battery is dead, the question is, what is the best way to bring it back to life?

Getting a boost with a good set of jumper cables will get the car started and, if you intend to do a lot of driving right away, the battery will probably recharge itself as you are driving. (See the section in this chapter on using jumper cables). Your charging system, consisting of an alternator and regulator, must be in good shape, however. (Cars made before the early 1960s were equipped with a generator, which has since been replaced by the alternator. These components are further explained in the Charging System chapter.)

If you are not planning to go anywhere after you jump-start your car's battery, you cannot take the chance that your car will start the next time you need it. If your battery has been drained of its electrical current for any length of time,

Here Is What You Will Need

Materials
- Water—Plain or Distilled

Tools
- Battery Charger
- Wrenches or Battery Pliers
- Battery Terminal Puller
- Battery Terminal Cleaner
- Hydrometer

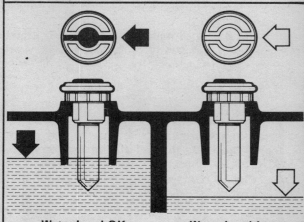

Water Level OK **Water Level Low**
When the fluid level in a cell is low, add water to bring it up to the proper level.

then it will probably need to be charged up.

A battery in good condition can be recharged by passing a specific amount of direct current through the battery. Fast charging and slow charging are the two most frequently used methods to do this. Slow charging induces a small amount of current, usually five to seven amperes, through the battery over a period of 12 to 14 hours or more. Fast charging will induce between 50 and 60 amperes through the battery in just an hour or two.

If it is at all possible, take the time to give your battery a slow charge. While this takes much longer than a quick charge, it is best for your battery in terms of preventing damage to the inside of the battery, and the battery will also hold its charge longer.

Fast charging will give your battery a quick boost, but it can be harmful to its health. The principle of quick charging is that the battery can be brought up to an acceptable rate of charge (not full charge) before the electrolyte reaches damaging high temperatures. The real question is whether or not you have the ex-

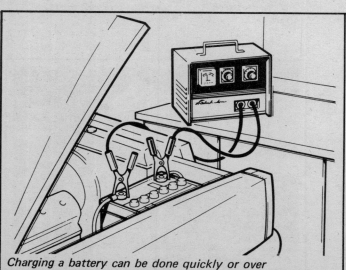

Charging a battery can be done quickly or over several hours. Slow charging is preferred, however.

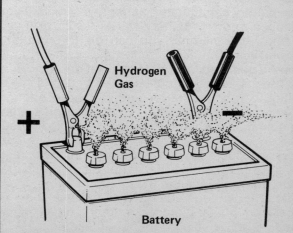

When charging a battery, be sure the hydrogen gas can escape. Your best bet is to remove the caps.

perience to cut back the charge rate soon enough to prevent damage. The more sophisticated equipment used by professional mechanics has protection devices to prevent overheating. Even after a fast charge, however, the battery should be brought up to its full state of charge by slow charging.

If you think a battery charger would be a good investment for you, then buy one that has an automatic cut-off, which prevents your battery from overheating, so that your battery can be allowed to charge overnight. Some of the more sophisticated units have rate-of-charge adjustments so that you can get a quicker charge if you so desire. Here is how to hook up and use a battery charger:

1. Remove the battery vent caps from the top of your battery. Vent caps are either pulled off or unscrewed by hand. This is important because the buildup of hydrogen gas in your battery during the charging process can be dangerous. If your car is equipped with a maintenance-free battery, one with no cell openings, you will need a charger that can handle this type of battery.

2. Make sure the battery fluid (called electrolyte) in each cell is up to the proper fill mark. The proper level will be indicated by a slot, notch, lip, or ring. If you can see the tops of the plates in the battery, or if the fluid level is below the fill mark, add water. **CAUTION:** Do not overfill! Also, if the water in your area has a high mineral content, use distilled water.

3. If you intend to leave the battery in the car while you charge it, disconnect both battery cables (negative cable first) to prevent damage to the electrical system and the accessories. (On cars that have a positive ground system, with the positive cable connected to ground, disconnect the positive cable first.) To remove the battery cables, use a wrench to loosen the nuts on the battery cable clamps. If the cable clamps do not pull off easily, use a battery terminal puller to get them off. Do not use a screwdriver or any other similar tool to pry the clamps off as this can result in a cracked battery case. With spring-type cable clamps, a battery pliers should be used to pull them off.

4. Clean the battery terminals with a battery terminal cleaner, as described in the Battery Maintenance section, so that the cables from the battery charger can make good contact. Just as electricity cannot get out past the corrosion, it also cannot get in.

5. Connect the positive (+) cable of the battery charger to the positive battery terminal, then connect the negative (-) cable of the charger to the negative battery terminal. Plug the charger cord into an electrical wall outlet or other 110-volt power source.

6. Turn the charger to the On position. If you have an adjustable unit, set it at a rate of between five and 15 amperes. Also set the charger for either a six- or 12-volt battery, whichever type you have. A six-volt battery has three cell openings in its cover, and a 12-volt battery has six openings. Each cell produces two volts.

7. If your battery charger does not have an automatic cut-off, you should have a hydrometer (battery tester) with a built-in thermometer to check the battery fluid

Battery chargers are easy to hook up, but must be done correctly. Just remember, positive to positive and negative to negative.

about once an hour, never allowing it to exceed 125° F. If you see the cells bubbling quite a bit, reduce the charging rate. The battery is fully charged when the specific gravity reading of the fluid in each cell is 1.260 at 80°F; see the accompanying chart of typical specific gravity ranges. (Specific gravity is the weight of that fluid in relation to the same volume of water. Both the hydrometer and specific gravity are explained in more detail in the Battery Testing section.) If you do not have a thermometer built into your hydrometer, you will need to feel the casing of the battery to determine if the fluid is getting too hot. Obviously, when you see the bubbling condition, you should lower the charging rate at once. Excessive heat can damage the interior parts and ruin the battery.

8. Once the charging process has been completed, turn off the battery charger and disconnect the charger's cables from the battery. Remove the charger cord from the 110 volt power source. Store the charger in a safe, dry place. Reconnect the battery cables—positive cable first. Replace the battery vent caps after first cleaning the vent holes.

If your battery is in sound mechanical condition, the battery charge should hold. If it does not, then you must track down the source of trouble. Some causes are improper regulator settings, a faulty alternator, excessive cranking from a defective starting motor, and bad wiring. You will learn more about these in later chapters.

TYPICAL RANGES OF SPECIFIC GRAVITY

1.260 Sp. Gr.	1.280 Sp. Gr.	100% Charged
1.230 Sp. Gr.	1.250 Sp. Gr.	75% Charged
1.200 Sp. Gr.	1.220 Sp. Gr.	50% Charged
1.170 Sp. Gr.	1.190 Sp. Gr.	25% Charged
1.140 Sp. Gr.	1.160 Sp. Gr.	Very little useful capacity
1.110 Sp. Gr.	1.130 Sp. Gr.	Discharged

Battery Efficiency In Cold Weather

If you have ever tried to start your car on a bitter cold day and it would not start even though your battery was fully charged and in top condition, it was probably the weather and not the battery that would not allow your car to start. Battery efficiency is greatly reduced as the temperature drops. Cold weather affects the chemical action in the battery by slowing it down. For example, a fully charged battery at 10°F is only half as efficient as a fully charged battery at 80°F. Therefore, it is absolutely necessary that a battery be fully charged for safe cold weather operation.

BATTERY EFFICIENCY AT VARIOUS TEMPERATURES

Temperature	Efficiency of a Fully Charged Battery
80°F	100%
50°F	82%
30°F	64%
20°F	58%
10°F	50%
0°F	40%
-10°F	33%

Schauer Sells Single Starting/Charging Unit

Once you get that dead battery in your car to start the engine, you will have to do something about charging the battery. Schauer Manufacturing Corp. offers a combination starter/charger. In addition to charging a dead battery, the company's Model 0141-01 engine starter/charger can put out a 50-amp starting charge, which is sufficient to turn over the average engine. Its 10-ampere recharge rate is adequate for charging the average battery in 2½ to 3 hours. Schauer also markets a larger engine starter/charger that produces a 20-amp recharging rate and a 60-amp starting charge. Both units work off standard house current.

Now You Can Maintain Your Maintenance-Free Battery

The Sure Start Power Peak maintenance-free battery from ESB Brands, Inc. is another battery that comes with removable vent caps so that water can be added should a failure of the voltage regulator or other electrical problems in the car create a situation in which water must be added. In normal use, however, maintenance-free batteries require only an occasional cleaning of the terminal posts.

No Spills With This Battery Carrier

A unique battery carrier that permits lifting side terminal batteries is available from Plews Division, Parker Automotive. Where conventional carriers will cause the battery to tilt, and possibly spill battery acid, this tool, Model 70-032, has extension arms that swivel toward the center line of the battery to permit a straight lift. A good battery carrier is an important safety device.

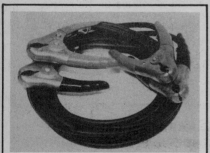

Cables Offer Color-Coded Clamps

It is a good idea to have a set of jumper cables in your trunk because you never know when your battery will go dead. Marquette Automotive Service Systems Group, offers deluxe booster cables in both 10-foot (Model 37-105) and 15-foot (Model 37-109) lengths. Wire size in both models is No. 4 copper. What makes these booster cables deluxe? They are designed to remain flexible in all types of weather, and the well-insulated clamps are color-coded and marked to reduce the safety hazard in starting a car with jumper cables.

Battery Fillers Make Adding Water Neat And Easy

Filling your car's battery with water can often be a messy chore when you use a makeshift jug or bottle. The neat and easy way to refill is to use the same kind of water container that service station attendants use to fill a low battery. Huffman Manufacturing Company makes two battery fillers that are like those used in professional garages. They are made of durable plastic that is tough to break and is impervious to most chemicals and normal temperature extremes. An automatic shut-off feature stops the water flow when the cell is filled, preventing overflow. Both models have a 2½ quart capacity. Model 2108 is red and Model 2110 is blue.

USING JUMPER CABLES

DURING THE COLD weather, there is one question that creates a bond within a neighborhood: ".... can you give me a boost?" To cement your friendship with neighbors, you must know what you are doing with your jumper cables.

Using jumper cables to start a dead battery from a healthy one is the most common method used to enliven the dead battery. Electrical current, sufficient to start the ailing car, is supplied through the jumper cables from the good battery. With jumper cables and power from the battery of any car having the same voltage, you can start your car with no trouble.

The procedure when done right is easy, but you can damage a car's electrical system by not connecting the cables correctly. If you have the talent to lift the hood of the car, you should be able to hook up the jumper cables correctly without any trouble. Here is how it should be done:

Here Is What You Will Need
Materials
● Water—Plain or Distilled
● Rag
Tools
● Jumper Cables
● Hydrometer

1. Be sure the booster battery and the run-down battery are of the same voltage. That is, both should have the same number of cells. For example, you should not jump a 12-volt battery with a six-volt battery. Remember, a six-volt battery has three cell openings, and a 12-volt battery has six openings in the cover.
2. To jump-start your car's dead battery, line up the two cars so they are facing each other. Do not allow them to touch, however, as this could lead to electrical shorts and dangerous sparks.
3. Remove the battery vent caps from both the run-down battery and the good battery. Look inside and check the electrolyte level

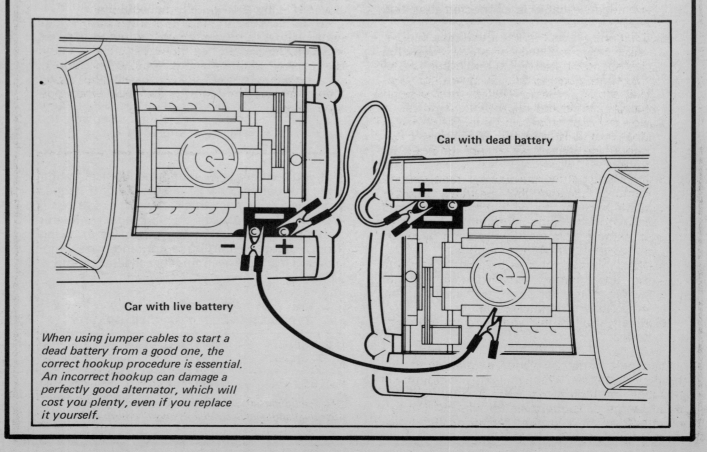

Car with dead battery

Car with live battery

When using jumper cables to start a dead battery from a good one, the correct hookup procedure is essential. An incorrect hookup can damage a perfectly good alternator, which will cost you plenty, even if you replace it yourself.

BATTERY AND STARTING SYSTEM

Battery Hold-Down Parts Fit Most Batteries

If you have battery hold-down assembly damage due to corrosion, you might consider replacing the assembly with one from TRW Replacement Division, TRW, Inc. The company manufactures a wide variety of hold-down brackets and frames that are coated with corrosion resistant vinyl.

Longer Jumper Cables For Hard-To-Get-To Places

Have you ever been in a spot where your jumper cables were not long enough to reach the battery of another car? If so, you would appreciate these 20-foot-long battery jumper cables, Model BC 9, from Standard Motor Products. With these cables, you can connect your dead battery to a car behind you, in front of you, or anywhere within 20 feet of you. These non-tangling "Siamese" construction, four gauge cables are made from extra flexible welding cable. Heavy-duty, insulated, color-coded clamps will not short if accidentally grounded. Twelve- and 16-foot cables are also available.

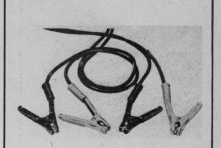

Cables Stay Flexible At -60°F

If you are looking for the convenience of 25-foot booster cables, consider the super heavy-duty cables (Model 3294) from Whitaker Cable Corp. Their thermal plastic insulation can withstand temperatures as low as -60°F. The conductors—No. 1 gauge copper with 600-amp capacity—are banded together so that they cannot tangle. The clamps—completely insulated steel with replaceable copper jaws—are designed to work on both side terminal and top post batteries.

Battery Terminal Conversions

Most of the newer batteries do not have battery terminals on top, but have postless terminals on the side. It is possible to buy replacement battery cables that will fit this type of battery if your former battery was the top-mounted, conventional type. If the battery cables for your particular car are not available when you need them, you can buy conventional battery terminals that screw into the side terminals of the new battery. These will accept your present battery cables perfectly. Christie Electric Corporation is one of the many manufacturers that make these post inserts.

Booster Cables To Get You Started

Winter or summer, you should always carry a set of jumper cables in your car. In fact, next to a jack and spare tire, they are the most useful type of emergency equipment you can store in your trunk. Essex Automotive Parts sells 8-, 12-, and 20-foot cables, which feature shock-resistant handles and large, spring-loaded alligator clamps. The clamps attach securely to both top-mounted terminals and side-mounted types. The long, insulated leads allow jump starts when the two cars are in a variety of positions. The Models are: 78-6 for the 8-foot cables, 78-5 for the 12-foot cables, and 78-7 for the 20-foot cables.

---

in both batteries. If the level is low, add water. Use distilled water if the water in your area has a high mineral content. Leave all vent caps off during the procedure and keep the holes covered with a rag. **NOTE:** If the battery fluid in the run-down battery is frozen, it should not be boosted. Using jumper cables could damage the battery and possibly cause an explosion.

4. Turn off the ignition switch and all accessories in the car that will not start to avoid any unnecessary power drains. Set the brake and place the gear selector in Park for cars with automatic transmissions, and in Neutral for cars with manual transmissions.
5. Connect one end of the jumper cables to the positive (+) battery terminal of the run-down battery. Connect the other end of this same cable to the positive (+) terminal of the booster battery. In most American cars, the positive terminal is the one with a red cable leading to the starter motor solenoid. The negative cable, usually black, is grounded to the engine block or car frame. **NOTE:** Some older cars and many import models use a positive ground system. The only difference is the positive cable is connected to ground and the negative cable is connected to the starter motor solenoid—just the reverse of a negative ground system. On this system, the negative cable is connected first and removed last.
6. Connect one end of the remaining jumper cable to the negative (-) battery terminal of the booster battery, and the other end of this same cable to the run-down car's engine block, or frame. Always connect positive to positive and negative to negative.
7. Now, try to start the run-down car. If the car does not start at once, the booster car should be started so as not to drain its battery.
8. Once you get the run-down car started and running, remove the negative booster cable from the engine block or frame, and then from the battery terminal of the booster battery. (On positive ground systems, this would be the positive cable.)
9. Next, remove the positive cable from the run-down battery, then from the booster battery. (On positive ground systems, this would be the negative cable.)
10. Finally, replace the vent caps on both batteries.

Many late model cars are equipped with side terminal batteries. When making a hookup on this type of battery, be very careful that the positive jumper cable does not slip off the terminal and touch a ground. Some of these ter-

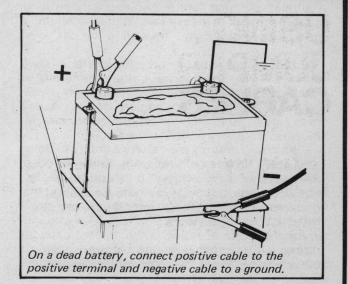

On a dead battery, connect positive cable to the positive terminal and negative cable to a ground.

minals are hard to reach and so small that the jumper cable clamp does not hold tightly.

After a car is boosted, it should be run for at least 20 minutes at highway speeds to charge up the battery. A battery tester (hydrometer) will tell you whether the battery has enough of a charge left to restart the car.

If your battery continues to go dead, or your alternator light or gauge indicates trouble, you will have to do some further checking of the battery and of the charging system, which will be covered in the Charging System chapter.

When purchasing a set of jumper cables, buy some with a good electrical conductor, such as copper. Copper carries electrical current much better than aluminum and most other metals. Also, make sure the cables are flexible. Good cables should not feel brittle or kink when you bend them.

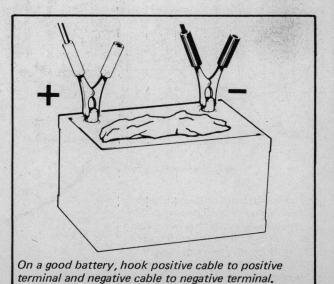

On a good battery, hook positive cable to positive terminal and negative cable to negative terminal.

Carriers Simplify Battery Removal

There are two ways to lift a battery out of a car and transport it somewhere else. One is by hand, a dangerous procedure because electrolyte overflow can damage skin and clothing. The other way— using a battery carrier—makes more sense. Whitaker Cable Corporation offers two types of battery carriers: the strap (Models 1046 and 1058) that can be conveniently connected to battery posts, and the grip (Model 1044) that is especially useful in carrying batteries that have side terminals. Using either type of battery carrier makes battery replacement much easier, as batteries are heavy and awkward to move.

Put An End To Battery Filling Drips

If you have ever tried to fill your battery with water and have ended up with the water everywhere but in the battery, you could have used a battery filler. The automatic battery filler, Model 75-030, from Plews Division of Parker Automotive prevents water from dripping on the top of the battery where it could cause surface discharge by aiming it directly into the cell opening. The blue polyethylene 2¼ quart container comes with a double-action fast-flow valve tip. It can also be used to safely fill the battery with acid. Plews also offers an economy battery filler, Model 75-033, that works via syringe action.

BATTERY SELECTION AND REPLACEMENT

WHEN BUYING a new battery, invest in one at least as large as the original equipment battery or the one you happen to be replacing, unless you intend to be disposing of the car in the relatively near future. And even under those circumstances, a heavy-duty battery can be a good sales point if you are selling the car yourself.

Batteries are rated in ampere hours. A standard one-year guarantee battery generally is rated as low as 35-40 ampere hours; a two-year guarantee is about 50 ampere hours, and a heavy-duty three-year or longer guarantee indicates 70 ampere hours or more.

This rating defines the battery's ability to deliver a given amount of amperage for a period of 20 hours at 80°F without a dropping of terminal voltage below 10.5 volts. A battery that delivers three amps for 20 hours, for example, is rated at 60 ampere hours.

Another form of rating is the reserve capacity rating, which establishes the amount of time a battery can deliver 25 amps while maintaining

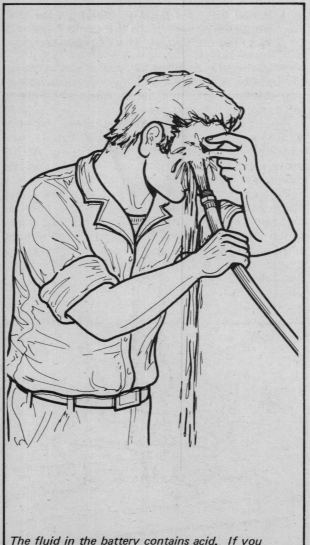

The fluid in the battery contains acid. If you get any in your eye, flush the contacted area with water.

terminal voltage of 10.5 volts at a temperature of 80°F. This reading is shown in minutes and is an indication of how long you can run your car with the charging system inoperative. If, for example, a battery operates for 90 minutes with an inoperative charging system before the battery voltage drops below 10.5 volts, the battery would have a 90 minute reserve capacity rating.

A third battery rating method is cold-cranking performance, which indicates how much current a battery can supply to the starter in extremely cold weather. The cold-cranking performance test shows the number of amps that can be drawn from a battery at 0°F for 30 seconds before the voltage drops to 7.2 volts. Ratings are expressed in amperes—for example, a 280 ampere battery.

As opposed to some parts of the car, such as belts and hoses, batteries are a highly competitive commodity at the retail level and often can be bought at substantial savings by watching for sales. For this reason, be aware of your battery's age and condition; be able to anticipate when it will be ready for replacement and you will be able to buy your new one at the best price rather than possibly be forced into buying one under emergency conditions when you cannot "dicker" over the price.

In addition to the sizes and capacities of batteries, there are several types to choose from. The pre-charged or wet-charged type, with the electrolyte fluid already in it, ready for installation, is most common.

The dry-charged battery has to have electrolyte added to it. This fluid comes with the battery in a plastic pour container. While the battery will be absolutely "fresh," never having had any electrolyte in the case, it does present the problem of filling. (See caution below.) Each cell is filled to the top of the plates. Then, after the bubbling has stopped, fill to the top level mark.

CAUTION: Battery fluid is a corrosive acid. Do not allow it to contact your eyes, skin, fabrics, or painted surfaces. Flush any contacted area with water immediately and thoroughly. Never expose a battery to an open flame or electric spark. Batteries generate a gas that is flammable and explosive. Always remove rings and watches when working around batteries and jumper cables to prevent the possibility of electrical burns. Be careful that metal tools or jumper cables do not contact the positive battery terminal (or any metal in contact with that terminal) and any other metal on the car at the same time. A short circuit could occur.

BATTERY AND STARTING SYSTEM

The Maintenance-Free Battery

IF YOU HAVE a car that is a few years old and you have been replacing the original parts such as tires, shock absorbers, and mufflers with the best you can buy, you probably are driving a car that is, in many respects, better than it was when it was new. That is one of the benefits the "automotive aftermarket" has to offer the motoring public.

A good example of this is the new "maintenance-free" battery, well worth considering when replacing your battery. Its main feature is that it should never need the addition of water. But keep in mind, there are various types of maintenance-free batteries, and unless you happen to be a chemical engineer, you might have trouble determining which kind you want.

There are some maintenance-free batteries that still have the water filler caps on the top. This is generally the "low-antimony" type that probably will cost less than the new calcium-lead battery and, according to some manufacturers, will last just as long as the more expensive type. Antimony is a chemical that is used with metals to harden them and increase their resistance to chemical action.

The maintenance-free battery, such as is now being used on General Motors cars and sold by some of the big retail companies, has no filler caps on top. Instead of the traditional lead-acid compound called electrolyte (which uses antimony in the mixture), this new type uses a calcium-lead approach that permits the manufacturers to seal the top of the battery. The calcium reduces the amount of gas that is produced by the charging action and the lack of antimony is supposed to eliminate the need to add water.

Whether you opt for the completely sealed maintenance-free battery or the less expensive type with the filler caps, you are probably still going to get a better replacement battery than what came in your car.

One of the benefits of all maintenance-free batteries is that there is little or no acid buildup. Therefore, there is a considerable reduction in the amount of corrosion on the terminal posts, cable clamps, and on the case itself. Nevertheless, it is still a good idea to check and clean the battery occasionally because there is an accumulation from other normal under-the-hood contaminants.

Because many sealed maintenance-free batteries do not have caps and holes for checking their condition with a hydrometer, a typical unit will have a test indicator to show its condition. When the indicator shows green, the charge is good. When it shows a dark color, it needs charging, and when the indicator is clear or a light color, the electrolyte level is too low to charge. Do not attempt to charge a maintenance-free battery under this condition. It must be replaced.

After charging a maintenance-free battery that uses these indicators, you may have to tip the battery slightly from side to side in order to get the green color to show, as gas bubbles may have collected around the test indicator.

If, after following instructions in the Battery Testing section, you find that your battery needs to be replaced, here is how it should be done:

1. Use a wrench to remove the hold-down frame bolts that secure the battery in the car. Planning ahead always makes for easiest serviceability. If you think that you may have to change the battery, go out at least a couple of hours before you are going to change it and cover the hold-down nuts with penetrating oil so they will be easier to remove.
2. Remove the battery cable clamps as outlined in the battery charging section.
3. Remove the old battery from the car. A battery strap carrier will make its removal much easier. Clean the hold-down frame with a baking soda and water solution. It is a good idea to paint this frame to retard further corrosion (any type of rust-inhibiting paint can be used).
4. Install the new battery, making sure that the same cables go to the same terminals as in the old battery. The negative terminal

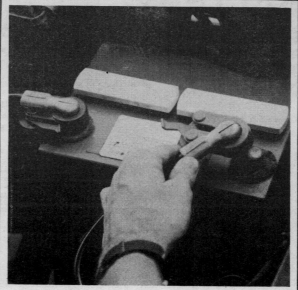

Always connect the positive clamp first and the negative clamp last.

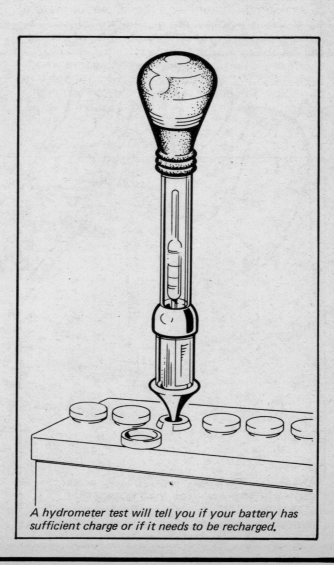

A hydrometer test will tell you if your battery has sufficient charge or if it needs to be recharged.

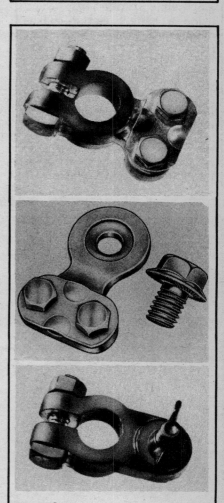

Maintenance-Free Battery Can Be Checked With A Hydrometer

Testing a maintenance-free battery can be a hassle if no provisions are made for getting to the battery fluid. Chloride Incorporated manufactures the No Hassle battery that offers a removable strip of safety vent caps, permitting the battery's state of charge to be checked easily with a standard hydrometer. As a maintenance-free unit, of course, the No Hassle battery provides all the features of its competitors: no need to add water, corrosion-free terminals, long shelf life, more starts than conventional batteries, greater cranking power, etc.

Battery Replacement Clamps

If you have broken, damaged, or heavily corroded battery clamps, you do not have to replace the whole cable, only the clamp itself. East Penn Manufacturing Company packages replacement clamps under the Deka brand name. Among the many types available are three universal clamps that fit positive or negative posts. They are Models 888L, C888L and 862-L. For replacing corroded terminals or for converting conventional clamps to fit side terminals, Deka offers replacement Model 999L. Just insert the stripped cable end into the threaded clamp and tighten. The protruding ring assures positive contact, and the recessed ring inside the protruding circle makes for precise positioning.

Cut Corrosion On Cable Connections

Many dead batteries are the result of heavily corroded battery connections. Keep an eye on those terminals and when the corrosion starts to form, get yourself a battery cleaning brush. One such tool is a handy little wire brush, available from K-D Manufacturing Company. Designed to make battery care as easy as possible, the K-D 206 battery brush does a fine job of cleaning away corrosion from both battery terminals and posts. It comes in a strong metal case to protect the wires from damage during storage.

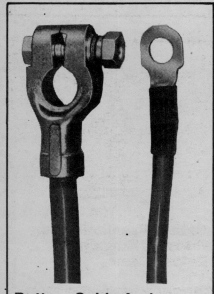

Battery Cable And Clamp Replacements

When you replace a battery, you should take careful look at your battery cables. Usually, they only need a thorough cleaning, but sometimes the entire cable needs replacement. Even a new battery will not give you top power if the inside of the battery cable clamp is out of shape because of frequent removal or cleaning. The Prestolite Company offers a wide variety of 12-volt, insulated battery cables to cover applications on most cars. To determine the length of a battery cable, you measure the distance between the center line of a hole in the clamp end and the center line of the hole in the lug end. Measuring in this manner will assure the proper choice of replacement cable.

Free Yourself From Battery Woes

If you would like to forget battery maintenance completely, there is a battery on the market that is designed to do just that. AC-Delco makes a battery that is sealed, which means that you never have to add water, so that case and terminal corrosion is virtually impossible. Most people are just concerned with the fact that the battery is maintenance-free. But for those of you who want to know the secret that makes it possible, we will explain. In conventional batteries, the grids are made with lead-antimony alloy. Antimony is used because it has the strength needed for the manufacturing process, but it is also the element that causes your battery to use water. The Freedom battery substitutes calcium for the antimony, which results in the same power output.

BATTERY SELECTION AND REPLACEMENT

is almost always the cable that is grounded against the engine block or frame. Only some older cars and import models have positive ground systems where the positive cable is connected to a good ground.

5. Always be sure that the new battery is fully charged after installation. Check the battery with a hydrometer. If the battery needs charging, refer to the section on charging for instructions.

There are several dangers to an insecurely mounted battery. One of the most obvious ones is the possibility of the battery falling off its perch on a sudden severe jounce. This could even cause an electrical fire.

However, another problem is the deterioration that can rapidly occur in an improperly mounted battery. Not only is there the danger of cracking the case, but you might also damage the battery by shaking the material on the plates loose, to a point where it piles up on the bottom of the battery, causing a short circuit. This, of course, will kill one or more of the cells.

After cleaning the battery terminals and whenever replacing a battery, you should apply a corrosion preventive to the cables and terminals. One quick way to do this is with a silicone spray,

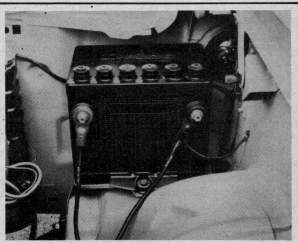

Batteries with their terminals mounted on the side rather than on top have less corrosion buildup.

but much more effective is the application of a special corrosion inhibitor that can be brushed on the metal. This is available from your auto parts store. You can also apply a heavy application of grease, or even standard petroleum jelly will do.

Many of the newer side terminal batteries have protective caps over the terminals to reduce their vulnerability to corrosion. These can help, but it is still a good idea to add your extra protection to this metal.

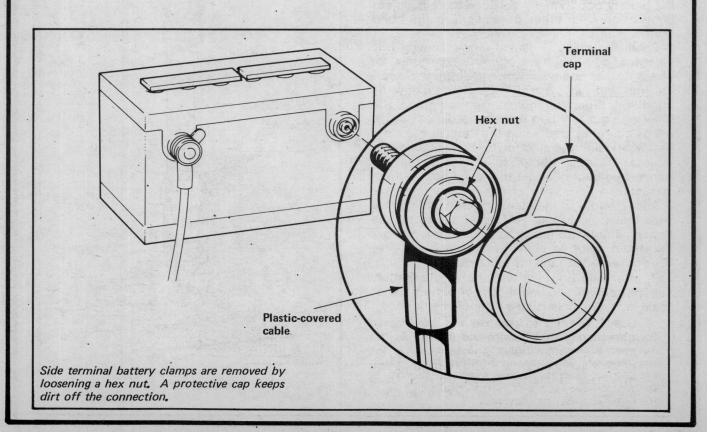

Terminal cap

Hex nut

Plastic-covered cable

Side terminal battery clamps are removed by loosening a hex nut. A protective cap keeps dirt off the connection.

REPLACING A STARTER AND SOLENOID

HERE IS A JOB that is not too difficult if you do not mind climbing under the car and lifting out a 10 to 15 pound motor. It is well worth the saving compared to the price of a starter motor replacement in most service shops. You can buy a good rebuilt or remanufactured starter for a good deal less than it would cost for a service shop to install a new one for you.

The starter motor is located underneath the car at the rear of the engine, usually on the driver's side of the car. It is bolted right to the flywheel housing. (The flywheel housing is the massive rear portion of the engine that houses the flywheel. The flywheel is the large heavy wheel at the end of the crankshaft on which are gear teeth.)

The job of the starter motor is to get the engine to crank. The battery supplies electrical current to the starter motor via the solenoid, where it is converted into mechanical power. A drive gear in the starter motor meshes with the gear teeth on the flywheel. The electrical current from the battery causes the starter motor drive gear to spin, which in turn causes the flywheel to turn. This sets the internal engine components in motion and the engine begins to start. (The ignition and

fuel systems also play equally important roles in getting the car started. You will learn more about their duties in their respective chapters.)

There are two common ways to engage the starter motor drive gear with the flywheel—the Bendix drive and the overrunning clutch drive. The Bendix drive uses inertia to engage the drive gear with the flywheel, while the overrunning clutch type uses a shift lever. In either case, as soon as the engine is started, the drive gear is disengaged from the flywheel and, along with the starter motor itself, is no longer needed until the next time you have to start your car.

The solenoid is a device used to engage the starter motor drive gear with the teeth on the flywheel. When the ignition key is turned to start the engine, electrical current is sent to the sole-

Here Is What You Will Need

Materials

- Starter
- Solenoid
- Lock Washers or Internal Tooth Washers

Tools

- Jack and Jack Stands
- Creeper
- Battery Pliers
- Wrenches
- Battery Terminal Puller

Remanufactured Parts Vs. New Ones

If you suspect your starter motor as the reason your car will not start, after thoroughly checking out the battery and all wiring connections, you will be glad to know that you can save between 20 and 25 percent by buying a rebuilt or remanufactured starter motor over buying a brand new one. Arrow Automotive Industries offers a line of remanufactured starter motors that are available through auto supply stores. Specific instructions on how to install the starter motor are included with each component. Quality remanufactured parts, in many cases, are just as good as new parts. They are tested and adjusted like new parts, and incorporate the newest engineering changes that the original part may not have had.

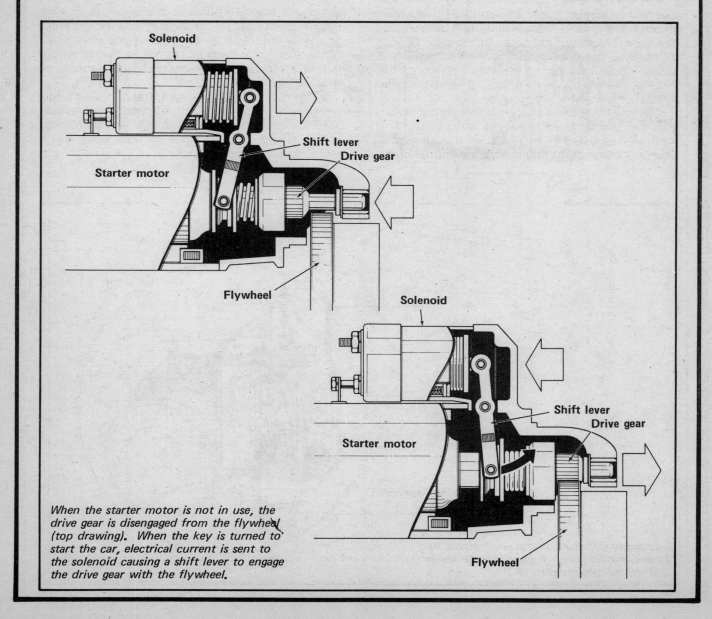

When the starter motor is not in use, the drive gear is disengaged from the flywheel (top drawing). When the key is turned to start the car, electrical current is sent to the solenoid causing a shift lever to engage the drive gear with the flywheel.

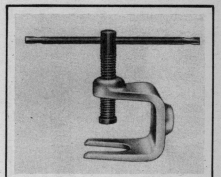

Battery Terminal Puller Prevents Damage To Battery Case

You must be careful when removing cable clamps from the battery terminals. Twisting can damage both. To remove the clamps properly, you need a battery terminal puller—especially if corrosion is present. Owatonna Tool Company makes a handy battery terminal puller that allows you to lift the clamp straight up off the post. Model 847-A is composed of a U-shaped steel bracket and a bolt with a T-handle. The bottom part of the bracket slips under the clamp, which positions the end of the bolt over the top of the battery terminal. Using the T-handle to screw the bolt down against the battery terminal lifts the bracket and clamp. The puller is designed to prevent damage to the battery case, and it has a special striking pad that takes the blow of a hammer when it is necessary to drive the bottom of the bracket under the clamp.

Portable Drive-On Ramp Makes Under-Car Service Easier

Working under a car can pose problems because of the close tolerances of parts and the lack of room for maneuvering, especially when replacing a starter. Auto Trend Products makes a dual purpose auto ramp and jack stand called the Super Jack Ramp that makes those hard-to-reach areas more accessible. Properly set up, you can drive your car up the ramps and rest it on the jack stands. The ramps can then be removed for more work area. Constructed of heavy steel, the ramp and jack stand will support in excess of 10,000 pounds. Auto Trend also markets separate jack stands in two sizes—12 and 15 inches. Called Super Stands, these stands offer several height variations and will support up to 3500 pounds.

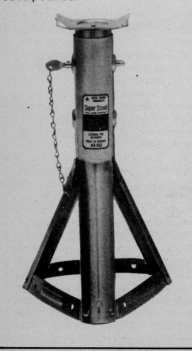

REPLACING A STARTER AND SOLENOID

noid that activates a plunger inside the solenoid. The plunger is connected to a shift lever that shifts the starter motor drive gear into and out of mesh with the flywheel.

The point to remember is that the starter motor and solenoid have important jobs to do and there is no room for abuse. If the car does not start after 30 seconds of cranking the engine, wait at least two minutes for the starter motor and solenoid to cool down before you try again. If the battery and its connections check out okay and all other systems are known to be in good working condition, you probably need a new starter motor or solenoid.

This decision is best left up to a professional mechanic. However, the actual replacement of a starter motor and/or solenoid is not a terribly complicated job.

Removing a starter motor varies from car to car and from model to model. For example, on some cars you will have to maneuver the starter motor around exhaust pipes and suspension linkage, which can be tricky without an air lift.

Solenoids are mounted either on the inner fender well or on the starter motor itself. There is

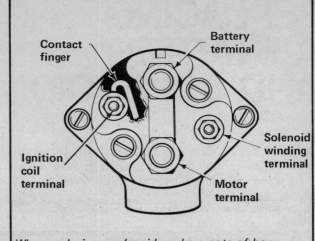

When replacing a solenoid, make a note of how the wires are connected so they can go back to the same terminals on the new one.

no problem in taking one off a fender well, but when the solenoid is mounted on the starter motor, the starter motor usually has to be removed to get at the solenoid.

In either case, the following procedures for removing a starter motor and solenoid are general procedures that can be used as good guidelines. By following our instructions and carefully

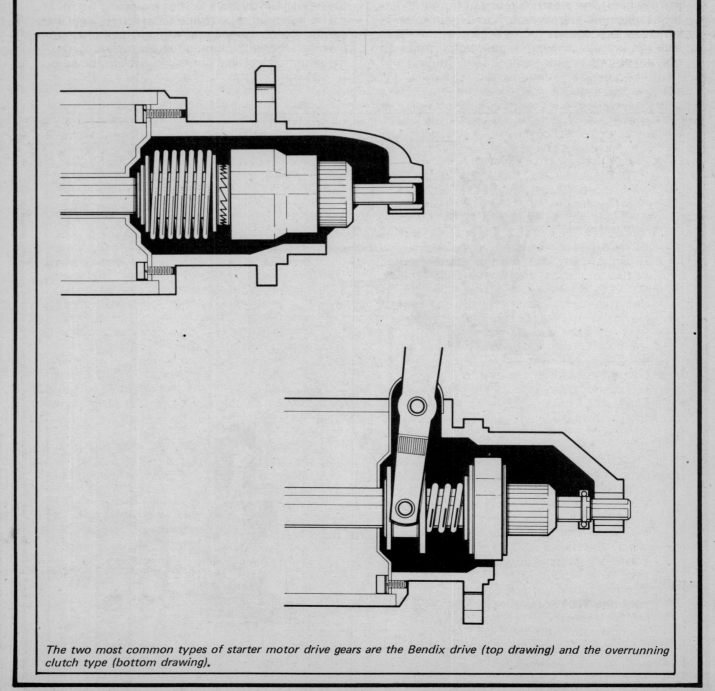

The two most common types of starter motor drive gears are the Bendix drive (top drawing) and the overrunning clutch type (bottom drawing).

The starter motor is located at the back of the engine. Most starter motors must be removed from underneath the car.

examining how the components are installed, you should not have any problems.

Some special equipment that will make your replacement job easier includes a jack, a pair of jack stands and a creeper. The jack will get your car high enough off the ground so that you will have more room to remove the starter motor. The jack stands will support the front end of your car while you are underneath it. And with a creeper, you can lie on your back and roll under the car to remove the starter motor.

1. Before you roll under the car to remove the starter motor, disconnect the ground cable from the battery terminal (use a wrench, pliers or battery terminal puller). Then locate your starter motor. It is usually near the bottom and rear of the engine on the driver's side of the car.
2. Brush off any dirt on the starter motor (watch your eyes). Use a wrench to remove all wires connected to the starter motor and solenoid. It is a good idea to tag these wires in some way so that you can be sure they go back to the same connections. Incorrectly connected wires can cause serious problems to the electrical system.
3. Loosen the starter motor mounting bolts, but do not take them all the way out. Find some way to support the starter motor so that you can brace yourself to accept its weight, approximately 10 to 15 pounds.
4. Now, remove the bolts and pull the starter motor forward and out. **NOTE:** On some cars, especially General Motors models, there may be a bracket on the top of the starter motor that braces it to the engine or is attached to one of the three starter motor bolts. This bracket must be removed before the starter motor can come out.
5. To install the starter motor, reverse steps two, three and four. Use lock washers or internal tooth washers on all wire connections. **NOTE:** Be sure the starter motor has a clean connection around the mounting bolt holes, without corrosion or paint.
6. Reconnect the battery ground cable and test the starter motor for normal operation by starting the engine.

General Motors Corporation cars and some Ford Motor Company and Chrysler Corporation products have their solenoid mounted on the starter motor, so the starter motor must be removed in order to replace the solenoid. This is done by following the procedure we have just described.

1. Once you have the starter motor and solenoid assembly out of the car, place it on a work bench and remove the two bolts that secure the solenoid to the starter motor.
2. At one end of the solenoid is a connection that attaches the starter motor field lead or leads to the solenoid. After removing this connection, rotate and remove the solenoid. **NOTE:** On the plunger, there is a spring that should be replaced when changing the solenoid.
3. Install the new solenoid, reversing steps one and two. Make sure that the spring seats properly on the plunger.
4. Secure all connections using lock washers or internal tooth washers.
5. Reinstall the starter motor and solenoid assembly as previously outlined.

Ford Motor Company and American Motors Corporation cars that have the solenoid mounted on the inner fender require the following procedure for removal.

1. Disconnect the battery ground cable.
2. Disconnect all wire connections on the solenoid. Be sure to tag them so you will not get confused when reconnecting them.
3. Remove the mounting bolts.
4. Mount the new solenoid in the same place as the old one.
5. Reconnect the wires using internal tooth or lock washers on all connections.
6. Reconnect the battery cable to the terminal.

Some Chrysler Corporation cars use a solenoid built directly into the starter motor and should only be changed by someone familiar with this type of starter motor and solenoid assembly.

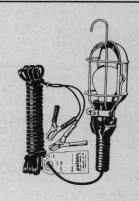

BATTERY AND STARTING SYSTEM

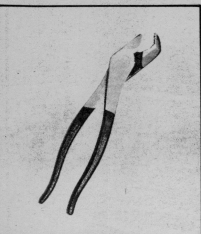

Removing Stubborn Battery Nuts

If your battery terminals have hex or square fasteners, battery pliers will make their removal quick and easy. Typical of battery pliers, the Wrench Grip Model T-14 from Teledyne AWD features a thin, tapered nose that can work to your advantage if the terminals or battery hold-down nuts are difficult to reach with your hand. Also, if you have rounded the edges of a nut, you can use the battery pliers to get a strong grip on the nut for removal. Battery pliers also serve as a general-purpose tool for use in other automotive repair and maintenance tasks.

Maintenance-Free Battery

Pocket-type separators inside the Gould maintenance-free battery allow the negative and positive plates to rest directly on the bottom of the tough polypropylene container. As a result, nearly twice as much electrolyte reaches the plates. The maintenance-free battery from Gould Inc., Automotive Battery Division, is available with either conventional terminals or with side terminals.

Be Careful When Making Hydrometer Measurements

Play it safe when using your hydrometer. Since the instrument will be filled with battery fluid called electrolyte—which contains highly corrosive sulphuric acid—you must take care not to let any of the fluid splash on yourself or on your car. Always wear gloves and safety glasses or goggles when working a hydrometer.

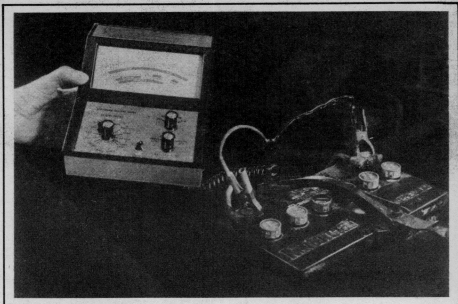

Electronic Battery Tester Combines Three Units Into One

Some home mechanics are not satisfied until they have the most sophisticated electronic testing equipment available. If you are into this type of testing equipment, Motorola Inc., has something for you. It is an electronic battery tester that does the job of load testers, cell voltmeters, and hydrometers. Model TBT1181W weighs only three pounds and includes readouts of 0 to 18 kilowatts and 0 to 16 volts. This unit has a color-coded "good/replace" scale, battery-temperature compensation, reverse polarity protection, and over-voltage protection. In addition to the complete battery check, it can also be used to check the starter motor and voltage regulator.

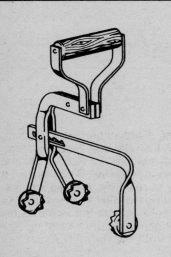

Ease Battery Replacement With A Battery Lifter

It is important that you use a battery carrier whenever you remove or replace a battery in your car. Batteries are filled with strong acid solutions that can cause severe burns on contact with your skin. Even if you do not spill the acid from the battery accidentally, the case sometimes becomes coated with an acid film after it has been in a car for a long time. Also, many batteries have been ruined when dropped while being lifted out of the car by hand. A battery carrier, manufactured by Essex Automotive Parts, adjusts to hold any battery securely—even those with side-mounted terminals. Model 79-27 features a comfortable handle that makes it easy to lift and carry even the heaviest car batteries.

General-Purpose Battery Chargers Get You Going When Your Battery Will Not

When your battery is low, and you know that the temperature will dip below the zero mark the next day, you will not have to worry about starting your car if you have a battery charger in your garage. Christie Electric Corporation makes a series of battery chargers that range in output from 4 to 20 amperes. The 10-ampere unit, Model C-61210, is adequate for most car owners, especially if energy conscious. There is a big jump in energy input from the 10- to 20-ampere models. The 10-amp model takes two amperes to operate, compared to four for the 20-ampere charger, Model C-61220. Also, the difference in weight between the two units is 15¾ pounds although the size difference is negligible.

Make All Tests With One Connection

Even though your car may be running fine now, there is always the possibility of a breakdown later on. Rather than taking the word of the repair shop mechanic, you can track down the problem source by using a quality tester. One such unit is available from Marquette Automotive Service Systems Group. The company's Model 42-125 BST (Battery/Starter Tester) features two 4½-inch meters, heavy-duty current leads with built-in voltage pickup leads, and voltage test leads for testing any electrical component or circuit in a car or truck. One of the meters is a voltmeter that tests six- through 40-volt systems with three test scales (0-2, 0-20, 0-40), while the other is an ammeter offering a 0-500 amperes range/amp-hour size scale. Easy to use, the company's battery/starter tester allows you to test energizer, conventional, hard top, and sealed batteries; starter solenoids; battery cable terminals; and alternator output.

Spreader, Reamer And Cleaner

If you have a conventional battery, with posts on the top, you will need tools to spread the clamps, ream the inside of the clamps, and clean the terminals. There is a tool on the market that can do all these jobs. The Terminal Clamp Spreader, Reamer and Post Cleaner sold by Teledyne AWD (catalog No. T-20-C) has a long handle that gives you extra leverage when reaming and cleaning battery terminals and cable clamps. This makes for quick removal of corrosion that could cause trouble in your electrical system.

BATTERY AND STARTING SYSTEM

Clean Batteries Last Longer

Corrosion on the battery terminals is one reason why an engine has trouble starting. Siloo Inc. offers two aerosol products that fight to control this problem. The manufacturer's battery cleaner, No. 24A, cleans away corrosion from the battery terminals, casing, cable connectors and hold-down frames. The company also makes a battery terminal protector, No. 46A, that helps to prevent any further buildup of corrosion on battery terminals. The benefits from taking care of your battery with these types of products include easier starting, longer battery life and improved battery output.

Drop Light Puts Light Where You Want It

For virtually any kind of auto repair work, a drop light, sometimes called a trouble light, is a basic piece of equipment. It allows you to put a great deal of illumination exactly where you need it. This particular light, Model 98-14, is sold by Essex Automotive Parts. It features a metal bulb cage to prevent bulb breakage, and a handy hook for hanging from the underside of the car's hood. The solid, metal shield on one side of the cage shades the light from your eyes to give optimum visibility.

Polypropylene Vs. Hard Rubber Containers

The Power Breed 60 battery, from Gould Inc., Automotive Battery Division, is built in a thin but tough polypropylene container. As a result, it contains more power-producing plates, bigger plates, and more acid than do the conventional batteries built in hard rubber containers. It delivers cold cranking power to 515 amperes, which is ample even for high-performance cars with big engines. Gang-type pull-out vent caps allow quick removal and replacement for faster battery servicing.

Battery Brush Cleans Side Terminals

Batteries that have side-mounted terminals do not have exposed posts, so they are less likely to accumulate corrosion. Occasionally, though, the threaded insert on the cable clamps plus the flat surface on the battery where contact is made with the cable clamp should be cleaned. Cal Van Tools markets a side terminal battery brush that can accomplish both these tasks. It features a pair of stainless steel brushes mounted in an acid-resistant plastic handle. The rectangular brush cleans the flat surface, and the circular brush on the other end of the handle cleans around the threaded insert.

Battery Terminal Cleaner And Protector

To clean those battery terminals and to keep them clean, Maywood Company makes two products you should know about. The company's battery terminal cleaner, No. S283, removes corrosion and grease to extend the strength of the battery for more trouble-free service. Simply spray on the cleaner, then wipe it off. The battery terminal coating spray, No. S284, protects the battery, cables, and connectors from moisture and acid corrosion.

Battery Replacement Cable For S/T Batteries

If you have a defective or worn battery cable, your car may fail to start even though your battery is in top condition. Standard Motor Products, Inc. makes a side terminal battery cable called the Ektrolead that replaces those found in most 1971 and later General Motors cars with side terminal batteries. It features a full-power connection with a high-conductivity connector. The cable's design provides good anticorrosion protection in addition to protection from shocks.

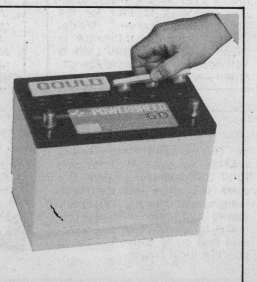

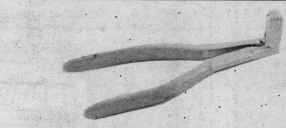

Charge Your Own Battery With This Medium Output Charger

When periodically checking your battery's state of charge with a battery tester, you may find that it needs recharging. This can be due to an overuse of accessories, extending cranking in cold weather, or accidentally leaving your car lights on for extended periods without running the engine. If you find yourself in this situation, you can save inconvenience and money by using your own battery charger. TRW Replacement Division, TRW, Inc.'s Model 679203 10-ampere medium output charger is a compact 10 inch x 6½ inch x 7½ inch unit, and can recharge a car battery in four to six hours. You just plug the unit into an AC outlet and attach the leads to your battery terminals. The unit is U/L tested and can provide a maximum battery charge of 12½ amperes.

Battery Clamp Spreader And Reamer

The only proper way to spread a battery clamp for removal is to use a plier-like tool designed specifically for that job. The Automark Division of Wells Manufacturing Corporation makes a tool, Model 51904 that features sharp metal teeth on the outside portion of the plier head. This makes it easy to ream the terminals by expanding the plier heads until they are tight against the inside of the terminal, and then twisting the tool until the metal is clean and bright.

Battery Condition Tester

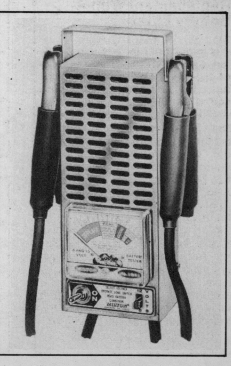

Easy-to-use battery tester from Milton Industries, Inc. can be used periodically to tell you if your battery is in a good or weak condition. Batteries can fail at the most inconvenient times and the cause can be nothing more than poor connections or worn cables. With Milton's Model 1260 battery tester, you can quickly locate the source of trouble and repair or replace the guilty culprit. If you suspect problems in the charging system, you can use this unit to check the charging rate and to determine if the rate is okay or too low. Advantages of this unit are a fast hookup with no outside power source and easy-to-read instructions printed on the meter face. It can be used on both six- and 12-volt systems.

Tight Connections Are Important

When connecting cables or wires to threaded terminals, be sure to use a lock washer under the nut. The preferred type is an internal tooth lock washer. This style has ten barbs around its inner circumference that bite into the connection, keeping it physically and electrically tight.

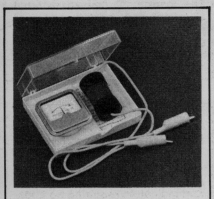

Short Circuit Detector 'Sees' Through Metal

One of the problems involved in finding a short in your electrical circuit is that wiring is generally concealed and difficult to reach. Cal-Van Tools, a division of Chemi-Trol Chemical Co., offers a detector that is able to locate short circuits in six- and 12-volt systems without removing a car's upholstery, body panels, etc. The Model 69 detector will also operate through metal door posts and rocker and door panels. It is small enough to fit in a shirt pocket and comes with instructions.

Test Light

Hastings Manufacturing Company's No. 1090 test light can be used to check out six- and 12-volt circuits with the power on. The instrument has a flexible wire lead with ground clip, and its sharp, pointed steel probe pierces insulation without damage to the wire. The test light, which uses a standard replacement bulb, has a high-impact plastic case.

Voltage Tester Accurate To 1/10 Volt

Hastings Manufacturing Company's Model 1786 voltage tester has a 0 to 16 volt scale that is large enough to make voltage tests accurate to 1/10 volt. The pocket-size unit serves common automotive applications. Its compact size allows you to make tests in difficult-to-reach locations. This tester's rubber case will not scratch or mar automotive finishes.

High-Low Voltage Test Light

K-D Manufacturing Co. sells a combination electrical troubleshooter and spark plug tester that can be used for high and low voltage applications. The device, which can trace electrical problems in your charging system, can be used on all six-, 12- and 24-volt systems. The voltage test light, Model 126, has a shock-proof handle. Replacement bulbs are available.

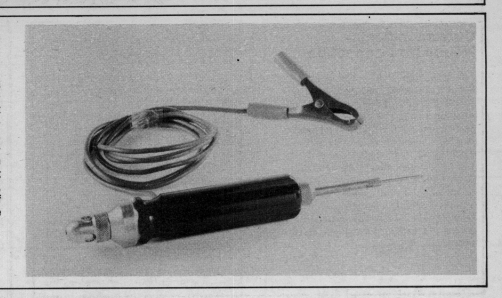

INTRODUCTION

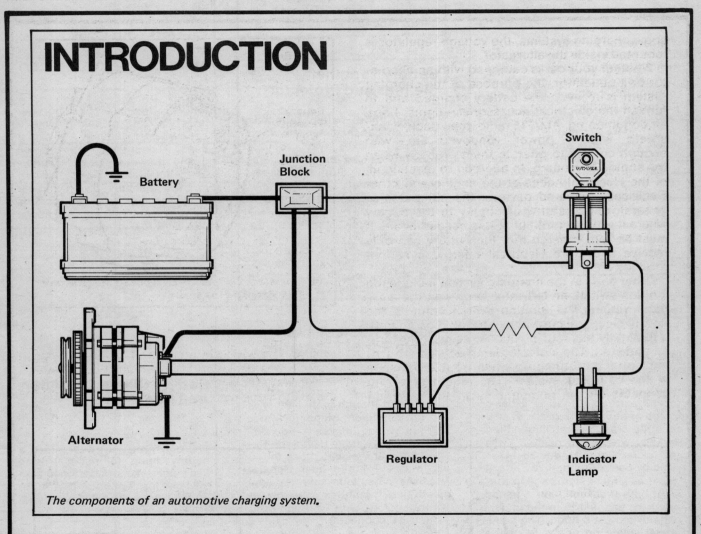

The components of an automotive charging system.

AS WE LEARNED in the battery chapter, the battery supplies the initial electrical current needed to start the engine. Once the engine is started, however, the electrical current is generated by an alternator or generator. Since about one-half of all automotive problems are electrically related, it is important to understand as much as possible about the function and basic repairs of the charging system.

The charging system basically consists of the battery, an alternator or generator, a voltage regulator and the necessary switches and wiring. For a complete discussion of the battery, see the chapter on Battery and Starting System.

In recent years, the conventional generator has been replaced by the alternator to keep up with the increased electrical demands of the newer cars. The alternator also has the capability of producing a greater level of electrical current at low engine speeds. Today, only some older cars and a few import models have a generator.

The alternator is a small, fat disc with fins around its edge. It is located near the radiator at the front of the engine, and is mechanically driven by a drive belt connected to the crankshaft pulley that turns the fan. A generator is located in the same place, but is more cylindrical in shape.

The voltage regulator is the "brains" of the charging system, in that it controls the amount of electricity produced by the alternator or generator. It prevents the alternator or generator from delivering too much current to the battery, a condition that can burn out all of the car's electrical components. The voltage regulator is silver or black, about three inches square and an inch high, with "Regulator" usually stamped on its top, and flat metal tabs or terminals at its bottom edge. Generally, it is mounted on or near the alternator or generator—sometimes on the fender well, sometimes on the firewall between the engine and the passenger compartment. In

CHARGING SYSTEM

Current Indicator Needs No Connection

An ammeter is necessary for alternator and starter diagnosis, and one that reads by induction rather than direct electrical connection is especially easy to use. The Model TE-569 Current Indicator Tester made by Filko Automotive Div. is such an instrument. It has two separate scales—one for alternator work, reading 75-0-75 amps, and another for starters, reading 400-0-400 amps.

Continuity Tester

Vaco Products Company's continuity tester, Model 70008, checks for defective controls, broken leads or lines in switches, motors and appliances. It allows you to test for the continuity of a circuit with the power off. A bulb in the tester's handle glows when the circuit is complete. The instrument features a 3-3/4 inch probe and a large, four-inch handle with a removable cap that stores a replacement bulb and battery. A 36 inch test lead and alligator clip are included.

Charging System Analyzer

Pocket-size charging analyzers are fine for some jobs, but for more exacting work, you need a professional-style analyzer such as the Model T-75 sold by C.E. Neihoff & Co. This model, which works on six-, 12-, 24- and 32-volt systems, has three voltmeter scales—0 to 4, 0 to 20, and 0 to 40—and a 0 to 100 ammeter scale. The instrument has an external shunt for easy hookup and field jumper connectors for all popular systems to simplify testing. All necessary adapters are included.

---

some charging systems, the voltage regulator is mounted inside the alternator.

Whether your car is equipped with an alternator or a generator, the purpose of the charging system is to keep the battery charged and to furnish the electrical accessories—lights, horn, air conditioning, AM/FM radio, tape deck, windshield wipers, power windows, etc.—with enough current to operate them properly when the engine is running. In addition to meeting all of the electrical needs of the engine and other electrically powered devices, the alternator or generator also returns electricity to the battery where it will be stored until it is needed again. It must be remembered that the battery can only receive and store electrical energy, it cannot produce it.

Other parts in the charging system include the ignition switch, an indicator lamp and the electrical wiring. The ignition switch controls the flow of electrical current by turning it on and off. It generally has four positions: accessories, off, on and start. The indicator lamp acts as a warning signal by lighting up when trouble develops in the charging system. The electrical wiring connects all the components in the charging

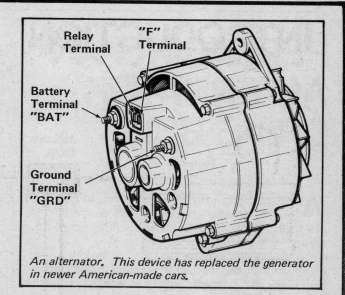

An alternator. This device has replaced the generator in newer American-made cars.

system. The wiring in a car is of different types and gauges designed for specific jobs. Therefore, always replace old wires with new ones that are of the same type, length and gauge.

Current Indicator Requires No Hookup

Auto mechanics know that current indicators requiring no hookup are very easy to use. This is why they have become popular. Hastings Manufacturing Co. sells a handy two-in-one indicator for checking both starter draw and generator output. You just hold it against the wire for either test. No connections are needed. The instrument, Model No. 1368, has clear dial markings and two scales, 80-0-80 and 400-0-400.

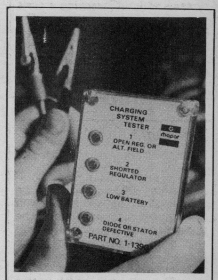

Mopar Analyzer Is Like A Minicomputer

Conventional charging-system testers require readouts in volts and amps, but Mopar's tester automatically compares the electrical output of the charging system to a preprogrammed set of specifications. Individual flashing lights indicate open regulator or alternator field, shorted regulator, low battery and diode or stator defects. The hand-held unit may also be used to test the diode trio on GM-style alternators. The new tester's part number is 1-1390, and it is available from the Chrysler Corporation.

A generator supplies current for the electrical system in older cars and some newer imported models.

Prevent Slippage With Belt Dressing

From time to time, you should apply a belt dressing to your alternator drive belt. A dressing, such as Permatex No. 120 made by Woodhill/Permatex, will prevent slippage and help prolong the life of the belt. The easiest type to apply is that which comes in an aerosol can. Permatex belt dressing comes in 14 ounce and five ounce aerosol cans and is applied to the drive belt at the pulley. It rids belts of foreign matter and stops glazing. Also, it contains no asphalt or resin.

Belt Dressing

To keep your alternator drive belt in good condition, you should occasionally treat it to an application of belt dressing, such as Belt-Ease manufactured by the American Grease Stick Co. This is a long lasting, clear belt dressing that adds traction, silences squeaks and helps to preserve the belt. The aerosol can (5.5 ounces) has a special spray-anyway valve that even works upside down. It is designed to let you pinpoint the stream with no messy overspray.

Mechanic's Light

Lighting is very important when working on your car because it makes the work easier and safer. Fluorescent type mechanic's lights are becoming increasingly popular because they are rugged, stay cool and offer glare-free illumination. New Era Products Inc. sells a very rugged light called the Master Mechanic's Light. It is resistant to water, oil, grease and vapor, and carries a 90 day warranty. Other features include an in-line, safety isolated ballast, an easily replaced 15 watt fluorescent lamp, clear protective

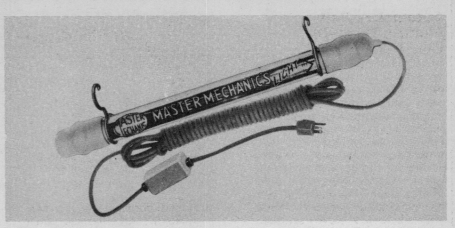

lamp enclosure and a built-in light reflector. It also has flexible, moisture resistant end caps and convenient hanging hook. The unit measures 22 inches overall and is UL approved.

REPLACING AN ALTERNATOR DRIVE BELT

A PROBLEM in the charging system can start out small and gradually get worse. There are indications, however, that will let you know when the system is malfunctioning.

An overcharged battery is a common indication that the charging system needs attention. An overcharged battery is indicated by the constant need for additional water. If this condition is not remedied immediately, your battery could be seriously damaged.

An undercharged battery can be just as serious. Indications are slow cranking of the engine and dim headlights.

Whether your car has an indicator light or an ammeter gauge in the dashboard, either of these devices will indicate early trouble. An indicator light should only come on when the ignition switch is in the On position with the engine not running. If it comes on while the engine is running or the ignition switch is off, then a problem exists in the charging system. The reading on the ammeter indicates if the battery is overcharging, undercharging or not charging at all.

If the battery is charged and in good condition, the drive belt is the next logical part to inspect, then the voltage regulator. If both the "charge" light and the "temperature" light are red, it means the drive belt is slipping or broken.

One of the biggest causes of charging system failure is a loose, overly tight or defective drive belt. (If this is not the cause of your problem, read the section on alternator testing in this chapter.) A loose drive belt means slippage, and the alternator will not produce enough power to charge the battery. So the red "charge" light on

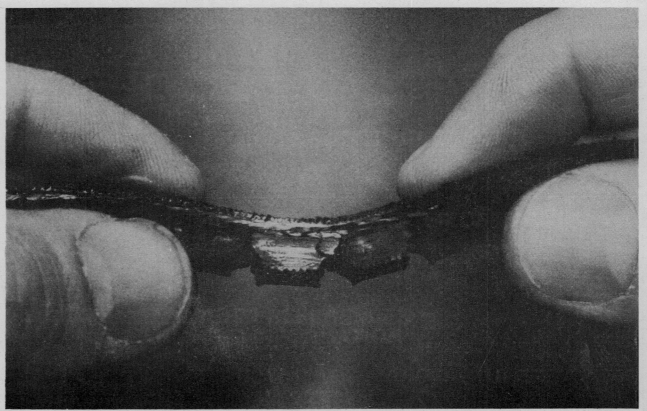

Alternator drive belts should be checked regularly. Usually, they last about three years. Inspect the belt for cracks, brittleness and oil on its surface.

Automotive Belts Feature Three-Ply Construction

When you replace an alternator drive belt on your engine, you might as well buy a top quality belt that will last a long time. The Goodyear Tire & Rubber Co. features a new line of belts with extra strong construction. The belts are constructed in layers. One outer layer is made of oil-resistant, rubber-impregnated tension fabric. This is a square, woven synthetic fabric designed to reduce surface fatigue and resist cracking. Beneath the tension fabric are low stretched cords. They are constructed for long flex-life and a great resistance to shock loads. Next comes a fiber reinforced insulation that provides greater strength and stability to the tensile cord members. Finally, there is a three-ply laminated fabric. This oil-resistant, rubber-impregnated three-ply fabric provides increased support for the tensile carrying cords and improved resistance to cracking and flexing. Goodyear belts are available at most automotive stores.

Here Is What You Will Need

Materials
● Drive Belt

Tools
● Drive Belt Tension Gauge
● Wrenches
● Pry Bar

---

the instrument panel may brighten and stay lit, the headlights will dim at idle speeds, and the battery will run down repeatedly. A drive belt that is too tight can burn out the alternator bearings and strain the water pump bearings.

Drive belts, like most parts made of rubber, usually last about three years. Many careful car owners replace the drive belt at three-year intervals to avoid both mechanical problems and electrical system damages. The only sound a loose drive belt makes is an occasional squeak or wail during acceleration.

You can check the drive belt tension with a belt tension gauge (available at auto supply stores). If you do not have a tension gauge, with the engine off, place your finger on the drive belt midway between the pulleys. Press on the drive belt with your finger. If the drive belt depresses more than 3/4 inch, then the drive belt is too loose and could be the cause of your charging system troubles. Inspect the drive belt for cracks, brittleness and oil on its surface. An oil soaked drive belt may appear tight, but it will still slip and prevent the battery from recharging. Here is the correct procedure for adjusting or replacing an alternator drive belt.

1. Use a wrench to loosen the alternator mounting bolt at the bottom of the alternator and the adjusting bolt at the top.
2. Slide the alternator towards the fan just enough to loosen the tension on the drive belt. If your car has other accessory units such as power steering, air conditioning or an emission control air pump, these belts may have to be loosened or removed in order to gain access to the alternator drive belt. Be sure to note which belt rides in which groove so you can reinstall them in the correct way.
3. Remove the old drive belt from the pulleys. Do not cut the drive belt to remove it unless you already have the correct replacement belt in hand. When buying a replacement drive belt from your auto supply store, be sure to get the correct size belt for your car.
4. Install the new alternator drive belt over the pulleys that it rides in. **NOTE:** If other belts are to be replaced, be sure you put the belts back on starting with the belt closest to the engine block. Do not try to stretch a new belt over the pulley with a screwdriver, as this will weaken it.
5. Tighten each belt using a pry bar to move the alternator away from the fan. Adjust the belt tension so that there is no more than 3/4 inch of deflection when you press down with your finger. Then tighten the mounting and adjusting bolts securely.
6. Start the engine and check to see that the belts are properly aligned and working okay. A few weeks after installing a new drive belt, you should recheck the tension, as new drive belts tend to stretch after installation.

A drive belt should not be too loose or too tight. You can check the belt tension with a belt tension gauge, which is available at auto supply stores.

Rechecking Belt Tension

When you replace an alternator drive belt, make sure the tension is correct. After a new drive belt has been in use for a couple of weeks, recheck its tension again. New belts have a tendency to stretch after a short time in service. A belt that is too loose will slip and become glazed, eventually resulting in belt failure.

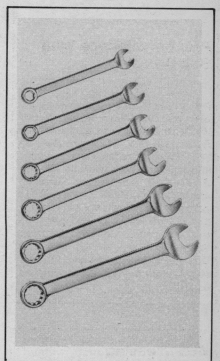

Combination Wrench Set Handy For Emergencies

If you are going to keep only a few tools in the car for emergency purposes, a good choice is to include a set of wrenches that have a box end and an open end. Duro Metal Products Co. manufactures a combination wrench set called Duro-Chrome Model 84115. Six wrenches are included: 5/16 inch, 3/8 inch, 7/16 inch, 1/2 inch, 9/16 inch, and 5/8 inch. The set is sold in a plastic pouch, which is handy for storage.

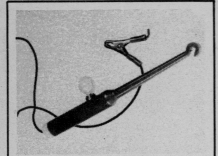

Circuit Tester Has A Long Hooked Nose

Thexton Manufacturing Co. offers a No. 120 Circuit-Chek Circuit Tester. This instrument is designed with a long hooked nose that allows you to check wires for current using only one hand. All you do is fasten the ground clamp to a clean surface and place the wire within the hook. Then you pull the tester to align the wire with the point and pull the trigger. If the circuit is live, the handle will light up. The long nose lets you reach areas that are not easily accessible—under the dash, in doors, through holes in the body, etc. The Circuit-Chek Circuit Tester is shock resistant with a tough, durable nylon body. The bulb and point are replaceable, and a probe is included for touch testing.

Electrical Analyzer For OEM Electronic And Standard Ignition Systems

When working on your charging system, you cannot get by without a good electrical analyzer. Peerless Instrument Company's Pulsar Model 250 analyzer can be used on six-, 12- and 24-volt electrical systems for testing alternators, generators, voltage regulators, batteries, alternator diodes and stators, short circuits, battery cables and solenoids, voltage drops, starter motors, circuit resistance and accessory current. The scale ranges on the 3-1/2 inch meter include 0 to 32 volts; 0 to 16 volts; 0 to 3 volts; 10-0-80 amps; and 0-400 amps. The unit also features a 5-1/2 inch D'Arsonval meter movement.

Current Indicator Registers Amperage Without Hookup

The Model 71 alternator and generator current indicator sold by Cal-Van Tools, a division of Chemi-Trol Chemical Company, makes it easy to check generator or alternator output. You just place the metal slots in the back of the device over the output wire from the generator/alternator with the engine running. Then you take a dial reading. The scale

reads from 75-0-75 DC amperes. The Lexan plastic-encased meter measures 2-3/8 inches by 2-3/8 inches.

Solid-State Analyzer For Do-It-Yourselfer

Triple-A Specialty Company sells a charging system analyzer that is designed specifically for the do-it-yourself mechanic. Tagged the Silver Beauty, the unit is about the size of a pack of cigarettes and indicates four conditions with flashing lights. It tells if there is an open regulator or alternator field, shorted regulator, low battery or diode or stator defective in the alternator. The unit can check all 12-volt systems.

TESTING THE ALTERNATOR AND VOLTAGE REGULATOR

IF YOUR alternator light comes on while you are driving down the highway, this usually means one of two things—your alternator is not supplying current to the battery, or the drive belt is loose or broken. A drive belt is easy to check, so do this first. If it needs to be replaced or tightened, follow the directions in the section on replacing a drive belt elsewhere in this chapter.

If your car is equipped with a generator rather than an alternator, take it to a qualified mechanic and have him check it out. There are several types of generator systems. Using the wrong testing procedures could give you inaccurate results or could even damage components.

Before performing any alternator tests, the battery must be fully charged. Use a hydrometer to test the battery's state of charge. If it is not fully charged, you will have to charge your battery as explained in the battery chapter. Once the battery is fully charged, you can go ahead with the alternator output test.

Performing an alternator output test will tell you whether or not your alternator is supplying current to the battery. It will also tell you if the alternator is at fault or if the voltage regulator is the cause of your problem. Testing the alternator requires no major mechanical work. It is a matter of properly connecting a voltmeter to the electrical system of your car and taking readings. The voltmeter measures the amount of voltage in an electrical circuit.

If you have little or no experience with working on the electrical system of a car, however, read every step very carefully and use extreme caution. If any instructions are unclear to you, having a professional mechanic do the work for you is preferable to the risk of shorting out expensive parts.

Here is a general procedure for checking the output of your alternator:

1. Disconnect the negative battery cable clamp from the negative battery terminal. (On positive ground systems, disconnect the positive cable clamp.) Side terminal battery cable clamps will come off by removing a hex-head bolt from the clamp with a wrench. Spring-type clamps require battery pliers to squeeze the tabs on the end of the clamp and to lift the clamp off the battery terminal. Conventional clamps can be removed by using a wrench to loosen a bolt on the clamp. A battery terminal puller will aid in lifting the clamp from the terminal.
2. Disconnect the field lead from the alternator. The field lead can be disconnected by pulling off a plug-on connector, or by removing a nut with a small wrench. This lead will generally be marked with an F on the alternator housing. If there is no mark, then you will have to find out which terminal is the field terminal through your car's service manual.
3. Clip one end of a jumper wire to this field terminal. You are now eliminating the regulator from the charging system to make the alternator charge at full output. Clip the other end to the terminal on the alternator marked BAT, which means battery.
4. Hook up the leads of the voltmeter—the red one to the BAT terminal on the alternator, and the black one to a good ground on the alternator frame.
5. Reconnect the ground cable to the battery terminal.
6. Turn off all the accessories and start the engine.
7. Note the reading on the voltmeter. A fully charged battery will read about 14 volts at idle. If the battery is low, you may have to speed the engine slightly above idle for a minute or two to start building up the voltage in the battery. If the voltage does not start climbing after a couple of minutes, you can be relatively sure that a problem exists in the alternator. If the voltage does

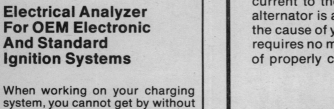

Here Is What You Will Need

Materials
- Sandpaper

Tools
- Hydrometer
- Wrenches
- Battery Pliers
- Battery Terminal Puller
- Jumper Wire
- Voltmeter
- Screwdriver

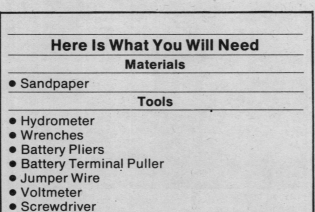

CHARGING SYSTEM

Full-Fielder Alternator Test Adapter

Here is a product that simplifies on-the-car alternator testing. It is the No. 304 Full Fielder alternator test adapter sold by Thexton Manufacturing Co. This gadget energizes the field circuit so that full alternator output can be measured. It bypasses the voltage regulator to isolate charging circuit problems. Easy to use, it inserts into the plug from the voltage regulator and accepts all standard Delco, Ford, and Chrysler voltage regulator units (except transistorized units). It works with all types of test equipment and is mistake-proof; the plugs cannot be inserted in the wrong position.

Current Indicator Works Without Hookups

A combination current indicator marketed by Sonco, a division of Mergo-Tronics Instrument Corp., can indicate starter, generator and alternator current without removing any cables or making connections. You simply place the instrument over the starter, generator or alternator cable and the unit shows the current being generated or consumed. The fully guaranteed instrument is calibrated.

Alternator/Generator/ Regulator Tester

If you do not have one of the newer, sophisticated electrical system analyzers that gives you a flashing light readout, you should at least have a basic alternator/generator/regulator tester. With an instrument such as Kar Check's Model 2043, you can measure the electrical performance of either alternator or generator charging systems, and the regulation of the electrical output on six- and 12-volt systems. The tester features color-coded scales for fast tests and easy-to-hook-up leads for safe use. It allows you to adjust the voltage regulator to end low battery or dead battery problems and also helps you to protect against burned-out bulbs, accessories, ignition points, ignition coil and resistor.

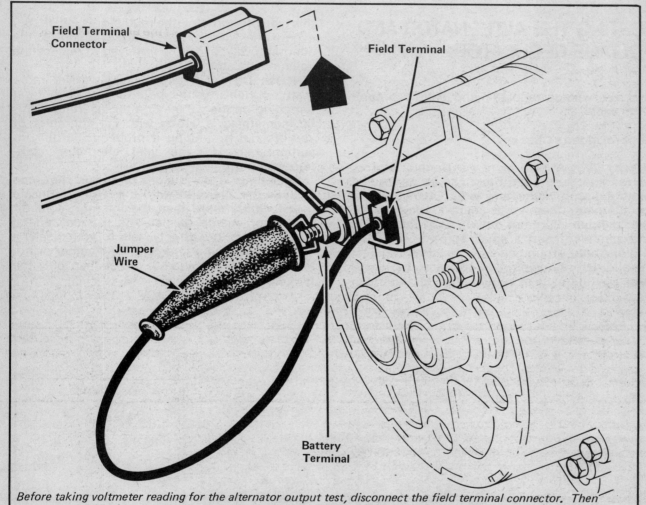

Before taking voltmeter reading for the alternator output test, disconnect the field terminal connector. Then connect one end of jumper wire to field terminal on the alternator; the other end of the jumper wire is connected to the battery terminal.

Professional Generator/ Alternator/Regulator Tester

If you do a lot of auto repair work, it is wise to invest in tools and instruments that are designed for professional use. Marquette manufactures a generator/alternator/regulator tester (Model 42-128) that is designed for heavy-duty use. It features two large, 4-1/2 inch meters. The voltmeter has three voltage ranges —0-2, 0-20, 0-40. It also has an expanded scale for reading voltage difference between upper and lower contacts or double contact voltage regulators. You can easily check voltage regulators to within 1/10 volt accuracy. The expanded scale range is 13-15.6 volts. The instrument's ammeter has a -10 to 100 amperes range. The instrument can quickly pinpoint any malfunction in alternators, generators, regulators and double contact regulators. It comes complete with a heavy-duty field rheostat, a heavy carbon pile, alternator adapter leads and battery post switch. Four different adapters for various alternators and generators are also available. The Model No. 42-128 is not a small machine. So, you might want to purchase the optional stand, Model No. 42-106.

start to climb, the regulator is causing the problem. **CAUTION:** Never let the voltage climb over 15 volts when performing this test, as this can damage the alternator or some other part of the electrical system.

One of the most common problems that results from a faulty voltage regulator is overcharging of the battery. An indication that your car is overcharging is if you are continually adding water to the battery or if a voltmeter reads 15 volts or higher when the car is running at idle. A defective battery can cause an overcharge condition too. So be sure the battery has been thoroughly checked out before blaming other parts of the charging system. If the battery

checks out okay and the alternator output test indicates a faulty voltage regulator, try this quick check before you replace the regulator.

8. Remove the mounting fasteners from the regulator with a screwdriver.
9. Use a piece of sandpaper to clean the area around the screws on the regulator and where it mounts on the body of the car.
10. Remount the regulator and start the car to see if the voltage reduces to a normal rate of charge. If overcharging still exists, install a new voltage regulator as covered elsewhere in this chapter.
11. Reverse steps one, two, three, four and five to disconnect the voltmeter and reconnect

CHARGING SYSTEM

Voltmeter Gauge Kit

A two inch voltmeter gauge kit, Model CP-7930, is made by the Sun Electric Corporation. It features solid-state circuit design, a 60-degree dial scale with a 10 to 16 volt range and chrome bezel. The kit also includes a single-unit mounting panel, wiring kit, and installation instructions with wire size recommendations.

AGR Tester Features Replaceable Meter

After using an ignition tune-up instrument for some time, a meter will occasionally malfunction. If this happens with the Milton Industries, Inc. Model 1206 AGR (Alternator, Generator, Regulator) tester, you simply buy a new meter cartridge to replace the faulty one: there is no need to buy an entire new instrument. The AGR tester also features a direct-reading volt and ampere scale, color-coded scales and switches, solid-state circuitry, and a complete set of leads that lets the meter perform all functions without the need for additional electrical harnesses.

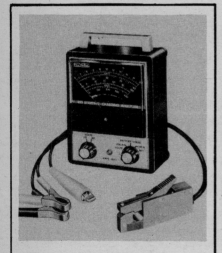

Professional Starting/ Charging Analyzer

Fox Valley Instrument Co. offers a professional starting/charging analyzer that features a unique clamp-on DC ammeter that simplifies starting and charging system tests. The ammeter is clamped over the battery cable or alternator lead so you can measure starter current drop or alternator output quickly and easily. The instrument allows you to test alternator output, alternator condition, starter current, regulated battery voltage, battery cranking voltage and ignition coil input voltage. The 4-1/2 inch meter covers 0 to 20 volts, 0 to 40 volts, 0 to 100 amps, 0 to 400 amps and alternator condition. The lead links are five feet long and the unit measures 2-5/16 inches by 5-1/4 inches by 6-13/16 inches. A 12-volt DC battery is required.

Circuit Tester

TRW, Inc. makes a low-voltage electrical tester that is ideal for automotive work. The insulated unit has a zinc-coated rod and durable, plastic outer construction. This tester is designed to penetrate the wire coating with minimum effort and damage and can be used on six- and 12-volt systems. For 24-volt systems, you merely replace the stock bulb with an accessory bulb included with the circuit tester. Instructions are included.

Pocket-Size Current Indicator

A current indicator that you can use anywhere is made by C. E. Neihoff & Co. To use, you simply place the Model T-52 induction meter over the wire to take a reading—no connections are necessary. The device, which checks alternator or generator output up to 75 amps, also indicates starter current drop. It features a color-coded "High-OK-Low" scale. The meter is calibrated up to 400 amps.

Professional Volt/Amp Generator/Alternator/ Regulator Tester

Sonco, a division of Mergo-Tronics Instrument Corp., has an extremely versatile hand-held tester, Model 2540, that will check alternator output, generator output, the voltage regulator and current regulator. The device's voltmeter has three voltage ranges; the ammeter reads 10-0-80 amps. The fully guaranteed tester features a chrome-plated die-cast housing.

TESTING THE ALTERNATOR AND VOLTAGE REGULATOR

the voltage regulator and battery ground cable.

General Motors Check

IF YOU OWN A 1973 or newer General Motors car, an alternator output test can be performed without disconnecting any wires. On the back of the alternator, there is a D-shaped hole used for checking full alternator output. Start the engine and carefully insert a small screwdriver blade into that hole, grounding the screwdriver against the alternator housing. This bypasses the regulator and the voltage should start to climb. On this type of alternator, the regulator is inside. So, even if the voltage does start to increase, the alternator will have to be removed to replace the voltage regulator.

NOTE: Do not insert the screwdriver more than 3/4 inch into the hole. If you do not get a reading on the voltmeter after inserting it this far, something is wrong with the alternator or you are not grounding it properly. Further insertion may damage vital alternator components.

Sometimes a parts store or repair shop can sell you the alternator with the regulator inside of it for little more than the internal regulator plus labor charge to install it. If your General Motors car is in warranty, talk to your dealer's service department to determine whether or not the whole unit is covered, rather than only the regulator.

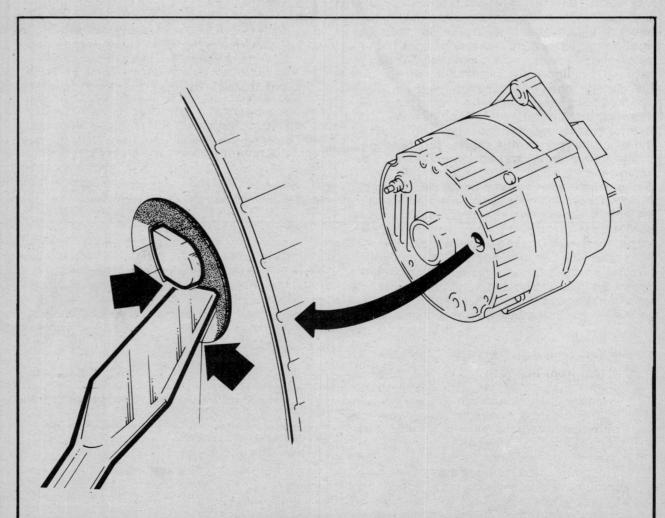

On 1973 or newer GM cars, you can check full alternator output without disconnecting wires. Insert a screwdriver blade no more than 3/4 of an inch into D-shaped testing hole. Blade must be grounded against alternator housing to bypass the regulator.

Alternator Cable Extender Eliminates Wire Splicing

If you replace your alternator with a model that is not an original factory equipment part, you may find that the wire leads are too short. This can be due to the connection plug being in the wrong "clock" position or because an obstruction blocks the wire's path. If you are working on a GM car, you can lick this problem with a GM alternator cable extender, available from Thexton Manufacturing Co. Two models are available—No. 570 fits GM cars through 1969, and No. 571 fits GM cars 1970 and up.

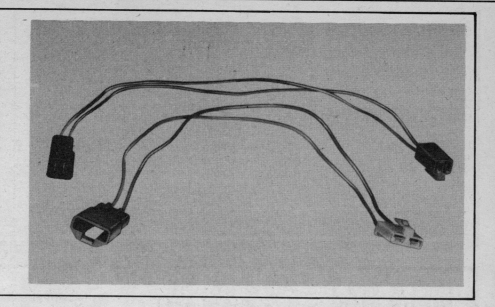

Remanufactured Alternators

Rayloc markets a complete line of remanufactured alternators to replace original equipment on virtually any car. Remanufactured alternators are less expensive than brand new ones and, generally, provide the same service and dependability. You might give this a thought when your vehicle's alternator needs replacing.

Replacement Voltage Regulator

Your car's electrical system is protected by the voltage regulator. If the regulator does not keep voltage constant, your electrical system is in big trouble. Wells Manufacturing Co. offers a full line of voltage regulators for charging circuit control. All the regulators are built with heavy steel bases and covers. Copper windings are used to reduce heating and to assure longer life. The contacts are silver alloys, tungsten or platinum alloys, whichever is required for the unit's particular application. Each regulator is individually checked and adjusted for proper mechanical assembly and individually adjusted at operating temperature. Models are available to fit most American cars.

REPLACING THE ALTERNATOR AND VOLTAGE REGULATOR

THE SYMPTOMS of troublesome voltage regulators and alternators are the general signs of electrical problems: the red "charge" light on the dashboard remains lit after the engine is started (or the ammeter shows a low reading), the lights dim significantly at idle, and the battery repeatedly runs down. If you have checked the battery connections, performed hydrometer tests, examined drive belts, tested pulleys for restrictions and sideplay, and checked the electrical system for shorts, you have pinpointed the problem to either the voltage regulator or the alternator.

If you have never worked with the electrical wiring of a car and have no experienced friend to assist you, you should consider leaving the repair of these parts to a trained mechanic. Once learned, however, the processes are easy.

An alternator is generally not too difficult to remove, so if you question its condition, remove it from the car and bring it to a parts store or to a rebuilder who can give it a thorough check.

Here is how to remove and replace an alternator.

1. Disconnect the negative battery cable clamp from the battery terminal (positive clamp if your car has a positive ground system). Use a wrench to loosen the bolt on the clamp. Remove the clamp from the terminal with a battery terminal puller if the clamp cannot be lifted off by hand. Do not hammer or pry the terminal or clamp. You could break or crack the battery case. If you have a spring-type cable clamp, use battery pliers to squeeze the tabs on the clamp and lift it off. Side terminal battery cables are removed by loosening a small hex bolt and unscrewing it from the battery.

2. Loosen the bolts that mount the alternator. There is usually one bolt that secures the alternator to the engine block and one adjusting bolt near the top.
3. Push the alternator towards the fan and slip the drive belt off.
4. Disconnect the wires that are attached to the alternator. Note and mark their location so that you will not get confused when you have to put them back.
5. Remove the mounting bolts and the alternator from the car.
6. After your alternator has been thoroughly checked, reinstall it by reversing steps one, two, three, four and five.
7. The drive belt must be properly tensioned when it is put back on. This is done by placing the belt on the pulleys. Using a pry bar, pull the alternator away from the fan until the belt is taut. Then tighten the mounting bolts.

Installing a new voltage regulator whenever an alternator is replaced is a good policy. The step may be unnecessary, but it does insure against the likelihood that the old regulator will be responsible for the ruin of the replaced alternator. **NOTE:** Many late-model cars have their voltage regulator mounted inside the alternator. Replacing this type of regulator is a job that should be left up to a professional mechanic. Here is how to replace an external voltage regulator:

CAUTION: The battery ground cable must be disconnected as previously outlined.

1. Locate the voltage regulator. It is usually mounted on the firewall or on the fender under the hood.

Here Is What You Will Need
Materials
● Alternator or Generator
● Regulator
Tools
● Wrenches
● Battery Pliers
● Battery Terminal Puller
● Pry Bar
● Screwdriver

Alternators Designed For Easy Repair

If you decide to buy a new alternator rather than a rebuilt unit, you might as well purchase one that will be easy to repair in the future. Motorola has a new line of alternators that feature a regulator and one-piece brush assembly that are removable without disassembling or pulling the alternator. Other features include a dynamically balanced rotor, permanently lubricated and sealed front ball bearing, epoxy-insulated stator for short prevention, silicon diodes and a standard 17mm shaft. The alternators are available to fit most GM, Ford, Chrysler, AMC, VW, Datsun and Toyota cars and light trucks.

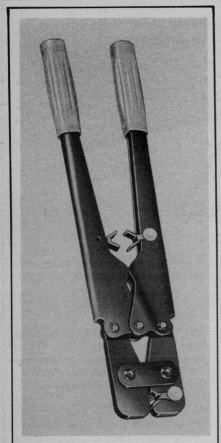

Make A Good Connection

The safest electrical connections are those that are strong and neat. To make these types of connections, you need a cutting, stripping and crimping tool such as Model 5998 by The Prestolite Co. This tool is made of tempered, blued steel and has insulated handles. It is marked for 10 to 22 gauge wire.

Ammeter Gauge Kit

An idiot light can tell you when something is definitely wrong with your charging system, but you need an ammeter if you want to spot problems before they become big trouble. Sun Electric Corporation makes an easy-to-read, two inch diameter unit, tagged Model CP7925, that is compact enough to fit nicely in most vehicles. The gauge has a range of plus and minus 60 amperes on a 60° dial scale. Also included in the gauge kit is a single-unit mounting bracket, lighting kit (including bulb), and an installation instruction sheet that details wire size recommendations.

Alternator Firm Gives Installation Tips

When replacing a Delco alternator, people often buy one with the wrong "clock" position and try to compensate for it by disassembling the unit and rotating the end plate. When this is done, spring-loaded brushes inside the alternator break, and the mechanic returns the alternator as a defective unit. To avoid this and other problems when installing a replacement alternator, the Progressive Armature Company sells its rebuilt alternators with a list of installation tips and a sheet showing the different clock positions of different alternators. In addition, the alternator box shows the clock position of the alternator it contains. Progressive suggests, by the way, that you adjust the wiring harness if the clock position is wrong. The company makes replacement alternators for late-model Ford, GM and Chrysler cars.

REPLACING THE ALTERNATOR AND VOLTAGE REGULATOR

2. Remove the wires, noting and marking their locations, from the voltage regulator.
   NOTE: Some model cars have a plug-type connector that, when removed, disconnects all regulator wires.
3. Remove the unit from its mounting. Use a screwdriver to remove the screws that hold it in place.
4. Attach the new voltage regulator in the same location as the old one and install the attaching screws.
5. Reconnect the wires in the same way.

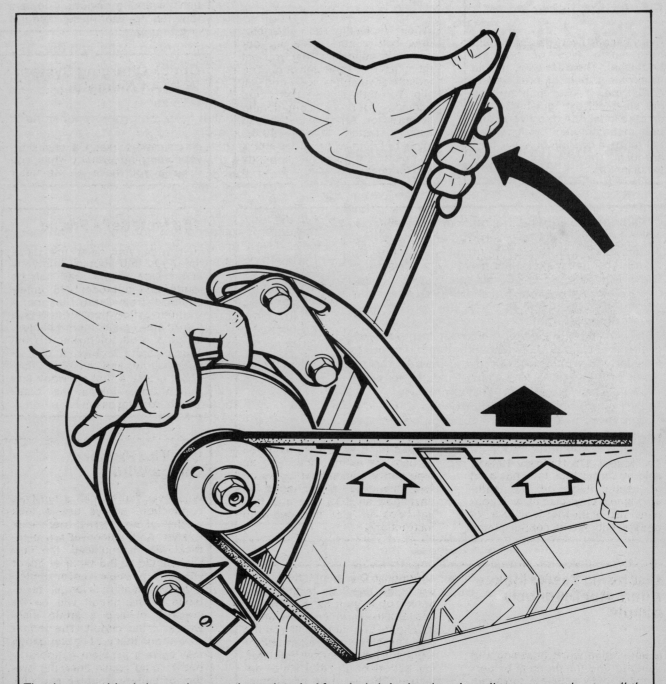

The alternator drive belt must be properly tensioned. After the belt is placed on the pulleys, use a pry bar to pull the alternator away from the fan until the belt is taut. Then tighten the alternator mounting bolts.

Heavy-Duty Fire Extinguisher

Every car and every garage should have some type of fire extinguisher. The best type, usable in a wide variety of fires, is the ABC type. These multipurpose dry chemical extinguishers such as the Model A5A-1, a five-pound unit manufactured by American LaFrance, a division of A-T-O Inc., are ideal. The A5A-1 is 20-3/8 by 5-7/8 inches.

Polarity Tester Doubles As Live Circuit Tester

If you are unsure which of your battery terminals is positive and which is negative, you should give it a polarity check. Reversing polarity can permanently damage your alternator diodes and can cause problems with transistor ignition systems, radios, voltage regulators, and many accessories in your car. This job can be done with a voltmeter. A simpler way is to use a polarity tester such as that sold by Standard Motor Products, Inc. Their easy-to-use Model PT-11 Polarity Tester can be used on six- or 12-volt systems. The unit consists of a needle probe and a ground lead. If the ground lead is connected to the negative terminal and the probe is touched to the positive terminal, the unit will indicate a voltage flow. The tester can also be used as a live circuit tester to trouble-shoot your car's electrical system.

Belt Tension Tester

When replacing an alternator drive belt or other belts on your car, it is important that you set them at the right tension. Too loose a drive belt is noisy and will slip. Too tight a drive belt could damage your air conditioning compressor. An easy-to-use belt tension tester, Model 740-88, made by Lempco Industries Inc. is compact and includes a handy clip for pocket carrying.

Emergency Warning Triangle

While driving down the highway, you may have noticed the new type of reflectors that trucks in interstate travel must use as emergency warning devices. They are required to use these triangles that meet Federal Motor Vehicle Safety Standard No. 125. These triangles also are available to the motoring public. Stimsonite, a division of Amerace Corporation, manufactures a set of three triangles, No. 13000. The triangles are effective night and day because they have a fluorescent coating and bright reflectors.

Check Charging System With An Ammeter

It is simple to keep a check on your charging system while you drive if you have an ammeter mounted inside the car. The Model UA-1106 ammeter gauge sold by Hastings Manufacturing Company features a two inch diameter illuminated dial with a 90-degree sweep. Calibrations are 60-30-0-30-60. The instrument has a chrome panel and a steel, zinc-plated case.

Highway Helper

The Model 375 Highway Helper, sold by Carter Hall, Inc., has a lot of useful items in its leather-grained, vinyl-clad case. It contains an eight-foot-long set of booster cables with copper-plated steel clamps and color-coded insulated handles, a tire inflater, an aerosol fire extinguisher, and an emergency blinker that works on two standard C batteries. A flashlight, an SOS flag and first aid book are also included with instructions.

Electronic Tester Makes Alternator Diagnosis Simple

In auto repair work, guessing and trying to find the problem by performing many separate tests can waste a lot of time. The TE-570 Alternator Tester made by Filko Automotive Div. eliminates guesswork and needless testing. Just hook it up to your car's alternator and look to see which of the unit's four lights brighten. It tells you the exact problem: open alternator or regulator field, shorted regulator, low battery or diode or stator defective. This is quite an accomplishment for an instrument you can hold in one hand!

The Motorist's Friend

Just what you need for those times you find yourself immobile at the side of the road can be found in the Model 475 emergency kit from Carter Hall, Inc. It includes battery booster cables, a tire inflater, an emergency blinker, an auto spotlight powered from your cigarette lighter, a gas siphon pump and an SOS flag. There is also a first aid book and instructions inside the black Texon carrying case.

Use The Proper Gauge Wire

Whenever you tighten a nut-type connection, always use a lock washer or an internal-tooth lock washer. And, whenever any electrical wire is replaced, the new wire should be the same length or shorter if possible—never longer. If the replacement is longer, resistance in the circuit will be increased, placing a strain elsewhere in the circuit. The longer wire or one that is of lighter gauge may solve a problem temporarily but it could cause charging system or battery troubles and give your vehicle weak cranking power in the future.

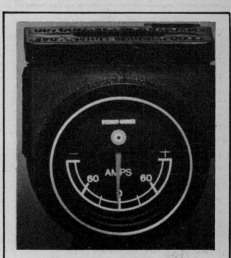

Ammeter Warns Of Charging System Problems

Idiot lights, found on most late-model cars, will tell you when your charging system has developed a problem. But the only way to notice small problems before they become major is to keep tabs on your charging system with an ammeter. Stewart-Warner's Model 82450 ammeter features an illuminated European face dial. It is a direct reading unit that reads from -60 amps to +60 amps. The unit includes an adjustable black polypropylene panel, lighting kit and complete instructions.

Taillight Sockets And Pigtails

Sometimes when your taillights go out or flicker occasionally, it is due to a corroded socket or worn wires. In many cases, you can repair the wire or clean the socket if it is corroded. But if the socket has been neglected for a long period of time, it is better to replace it. Microdot Products sells sockets and pigtails that will fit all domestic cars, including Chrysler brands and most trucks. It is easy to find the right unit for your car because Microdot provides dealers with an application guide for

quick selection of the proper sockets and pigtails. Sockets are available for headlights, brake lights, back-up lights, turn signals and cornering lights, in addition to taillights.

Hot Line Seeker

For trouble-shooting your auto's electrical system, a circuit and polarity tester is a necessity. Sonco Manufacturing, Inc. makes a Model 150 that can help you check

your wiring system for shorts, poor connections, battery condition, faulty accessories and blown fuses. You can even use it to set your timing and make other adjustments. It works on negative-ground six- or 12-volt systems. Instructions are included.

GM Circuit Breakers

If you find that your General Motors car needs a new circuit breaker of the plug-in type, you can acquire it from Littelfuse Inc. This new fuse holder is their Model No. ACB30 and is a direct factory replacement for all 1977 full-size Buicks, Cadillacs, Chevrolets, Oldsmobiles and Pontiacs.

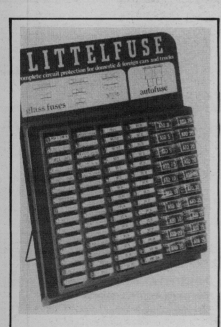

New Fuse For 1977 GM Cars

If you've got a 1977 full-size Buick, Cadillac, Chevrolet, Oldsmobile or Pontiac, you may have noticed that you cannot use the same kind of fuse used in other cars. These newer vehicles take ATO fuses that plug in with two prongs. Autofuse ATO fuses, made by Littelfuse, are available in 3 amp, 5 amp, 7-1/2 amp, 10 amp, 20 amp and 25 amp sizes.

INTRODUCTION

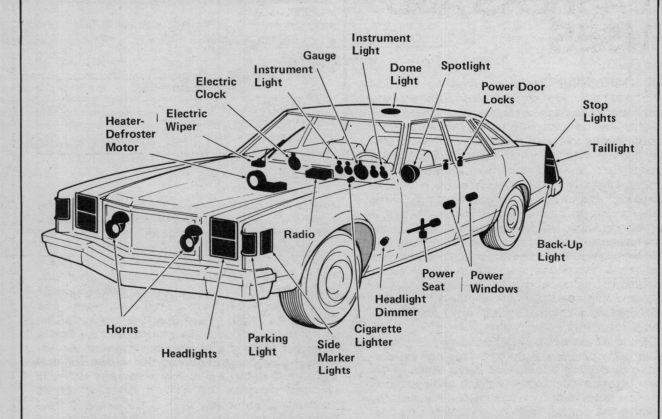

A quarter of a century or more ago, cars had few options or accessories. Today, however, there are many standard or optional items of equipment that sooner or later may malfunction.

IF YOU WERE to look at the catalog of a standard-size automobile of the early 1940s, you would find that very few options or accessories were available. Things we take for granted on cars today—radio, heater, even turn signals—had to be specially ordered by the customer.

Options, such as air conditioning, power steering and power brakes, automatic transmission, power windows and automatic door locks, still must be specified by the car buyer, but they are quickly becoming standard equipment on most full-size cars.

Other accessories, including AM-FM radio (some with stereo), automatic speed control, and other comfort or entertainment features, also are gaining in popularity.

Whether these electrically operated options and accessories are installed by the car manu-

facturer as original equipment or added later by the car dealer or some independent installer, service and repair occasionally are necessary.

We will not attempt to explain all of the various services that might be performed to option and accessory items. In this chapter, however, we will offer some of the checks, services, repairs and installation advice to assist you in coping with a well-equipped automobile.

Because many of the components discussed are built into the automobile and involve complex wiring, panels, etc., you may find it more practical to have an experienced mechanic work on such things as electric window circuitry, automatic speed control and other instrument repairs. But, if you are nimble, flexible and patient enough to work in close quarters under the instrument panel, there is plenty you can accomplish on your own.

LUBRICATION

Grease Cartridge

One of the best types of grease you can use to lubricate your vehicle's suspension system is lithium grease. Balcrank Products Division of Wheelabrator-Frye, Inc. sells a versatile 14-1/2 ounce cartridge that contains a high-quality, multipurpose lithium grease. It fits any standard-size cartridge grease gun. Grease cartridges cost a little more than bulk grease, but are cleaner to use.

Removing Those Messy Oil Spots

Here is an effective means of cleaning oil spots from your driveway or concrete floor. Wipe up as much of the oil or grease as possible with rags. Using oil absorbent such as garages use (Oil-Dri, Speed-Dri, etc.), sprinkle a light coating on the spots. Then, using a block of wood such as a 2 x 4 about six inches long, rub the absorbent into the spots. The scrubbing action disintegrates the granules, forces them into the pores of the surface and picks up the stain. Then sweep up and your floor is clean! A second treatment may be necessary if the spot is stubborn.

Grease Gun Leaves One Hand Free

The smaller size grease guns, which can be operated with one hand and hold grease cartridges of about three ounces, are becoming increasingly popular. Model 119 Micro One Hand Grease Gun from J-Mark Quality Products, Inc. is an especially powerful model, developing 7500 psi pressure and enough volume per stroke to grease anything with a grease fitting. The three ounce cartridges it uses make loading the gun quick and neat.

Oil With A Pistol

For automotive repair maintenance, oil packaged in a commercial squeeze can just cannot cut it. The spout is not normally long enough, and squeezing the can cannot give you a steady stream of oil for lubricating hard to reach parts. Pistol type oilers are the best, and Balcrank Products Division offers six different models. One in particular, Model 351, has a six ounce capacity and a six inch spout. This nickel-plated model is great for all-around auto work. And it comes in handy around the house, too!

must put in grease fittings before you can do your own lubrications. Installing the fittings, however, requires special tools, so it would be practical to have a service center grease your car the first time greasing is needed, and to have them install fittings at that time. Thereafter, you can do your own grease jobs. Here is how to grease the fittings of your car's chassis.

1. If you do not have access to a professional lift, buy, borrow or rent a pair of ramps. These make the easiest and safest perch for your car when lubricating the chassis. You can also use a jack with a pair of jack stands. Also, a creeper will allow you to move around under your car from fitting to fitting. **NOTE:** When lubricating ball joints, it is advisable to take the weight off the load-carrying joint by raising the front wheels off the ground. This allows the chassis grease to get into places that would otherwise have been inaccessible because of the pressure of one surface against the other. To determine how to jack it up, note the location of the coil spring. If it is above the upper control arm, lift from below the frame. If it is between the two control arms, jack from under the lower control arm.

   NOTE: Some fittings are difficult or impossible to reach without a flexible attachment for the gun and/or a swiveling elbow. If these do not come standard with your gun, consider buying them right off to avoid having to make a second trip to the auto parts store later on.

2. If you are not sure where the various grease fittings are located and if you do not have a factory shop manual, visit a local service station and ask to see their lubrication guide.

3. Carefully wipe off the grit and dirt with a rag from each of the grease fittings before using a grease gun to grease these fittings. **NOTE:** Late-model cars with extended service intervals have plugs where the grease fittings normally would go. Assuming this is the first grease job your car has had, it will be necessary to remove these plugs with a wrench and replace them with standard grease fittings. Standard grease fittings are available with straight, 45° or 90° angle ends. The various angled ends allow for easy accessibility in confined areas of the chassis. These are available at auto supply stores.

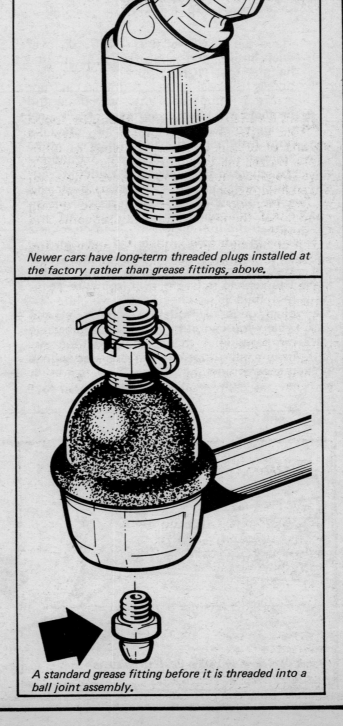

Newer cars have long-term threaded plugs installed at the factory rather than grease fittings, above.

A standard grease fitting before it is threaded into a ball joint assembly.

Innovative Grease Gun

Many small grease guns that are designed for use with one hand have a trigger and handle at the rear of the gun. This does not allow you to push the gun against the fitting very easily. The CD-2 Pusher from Alemite Division of Stewart-Warner is designed so that you wrap your fingers around the front of the cartridge-holding cylinder and push a lever, using your palm, against the back of the cylinder. This allows you to hold the gun against the fitting with maximum pressure while pumping grease. The CD-2 Pusher carries the Model No. 4160 and uses three ounce grease cartridge tubes.

Disposable Shop Towels

Lubricating your car often turns out to be one of the chores of automotive work. That is why the home mechanic should keep a good supply of rags and towels in his or her garage. Clean Rite Products Company, a division of Max Rittenbaum, Inc., sells nonwoven, disposable shop towels in packages containing 100 to 1200 towels, and in various sizes. Made of bonded textile fibers, the towels are absorbent and durable enough to be used several times.

LUBRICATION

Grease Gun

If you plan to do your own auto lubrication, one of the first items you should have is a hand-operated grease gun. Balcrank Products Division of Wheelabrator-Frye, Inc. offers their Model 2274-806042 spring-primed cartridge gun for either cartridges or bulk grease. It has a 20 ounce bulk grease capacity and develops 10,000 pounds working pressure. The gun features a curved hydraulic adaptor.

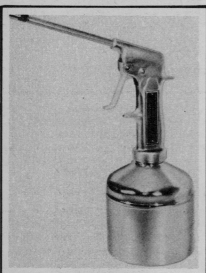

Large-Capacity Spring Oiler

It is frustrating to pick up your oil can and find that it is empty just when you need it. Using a spring oiler like Balcrank Products Division's Model HWA524-80115 with a one quart capacity means that you run out of oil less often. It has a hand-trigger type mechanism and a long spout to reach difficult places.

Grease Cartridge For General Automotive Use

If you own a grease gun that uses a cartridge, it is always good to pick up a few cartridges whenever you are at an automotive store. J-Mark Quality Products, Inc. makes a 14-1/2 ounce grease cartridge, Model 11, typical of the cartridges you find on the market. It contains a heavy duty, all-season, all-purpose grease called Dura Lith. The cartridge fits most standard size combination grease guns.

Oil Treatment For High-Mile Cars

If your car has plenty of mileage on it and is burning too much oil, CD-2 Oil Treatment made by the Alemite Division of Stewart-Warner may remedy the problem. But if excessive oil burning persists, you may require an engine overhaul.

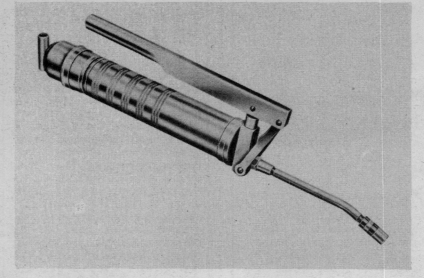

Hand Grease Guns

You can save money several times a year if you do your own chassis lubrication. All it takes is a hand-pump grease gun and a grease cartridge. Brookins Service Station Equipment Division of Balcrank Products offers a spring-primed, high-pressure lever gun with an 18 ounce capacity. Model 2271X has a seven-inch curved hydraulic adapter and develops 10,000 pounds working pressure. It handles all types of commonly used lubricants.

Roadrunner Jack

Any active home mechanic should invest in a service jack like garages use. It makes almost all jobs easier. But one does not have to go to the expense of buying a heavy-duty model. In fact, it may be better to buy one that has a capacity between one and two tons. The Watco Roadrunner Model W1 service jack, sold by the Watervliet Tool Co., is made for the do-it-yourselfer. The jack weighs only 33 pounds and measures only 23-1/2 inches long. It has a 1-1/4 ton capacity, a 4-1/4 inch low saddle point, a 16-1/2 inch high saddle point, and a saddle diameter of 1-1/2 by 3-3/4 inches. The highest point of the chassis is 4-3/4 inches, which makes it easy to use even when there is low ground clearance on the vehicle to be serviced. The service jack's chassis is eight inches wide; the handle length is 22-3/4 inches. The Roadrunner jack comes with a 90-day guarantee.

CHASSIS LUBRICATION

4. Place the nozzle of the grease gun over each fitting and apply pressure to the handle. **CAUTION:** Apply pressure cautiously. Excessive chassis grease can rupture the rubber boot that surrounds and protects the bearing surfaces. Apply only enough pressure until you begin to feel the boot distending from the chassis grease application. If it breaks from extra pressure, it must be replaced. On fittings without boots, look for the chassis grease to come out when sufficient chassis grease has been applied.

5. Part of the lubrication job is to check the level of rear axle lubricant in the rear axle (or differential) housing. You will have to crawl underneath the car to do this. **NOTE:** The vehicle must be level to insure accurate fluid level check. You will find the plug, generally with a square inset into which you can put a 3/8 or 1/2 inch drive ratchet wrench to unscrew it. Other cars have a plug that can be loosened with a regular wrench.

Remove the rear axle plug and check the lubricant level with the tip of your finger. If you can reach it, you have enough fluid. If not, it is best to have this topped off by a service station because it is sometimes difficult to get the fluid into the upper hole without the proper equipment.

No lubrication job would be complete without paying some attention to the various hinges, springs and fluid levels for your car.

Pay particular attention to door hinges and locks. A special dry lubricant is available from your auto parts store for this purpose. Simply spray the lubricant on each door hinge, working the door back and forth to be sure the lubricant can do its job to stop squeaks.

The same holds true for door locks. A little dry lubricant on each lock will prevent sticking.

Hood and trunk lid hinges require attention from time to time as well. Here again, a squirt of dry lubricant will eliminate and/or prevent squeaks.

Don't forget the power steering pump fluid level and the automatic transmission fluid. Refer to your owner's manual for the correct fluid to be added and instructions for checking.

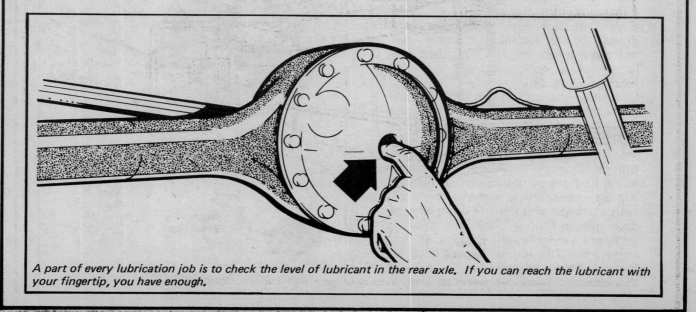

A part of every lubrication job is to check the level of lubricant in the rear axle. If you can reach the lubricant with your fingertip, you have enough.

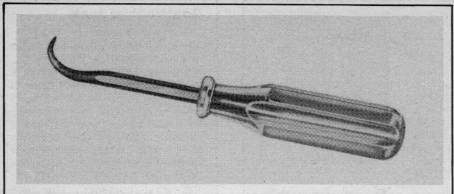

Cotter Pin Puller

When the home mechanic encounters hard-to-reach or stubborn cotter pins, such as those on a wheel hub, he generally has to improvise to remove them. For a small cost, you can make this job a lot easier by buying the right tool. Cal-Van Tools, a division of Chemi-Trol Chemical Company, markets a cotter pin puller, No. 352, that looks like a screwdriver but has a rolled hook that provides good leverage. The tool is 5/16 by 7-1/2 inches long.

Wheel Chocks

Whenever you jack your car, you should always block the wheels. While you can use a large wooden block to do this, a more professional approach would be to use wheel chocks. The Watervliet Tool Company makes a set of wheel chocks that are made of light-

weight aluminum. A pair weighs only three pounds. One pair holds weights up to 20,000 pounds, even though they are only 5-1/4 inches high by six inches wide by seven inches long. The chocks do not have sharp edges to cut tires, and they meet or exceed OSHA requirements and SAE standard J-348.

REPACKING FRONT WHEEL BEARINGS

BECAUSE THEY are generally ignored until it is time for brake work, the front wheel bearings are one of the most badly neglected parts on an automobile. The need for periodic maintenance on front wheel bearings cannot be overemphasized. One of the functions of the front wheel bearings, when correctly adjusted and serviced, is to allow the tire and wheel to rotate smoothly, quietly and with minimum friction. The front wheel bearings are designed to withstand tremendous load forces over a wide range of road and speed conditions—which would include side thrust when cornering as well as the severe shocks encountered when the vehicle hits chuck holes, curbs or other obstructions. General dependability of the vehicle, braking,

steering and handling would all be affected if the wheel bearings should fail.

Wheel bearings should be serviced every 15,000 to 20,000 miles or as specified by the manufacturer. Servicing every 12,000 miles is not an uncommon practice if the vehicle is used in heavy-duty applications or is subjected to extreme climatic changes. Proper servicing of the front bearings would include disassembly, cleaning and inspection, repacking and correct wheel bearing adjustment.

Each front wheel is supported by an inner and an outer wheel bearing assembly. The rear wheels also have bearings, but since servicing of these bearings requires the removal of the axle shafts, this should be left to a repair shop and a qualified mechanic. However, if you do want to remove the axle shafts, this is covered in the chapter on Transmission, Differential And Rear Axle.

The front wheel bearings must be tight enough to retain proper wheel alignment but loose enough to permit free rotation of the wheel. It is a big assignment for a small bearing; they deserve more care than they generally receive.

Easy Way To Keep Your Garage Floor Oil Free

Cleanliness is the trademark of a good mechanic. You can keep your garage floor free of oil by using an absorbent such as Oil-Dri, manufactured by the Oil-Dri Corp. of America. To take care of an oil spill, you just cover the spill with about an 1/8 inch layer of Oil-Dri and sweep it away when the material darkens from the oil. You can even remove oil or grease that has caked into a thick hard layer by emulsifying with a nonflammable solvent and then treating it with Oil-Dri as if it were an oil spill. Oil-Dri absorbents are chemically inert calcined mineral granuals; they are nontoxic, nonflammable and safe to handle and to use. The absorbent can be used to absorb lubricating oils, cutting oils, grease, water and practically any kind of liquid.

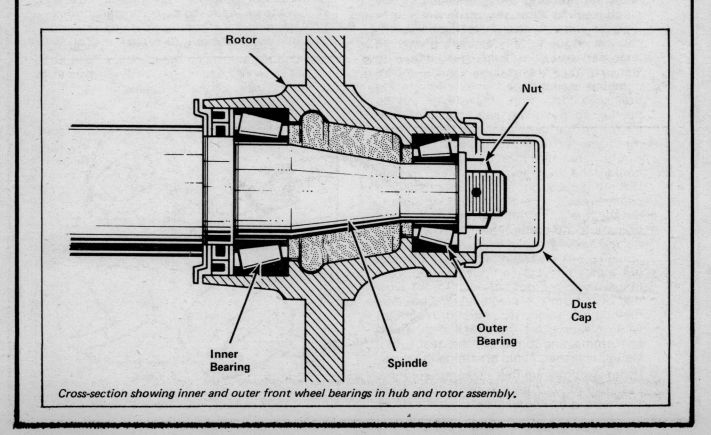

Cross-section showing inner and outer front wheel bearings in hub and rotor assembly.

Seal Puller

Popping off oil and grease seals can be a real hassle if you do not have the right tool. Lisle Corporation manufactures a seal puller, Model 56750, designed to make this job easy. You simply insert the tip of the tool behind the oil or grease seal, press and pull. It eliminates the pounding, hammering and digging that may damage bearings. Two sizes of tips fit nearly all seals.

LUBRICATION

A Handy Way To Carry And Store Tools

If you are not organized, you can spend more time looking for a tool than it takes to do the job you have at hand. Even if your entire garage is organized but you tend to lay tools on the floor while doing a particular job, you can waste time when that critical wrench (that you just had in your hand!) goes astray. Rubbermaid Specialty Products, Inc. makes a small portable tool box called the Tool Tote. It has three large compartments to separate and organize tools. And it is lightweight, durable and easy to carry with a built-in handle. It will last for a long time because it will not rust or corrode. The Tool Tote Model 3153 comes in black.

Packer For Front Wheel Bearings

The old method of packing front wheel bearings by holding the bearing in the palm of your hand is very inefficient compared to the job that you can do if you have a bearing packer. Rinck-McIlwaine, Inc. makes a heavy-duty bearing packer that makes packing front bearings fast, clean and efficient. It is equipped with a standard grease fitting and may be used with either power or hand operated grease guns. The device will handle bearings from a minimum of 25/64 inch interior diameter to a maximum overall diameter of five inches, and with a minimum and maximum working height between cones from 0 to 2-1/8 inches. Ask for Model 640.

Wheel Bearing Lubricant Includes Instructions

CD-2 wheel bearing lubricant comes in one-pound cans that give you a bonus. On the back of the can is a full set of instructions on how to repack wheel bearings the proper way. It even includes a diagram showing you how to disassemble the wheel to remove the bearing. CD-2 wheel bearing lubricant is made by Alemite, which is a division of Stewart-Warner.

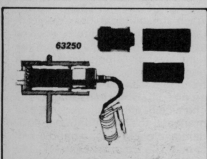

Inner Wheel Bearing Packer

Repacking inner wheel bearings on a car that has disc brakes can be a time-consuming job because you usually have to remove the disc brake assembly first. Lisle Corporation, however, makes an inner wheel bearing packer, No. 63250, that can save you plenty of time. You simply attach the tool to the spindle and pump the grease through the tool. The old grease is forced out and new grease is packed in. Removal of the brake assembly is not necessary. This tool, designed not to harm the inner seal, works well on both domestic and foreign cars.

REPACKING FRONT WHEEL BEARINGS

Drum Brakes

HERE is how to repack front wheel bearings on cars equipped with drum brakes:

1. Jack up the car and secure it with jack stands. Put a wooden block behind a rear wheel to prevent the car from rolling. Since the wheels must be removed in order to replace the wheel bearings, jack the car high enough to get the wheel off.
2. Remove the wheel cover. Most can be removed by prying them off with a big screwdriver. Remove the wheel and tire assembly. This will allow for easier removal of the drum and hub assembly and reduce the possibility of damage to the brakes and bearing parts. Place the lug nuts in the wheel cover for safe keeping.
3. Remove the dust cap. Use large water-pump pliers in combination with a screwdriver. Grip the dust cap with the pliers and pry it off with the screwdriver.
4. Remove the cotter pin.
5. Use a wrench to remove the adjusting nut and washer. (If the nut does not want to come off by turning it counterclockwise, try turning it clockwise.)
6. Rock the drum and hub assembly to work the outer bearing loose. (Use care to avoid having the bearing fall out on the floor. Have your hand ready to catch it.) Place the outer bearing, washer and spindle nut on a clean rag.
7. Slide the hub and drum assembly off. Be careful not to allow the inner bearing to drag on the spindle. If resistance is encountered during the removal, it may be necessary to back off the brake adjusting star by using a brake spoon. On late-model cars that are equipped with self-adjusting brakes, a long, thin screwdriver will be needed to push the self-adjusting lever away from the star wheel. **CAUTION:** While the drum and hub assembly is off of the car, be careful not to allow grease or dirt to contact the drum surface or brake linings. Dirt or grease on these surfaces could cause brake drag or loss of braking action.
8. Set the hub and drum assembly aside and prepare to do a little cleaning. **CAUTION:** As brake linings wear, they create dust that contains 3 to 6 percent asbestos. This can get into your skin, or, worse, into your lungs if you are not careful. Do not blow this dust from the mechanism. The ideal method is to wear a face mask or respirator while cleaning off the brake mechanism and drums, and to remove the dust with a vacuum cleaner. Avoid breathing the dust!
9. Using a nonflammable cleaning solution, available at your auto supply store, wash the bearing free of all grease. This is just a matter of sloshing it up and down in the solution until all the grease has dissolved.
10. Place the bearing on a clean surface and let it air dry.
11. Inspect the bearing for wear conditions such as cracks, chipping, nicks, scratches, flaking of the bearing surface or corrosion (which should not happen except in the driest of situations). If they are bad, they should be replaced. New bearings will have to be repacked before installation.
12. Assuming your bearing is in good condition, you are ready to repack it. You will

Here Is What You Will Need

Materials
- Clean Rag
- Face Mask or Respirator
- Nonflammable Cleaning Solution
- Inner and Outer Front Wheel Bearings
- Inner Wheel Bearing Seals
- Wheel Bearing Grease
- Cotter Pins

Tools
- Jack and Jack Stands
- Wooden Blocks
- Big Screwdriver
- Water-Pump Pliers
- Wrenches
- Brake Spoon or Long, Thin Screwdriver
- Vacuum Cleaner
- Hammer
- Wooden Stick or Brass Drift
- Pliers
- Ruler
- Torque Wrench

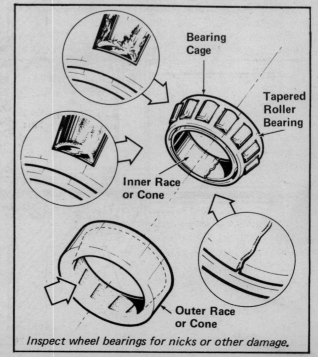

Inspect wheel bearings for nicks or other damage.

LUBRICATION

Beam-Type Torque Wrench

For certain automotive jobs, such as replacing cylinder heads and repacking wheel bearings, you must have a torque wrench. There are two types of torque wrenches. One is a micrometer type that will click when you reach the proper pressure. Less expensive torque wrenches are the beam type. These have a pointer that extends from the head down to the handle where a scale is located. You apply pressure until the pointer reaches the appropriate point on the scale. K-D Tools makes a beam-type torque wrench, Model 2388, that will measure from 0 to 150 foot-pounds and from 0 to 20 meters/kilogram. It is 19 inches long and has a 1/2 inch drive. The small, 7/8 inch head diameter assures easy access in tight spots.

To remove the inner bearing (left), tap the inner core lightly with a hammer and wooden stick or brass drift. To install the inner wheel bearing seal, tap it gently (right) with a wooden block being careful not to twist it.

need special wheel bearing grease for this, available at auto parts stores. Place a gob of grease in your hand and work it into the bearing. Also coat the inside of the hub and spindle lightly with grease.

13. Set the bearing aside on a clean surface and remove the inner bearing. This is done as follows:
    a. With the inside of the brake drum facing down, tap the inner cone or race lightly with a hammer and a wooden stick or brass drift.
    b. When the bearing is loosened sufficiently, remove it and its seal by hand.
14. Follow the same cleaning, inspection, and packing procedure as outlined for the outer bearing.
15. Replace the repacked inner bearing into its place in the hub.

16. Obtain a new inner wheel bearing seal from your auto supply store. Install the new inner seal, inner side lightly coated with grease, by tapping it gently with a wooden block. Be careful not to twist it as it is forced into its position. A bent or broken seal is as good as none at all and will permit grease to leak out when the bearing gets hot.
17. Slide the drum and hub assembly onto the spindle.
18. Replace the outer bearing, the washer and the adjusting nut.
19. Follow the procedure outlined in this section under Wheel Bearing Adjustment for drum type brakes.
20. After following the outlined procedure on adjustment, install a new cotter pin through the spindle nut and spindle. Bend

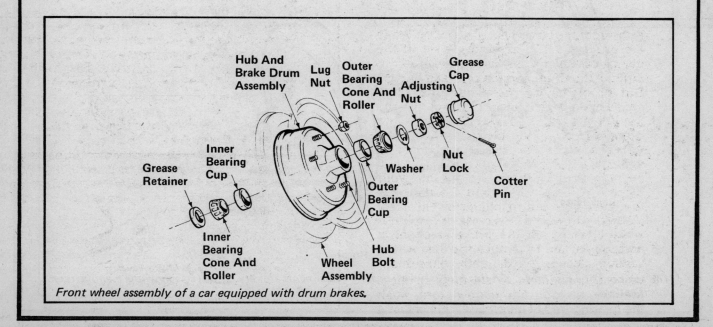

Front wheel assembly of a car equipped with drum brakes.

Labels: Hub And Brake Drum Assembly, Lug Nut, Outer Bearing Cone And Roller, Adjusting Nut, Grease Cap, Inner Bearing Cup, Grease Retainer, Washer, Nut Lock, Cotter Pin, Inner Bearing Cone And Roller, Outer Bearing Cup, Hub Bolt, Wheel Assembly

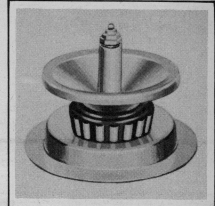

Wheel Bearing Packer

You may pack your front wheel bearings only once every 20,000 miles, but when you do it, a wheel bearing packer comes in handy. You just insert the roller bearings in the packer and hook up the packer's nipple to a regular grease gun. A model such as the LP-103-811231, made by Balcrank Products Division of Wheelabrator-Frye, Inc., is easy to use. The packer handles automotive ball or roller-type bearings from 5/8 inch interior diameter to 1/4 inch overall diameter.

Grease Cap Puller

Pulling grease caps from wheel hubs is a time-consuming chore if you use a makeshift tool like a screwdriver. In addition, this may damage the cap. A better way is to use a grease cap puller like Hastings Manufacturing Company's Model 1880. The thin jaws of this tool slip behind the grease cap and a wedging action forces the cap away from the hub. The end of one handle is flat for easy removal of the wheel cover.

Wheel Bearing Grease Comes In Tub

Since you only pack your wheel bearings once every 20,000 miles or so, you might as well use a high quality grease. LubriMatic Products offers a 16 ounce tub, No. 120, of specially formulated grease for wheel bearings and similar applications. The plastic tub has a reclosable lid for convenient, nonmessy application and storage.

LUBRICATION

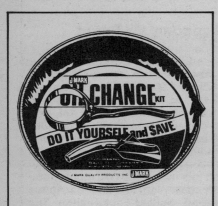
REPACKING FRONT WHEEL BEARINGS

the ends around the nut with pliers so that it will not come out.

21. Reinstall the dust cap, tire and wheel assembly and wheel cover. Your job is complete.

   NOTE: Some vehicles come equipped with spring static suppressors in the dust cap. Be sure that the ends of the cotter pin do not contact the suppressor.

Wheel Bearing Adjustment

MANUFACTURER'S specifications should always be followed. If specifications are not available, these basic guidelines for wheel bearing adjustment should be followed:

1. With a ruler, measure the hub bore size for the outer bearing.
   a. If the bore size is 1-3/4 inches or more, tighten the spindle nut using a torque wrench to 17 foot-pounds while rotating the wheel by hand.
   b. If the bore size is less than 1-3/4 inches, tighten the spindle nut using a torque wrench to 8 foot-pounds while rotating the wheel by hand.
2. After tightening the spindle nut to the specified torque, back off the spindle nut 1/6 to 1/4 turn to obtain proper cotter pin alignment between the cotter pin hole in the spindle nut and the cotter pin hole in the spindle.

   NOTE: If drum brake adjustment was altered during the repacking procedure, proper brake adjustment will be necessary. This is covered in the Brakes chapter.

Disc Brakes

THE PROCEDURE for repacking and inspecting front wheel bearings on disc-type brake equipped vehicles is basically the same as on drum-type brakes, with one exception: The disc brake caliper must be removed before the rotor and hub assembly can be removed.

Each manufacturer has a different type of caliper mounting system. Generally, it is a matter of locating and removing the caliper mounting bolts or threaded caliper guide locating pins that attach the caliper to the steering knuckle or mounting bracket. During the removal of the caliper, it is not usually recommended that the hydraulic brake line be disconnected from the caliper. Doing so will make it necessary to bleed the front brake system. Do not, however, allow the caliper to hang from the brake line. Support the weight of the caliper with a piece of wire.

NOTE: When installing the caliper, be sure to use a torque wrench. Be aware of which bolts you are tightening. For instance, the caliper mounting bolts that secure the caliper directly to the steering knuckle, as found on some Ford vehicles, require approximately 100 to 135 foot-pounds of torque, while threaded caliper locating pins, as found on some General Motors cars, require 25 to 35 foot-pounds of torque. Use of the incorrect torque specification will result in damaged components if overtorqued or in a caliper working loose if undertorqued.

Wheel bearing adjustments on cars equipped with disc-type brakes are very critical. Follow the manufacturer's specifications. If specifications are not available, use the basic guideline in this section under Wheel Bearing Adjustment. All other procedures for repacking the front wheel bearings on disc-type brakes are the same as for drum-type brakes.

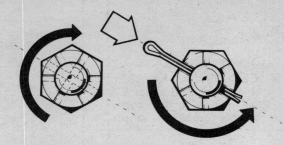

After tightening the spindle nut to specified torque, back it off 1/16 to 1/4 turn to obtain the proper cotter pin alignment.

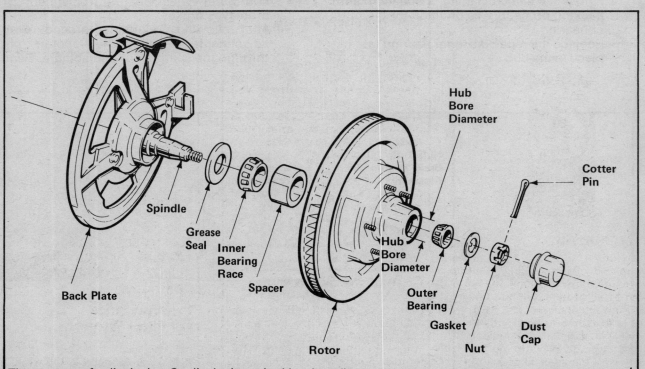

The anatomy of a disc brake. On disc brakes, wheel bearing adjustments are very critical so follow the manufacturer's specifications.

LUBRICATION

Imperial Motor Oil

Multi-grade motor oils have become increasingly popular in recent years. They are designed to keep the proper viscosity through a wide range of temperatures. Imperial Multi-Grade Motor Oil, produced by the Amalie Refining Company, is such a motor oil. It comes in SAE grades 5W-20, 10W-30, 10W-40, 20W-40 and 20W-50.

Mechanical Oil Pressure Gauge

A drop or a sudden rise in oil pressure can spell trouble for your engine. You can keep track of it if you have an interior-mounted mechanical oil pressure gauge like the Model AU-1144 sold by Hastings Manufacturing Company. This is a two-inch illuminated dial with a 27-degree dial sweep and chrome panel. It measures 0 to 800 pounds of pressure. The gauge also has a zinc-plated steel case and comes with a complete installation kit, including 72 inches of nylon tubing.

Oil Treatment

Bardahl's No. 2 is an additive that the manufacturer recommends be added to oil at each change and once between changes. The treatment is designed to give body to the oil, place a film on moving engine parts, quiet clattering engine noises, increase oil pressure, combat additional wear, and help restore lost compression and power.

Cap-Type Oil Filter Wrench

Oil filter wrenches are generally inexpensive tools, and a home mechanic may try several different types before he finds the one that serves him best. The Model 1873 cap-type wrench sold by Hastings Manufacturing Company is a 15-sided cap wrench that matches the contour of the filter. The top of the tool has two openings for a ratchet, sliding T-driver or a hinged handle.

High-Performance Oil Treatment

Union Carbide Corporation's High-Performance Oil Treatment was developed to reduce oil consumption, increase the viscosity index of the base oil, and prevent undesirable thinning out at high temperatures. It is formulated to improve load-carrying ability and minimize wear. The product, available at local auto parts stores, is sold in 15 ounce cans.

Oil Pressure Gauge

Too high or low an oil pressure can cause severe damage to your engine. To keep an eye on the pressure while you drive, you need an oil pressure gauge. Stewart-Warner's Model 82451 has a heavy-duty link-Bourdon tube mechanism that reads from 10 to 90 psi oil pressure. It is easy to mount in your car because it includes an adjustable black polypropylene panel. Also included is an installation kit, lighting kit and complete instructions. The dial is illuminated.

Crankcase Drain Plugs

Crankcase drain plugs may leak after many years of use. One solution may be to purchase an oversize, self-tapping drain plug. TRW Replacement Division sells such drain plugs with a fiber washer. They come in a wide assortment of sizes.

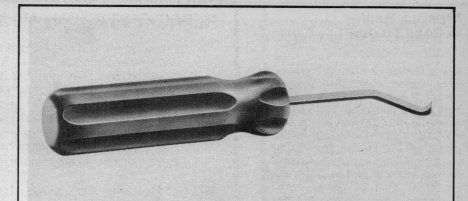

Oil Filter Gasket-Removing Tool

Cal-Van Tools offers the Model 348 oil filter gasket-removing device for use on cars with removable filter elements. The shape of this tool is specially designed for quick gasket removal using its sharp cutting edge. It permits installation of new elements without detaching the mounting plate. The tool also features a large, comfortable red plastic handle and heat-treated alloy blade.

Super-Duty Motor Oil

Often, motorists have a preference for a certain brand of motor oil because it has worked well for them in the past. There are a lot of followers of Wolf's Head Oil Refining Company's motor oil. The firm has been in business since 1879. Their Super-Duty Motor Oil is a high-detergent, multi-grade oil formulated for hard, long-distance driving in all kinds of weather.

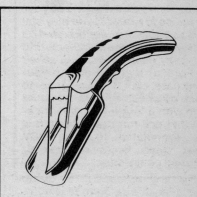

Economy Oil Spout

By adding your own oil when you need it, you can save quite a bit of money, especially if you buy automotive oil in bulk. If you are going to add your own oil, you might as well have the convenience of an oil spout. J-Mark Quality Products, Inc. makes an economy lube spout. The spout on this model is 8-1/2 inches long for convenient use, and it features strong, welded construction. The zinc lustron finish adds to the unit's durability.

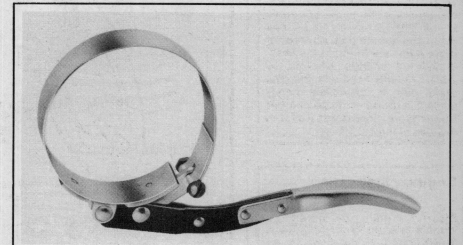

Friction-Grip Oil Filter Wrench

K-D Tools' Model K-D 190 wrench will remove disposable oil filters from 3-7/16 to 3-3/4 inches in diameter. Designed not to puncture or crush the filter, the tool features a positive friction grip with enough leverage to exceed normal requirements. For extremely close quarters, the band can be disassembled at the bolt, wrapped around the filter and reassembled for use.

LUBRICATION

Heavy-Duty Filter Wrench Features Swivel Handle

The key to removing stubborn oil filters is to have a heavy-duty filter wrench. Owatonna Tool Co. makes one that is designed to handle oil, fuel and coolant spin-on filters up to six inches in diameter. Its rugged nylon strap holds firmly and will not slip. In fact, the more leverage applied, the tighter it grips. The special swivel handle and 3/8 inch square drive end let you clear obstructions around the filter easily. Order it by Model No. 7062.

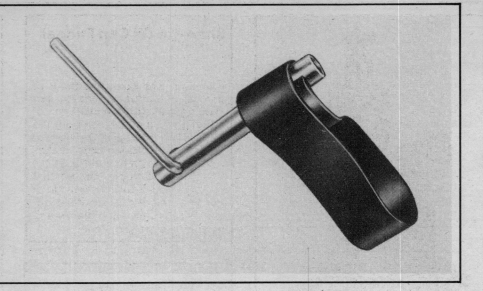

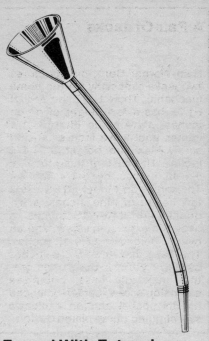

Funnel With Extension Hose

If you have a van or motor home, you might find it necessary to get a funnel with an extension hose for filling your crankcase with oil. Model No. 650 made by J-Mark Quality Products Inc. is a rigid vinyl funnel and has a tip that includes a 15 inch polyflex hose.

A Drain Pan That Can Take It

One of the handiest items to have around the garage is a simple drain pan. It should have a low profile yet hold a large quantity of fluid. It also needs to be durable because it is going to take a lot of abuse. J-Mark Quality Products, Inc. sells a galvanized utility drain pan that is ideal for catching drained automotive fluids. It is their Model 59 that holds 10 quarts.

Immersion Type Oil Pan Heaters

In cold areas of the country, motorists have many different opinions of what type of heater to use to help start their car more easily. Many choose the immersion type oil pan heater such as Model Nos. 150 and 151 sold by Mastermotive, Inc. This type of heater installs in the oil pan, heating the oil to let it flow easier and giving quicker lubrication without power-robbing drag. The heaters can be installed on steel or aluminum oil pans. A cord guard and installation instructions are included with both models. Model 150 is a 150 watt/120 volt unit and Model 151 is a 200 watt/240 volt unit.

HD-1 Motor Oil

If you prefer a straight weight motor oil, you might consider HD-1 motor oil from Amalie Refining Co. It is a premium quality motor oil blended from selected base stocks and from detergent/dispersent, antiwear, antioxidant, rust and corrosion inhibitors and antifoam additives. It comes in SAE grades 10W, 20W, 30W, 40W, and 50W.

Oil Drain Plug Stops Leaks

After you change the oil in your car, you should let the engine run for a while to make sure that there are no leaks at the oil drain plug. If the plug is tightened correctly and it still leaks, you may need to purchase a replacement drain plug. J-Mark Quality Products, Inc. makes a 1/2 inch double oversize replacement plug that can do the job. These plugs are available for a wide variety of cars, so you should be able to find the one that fits yours.

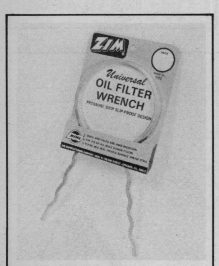

Universal Oil Filter Wrench

Zim Manufacturing Company makes a unique oil filter wrench that allows you to easily regulate the pressure that is applied to the walls of the filter. There is not much danger of crushing the oil filter with their Model 991 universal oil filter wrench. You can quickly adjust the wrench to the size of the filter and regulate the pressure on the filter with your grip. The wrench is made of plated and heat-treated spring steel and should offer many years of good service.

Old Timer Motor Oil

Kendall Refining Company was the first manufacturer to market multi-viscosity oils nationally. That was back in 1953, and they are still providing the consumer with top quality multi-grade oils. One of their latest is Kendall Superb Motor Oil. It has a 10W-20W-30 weight designation and exceeds car manufacturers' warranty requirements. It is also available in the following SAE grades: 5W-20, 10W-40 and 20W-40 in one quart cans.

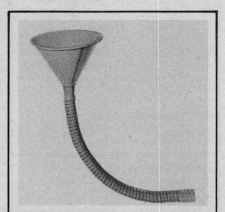

Funnel Makes Adding Fluids A Neat Chore

A funnel, especially one with a flexible spout, is necessary when adding transmission fluid to most cars. Brookins Service Station Equipment Division of Balcrank Products has Model 1151 that has a 12-inch flexible spout and comes in capacity sizes from 1/4 pint to six quarts.

Use A Funnel To Prevent Spills

It is always good to have a few funnels in different sizes on hand. One just cannot do all the jobs that you encounter when working on an automobile. A large one may not fit in the space that you are working in, and a small one sometimes makes the job take forever. Brookins Service Station Equipment by Balcrank Products makes pregalvanized funnels in four sizes. Their Model 543 is a one pint capacity funnel with a diameter of 5-1/4 inches. If you need a one quart model, choose their Model 545, which has a diameter of 6-3/4 inches. Model 546 holds two quarts and has a diameter of 8-3/8 inches, while their four quart model, No. 547, measures 9-3/8 inches in diameter.

LUBRICATION

A Pair Of Jacks

Hein-Werner Corp. manufactures two jacks especially for the home mechanic. Their 1-1/2 ton Model E1.7F has a low height of seven inches, a hydraulic lift of 5-1/4 inches and a two-inch extension screw. Maximum height is 14-1/4 inches. The base of this model is 5-1/16 inches by 3-1/4 inches. The three-ton Model E3.9A has a low height of nine inches, a hydraulic lift of 6-9/16 inches, a two-inch extension screw, and an overall height of 17-9/16 inches. The base measures 5-5/8 inches by 3-3/4 inches. Both units feature malleable base, one-piece extension screw, center-balanced handle socket and an exclusive self-aligning pump piston design.

Engine Treatment

Rislone is an engine treatment product that you add to your engine's oil. The Shaler Company formulated Rislone to help remove the cause of noisy valve trains, low compression, sluggish and rough operation, and lost power. It is made to promote longer engine life and continued efficient power performance through engine cleanliness and proper lubrication. If you have a noisy valve or lifter, Rislone might do the trick.

Multipurpose Product

Woodhill/Permatex makes DLF No. 109, a multipurpose product with a multitude of applications. DLF is a demoisturizer that dries wet metal surfaces. It also is a lubricant that cuts friction and quiets squeaks. In addition, it can free rusted and frozen parts and protect metal against oxidation. It is available in five and 14 ounce aerosol cans.

Graphite Lock Fluid

There is nothing like a stuck or frozen lock to annoy you. American Grease Stick Company, Inc. makes Lock-Ease, a graphite lock fluid that seals out moisture and protects against freeze-ups. It also helps locks to work easier, prevents sticking and guards against rust and corrosion. The product is available in 3.4 ounce squeeze cans and four ounce aerosol cans that include a snorkel for easy application.

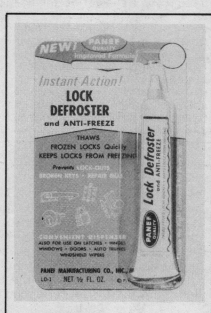

Lock Defroster

Most motorists know the trick of heating a key with a cigarette lighter and then inserting it into a keyhole to defrost the lock. This may get you in, but it will not prevent the lock from freezing up again. It is much better to use a lock defroster such as that made by Panef Manufacturing Co., Inc. Their lock defroster, which comes in 1/2 ounce tubes, will not harm paint finishes. The tube has a pointed nozzle and can dispense a drop or a stream directly into a key slot.

Snap-On Oil Can Funnel

Someone was bound to think of this one. It is a funnel that you can snap onto the top of a quart can of motor oil so that you can pour the oil easily. Automark Division of Wells Manufacturing Corp. makes a snap on oil can funnel No. 51714 that also includes a cap, so that you can store a partially full can of oil. The funnel has an offset design for hard to reach places and is molded of polyethylene.

Three-Piece Oil Change Kit

If you are looking for an economical way to get started in the world of do-it-yourself auto repairs, you might take a look at the Handee Oil Change Kit made by J-Mark Quality Products, Inc. The kit, Model No. 666, includes a utility drain pan, a can spout that has a zinc lustron finish and welded construction, and an oil filter wrench that is zinc plated and fits all standard size filters.

Versatile Spray

The WD-40 Company makes an extremely versatile spray. It can take the place of penetrating oil, light lubricants, grease sticks, rust preventives, graphite and silicone spray lubes. WD-40 is formulated to have an ultra-high surface attraction to metal. This characteristic enables it to creep under moisture to establish a protective barrier between moisture and the metal part. On your car, you can use it wherever you would use a light lubricating oil to stop squeaks and to make parts work smoothly. It also is good for freeing stuck or rusted metal parts, bolts connectors, operating controls and linkages. It will lubricate locks. If your car is having trouble starting due to moisture, you can often remedy the problem by spraying the ignition wires, coil, spark plugs and distributor cap with WD-40.

Heavy-Duty Jack Stands

Working under a car can be dangerous, so it is wise to invest in a quality set of jack stands for such repair work. Strongarm heavy-duty jack stands, made by Armstrong Hydraulics Inc., are available in two- and five-ton capacities. The two-ton model, No. 2T, has a low height of 11 inches and a high height of 17-3/4 inches. A pair weighs 13 pounds. The five-ton model, No. 5T, has a low height of 14-3/4 inches and a high height of 25 inches. A pair weighs 27 pounds. Such stands are also excellent for vehicle storage.

Heavy-Duty Filter Wrench

It is wise to change your oil filter at least every other time you change your oil. To make this chore simpler, a heavy-duty filter wrench such as the Nun-Better Model 12-807, sold by Rittenbaum Brothers, Inc., may be the answer for you.

Heavy-Duty Pouring Spout

Rittenbaum Brothers, Inc. manufactures a heavy-duty pouring spout for cans under the Nun-Better trade name. The Model 12-822 spout is eight inches long and has a gasket to reduce leakage. The device eliminates messy spills when adding oil to your car.

Water Temperature Gauge

It is very beneficial to have a water temperature gauge in your car, especially if you run your car in hot climates or tow a trailer. Stewart-Warner makes a compact model called the No. 82452 water temperature gauge. It can read coolant temperatures from 120° to 270° F. The 12-volt zener-diode-regulated bimetal mechanism works with negative ground systems only. The gauge includes an adjustable black polypropylene panel, 1/8 inch temperature center with adaptors for 1/2 inch and 3/8 inch temperature connections, a lighting kit and complete instructions. The gauge is illuminated for easy reading at night.

Make Your Own Gaskets

When working on your car at odd hours, you sometimes discover that you need a certain gasket but the auto supply stores are closed. At such times, a gasket and washer cutting tool kit such as the one made by Kastar, Inc. can be a time-saver. The Model 550A gasket and washer cutting tool kit includes a gasket and washer cutting tool, five blades of high-carbon hardened and tempered steel, an eight by nine inch corrugated cutting board, three sheets of cork gasket material (eight by nine by 1/16 inches) and three sheets of gasket material (eight by nine by 1/32 inches).

Engine Oil Coolers

If you pull a trailer with your auto or own a motor home, you may be able to use an auxiliary oil cooler such as those made by Dunham-Bush, Inc. The firm's Kool-Mor oil coolers feature a series of fins inside the tubing designed to force hot oil to swirl and not to cling to the tubing, which would reduce efficiency.

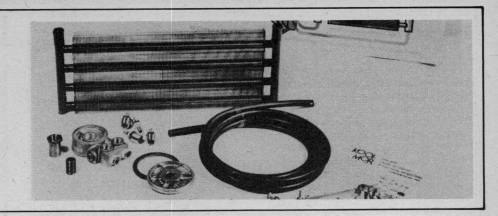

INTRODUCTION

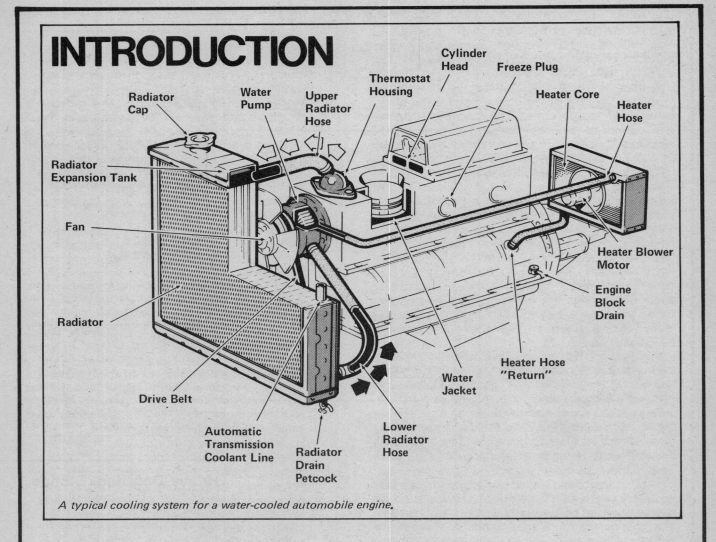

A typical cooling system for a water-cooled automobile engine.

THE INTERNAL combustion engine, which powers almost all automobiles, works on the principle of "burning inside." The burning of the air/fuel mixture in the engine creates a tremendous amount of heat—enough heat to melt an average 200 pound engine block in 20 minutes. In normal driving, temperatures inside the engine may be as high as 4500°F. Pistons may run 200° or more above the boiling point of water.

The function of the cooling system is to keep the engine at a temperature where it performs best. Two methods are employed to regulate this performance—water-cooling systems and air-cooling systems. Water-cooling systems, by far the more common, are used in almost all American-made cars. Air cooling is common in some foreign car makes, the largest number being Volkswagen. (VW, however, recently decided to water-cool some of their engines.) Cars with engines in the rear often have an air-cooling system. The principal clue is the lack of a radiator. Because of its dominance in auto design, the water-cooled engine will be the focus of this chapter.

For efficient operation, each automobile engine has an optimum temperature range. Without an efficient cooling system, the engine's own heat would destroy it in minutes. On the other hand, a certain amount of engine heat is desirable to preheat the air/fuel mixture for better combustion in the cylinders. Anyone who has noticed the rough running of a cold engine has experienced the importance of temperature control.

The block of a water-cooled engine is hollow around the cylinders. This space is filled with coolant, and the cylinders are thus enclosed in a "jacket" of coolant. (Coolant is made up of a mixture of antifreeze and water; a 50/50 mixture is normally recommended.) The coolant picks up heat during its circulation through the passages of the jacket and is forced to the radiator by the action of a water pump.

The radiator is a grilled nest of thin pipes, or tubes, and metal fins. The coolant is pumped through the tubes. At highway speeds, the outside air rushing between the tubes and over the fins cools the solution, dissipating the heat. At low speeds and at idle, a belt-driven fan forces

Push-Pull Gasket Scraper

Removing a gasket that has been on the car for many years is usually difficult. A push-pull gasket scraper, such as the No. 323 from Thexton Manufacturing Co., is designed for easy removal of manifold gaskets, water pump gaskets, valve cover gaskets, thermostat housing gaskets, head gaskets, differential cover gaskets, and en-

gine and transmission oil pan gaskets. The tool has a straight blade for pushing and a curved blade for pulling. The blades are made of

hardened and sharpened spring steel, and the tool has a comfortable vinyl grip.

Cool Your Engine

If you have an air-conditioned car or a vehicle that is used to pull trailers, you need an extra efficient cooling system. In the event that you notice slight overheating of your coolant, you may be able to remedy the problem somewhat by adding Enginkool made by Siloo Inc. It is made to dissipate heat from the engine when added to your regular coolant. Enginkool comes in 32 ounce cans.

SERVICING THE THERMOSTAT

BECAUSE ENGINE performance is so directly related to operating temperature, the thermostat plays a vital role under the hood. The thermostat is a temperature-sensitive device that partially closes to prevent coolant from reaching the radiator when the engine is cold. This speeds up the heat-up process. Later, it opens wide when the engine is warm to allow maximum flow and cooling of the coolant.

When the cooling system is clean and operating at normal temperatures, it can last for years. But it also can be a source of underheating or overheating problems. If a thermostat sticks in the open position, the car heater will generate insufficient heat in winter. If the thermostat fails to open, overheating will result. It is easy to find out whether or not the thermostat is creating your cooling system troubles. Here is how to go about it.

Here Is What You Will Need

Materials
- Block of Wood
- Kitchen Pan
- Water
- Thermometer
- Thermostat and Gasket
- Lint-Free Rag
- Gasket Sealer
- Hose Clamps

Tools
- Screwdriver
- Pliers
- Wrenches or Ratchet Wrench and Sockets
- Hammer
- Scraper

1. Drain the cooling system radiator. See the section in this chapter on Cooling System Flushing for instructions.
2. Find the thermostat housing, which contains the thermostat. It is generally located on the engine block at the top front of the

Stainless Steel Thermostats

Without a properly working thermostat, your cooling system cannot keep your car's engine at the correct operating temperature. The main enemy of automotive thermostats is erosion from the flow of coolant and corrosion in today's car. Ideal Corp. makes a line of six thermostats with structural components and springs of 316L stainless steel, which provides extremely high resistance to erosion. The stainless steel construction also gives the units a tensile strength of about 70,000 psi. Ideal thermostats are also manufactured with a die-stamped, one-piece bridge and flange that eliminates the stress points that can occur with ordinary two-piece thermostats. The six thermostats in the line cover over 90 percent of all passenger car applications. They are available in two sizes (2-1/8 inches - 54.2 mm; 2-1/2 inches - 63.5mm) and three temperatures (160° F, 180° F and 192° F).

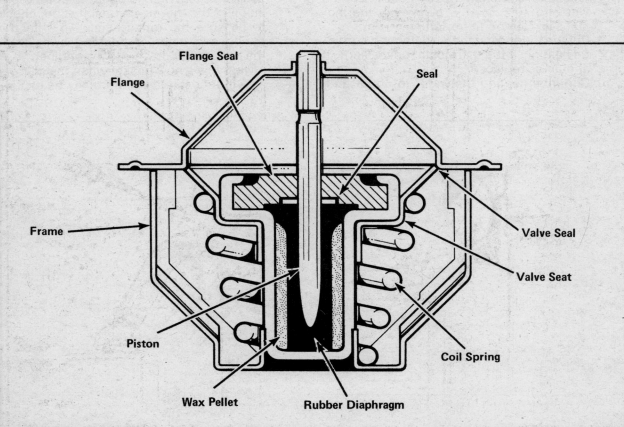

Cross-section of a thermostat, a temperature-sensitive device that partially closes to prevent coolant from reaching the radiator when the engine is cold. Once the engine is warm, it opens wide.

Gasket Sealer In An Aerosol Can

If you are tired of applying a gasket sealer with a brush, you might try High Tack Spray-A-Gasket adhesive sealant No. 99, made by Woodhill/Permatex. It sets fast and remains tacky to hold gaskets in place. It resists gasoline, oil, kerosene, lubricating oils, water, steam and glycol-water mixtures. It works in a temperature range from -65° to +500°F and withstands pressures to 5000 psi. The liquid has a red color for uniform coverage control, and it can be used on all metals and any gasket material. Six and 12 ounce aerosol cans are available.

Cooling System Leak Stopper

Sometimes minor leaks in your cooling system can be remedied with the use of a leak stopper and radiator sealer. Silver Seal Leak Stopper made by Silver Seal Products Co. Inc. is said to be effective on radiators, hoses, the block, and internal parts of the engine such as scored cylinders. It has a metallic sealer with a carrying agent that stays in suspension until carried to the leaking area. Fine metallic particles form a bridge held together with a plastic binder, activated when exposed to the atmosphere. Ten minutes of engine operation complete the sealing cycle.

Hose Clamp Strengthens Under Tension Like A Square Knot

Ideal Corporation's Combo-Hex hose clamps come in enough sizes to literally cover applications anywhere on your car. They feature a wide, 9/16 inch band with rounded edges to protect the hose. You do not have to worry about this clamp rusting because the band is made of stainless steel and so is the housing. Adjustment is made with a deep slotted, safety collared 3/8 inch hex head screw. This screw in the 54 Series is cadmium plated carbon steel, and in the 64 Series, it is made of stainless steel. Sizes are available to fit hoses with a diameter from 1/2 inch to seven inches.

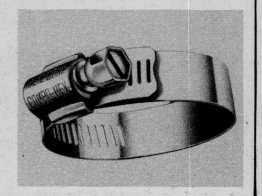

SERVICING THE THERMOSTAT

engine. It is connected to the upper radiator hose.

3. Remove the upper radiator hose clamp at the thermostat housing. Use a screwdriver to loosen the screw on the clamp. If you have a spring-type clamp, use a pliers to remove it. Slide the clamp along the hose out of the way.

4. Remove the two bolts that secure the thermostat housing to the engine block. If you cannot fit a wrench over these bolts, use a ratchet wrench and the proper size socket.

5. Lift off the thermostat housing. This may require some gentle tapping, as the gasket may have hardened. Put a block of wood against the housing and tap gently with a hammer until it comes loose.

6. Lift the thermostat out of its seat in the engine block.

7. Determine the temperature range of the thermostat. This is usually stamped on the thermostat itself. The lower temperature is the point at which it should begin to open. The higher temperature marks the full-open position.

8. Place a pan of water on a stove or hot plate and insert a kitchen thermometer. Heat the water to 10°F or 15°F below the thermostat's low temperature setting.

9. Put the thermostat in the water and continue heating. If the thermostat opens early, it should be replaced.

10. Continue heating the water to about 20°F above the low temperature setting for the thermostat. It should open fully. If it does not, it should be replaced.

11. Before installing a new thermostat, you may have to scrape the old gasket off the mounting surface on the engine block. Stuff a lint-free rag into the engine block opening before you scrape the gasket surface. This will prevent small parts of the gasket from falling into the opening. **CAUTION:** Most thermostats look alike, so there is a possibility of buying and installing one that is not engineered to the temperature range of your specific engine. Double-check the part specification of your car before leaving the auto parts store. Even the best of parts salesmen can make mistakes, and it is just one more trip back to correct the situation. Or worse, you might not discover the problem until the unit is installed. Remove the rag.

12. Place the thermostat into its seat in the engine block. Some thermostats have a flange that must be set in a groove for proper alignment. A thermostat will have Front, Up or To Rad stamped on it. This portion of the thermostat must face the radiator. It is possible to get one upside down in the housing if you ignore these markings. Be sure that you do not make that mistake. When in doubt about the position of the thermostat installation, check to be sure the unit is installed with the spring and actuator pointing away from the radiator (or down into the engine).

13. Always use a new gasket when installing a new thermostat. It will normally be includ-

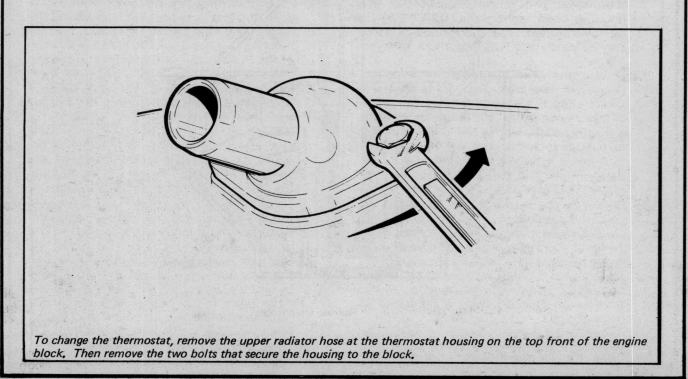

To change the thermostat, remove the upper radiator hose at the thermostat housing on the top front of the engine block. Then remove the two bolts that secure the housing to the block.

Gasket Cement

In addition to a wide variety of auto body products, Dynatron/Bondo Corporation also makes a pliable No. 2 gasket cement. It is easy to use and easy to replace. The product comes in 1.5 ounce tubes and is listed as product No. 918.

Engine Block Heater Installs With A Screwdriver

Mastermotive, Inc. makes a line of engine block heaters in 400 and 600 watt capacities. They have long-life heating elements, non-corrosive parts accurately machined for a positive fit, and O-ring seals to provide safe, sure protection from leaks. Each engine block heater also includes a

six foot, three wire detachable power cord. The installation is very quick and easy. Each unit has a positive locking assembly.

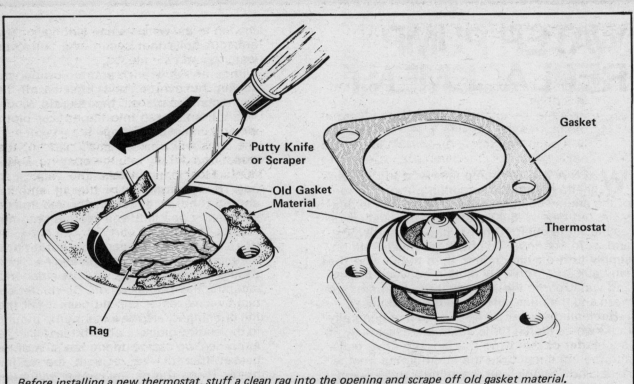

Putty Knife or Scraper

Old Gasket Material

Rag

Gasket

Thermostat

Before installing a new thermostat, stuff a clean rag into the opening and scrape off old gasket material. Seat new thermostat properly, apply sealer to both sides of gasket and place it over the thermostat before replacing the housing.

Radiator Thermometer

If your water gauge or idiot light indicates that your car is overheating but it never boils over, it may be that the gauge, idiot light or sending unit is malfunctioning. An easy way to determine this is to use a radiator thermometer such as the one made by Cal-Van Tools, a division of Chemi-Trol Chemical Company. The firm's No. 732 thermometer, which also can check thermostats, is calibrated in Centigrade and Fahrenheit scales and has a 4-1/2 inch thermotube.

ed in the package. Coat both sides of the gasket with a gasket sealing compound to insure a leak-proof fit. Then carefully place the gasket over the thermostat and the mounting surface of the engine block.

14. Place the thermostat housing over the thermostat and gasket. Install the two housing bolts and tighten. **CAUTION:** Do not overtighten. The thermostat housing can be easily cracked or broken by over-tightening.

15. Unless your hose clamps are in excellent condition, use new ones. Slide the hose clamp onto the hose and place the upper radiator hose over the thermostat housing. Slide the clamp along the hose until it is about one inch from the end of the hose. If you have a spring-type clamp, you will need a pliers to do this. On screw-type clamps, tighten the screw securely.

16. Once you are satisfied that all hose connections are secure, it is time to refill the cooling system. Be sure the petcock drain on the bottom of the radiator is shut tight, or the lower radiator hose is secure. Fill the system with a 50/50 mixture of water and antifreeze. (Refer to the section in this chapter on Cooling System Flushing for instructions.)

17. Reinstall the radiator pressure cap. Start the engine and let it run for 15 or 20 min-

utes. This will allow the engine to reach its normal operating temperature. With the engine still running, check for leaks where the upper radiator hose and thermostat housing are joined. Also check around the thermostat housing and engine block connection. If there are no leaks, your job is done. If a leak is present, try tightening the hose clamp some more. If the leak is at the housing to block connection, use a wrench of the proper size and carefully turn each bolt in quarter-of-a-turn increments. If after a couple of turns on each bolt the leak does not stop, you will have to remove the housing and start over.

18. If there are no leaks, shut off the engine and let it cool. Remove the radiator pressure cap. **CAUTION:** Some pressure will remain in the cooling system. Be careful. Slowly turn the radiator pressure cap to the first notch to relieve this pressure. Place rags around the radiator pressure cap to prevent coolant from splashing out and possibly burning you.

19. Recheck the cooling system level. Any air pockets that were in the cooling system before it was put under pressure will now have been filled. The system should be filled to within one inch below the radiator filler neck. Add coolant as necessary.

20. Reinstall the radiator pressure cap.

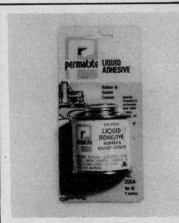

Nonhardening Gasket Cement

For some gasket applications, such as cooling system thermostats, you need a gasket cement that is nonhardening. The Durkee-Atwood Company makes a Permatite brand liquid adhesive rubber and gasket cement that does just this. It is a special tacky adhesive for applying rubber and other gasket materials to glass, plastic, metal, wood or fabric. It also acts as a reactivator for enlivening dry adhesive.

Water Pump Lubricant Takes Out The Squeal

If you are experiencing water pump squeal, you might try some Woodhill/Permatex water pump lubricant and radiator antirust No. 38M. It comes in 12 ounce cone-top cans and is designed to stop water pump squeal by lubricating the pump parts. It is also designed to eliminate rust by coating metal surfaces and is formulated to keep water clean. It is noncaustic, nonacid and harmless to rubber and metal.

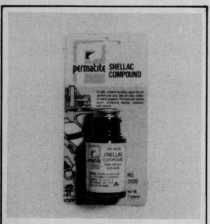

Gasket Shellac Compound Comes In Swab Bottle

Shellac compound is commonly used for all types of heat gaskets, manifold gaskets and water connections. Permatite gasket shellac compound, made by Durkee-Atwood Co., is such an adhesive. It withstands heat, water, oil and gasoline, and retains its plasticity after it has set. The two ounce bottle includes a swab for easy application.

Cure Radiator Leaks

Casite Leak-Stop, manufactured by Hastings Manufacturing Co., contains an exclusive sealing ingredient that stops cooling system leaks immediately. It also prevents rust and corrosion, lubricates the water pump and will not cake, harden or rot. The product is claimed to be harmless to hoses, metal and paint.

Heater And Radiator Hose Slitter

Using a hose slitter can speed up hose replacement considerably. Thexton Manufacturing Co.'s No. 318 has double cutting edges, which allow you to slit the hose by pushing or pulling. The angle blade pulls into the material, requiring very little pressure. The design enables you to cut heater hoses right up to the fire wall, and the comfortable vinyl grip makes the whole job less of a chore.

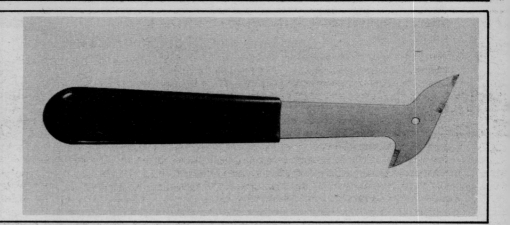

WATER PUMP REPLACEMENT

WHEN A WATER pump fails, you will usually hear a rattling noise coming from the front of the engine compartment. Overheating is possible, but before this develops, a leak usually is visible at the pump. Other failure signs are loose and worn bearings. To check for this condition, simply turn off the engine, then try moving the fan back and forth. Any motion between the fan and water pump indicates that the bearings are worn and the pump should be replaced.

Replacing a water pump is a job that generally looks worse than it turns out to be. Essentially, it is a matter of removing the fan, the drive belts, and the bolts that hold the pump to the engine. Here is how to go about replacing a water pump:

1. Remove the radiator pressure cap. (This will allow the coolant to drain easier.) Use a pliers to loosen the petcock—located near the bottom of the radiator. If you want to reuse this coolant, drain it into a clean pan. Once the coolant has completely drained out of the radiator, tighten the petcock. **NOTE:** The 1972 Chevrolet Vegas, most 1973 Oldsmobile Omegas and most 1973 Chevrolet and Pontiac models do not have a radiator drain petcock. To drain this type of radiator, you will have to remove the lower radiator hose as described in step 3.

2. Next, you will have to remove all drive belts; you will need a wrench for this job. A complete discussion on this subject is covered in a section called Replacing A Fan Belt elsewhere in this chapter.

3. Remove all hoses connected to the water pump. There may be up to three hoses: lower radiator hose, heater hose and a bypass hose. It is a good idea to mark each hose, so you will know where they go back on. On hoses with screw-type clamps, loosen the screw with a screwdriver and slide the clamp back along the hose and out of the way. With spring-type clamps, you will need a pliers to squeeze the ends of these clamps in order to slide them back along the hose. Once the clamps are out of the way, try to twist each hose off its mounting. This may require a little extra effort. If you cannot get them loose, you will have to cut them off with a sharp knife. If you do this, however, the hose must be replaced.

4. Use a wrench to remove the bolts that hold the fan to the water pump. Normally, there are four bolts that secure the fan to the water pump.

5. With a ratchet wrench and the proper size socket, remove the bolts that secure the water pump in place. There should be anywhere from four to seven bolts holding the water pump in place.

6. Lift out the water pump. **NOTE:** In some rare cases, it may be necessary to remove the radiator in order to get the water pump out. This generally is a matter of removing shrouds, hoses and radiator mountings. This job is best left to a professional mechanic.

7. Use a scraper to scrape the old gasket from the mounting surface on the engine block. Stuff a lint-free rag into the opening while scraping the old gasket off. Do not let any bits and pieces of the old gasket fall into the opening where the water pump mounts to the engine block. Remove the rag.

8. Apply sealing compound to the side of the gasket that fits up against the engine block. Place the gasket on the mounting surface of the engine block. Then coat the other side of the gasket with the sealing compound.

9. Position the water pump over the gasket and mounting surface. Install the water pump mounting bolts by hand and tighten. Use the ratchet wrench and the proper size socket to tighten the bolts securely. **CAUTION:** Water pumps are very similar in appearance, so be sure you get the right

---

Here Is What You Will Need

Materials

- Drain Pan
- Lint-Free Rag
- Gasket Sealer
- Water Pump and Gasket
- Heater Hose
- Hose Clamps
- Sandpaper
- Antifreeze
- Water

Tools

- Pliers
- Wrenches
- Screwdriver
- Sharp Knife
- Ratchet Wrench and Sockets
- Scraper
- Pry Bar
- Cooling System Pressure Tester

COOLING AND HEATING SYSTEM

Radiator Petcock Socket

Radiator petcocks have a wing-type nut that you can normally loosen with your hand. But sometimes you run into very stubborn ones that need a tool to open. Many mechanics use pliers, but this sometimes causes twisting and breakage of the petcock ears. An easier way is to use a radiator petcock socket. Thexton Manufacturing Co.'s No. 326 has a 3/4 inch hex that allows the use of open end, box end or socket

wrenches. An O-ring holds the socket securely in the wrench. This socket saves a lot of time when you are servicing your cooling system.

Versatile Gasket Cement

The Maywood Company makes a gasket cement that can be used for gaskets as well as threaded fittings and hose connections. Unlike many other types of gasket cement, Maywood's No. S276 sprays on from a one pint aerosol can, doing away with gooey cans and messy brushes. It is made to hold a gasket in place firmly and to eliminate slipping and misalignment.

New Line Of Fan Clutches

Arrow Automotive Industries recently introduced a new line of fan clutches for passenger cars and light trucks. Some mechanics recommend that you change your fan clutch whenever you change your water pump. The clutch feathers the fan so that it is not running at high speed when the car is.

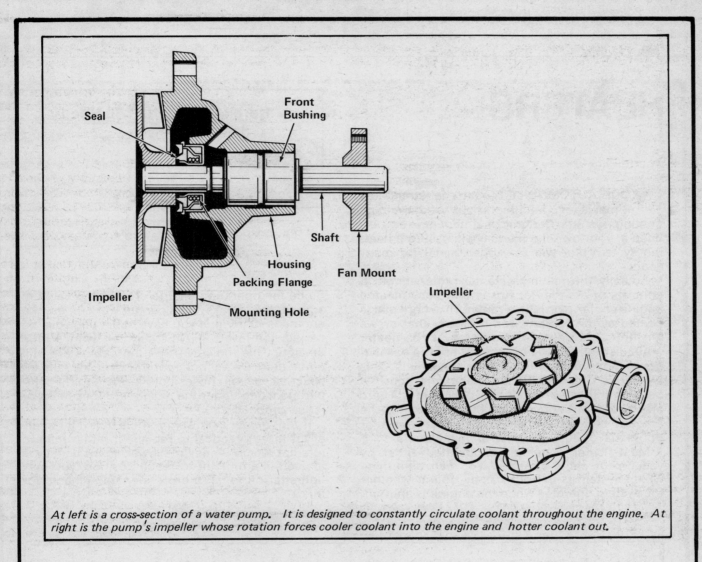

At left is a cross-section of a water pump. It is designed to constantly circulate coolant throughout the engine. At right is the pump's impeller whose rotation forces cooler coolant into the engine and hotter coolant out.

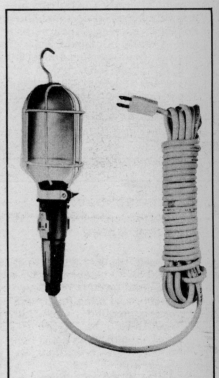

Without A Trouble Light, You Are In Trouble

Even if you are working in bright daylight, the nooks and crannies that you find in the engine compartment of your car remain dark. So, for almost any kind of automotive repair work, you need a good trouble light that allows you to illuminate the part of the car that you are working on. Filko Automotive Division makes two models of trouble lights, each rated at 10 amps and 125 volts. They have a molded plug, jacketed cord, and a plastic handle with a side outlet, guard and switch. Model 4702 has a 25 foot cord, and Model 4703 has a 50 foot cord. Both trouble lights are UL listed.

replacement pump for your car. Take the old one with you to the auto supply store if you can. **NOTE:** You can save yourself about half the price of a new pump by installing a rebuilt unit. Generally, these will work as well as a new one. Check with your auto supply store for information on rebuilt or remanufactured parts.

10. Place the fan over the end of the new water pump and install the mounting bolts. Tighten them securely with a wrench.

11. Replace all hoses. If you had to cut any to remove them, you will have to install new ones. See the section on Hose Removal and Installation. Always use new hose clamps unless the old ones are still in excellent condition. Scrape or sand any sealing compound off the hose mounting surfaces. Place a new clamp over each hose. If the old ones are being reused, be sure they are on the hoses before you reinstall them. Slip each hose onto its proper mounting and slide the hose clamps to within one inch of the ends of each hose. On

screw-type clamps, tighten the screw securely. Spring-type clamps require a pliers.

12. The fan belts can now be put back on. You will need a pry bar for this task. There is a complete discussion of belt replacement in another section called Replacing A Fan Belt.

13. Fill the radiator with the coolant you drained from the radiator. You can add new coolant if your radiator coolant protection level is low. Add a 50/50 mixture of antifreeze and water. If you want to check the antifreeze protection level, you will have to let the new antifreeze mix with the old coolant. Do this by driving the car for approximately 20 to 30 minutes. Use an antifreeze tester to determine the protection level. See the section in this chapter on Checking Your Antifreeze for specific instructions.

14. Replace the radiator pressure cap.

15. Start the engine and visually check for leaks. If you did your job carefully, you should not have any problems.

Gasket Cement Contains Copper

Marvel Oil Co. makes a gasket cement you can use on metal, asbestos, cork and paper gaskets. It also can be used on hoses and threaded fittings. The primary feature of this gasket cement, which comes in a seven ounce aerosol can, is that it contains copper to improve heat transfer and eliminate hot spots. The cement sets up in 60 seconds but remains tacky for easy positioning. The cement is designed for large and hard-to-hold gaskets and provides effective sealing properties from -65°F to 500°F.

Nonhardening Gasket Plastic

When you replace cooling system hoses, you must use an adhesive sealer at the hose connections. Durkee-Atwood makes Gasket-Eze No. 2. It is a nonhardening gasket plastic that preserves all types of solid gaskets and forms a tight leak-proof seal. You can also use it on cover plates and any threaded connection.

Low Cost Radiator Hose Heaters

Coolant heaters that merely mount in the lower radiator hose are less expensive than the type that includes a pump to circulate heated coolant throughout the system. Phillips Division of James B. Carter Inc. makes a lower radiator hose heater that is available in five models. Model 125 is a 500 watt unit that fits a 1-1/4 inch hose. Model 150 is a 750 watt unit that mounts in a 1-1/2 inch hose. Models 175, 200 and 225 are 750 watt units that mount in 1-3/4 inch, 2 inch and 2-1/4 inch radiator hoses respectively. All operate on 120 volts.

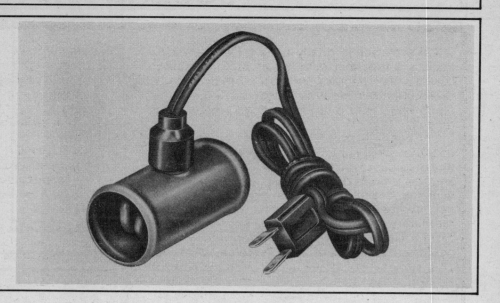

HEATERS

YOUR AUTOMOBILE'S heater is, strange as it may seem, an integral part of the engine cooling system. Periodic maintenance as outlined in your owner's manual will assure a heating system that will stay operational for many years.

Actually, the heating system is rather simple. It consists of a series of hoses that carry heated engine coolant through a radiatorlike core that is heated by the coolant, and a blower that draws air through a network of ducts over the heater core, distributing the heated air into the passenger compartment or toward the windshield. This blower is operated by an electric motor that usually is located under the dashboard. There also is a heat control valve that determines the amount of heat available and some vanes or doors that direct the heated air in the ducts.

Most heater systems are operated either by vacuum or cable controls. You can determine which system is in your car by noting whether the system operates when the engine is shut off.

Since the operating engine creates the vacuum source, a vacuum system cannot work unless the engine is running. If you have cable controls, be certain the levers move freely but with a little tension. This indicates that the cables are still connected. On vacuum control cars, visually inspect all vacuum hoses both in the engine compartment and under the dashboard for breaks or loose connections.

If your heater's blower motor is noisy, it generally is more practical to replace it rather than to attempt repair. Since the blower motor usually is located in a difficult-to-reach position, you may be better off to get a professional mechanic for this job.

Here Is What You Will Need

Materials

- Fuse
- Antifreeze
- Water
- Rags

Tools

- Safety Goggles

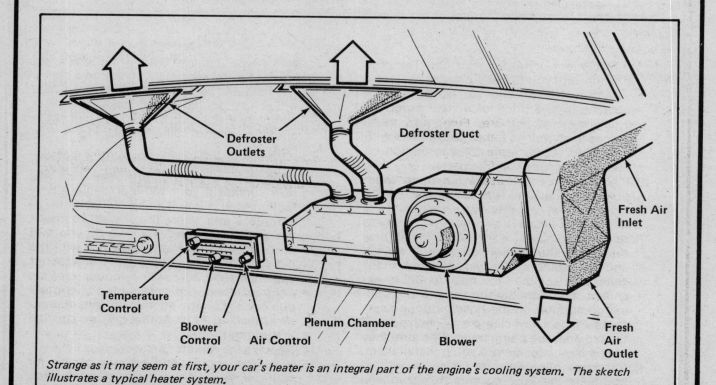

Strange as it may seem at first, your car's heater is an integral part of the engine's cooling system. The sketch illustrates a typical heater system.

If the blower is totally inoperative, however, there is a fuse that controls its motor. Usually, the fuse is in the fuse box under the dashboard. Check it and, if required, replace it with one of equal value before proceeding with any system repairs.

One common problem with a heating system is coolant leakage. Just as the engine cooling system uses hoses and connections that sometimes spring a leak, so does the heating system. Whenever the heater hoses deteriorate or the connections become loose, coolant seeps out. This reduction of available fluid affects the heating system. Heat levels may become erratic, or there could be a total loss of heat. Therefore, all hoses and connections should be kept in top shape for efficient heater operation.

Before making any heating system checks, be certain the cooling system (radiator) is full of coolant. Most people keep antifreeze in their cars all year round. If the cooling system is equipped with an overflow tank, check the coolant level in the tank and bring it up to the proper level if necessary.

CAUTION: Never remove the radiator's pressure cap from a hot system. In fact, always use caution when removing a radiator pressure cap. Safety goggles are a wise precaution. Since the system operates under pressure when hot, removing the radiator pressure cap might cause hot coolant to blow out of the radiator and severely burn you. If you must open the cap when the system is hot, use several layers of rags for protection. Depending on the type of radiator pressure cap, there may be two ways to relieve the pressure. Some radiator pressure caps have a lever or a button for this purpose. Flipping the lever up or holding the button in will release the pressure buildup. Other radiator pressure caps, meanwhile, are designed to be turned counterclockwise to a notch. Once the pressure has been relieved, you push the cap down and turn it counterclockwise for removal.

If there is no overflow tank on the cooling system, remove the radiator pressure cap — observing the same precautions emphasized earlier — and, if necessary, add coolant until the fluid level is about one-half inch below the filler opening. Most manufacturers recommend a coolant concentration of 50 percent antifreeze and 50 percent water.

You also should be certain the engine is at normal operating temperature before heating system checks are made. Allow the engine to run for about 20 minutes. Then, to check for low heat or no heat at all, follow these steps:

1. Determine whether coolant is flowing through the heater core. First, turn the heater to 'on' and the temperature to 'hot.' Feel the two heater hoses. These are long hoses coming from the front of the engine that connect to the heater core on the engine side of the fire wall. Generally heater hoses are about one inch in diameter. With the heater system operating, both heater hoses should be hot to the touch.
2. If the heater hoses are only warm (and there is coolant in the radiator and the engine is at operating temperature), you may have a malfunctioning thermostat in your cooling system. It may not be allowing the coolant to reach the proper temperature. Replace the thermostat. This procedure is outlined in the section in this chapter on the thermostat.
3. If one heater hose is hot and the other is not, or is only warm, you most probably have a restricted heater core. Sometimes,

this condition may be corrected by flushing out the entire cooling system with one of the products designed for this purpose. They are available at your auto supply store. Refer to the section in this chapter for instructions on how to flush the cooling system.
4. If, however, flushing does not solve the problem, you may have to have the heater core removed and repaired by a radiator shop.

Some automobiles, meanwhile, have a heater control valve attached to one of the heater hoses. Locate this valve by following each of the hoses from one end to the other. If a heater hose is hot on one side of this valve and only warm (or cool) on the other, the valve may be defective or be inoperative due to faulty cable or vacuum operation. Here are some steps to determine the nature of the problem:

1. If your heater system is cable-operated, have someone in the car move the temperature control from 'low' to 'high' as you closely watch the control valve. If the cable connected to it does not move, it is either broken or it has come loose at the lever end.
2. Inspect the cable connection at both ends. If they are secure, the cable is broken and must be replaced by a mechanic. Otherwise, resecure the cable.
3. If the car's system is vacuum-operated, have someone move the temperature control from 'low' to 'high' with the engine running. Observe the control valve.
4. If it does not operate, check for vacuum leaks and repair them. Otherwise, have a mechanic replace the heater control valve.

If both heater hoses are hot, you then know the coolant is flowing through the system. However, if there still is no heat, one of the 'blend doors' may not be working properly. A blend door is like a 'flapper' valve or vane that directs the passing of air in the heat duct. If this does not open or close properly, heat may not be directed into the passenger area (or you may not be able to shut off the heat) properly.

To check this:

1. Follow the heater duct, usually under the dashboard, and locate the blend door or doors.
2. Make certain they swing freely on their hinges.
3. If the system is cable-operated, make sure the cable is securely connected to the door.
4. If the blend doors are vacuum-operated, check for leaks and repair them, replacing any defective vacuum hoses.

Sometimes, a heating system will produce heat all the time, regardless of where the control levers are positioned. In such a case, check the heater control valve for operation as outlined previously. If the valve is stuck in the open position and the controls to the valve are operating, have the valve replaced. Also check the blend doors. If they are not closing fully, heat will be delivered into the passenger compartment at all times. Once again, check the controls, especially the door itself for warpage or sticking hinges. If you cannot get the doors to close properly, you should have your professional mechanic check them out.

Molded Radiator Hoses Replace Original Equipment

The Goodyear Tire & Rubber Company makes a line of molded radiator hoses that are preshaped for specific application and constructed to original equipment manufacturer's specifications. They are molded to provide a full flow through tight bends, ease of application and to relieve stress in radiator connections. Tubes and covers are especially formulated to resist heat, ozone and chemical coolants. The premium synthetic knit reinforcement provides burst limits exceeding SAE standards.

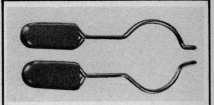

Radiator Hose Removal Tool Set

Radiator hoses can be tough customers when it comes to removing them. In fact, it may be difficult to remove the hose without damaging the hose or nipple. Thexton Manufacturing Company sells a radiator hose removal set No. 317 that can save you time when you are servicing your radiator or water pump. The tool has a finger that slips between the hose and the pipe, and slides around to separate for easy removal without damage to the hose or nipple. Two tools, right hand and left hand, are included in the set. These allow 360 degree separation even in confined areas. They are made of durable spring steel and have a comfortable vinyl grip.

Hose Clamp Pliers

Trying to remove spring-tension clamps on your cooling system hoses with regular pliers is a tough chore. Proto Professional Tools, a division of Ingersoll-Rand, markets hose clamp pliers that feature two-position jaws that grip a full range of clamp sizes. The pliers are available with or without plastic-coated handles. Model 252 measures 7-3/4 inches long; Model 252G with plastic-coated handles measures 7-13/16 inches.

FUEL SYSTEM

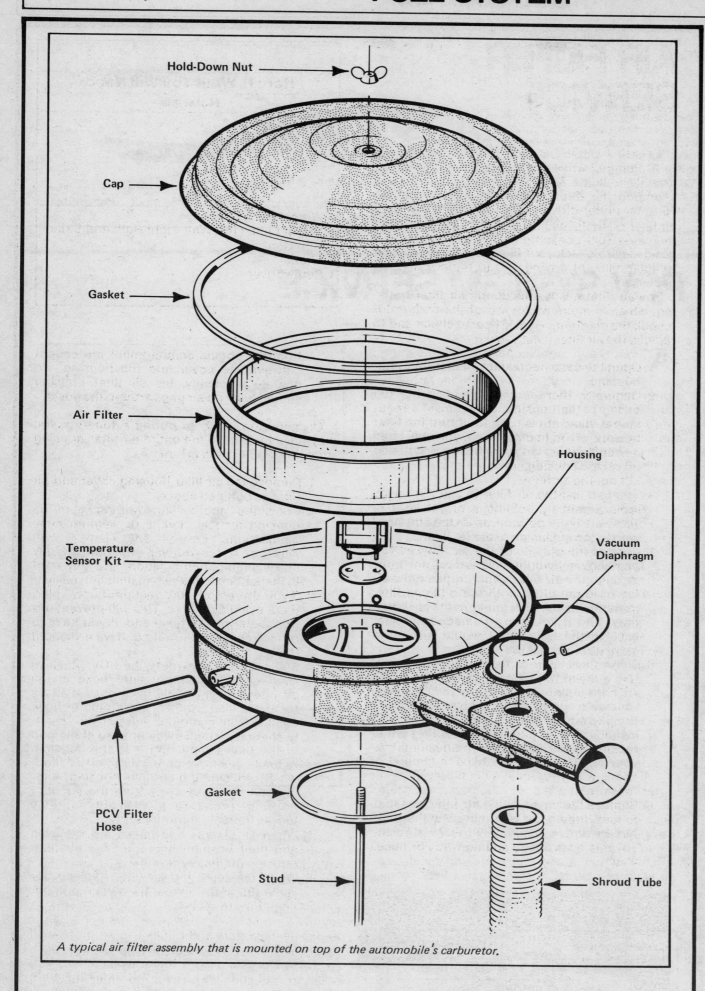

Hold-Down Nut

Cap

Gasket

Air Filter

Temperature
Sensor Kit

PCV Filter
Hose

Gasket

Stud

Housing

Vacuum
Diaphragm

Shroud Tube

A typical air filter assembly that is mounted on top of the automobile's carburetor.

Do Not Modify Air Cleaners

The air cleaner housing and cover should not be "re-engineered" by the home mechanic. The proper filter should be installed so that the lid fits snugly against the housing. Any alterations may lead to poor engine performance, especially during the cold engine warm-up period.

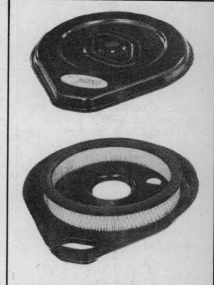

Air Filter Assembly Will Save Money

If you own a Chevrolet Chevette, Monza or Vega, or a Pontiac Astre or Sunbird, you know that the air filter and housing assembly for your car must be replaced as a complete unit. There is, however, an alternative. Hastings Manufacturing Company offers a replacement assembly that consists of a two-piece, all-metal housing plus a replaceable air filter element. The cost of the three-piece Hastings assembly compares favorably with that of an original-equipment replacement. But once the Hastings assembly is installed, all you have to purchase in the future is the inexpensive air filter element.

New Fuel Pumps

Arrow Automotive Industries recently added a new line of fuel pumps for passenger cars and light trucks to their product offerings. They may be worth considering if the fuel pump in your car needs replacement.

Use Caution When Replacing Air Cleaner

When replacing your car's air cleaner, be careful not to overtighten the wing nut securing it to the carburetor. It is possible to damage the carburetor since the air cleaner stud is threaded into the carburetor casting. It can be warped by excessive pressure.

maker's recommendations. Here is how:

1. To remove the air filter housing cover, loosen the nut in the center of the cover and remove the cover.
2. Remove the wire mesh filter element.
3. Remove the filter housing from the carburetor by lifting it off.
4. Clean the wire mesh filter element with solvent and let it air dry.
5. Empty the oil from the filter housing into a

suitable container and clean out any sediment that may be present in the bottom of the housing. Do this by washing the unit with solvent (not gasoline!) and wiping with a clean cloth.

6. Replace the housing on the carburetor.
7. Put clean engine oil in the housing up to the level marked on the housing.
8. Reinstall the wire mesh filter element.
9. Reinstall the housing cover and tighten the nut with a proper size wrench.

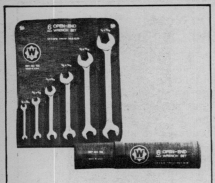

Six-Piece, Open-End Wrench Set

Box wrenches are generally easier to use than open-end wrenches, but only open-end wrenches can be used when you are dealing with pipes and tubing. A six-piece set from Wright Tool and Forge Company, No. 736, includes 12 wrench sizes that are most commonly used on automobiles. These are 1/4, 5/16, 3/8, 7/16, 1/2, 9/16, 5/8, 11/16, 3/4, 13/16, 7/8 and 15/16 inch. They are packaged in a handy tool roll.

Miniature Pliers Set

K-D Manufacturing Company sells a miniature pliers set, No. 11K3, for precision work. These pliers may look like toys, but they are designed for serious mechanical work. The set includes a standard-type pliers, parrot-nose pliers with a 3/8 inch maximum opening, and needle-nose pliers. All are about 3-3/4 inches long.

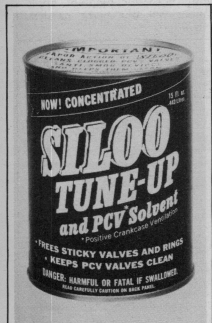

Solvent Cleans PCV Valves By Vapor Action

Siloo, Inc. makes a tune-up and PCV solvent that is formulated to give your car an on-the-road tune-up. The product is designed to dissolve gum and sludge deposits and to free sticky valves and rings. Siloo Tune-Up and PCV solvent comes in 15 ounce, one quart, five gallon and 55 gallon sizes.

Combination Slip-Joint Pliers Have Many Uses

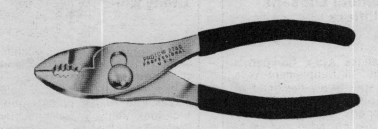

For big and small jobs, combination utility pliers have many uses. You can use them to grip bolts, twist and cut wire, bend sheet metal and loosen stripped fasteners. Proto Tool Division of Ingersoll-Rand offers combination slip-joint pliers in eight lengths from 5-3/8 to 10-1/16 inches. They have two jaw positions and a sheer-type wire cutter. The chrome-plated tools come with or without Plastisol-dipped handles.

PCV SYSTEM SERVICE

AS YOUR automobile operates and the combustion process is taking place, a highly corrosive gas is produced. In addition, for every gallon of gasoline burned, more than a gallon of water is formed. During the last part of the engine's combustion stroke, some unburned fuel and products of combustion (water vapor, for instance) leak past the engine's piston rings into the crankcase. This leakage is the result of four things:

1. High pressures in the engine combustion chamber. This condition is created by the normal compression stroke in the engine under operation.
2. The necessary working clearance of piston rings in their grooves. Without this normal ring clearance, the engine's piston rings would not have room to expand from heat created by normal engine operation and seal properly against the cylinder walls.
3. The normal shifting of piston rings in their grooves that sometimes lines up the clearance gaps of two or more rings. This, too, is a normal condition. As the piston rings continue to turn in their grooves, the situation will correct itself.
4. The reduction in piston ring sealing contact area as the piston moves up and down in the cylinder.

This leakage into the engine crankcase often is referred to as "blow-by." This blow-by must be removed from the engine before it condenses in the crankcase and reacts with oil to form sludge. If sludge does form and is allowed to circulate with the engine oil, it will corrode and accelerate the wear of pistons, piston rings, valves, bearings and other internal working parts of the engine.

Complete burning of the air/fuel mixture in the engine never occurs, so blow-by carries a certain amount of unburned fuel from the engine's combustion chamber into the crankcase. If this unburned fuel is not removed, the oil in the crankcase will be diluted. And, oil diluted with gasoline will not lubricate the engine properly, causing excessive wear.

The combustion gases that do enter the engine crankcase are removed from the crankcase by means of a system using engine vacuum to draw fresh air through the crankcase. This system is called Positive Crankcase Ventilation (PCV).

This fresh air, which dissipates the harmful gases, enters through the air filter on top of the carburetor or through a separate PCV breather filter located on the inside of the carburetor air filter housing.

Since the vacuum supply for the PCV system is from the engine's intake manifold, the air flow through this system must be controlled in such a

Filtered Air ◢

Blow-By Gases ◇

Combustible Mixture ▨▨▨

Filtered Air and Blow-By Gases - - - ►

The sketch depicts how a typical PCV system uses engine vacuum to remove combustion gases.

Here Is What You Will Need

Materials
- PCV System Hose
- PCV Valve Solvent or Lacquer Thinner
- Engine Oil
- PCV Valve
- PCV Breather Filter

Tools
- Pliers
- Screwdriver
- Sharp Knife
- Wrench

FUEL SYSTEM

Detergent Oil Supplement Loosens Valve Lifters

United States Aviex Company's Detergent Oil Supplement is a product specifically designed to impart a high detergency and antirust property to oil. It is formulated to free corroded and sticking hydraulic valve lifters. If you have a problem with a sticking lifter, you might try this product.

Push-Button, Slide-Lock Utility Knife

Using your good pocketknife around the garage can ruin it in short order. A better tool to use is a utility knife that has replaceable blades. The No. 689 push-button, slide-lock utility knife, made by Proto Tool Division of Ingersoll-Rand, gives you instant fingertip control of four blade positions. Its large handle also gives

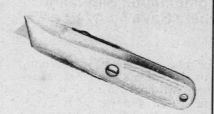

you a better grip. Each knife comes with five No. 692 heavy-duty blades that can be stored in the handle.

way that it varies in proportion to the regular air/fuel ratio being drawn into the intake manifold through the carburetor. Otherwise, the additional air being drawn into the system would cause the air/fuel mixture to become too lean for efficient engine operation.

The air flow through the PCV system into the intake manifold is regulated by the PCV valve. This valve, along with the necessary piping (metal tubing or rubber hose) and the intake breather filter, comprise the PCV system.

The PCV valve varies the amount of air flow through the system according to engine operation such as idle, cruise, acceleration, etc. The PCV valve itself consists of a coil spring, a valve and a two-piece body that is crimped together. The valve dimensions, spring tension and internal dimensions vary according to the engine they are used on to produce the desired air flow requirements. For this reason, when replacing a PCV valve, it is important to get the valve that is specifically designed for your car's engine.

The PCV system has three major benefits. It eliminates harmful crankcase gases by rerouting them through the intake manifold. It also reduces air pollution by not allowing these gases to enter the atmosphere. And, it promotes fuel economy. The recirculated gases in the system are a combustible mixture. In effect, it becomes fuel for the engine when added to the air/fuel mixture entering the intake manifold from the carburetor.

Consequently, an inoperative PCV system could shorten the life of the engine by allowing harmful blow-by gases to remain in the engine, causing corrosion and accelerating wear.

Let us now take a closer look at how the PCV system operates (see illustration). First, outside air enters the carburetor air filter housing and is filtered by the PCV system breather filter in the carburetor air filter housing. It then enters the

engine crankcase by means of a tube or rubber hose through the engine valve cover. The air then circulates through the engine crankcase and mixes with blow-by gases. The air is drawn out of the engine crankcase by intake manifold vacuum, through the PCV valve and into the engine intake manifold.

While the illustration is general, all PCV systems operate essentially the same. Note that the PCV valve itself is located in the hose or tube that is connected between the engine valve cover and a vacuum source fitting at the intake manifold below the carburetor. Depending on the particular engine, the actual location of the PCV valve will vary. It may be inserted into a rubber grommet in the engine valve cover, or it may be closer to the intake manifold with rubber hoses connected to each end of the valve. If you have any doubt as to the location of the PCV valve on your vehicle, ask your professional mechanic or a knowledgeable person at your auto supply store.

Note, too, how fresh air enters the PCV system from the carburetor air filter housing. There is a rubber hose or tubing with one end connected to the air filter housing and the other end connected to the engine (usually at the valve cover). (The valve cover is a long box-shaped object about the length of the engine. It is held to the engine by several screws along its mounting surface.) Four- and six-cylinder engines will have one valve cover; eight-cylinder engines will have two, one on each side.

Car makers may vary on their recommendations for PCV system servicing and PCV valve replacement. But, as a general rule, you should check the PCV system for satisfactory operation every 12 months or 12,000 miles of driving, whichever comes first. Also, the PCV valve should be replaced at least every 24 months or 24,000 miles of driving, whichever comes first.

Safety Valve On Cleaner

To clean a carburetor's linkage well, a product must be strong. And most good carburetor and choke cleaners are solutions that are harmful if they are swallowed or come in contact with the eyes. CD-2 Choke and Carburetor Cleaner, made by the Alemite Division of Stewart-Warner, features a child-resistant closure and directional spray top for safety. The aerosol can, which includes a spray hose for pinpoint application, will not harm catalytic converters.

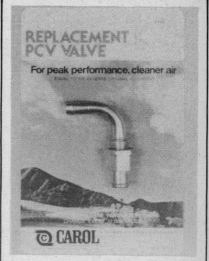

PCV Valves Do Not Last Forever

If your car is idling roughly, it may be that your PCV valve needs replacement. The Carol Cable Co., a division of Avnet, Inc., manufactures a line of replacement PCV valves. Since the vehicles that the valves will fit are listed on the front of the package, you will find it easy to select the one designed to fit your car.

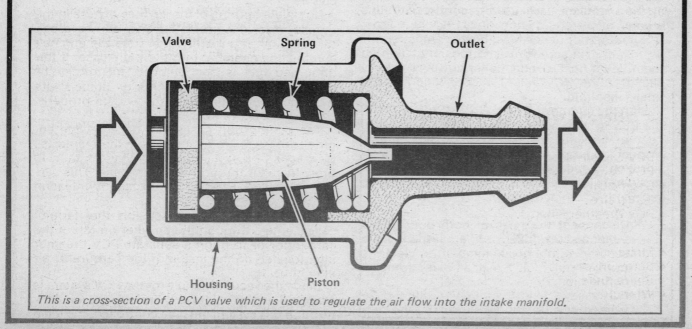

This is a cross-section of a PCV valve which is used to regulate the air flow into the intake manifold.

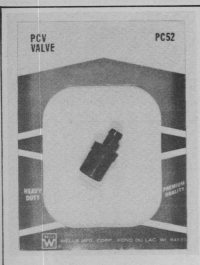

Replacement PCV Valve

Whenever you give your car a tune-up, you should check the PCV valve (positive crankcase ventilation valve). This is really an easy job. All you have to do is remove the valve and shake it. If it rattles, it is most likely good. If it does not, it needs to be replaced. Wells Manufacturing Corp. makes Ampco replacement PCV valves for most Buick, Chevrolet, Oldsmobile, Pontiac, Chrysler and Ford Motor Company cars.

Solvent For Chokes And Carburetors

Spray-on cleaner for automatic chokes and carburetors is formulated to tackle dirt, gum, varnish, oil and grease accumulations. Marvel's Automatic Choke and Carburetor Cleaner, available from the Marvel Oil Co., Inc., comes in 12 ounce cans. It also will clean grime from PCV valves. You just remove the valve from its socket, spray the cleaner into both ends of the valve and blow it out with an air hose.

Engine Tune-Up

Wynn's Friction Proofing Supply, Inc. manufactures an additive called Engine Tune-Up to free and quiet mechanically sound hydraulic valve lifters that are sticking due to crankcase deposits. Its formula includes solvents, ketones and alcohols that help restore lost engine performance. The product is added to the crankcase oil. A 15 ounce can is sufficient for one application.

PCV SYSTEM SERVICE

If you operate your car under dusty conditions, subject your engine to long periods of idling or make mostly short trips in cold weather, you should check your PCV system more often.

You may be having trouble with your PCV system if you have a rough-running engine at idle speed, discover oil in the air filter housing, find oil leaks at any of the PCV system hose or tube connections, or see oil leaks around the engine. Also, when you check the oil level of your engine and find that it is sludged up or appears to be diluted with gasoline (you can smell it), you probably have problems with the PCV system.

Checking The PCV System

IF YOU experience any of the symptoms described, a check of the PCV system is in order. Here is how to do it: **NOTE:** Before you replace a PCV valve or hoses, take a few minutes to look over the entire system. Locate the hoses in the system and locate the PCV valve. You will see that one hose is connected to the carburetor air filter housing and to the engine at the valve cover. This hose carries filtered air from the carburetor air filter to the engine crankcase. It seldom needs service, other than making sure the connections are secure. The line formed by this hose is unrestricted and never contains the PCV valve.

Next, you will see a hose connected between the engine valve cover and a fitting at the intake manifold just below the carburetor hose. The PCV valve will be installed as part of this line. Usually, the PCV valve will be installed in the end of the hose at the engine valve cover. However, the PCV valve will always be located somewhere in this line. Because the crankcase vapors and other contaminants are being drawn through the PCV valve and hose into the intake manifold, system problems are usually confined to this area.

Some rubber hoses have hose clamps requiring pliers or a screwdriver to loosen or tighten them. Most hose connections, however, simply slip over the PCV valve or connection at the intake manifold.

Start the engine and listen for vacuum leaks in the PCV system hose. If there is a leak, you will hear a slight hissing sound. Stop the engine. Inspect the hoses for cracks or any sign of deterioration. Since the PCV system must be airtight to operate efficiently, a leaking hose must be replaced. To replace a hose:

1. Disconnect the hose at both ends using either a screwdriver or pliers if the hose is secured with a hose clamp. If no clamp is used, simply pull the hose away from its connection. Remove the hose.
2. Purchase a length of PCV system hose from your auto supply store. Tell the person behind the counter the make and model car you are working on. In this way, he will be able to give you the correct diameter hose. Or, take the old hose with you and buy only the length that you need.
3. Using a sharp knife, cut the new hose to the same length as the one you removed.
4. Install the new PCV system hose, reversing step 1.

Testing The PCV Valve

HAVING visually checked out the PCV system and having replaced any defective hose, the next step is to test the PCV valve. Here is how to do it:

1. Open the hood and remove the air filter housing as outlined in the chapter on Air Filter Service. You may need a wrench or pliers to remove the air filter housing cover nut.
2. Look at the area near the carburetor base. There will be a hose about 3/4 of an inch in diameter. The PCV valve will be located near the carburetor end of this hose or at the other end entering the engine valve cover through a rubber grommet.
3. Start the engine and let it run at idle speed.
4. Using your hand, pinch the hose connected to the PCV valve. If the valve is operating, you will be able to hear the engine idle speed decline. If the engine idle speed does drop, the PCV system and valve are operating satisfactorily. Stop the engine and reinstall the air filter housing.
5. If no drop in engine speed is noted, remove the PCV valve from the engine. Either pull it from the rubber grommet in the engine valve cover by using pliers and wiggling it back and forth, or use pliers to remove it from the vent hose. In some instances, the hoses can be pulled off the valve at both ends. **NOTE:** If the grommet comes out with the PCV valve, it can be difficult to replace it. Soaking the grommet with engine oil will make it easier to reinstall.
6. Place the PCV valve in a cleaning solution for about 15 minutes. Use a solvent sold for this purpose or lacquer thinner to clean the PCV valve. **CAUTION:** Do not use gasoline! It is too hazardous.
7. After about 15 minutes, remove the PCV valve from the solvent and allow it to dry.
8. Reinstall the PCV valve and reconnect the hose, using pliers or a screwdriver to secure the hose clamp if necessary. Otherwise, slip the hose over its connections.
9. Start the engine and repeat step 4.
10. If no drop in engine speed is noted, replace the PCV valve.

Replacing The PCV Valve

IF THE PCV valve must be replaced, here is how to do it:

1. Locate the PCV valve as explained earlier.

FUEL SYSTEM

Metric Seven-Piece Combination Wrench Set

As a starter set, the Challenger No. 6100M seven-piece metric combination wrench set, made by Proto Tool Division of Ingersoll-Rand, offers a good selection. The wrench sizes in the open-end and box-end style are: 9mm, 10mm, 11mm, 12mm, 14mm, 17mm, and 19mm. These sizes were picked to give the beginner the tools that are most frequently used in automotive repair. They come packed in a vinyl roll-up kit.

Multipurpose Pliers

Proto Tool Division of Ingersoll-Rand offers 10 inch multipurpose pliers that can be used for a variety of garage uses. These are channel-lock pliers with an adjustable slip-joint.

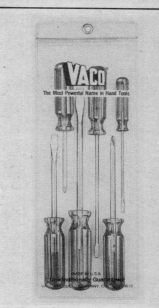

Combination Screwdriver Set

You have to be careful when selecting a screwdriver set. If the set does not contain the sizes that you will use most frequently, you may be better off buying the screwdrivers individually. Vaco Products Company has a six piece set, No. 89003, that includes both regular slotted and Phillips-type blade drivers that may fit your requirements. The set includes a 9/64 by four, a 3/16 by six, a 1/4 by six and a 5/16 by six inch blade, and the No. 1 by three inch and No. 2 by four inch Phillips driver blade.

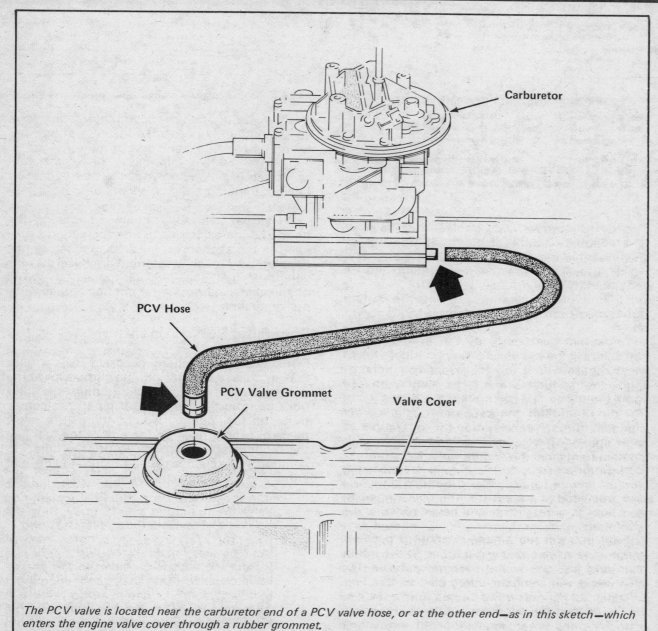

Carburetor

PCV Hose

PCV Valve Grommet

Valve Cover

The PCV valve is located near the carburetor end of a PCV valve hose, or at the other end—as in this sketch—which enters the engine valve cover through a rubber grommet.

2. Disconnect the PCV system hose from the PCV valve. This may be done by simply pulling the hose from the valve or by removing a hose clamp with pliers or a screwdriver and then pulling the hose free of the valve.
3. If the valve is in-line, use pliers to remove it or just pull off the hoses, depending on the hose connection. If the valve is located in a rubber grommet in the engine valve cover, remove it with pliers. Wiggle it back and forth while pulling it from the grommet. **NOTE:** If the grommet comes out with the PCV valve, it can be difficult to replace it. Soaking the grommet with engine oil will make it easier to reinstall.
4. Purchase the correct PCV valve for your car's engine.
5. Replace the new PCV valve by reversing steps 2 and 3.
6. Reinstall the air filter housing as outlined

in the chapter on Air Filter Service.

Replacing The Breather Filter Element

ON MOST model cars, there also is a breather filter element for the PCV system. It is located inside the air filter housing. If your car is equipped with one, this element also should be replaced periodically. Consult your owner's manual for replacement recommendations. To replace this breather filter element:

1. Remove the air filter housing cover using pliers or a wrench, if necessary, to remove the hold-down nut.
2. Remove the air filter.
3. Remove the PCV breather filter retaining clip with pliers.
4. Remove the PCV breather filter.
5. Purchase a new PCV breather filter and replace it by reversing steps 1 through 4.

Pow-R-Bak

The Marvel Oil Company makes a heavy concentrate that blends with all crankcase oils to improve viscosity. The oil treatment, called Pow-R-Bak, was developed to reduce oil burning and exhaust smoke, restore compression and power, and keep oil screens and crankcases clean. It contains a sludge dispersant formulated to keep oil pump screens and crankcases clean by holding sludge in suspension. This helps maintain proper oil pressure and provides a free flow of oil to the engine. Pow-R-Bak comes in one pint cans.

Six-Piece Combination Wrench Set

The combination wrench is one of the more versatile tools to have in your tool box. It also is handy to keep in your trunk, since you have your choice of using either the open end or the box end. S-K Tools, a division of Dresser Industries, Inc., has a set that includes six combination wrenches, No. 1706, in sizes from 7/16 to 3/4 inch in increments of 1/16 inch. The tools are made of C-series alloy and are packaged in a tool roll.

Professional Screwdriver Set

S-K Tools, a division of Dresser Industries, Inc., manufactures a six-piece screwdriver set, Model 70600, that meets the requirements of professional tradesmen. It contains a No. 2, 1/4 by 4 inch Phillips; a stubby, square-blade 1/4 by 1-1/4 inch; a square-blade 5/16 by 6 inch; a round-blade 1/8 by 3-1/2 inch; a round-blade 1/4 by 6 inch; and a round cabinet blade 3/16 by 6 inch.

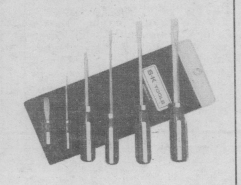

Fuel Filter Pliers

Removing two-inch fuel filters is much easier if you have fuel filter pliers. Hastings Manufacturing Co. makes Model 1796 fuel filter pliers that not only help you remove two-inch fuel filters, but also come in handy when working on radiator hoses, front wheel dust caps, master cylinder caps and other small cylindrical objects. It is designed with three sets of teeth for a good grip.

Checking Your Fuel Filter

An easy way to check if your fuel filter is clogged is to blow through it. A clogged filter will noticeably restrict the movement of air through it, while a clean one will not.

Gasoline Filters

Your automobile's carburetor is a delicate mechanism that is easily damaged by foreign particles in the fuel. For this reason, you should always be certain that your gas filter is clean. Check your owner's manual to see when it should be changed. Kem Manufacturing Company, Inc. makes replacement fuel filters for virtually any make of car—domestic or foreign. You can find them at your automotive parts store.

Fuel Filter Replacement

A clean fuel filter helps your fuel pump maintain a constant pressure in the fuel system. A dirty or clogged filter spells trouble, so you should replace it whenever your car owner's manual recommends. The Carol Cable Company sells a complete line of replacement fuel filters, and you are sure to find one among them for your vehicle.

FUEL FILTER REPLACEMENT

TO RUN properly, an engine must have an adequate supply of fuel at all times. And, this available fuel must be as clean as possible. As it passes through the fuel system, fuel is regulated by small orifices or jets. If dirt or any other foreign particles are present, the system could clog up, causing engine performance to suffer.

To prevent this possibility, car makers install fuel filters in the system. To keep the fuel system clean, these filters must be replaced according to the manufacturer's recommendations, or more often if engine performance declines.

A dirty fuel filter can cause an engine to act sluggish during acceleration or operation at high speeds. It also can be so clogged with contaminants that the engine will not operate.

Throughout the years, car makers have used several types of fuel filters. The most common one consisted of a porous, ceramic-like element enclosed in a glass housing. Fuel entered the glass housing from the top and was filtered as it passed through the element and into the carburetor. Servicing was performed by removing the glass housing when it looked dirty and by cleaning or replacing the filtering element.

Today, all car makers use some form of in-line fuel filter. The filter element is either enclosed in a housing and is replaceable, or the entire unit—housing and element—is replaced.

While some older General Motors cars had a fuel filter at the end of the fuel line in the fuel tank, most filters are now located on the engine somewhere between the fuel pump and the carburetor. General Motors incorporates an internal fuel filter, mounted in the fuel bowl behind the fuel inlet nut. Ford Motor Co. cars have fuel filters screwed directly into the carburetor.

Chrysler Corp. and American Motors cars have an in-line fuel filter located in the fuel line between the fuel pump and the carburetor.

Since there are differences in the replacement of fuel filters depending upon the type of car you have, manufacturers' models will be treated separately.

On all cars, however, begin by opening the hood and removing the air filter housing as outlined in the section on Air Filter Service in this chapter. **CAUTION:** A potential fire hazard exists whenever fuel lines are disconnected. Avoid open flames and working in confined areas without ventilation.

Ford Filter Replacement

FORD MOTOR Company generally uses a filter that is screwed directly into the carburetor at the end of the fuel line. Gasoline enters the filter housing from the fuel line (or pipe) that comes from the fuel pump. Usually, there is a short piece of rubber hose on the end of the fuel line that connects the fuel line to the fuel filter. In addition, hose clamps usually secure the hose at either end. To replace this filter:

1. Obtain the proper fuel filter replacement from your auto supply store before removing the old one.
2. Locate the fuel filter. It is a round, can-like unit that is about one inch in diameter.
3. Place a clean rag between the fuel filter, connecting hose and the intake manifold. This will help prevent a potential fire hazard by absorbing any gasoline loss during the removal of the fuel filter. Disconnect the fuel line hose from the end of the fuel filter by removing the hose clamp. Use pliers or a screwdriver, depending on the type of clamp. After the clamp is removed, pull the hose free of the fuel filter.
4. Remove the fuel filter from the carburetor. This is accomplished by unscrewing the filter counterclockwise. You may have to use a wrench on the end of the filter to turn it. Discard the entire fuel filter.
5. Install the new fuel filter. This is done by screwing the filter clockwise into the carburetor by hand. Use a wrench only to tighten the filter slightly.
6. Reinstall the fuel line hose located on the end of the fuel line by pushing it onto the end of the fuel filter. Tighten the clamp. Remove any gasoline that may have spilled onto the intake manifold with the rag and then discard the rag in a safe place.
7. Start the engine and check for fuel leaks. Repair any leaks by tightening the filter or hose clamp as necessary.
8. Reinstall the air filter housing.

Here Is What You Will Need

Materials

- Fuel Filter
- Fuel Line Hose
- Clean Rags

Tools

- Pliers or Screwdriver
- Open-End Wrenches
- Flare-Nut or Tubing Wrenches, 9/16 or 5/8 Inch

FUEL SYSTEM

Open-End Wrench Set Starts On The Small Side

Blackhawk Hand Tools markets a forged wrench set, Model EW-105, with open-end sizes from 1/4 through 7/8 inch. Five double-ended wrenches are included in the set, each offering the choice of two openings. The sizes are: 1/4, 5/16, 3/8, 7/16, 1/2, 9/16, 5/8, 3/4, 13/16 and 7/8 inch.

Spray Degreaser

It is tough to spot leaks and other problems on your engine when it is dirty. Every once in a while, you should use a spray degreaser on your engine such as that made by Valvoline Oil Co., No. 945. It provides a simple, easy method of dissolving grease or oil and dirt from automotive parts. You just spray it on. It comes in a 15 ounce aerosol can.

Fuel Line Filter Wrench

A clogged fuel line filter will bring your vehicle to a stop. And, foreign particles in the fuel line can make your engine act sluggish or even damage your car's carburetor. The easy way to remove the fuel line filter is with a special wrench that looks much like the kind used to remove oil filters—only smaller. J-Mark Quality Products, Inc. has a Model 351 heavy-duty fuel line filter wrench that makes removing and replacing fuel line filters a snap.

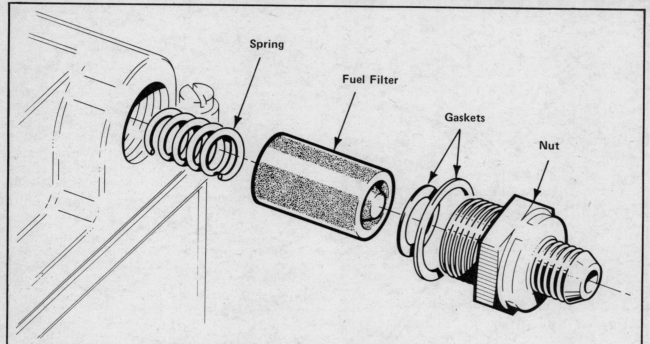

Most GM cars have the fuel filter housed in the carburetor where the fuel line from the fuel pump is connected. Only the filter element, generally made of bronze or paper, need be replaced.

Replacement Vapor Emission Filters

Most late-model passenger cars are equipped with evaporative emission control devices to prevent the escape of gasoline vapor. If the device on your auto has a replaceable air intake filter located in the charcoal canister, you can obtain a refill from Hastings Manufacturing Company. It is a good practice to replace the vapor emission filter about every 10,000 miles, along with the PCV valve and carburetor air filter.

General Motors Filter Replacement

MOST GENERAL Motors cars have the fuel filter housed right in the carburetor where the fuel line from the fuel pump is connected. Generally, the fuel filter element is made of bronze or paper. In this case, only the element itself is replaced. Be sure to obtain the correct replacement element from your auto supply store before removing the old element. To replace this fuel filter:

1. Locate the fuel line (pipe) that comes from the fuel pump to the carburetor.
2. Place a clean rag between the fuel inlet nut at the carburetor and the intake manifold. This will help absorb any gasoline loss during removal of the filter. Disconnect the fuel line at the carburetor. You will need two wrenches for this, about a one inch open-end wrench and a flare-nut or tubing wrench, usually 9/16 or 5/8 inch in size. Using the flare-nut wrench, loosen the nut on the end of the fuel line. If the larger nut on the carburetor also turns, prevent it from turning with the open-end wrench. This will be necessary to prevent damage to the fuel line when disconnecting it.
3. With the fuel line disconnected, loosen the larger nut on the carburetor with the larger wrench. This one holds the fuel filter. There is a light spring inside the filter element housing that could pop out if you are

not careful, so remove this nut slowly. Also, notice the direction the old fuel filter is facing as you remove it. It usually is marked in some way as to the direction of fuel flow.
4. Install the new fuel filter in the carburetor (do not forget the spring) and tighten the nut that holds it in the housing with the wrench.
5. Reconnect the fuel line to the carburetor and tighten the nut with the flare-nut wrench. Remove any gasoline that may have spilled on the intake manifold during the removal and installation of the filter.
6. Start the engine and check for fuel leaks. Repair them if necessary by tightening the nuts on the fuel line and carburetor.
7. Reinstall the air filter housing.

Chrysler, AMC Filter Replacement

CHRYSLER and AMC generally use an in-line fuel filter. This is a canister-type filter that is completely discarded. There will be rubber hoses on both ends of the filter, so you will have hose clamps, either spring-type or screw-type to loosen. To replace these fuel filters:

1. Purchase the proper fuel filter at your auto supply store.
2. Locate the filter. It will be in the fuel line

New Filter Keeps Fuel System Clean

To keep your engine running smoothly, you must keep your fuel free of contaminants. You should replace your fuel filter at intervals recommended in your auto owner's manual. It is a simple operation. Failure to do so may result in a big repair bill. The Wix Corporation offers a complete line of filters for most American-made cars.

FUEL FILTER REPLACEMENT

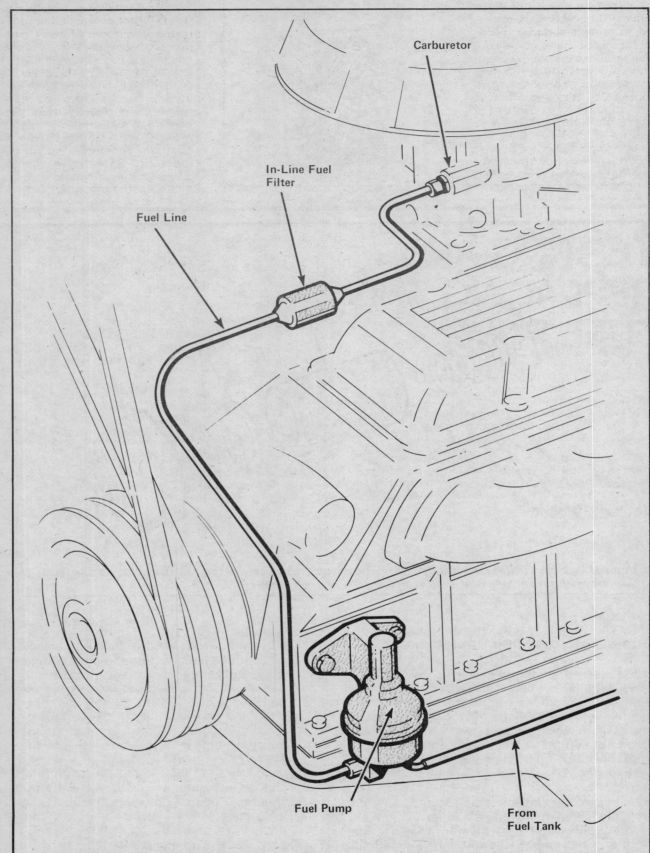

Carburetor

In-Line Fuel
Filter

Fuel Line

Fuel Pump

From
Fuel Tank

Chrysler and AMC generally use an in-line type of fuel filter. When installing a new filter, note the direction of fuel flow marked on the filter housing so that it is installed in the correct position.

Gum Chaser

If your car is performing poorly due to a dirty carburetor, a cleaner added to your gasoline may help. Gum Chaser, GC16, made by Gold Eagle Co., is designed to remove gum, varnish, lead, carbon and moisture from the carburetor. No carburetor dismantling is necessary. Gum Chaser, which comes in one pint cans, may be added to the gas tank or through the carburetor gas or air intake. It contains no oil and leaves no residue.

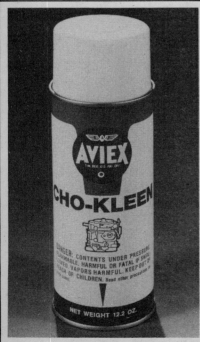

Clean Your Carburetor Before You Adjust It

It is impossible to adjust a carburetor that is dirty or that has dirty linkage. So, before adjusting, you should use a cleaner such as Cho-Kleen made by United States Aviex Company. You can use this product to clean your choke, anti-smog valves, automatic choke controls, needle valve jets and PCV valves. It comes in 14 ounce aerosol cans that provide several applications.

(pipe) that leads to the carburetor from the fuel pump.
3. Loosen the hose clamps on either end of the fuel filter, using a pliers or screwdriver, depending on the type of clamp.
4. Remove the fuel filter by pulling back the rubber hose on either end of the filter housing. Note the direction of fuel flow as marked on the filter.
5. Inspect the rubber hoses for signs of fuel leakage, cracking or other deterioration of the hoses. Replace as necessary, obtaining

the correct hose from your auto supply store.
6. Install the new fuel filter. Note the direction of fuel flow marked on the filter housing. Install it in the correct position. Place the hoses over the filter housing inlet and outlet. Tighten the hose clamps just enough to prevent fuel leakage.
7. Start the engine and check for fuel leaks. Repair them if necessary by tightening the hose clamps.
8. Reinstall the air filter housing.

"Does Everything" Oil

Kendall CML "Does Everything Oil," made by a division of Witco Chemical Corporation, is formulated to protect surfaces, penetrate corroded parts, drive out moisture and lubricate. You can use this product to quiet annoying hinge squeaks and loosen hard-to-open locks as well. In addition, the oil is designed to free rusted parts, stop moisture-induced problems in electrical units and engine ignition systems, and even protect tools from rust and corrosion. The product comes in two and 12 ounce aerosol dispensers.

Clean Your Carburetor Linkage

Your carburetor has a linkage system that cannot function properly unless it is clean. At every tune-up, and sometimes in between, you should use a cleaner such as Carb'n Choke Cleaner made by Bardahl Manufacturing Corp. This aerosol cleaner helps you spray away carbon deposits from your carburetor and varnish from your linkage. You also can use it to clean the carburetor throat. It is formulated to dissolve varnish, gum and sludge to help your engine run more efficiently.

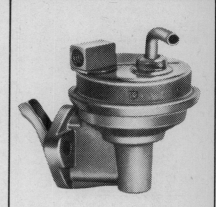

New Or Reconditioned Fuel Pumps

When you must replace your fuel pump, you have a choice of buying a new or reconditioned model. Kem Manufacturing Co., Inc. offers both. Their Ren-O-Vated pumps are reconditioned to the same specs as new Kem fuel pumps. In fact, all internal parts are new—gaskets, springs, valves, diaphragm assemblies and rocker arm pins. Body castings, covers and rocker arms are refinished and inspected. Worn parts are replaced by new components. Finally, the pumps are wet and dry tested under pressure. New Kem pumps look like the original from the outside, but the company stresses it has improved the interior. For example, the pumps feature a new design fuel valve seat for improved flow, and valve discs are made of molded rubber that is impervious to gasoline.

TESTING AND REPLACING THE FUEL PUMP

THE FUEL pump is the device that causes the fuel in the fuel tank to be moved from the tank through the fuel lines or pipes to the engine's carburetor. Basically, there are two types of fuel pumps—mechanical and electrical. These will be treated separately.

Mechanical Fuel Pump

THE MECHANICAL fuel pump is the one found on most cars. Usually, it is located on the engine block near the front of the engine. If you have difficulty locating the fuel pump, simply follow the fuel line (pipe) leading from your carburetor. The fuel line will be connected to the fuel pump.

Mechanical fuel pumps are also referred to as the diaphragm type because there is a diaphragm inside the pump that is actuated by the engine's camshaft. As the camshaft rotates during engine operation, a shaft or lever in the pump is moved up and down or back and forth, depending on the fuel pump's position on the engine. This causes the diaphragm to move back and forth, drawing fuel from the fuel tank, through the fuel lines and to the carburetor.

Years ago, fuel pumps were built to be disassembled and rebuilt. This is not the case today. Therefore, if the fuel pump does not operate, replacement is necessary.

Fuel pumps are designed to deliver a certain amount of fuel to the carburetor with a certain amount of pressure. Any pump that fails to do this must be replaced.

Other factors, however, can sometimes affect fuel pump operation. Leaks—air or fuel—will cause the pump to function improperly. A visual inspection of the entire fuel system is in order before any volume or pressure tests are made of the fuel pump. Also, if you suspect you are not getting the proper amount of fuel to the carburetor, make certain your problem is not caused by a clogged fuel filter. Refer to the section on fuel filters and make appropriate repairs or replacements before proceeding with fuel pump tests.

CAUTION: A potential fire hazard exists whenever fuel lines are disconnected. Avoid open flames and working in confined areas without ventilation.

Here Is What You Will Need

Materials

- Fuel Line
- Fuel Line Hose
- Quart Container With Graduated Scale
- Fuel Pump and Gasket
- Clean Rags
- Gasket Sealer
- Fuse
- Gas Cleaning Chemicals

Tools

- Safety Goggles
- Flare-Nut Wrenches
- Open-End Wrenches
- Flashlight
- Hand Tire Pump
- Fuel Pump Pressure Gauge
- Putty Knife or Scraper
- Pair of Mechanical Fingers
- Voltmeter

Visual Inspection

VISUAL INSPECTION involves getting under your car to check the fuel system, so you should be prepared with appropriate clothing and safety goggles.

1. Starting at the fuel tank, locate the fuel line (pipe) at the front of the tank. This is the line that runs to the fuel pump.

Fuel Pump | Actuating Arm

Fuel Pump Inlet From Fuel Tank

Fuel Pump Outlet To Carburetor

The fuel pump is a device that moves the fuel from the fuel tank to the engine's carburetor via the fuel lines.

Metamorphic Spray Lubricant

Grease is generally not easy to apply. But that is not the case with Lubrimatic Products' Lubrimist spray lubricant. Lubrimist, which comes in a 15 ounce spray can, is for lubricating and for preventing rust on any metallic surface. You can apply it to cables, hinges, pulleys, linkages, nuts, bolts, and other parts where lubrication and rust prevention are desired.

Four Tools In One

If you are looking for an extremely versatile tool, the lever-wrench pliers from Proto Tool Division of Ingersoll-Rand are a good candidate. The No. 3093 is four tools in one. You can use it as a powerful hand vise clamp, pipe wrench and pliers. The straight, lever-action jaws lock in a holding position with applied pressure up to one ton. A quick release feature removes the pressure instantly.

Plain Soap Is Not Good Enough

Ordinary soap is not strong enough to remove the kinds of grease and grime you get on your hands during automotive work. To clean your hands, you need a waterless hand cleaner such as that offered by United States Aviex Co. Aviex Lotion Hand Cleaner has a chemical and a buffering formula to remove stubborn dirt. Because it is water-soluble, it can be used with or without water.

Adjustable Wrenches Can Be Repaired

Because adjustable wrenches have moving parts, the mechanisms may need replacement after long, hard use. A line of adjustable wrenches made by Indestro, a division of Duro Metal Products Co., features replaceable parts that are available from the manufacturer. Parts available include the jaw, screw, worm and spring. These wrenches include models from four to 15 inches long and with maximum jaw openings from 1/2 to 1-11/16 inches.

THROTTLE LINKAGE

Here Is What You Will Need

Materials
- Carburetor Cleaner Spray
- Lubricant
- Idle Return Spring

Tools
- Wrench
- Pliers

THE THROTTLE linkage plays an important role in the overall operation of the automobile engine because it links the driver and the engine. The linkage is attached to the carburetor. A throttle cable connects this linkage to the accelerator pedal. A driver depressing the accelerator pedal moves the throttle linkage, which opens the throttle valve in the carburetor. This action allows more air and fuel to enter the carburetor intake, increasing the speed or revolutions per minute (rpm) of the engine. Releasing the accelerator pedal reverses the process and slows the engine.

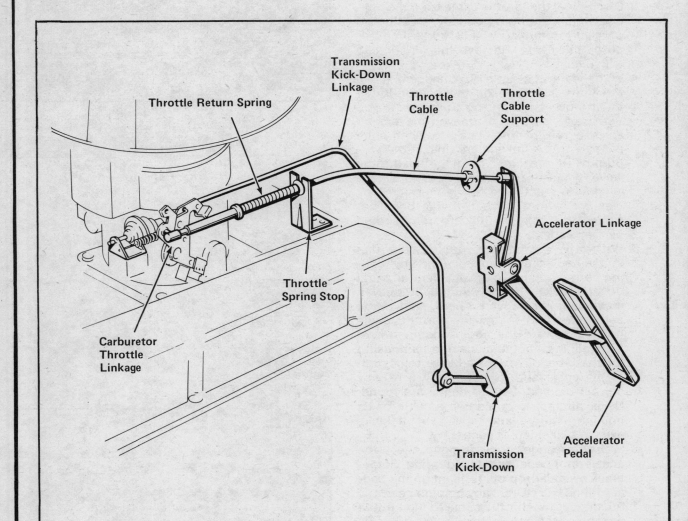

The throttle linkage connects the accelerator pedal to the carburetor. When the accelerator pedal is depressed, the linkage moves and allows more air and fuel to enter the carburetor, increasing the engine's speed.

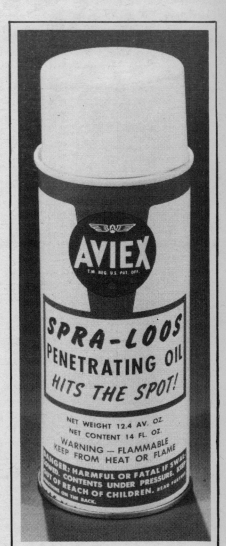

Penetrating Oil Reduces Frustration

You can save a lot of time and trouble by using a penetrating oil, such as Spra-Loos sold by United States Aviex Co. It is a lubricant and penetrant designed to treat corrosion, oxidation and lack of lubrication.

Combination Pliers

Every tool box needs all-purpose, combination pliers. S-K Tools, a division of Dresser Industries, Inc., has Nos. 7206, 7208 and 7210 to fill this niche. No. 7206 is six inches long. 7208 is eight inches long and 7210 is 10 inches long. All have nickel-chrome plating with vinyl cushion handles.

FUEL SYSTEM

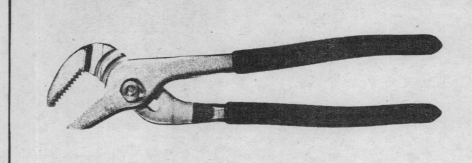

Check Accelerator Pump Action

Here is a way to check your accelerator pump action: With the engine stopped, remove the air cleaner and look into the carburetor. Slowly open the throttle. You should see a fine stream of fuel (or two if you have a two- or four-barrel carburetor). The flow should not be weak or a series of drips but rather strong. Poor acceleration response may be caused by inadequate pump action.

C-Joint Utility Pliers

Cal-Van Tools Division of Chemi-Trol Chemical Co. offers three sizes of C-joint utility pliers made of drop-forged, alloy steel. The No. 460 pliers have a length of 6-1/2 inches and four adjustments from 3/16 to one inch. The No. 461 is 10 inches and has five adjustments from 1/4 to 1-1/2 inches. The No. 462 is 12 inches and has seven adjustments from 3/8 to 2-1/2 inches.

Short-Handled Combination Wrenches Work In Tight Quarters

Usually, it is best to have a wrench with a long handle because this gives you plenty of leverage for loosening tight fasteners. But if you only have long-handled tools, you will find that often there is not enough clearance to use them. Indestro, a division of Duro Metal Products Co., sells a six piece combination wrench set that includes wrenches with openings from 7/16 through 3/4 inch, and that have an open and a box end. These tools are about half the size of standard tools sold by Indestro. They work well in situations where you have to sacrifice some leverage for some working room. The set, No. 770-6PK, comes with a compartment pouch.

Combination Slip-Joint Pliers Come In Many Sizes

Challenger combination slip-joint pliers by Proto Tool Division of Ingersoll-Rand are available in a variety of lengths for different situations. Sizes are 5-3/8, 6-3/8, 8 and 10 inches. The chrome-plated pliers are also available with Plastisol-dipped handles.

THROTTLE LINKAGE

For efficient and safe engine operation, the throttle linkage must operate smoothly without sticking or binding. Signs of linkage problems include: a) Engine will not return to idle speed when accelerator is released; b) engine idle speed is unsteady; c) engine will not reach full rpm.

If any of these problems are experienced:

1. Remove the air filter housing as described in the section in this chapter on Air Filter Service. You may need a wrench for this task.
2. Locate the throttle cable connection to the throttle linkage at the carburetor. Usually, it is connected on the driver's side of the carburetor.
3. Disconnect the throttle cable from the linkage at the carburetor. Usually, a cotter pin or clip resembling a tiny horseshoe secures the cable. Remove the pin or clip with pliers.
4. With the throttle cable disconnected, move the throttle linkage on the carburetor. It must move back and forth freely. If you detect any binding or uneven movement, spray a solvent formulated to clean such linkage on the linkage and inside the carburetor at the shaft holding the throttle valve in place. Often, any binding or uneven movement here can be corrected by cleaning with a solvent. If this does not correct the problem, the carburetor should be replaced.
5. With the carburetor cable still disconnected from the linkage (and any binding corrected), move the accelerator pedal up and down. If any binding or uneven movement is discovered here, start at the carburetor and follow the throttle cable housing toward the engine compartment fire wall. Inspect the cable and its housing for sharp bends or kinks. Minor relocation of the cable and its housing will usually correct binding if sharp bends are found. Never attempt to straighten a cable or its housing if there are kinks in it. If kinks exist, replacement is necessary.
6. In the passenger compartment, check the accelerator pedal and its mounting. Sometimes a small drop of lubricant on the pedal's hinge will correct any binding here.
7. Reconnect the throttle cable to the throttle linkage on the carburetor.
8. Have someone depress the accelerator all the way to the floor while you check at the carburetor to see if the throttle valve goes to the full open position when the accelerator is depressed. Use a wrench to adjust the throttle cable (turn the adjusting screw clockwise or counterclockwise as necessary) to obtain a full open throttle valve position.
9. Release the accelerator pedal, allowing it to return to the idle position. If it does not return to the idle position smoothly, replace the idle return spring on the carburetor. The idle return spring is attached to the carburetor end of the throttle linkage.
10. Install the air filter housing.

With the air filter housing removed, the throttle linkage, which opens and closes the throttle valve, can be seen.

Tune-Up Kits For American Carburetors

Carburetor rebuilding is not a simple task the occasional do-it-yourselfer should attempt. But if you have the skill required to service carburetors, Allparts, Inc. has a line of Auto-Mech kits designed for a wide variety of American-made cars. Each carburetor tune-up kit contains all the necessary parts for this chore, including a resilient-tipped needle and seat assemblies.

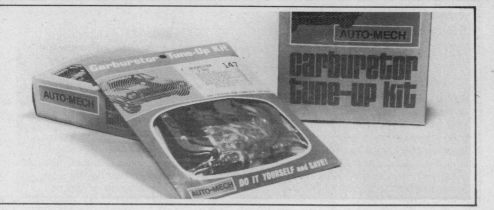

CARBURETOR REPLACEMENT

AS EXPLAINED in an earlier section, the carburetor of an automobile engine is a complex device. It is responsible for maintaining the proper air/fuel mixture for the engine under a wide range of operating conditions.

The carburetor also is probably the most misunderstood component on your car. It often is blamed for problems or conditions that are really the fault of some other system in the engine. Such things as rough running, hesitation during acceleration, poor gas mileage or lack of power certainly could be symptoms of carburetor trouble but more often than not, they could be corrected by investigating the ignition system. Or, a simple carburetor adjustment, as outlined in this chapter, could restore the engine to good running condition.

In other words, far too many carburetors are replaced unnecessarily. A good mechanic will exhaust every other possibility to correct a poorly running engine before replacing the carburetor.

If it is determined that your carburetor is defective, however, replacement is not so complicated that it cannot be performed by most do-it-yourselfers. Remember, however, every car maker has its own carburetor design, so carburetor removal and replacement procedures will vary to some degree. As a general rule, though, the guidelines presented here will apply to most installations.

Before you begin to replace the carburetor, secure the correct replacement unit from your auto supply store. A remanufactured carburetor is your best bet. For the most part, these units are of high quality and considerably less expensive than a new unit. Be prepared to pay a deposit for your old carburetor as well as the price of the remanufactured unit. This deposit assures the auto supply store that you will return the old unit, which they must send back to a supplier for remanufacturing. Your deposit will be returned to you when you bring in the old unit.

Here is how to replace the carburetor:

1. Open the hood and remove the air filter housing as described in the chapter on Air Filter Service. You may need a wrench for this task.
2. Disconnect the fuel line at the carburetor. This is the line between the fuel pump and the carburetor. Use two wrenches for this task to prevent damage to fuel line fittings. Loosen the fitting on the end of the fuel line with a flare-nut wrench. **NOTE:** A flare-nut wrench looks like a box-end wrench with a section of the box cut out so that the wrench may be placed around a fluid line and then moved into position to loosen or tighten a fitting. If the larger fitting on the carburetor also turns, use an open-end wrench to keep it from turning. This is necessary so you will not damage the fuel line when disconnecting it.
3. Disconnect all other hose connections. Mark these hoses so that it will be easier to reconnect them to the new carburetor. **NOTE:** There may be wires to such things as a transmission kick-down switch and/or an air conditioning idle speed up switch or an anti-dieseling solenoid. Be sure to mark each of these wires as they are removed so that you can replace each wire correctly.
4. Disconnect the throttle cable from the throttle linkage at the carburetor. Usually, this is held in place by a cotter pin or a clip that resembles a tiny horseshoe. Use pliers to remove the clip or pin.
5. Disconnect the choke cable from the choke linkage at the carburetor. Here, too, there will either be a clip or pin. Use a pliers to remove it. Also, mark the location of the choke rod on the carburetor. Sometimes, it can fit into more than one hole.
6. Using a wrench of proper size, remove the carburetor's mounting bolts, turning them counterclockwise. These bolts are at the base of the carburetor and secure the component to the engine intake manifold. Depending upon the type of carburetor, there will be two or four mounting bolts.
7. With the mounting bolts removed, lift the carburetor upward and remove it from the engine compartment. **NOTE:** Usually, there is a gasket between the carburetor and the intake manifold. Sometimes this gasket

Here Is What You Will Need

Materials

- Carburetor
- Clean Rags

Tools

- Box-End, Open-End and Flare-Nut Wrenches
- Pliers
- Small Hammer
- Putty Knife or Gasket Scraper

Not All Four-Barrel Carburetors Are Alike

Carburetors are rated by the cubic feet per minute (cfm) volume of air intake. Holley Carburetor Division of Colt Industries offers a wide range of four-barrel carburetors with cfm ratings to match the needs of various engines. Just recently, the firm updated their small, four-barrel, 390 cfm RV model for universal coverage on V-6 or in-line six-cylinder or small V-8 engines. They also make a larger RV four-barrel, the 600 cfm Model 4160, that has been updated for 1975-1976 General Motors, Ford and Chrysler vehicles. The company recommends the Model 4160 for heavy vehicles beyond the capacity of the smaller 450 cfm Model 4360. There also is a revised racing version four-barrel available that has a 1050 cfm rating. This is Model 4500, which is designed for single four-barrel, small block applications in drag racing.

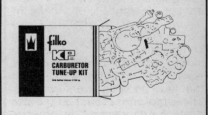

Tune-Up Kit For Carburetors

Your car's carburetor consists of a complex array of parts. If it is causing you trouble that a simple adjustment will not cure, the carburetor may need rebuilding. Taking apart and reassembling a carburetor requires confidence and plenty of skill. But if you have the know-how, Filko Automotive Products, a Division of F & B Manufacturing Co., can provide you with a tune-up kit containing all the necessary parts and instructions to overhaul original carburetors on American-made and foreign-made cars.

Carburetors Designed For Do-It-Yourselfers

Holley Carburetor Division of Colt Industries offers replacement carburetors aimed at economy-conscious, do-it-yourself motorists. The Economaster line has models for most popular American Motors, Chrysler, Ford and General Motors vehicles produced during the past 13 model years. The carburetors come with step-by-step instructions.

Fuel Line Fitting For Quadrajet Carburetors

A self-tapping fitting from Thexton Manufacturing Co. allows you to repair stripped fuel line threads without removing the carburetor. It also eliminates the cost of replacing the carburetor casting. The plated, hardened fuel line fitting, which will accept standard filter elements, is available in three sizes for GM quadrajet carburetors: No. 506 (3/8 inch); No. 507 (5/16 inch); No. 508 (long filter).

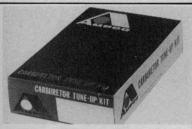

Kit For Rebuilding Carburetors

Depending on the model, carburetor rebuilding can be a complicated task that requires a skilled specialist. But the advanced home mechanic who knows what he is doing may want to tune up his carburetor when necessary, especially if it is a less complex unit. Wells Manufacturing Corporation markets a series of Ampco carburetor tune-up kits complete with resilient needle and seat assemblies, pump plunger, gasket and instruction sheet. Each kit is sealed to keep gaskets and other parts fresh for precision fit.

Tune-Up Kit Offers Step-By-Step Guide

When you select a carburetor rebuilding kit, you should find one that includes complete step-by-step instructions. Such kits are offered by the Hygrade Products Division of Standard Motor Products, Inc. Their Jiffy Kits, which are available for about 90 percent of all passenger cars and trucks, will tune Carter, Ford, Holley, Rochester and Stromberg carburetors and many on imported models. Kits include gasket, pump pistons, economizer valves, needles in seats and gauges. Instructions feature an "exploded" view of parts, with each one identified. Gaskets and smaller parts are sealed in separate plastic bags to protect against damage or loss.

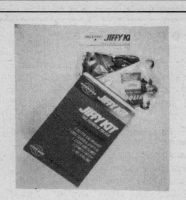

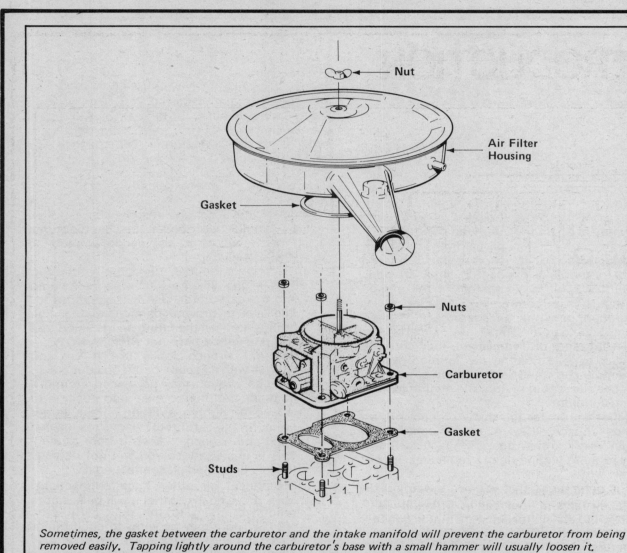

Sometimes, the gasket between the carburetor and the intake manifold will prevent the carburetor from being removed easily. Tapping lightly around the carburetor's base with a small hammer will usually loosen it.

CARBURETOR REPLACEMENT

will prevent the carburetor from being removed easily. If this is the case, use a small hammer to lightly tap around the base of the carburetor to loosen it.

8. As you remove the carburetor, see if there is one or more gaskets or metal plates between the carburetor and intake manifold. Make a note of this for reinstallation.

9. Place a clean rag into the intake manifold inlet and scrape the carburetor mounting surface clean of any old gasket material. Use a putty knife or gasket scraper. Do not allow any of this material to fall into the intake manifold.

10. When clean, remove the rag from the intake manifold and position a new carburetor gasket. It will be supplied with the carburetor. At this time, also reinstall any other gaskets or metal plates as in step 8.

11. Place the replacement carburetor on the mounting surface and insert and thread the carburetor mounting bolts by hand. Do not tighten them.

12. With the carburetor still loose, reconnect the fuel line to the carburetor. Tighten the line, using two wrenches as outlined in step 2.

13. Use a wrench of proper size and tighten the carburetor mounting bolts. Be careful not to overtighten them. You could crack the carburetor mounting flange. Just snug the bolts to secure the carburetor.

14. Reconnect the throttle cable to the throttle linkage at the carburetor.

15. Reconnect the choke cable to the choke linkage at the carburetor.

16. Reconnect all hoses and wires to the carburetor.

17. Start the engine and check for fuel leaks and repair them if necessary.

18. Adjust the carburetor idle speed and air/fuel mixture as outlined in the section on Adjusting The Carburetor.

19. Install the air filter housing.

Use A Fender Cover

With all the reaching and stretching you have to do to reach ignition system components under the hood of a car, you could scratch your fender. To prevent this, you might get a fender cover like the Model 21-4000 from Clean Rite Products Co. The washable cover measures 36 by 42 inches. The firm also offers Model 21-4001, a vinyl fender cover measuring 36 by 24 inches. It includes a tool holder.

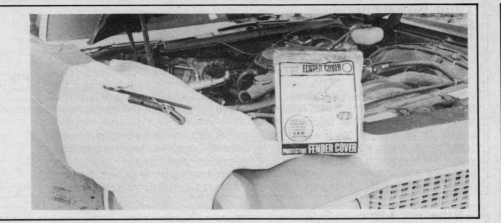

INTRODUCTION

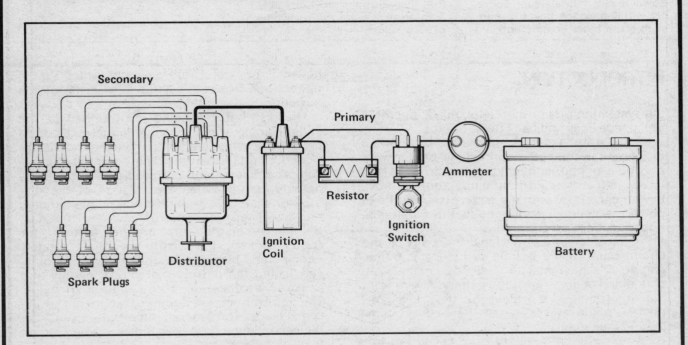

Secondary
Primary
Ammeter
Resistor
Ignition Switch
Battery
Ignition Coil
Distributor
Spark Plugs

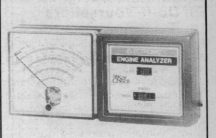

Karcheck Electronic Engine Analyzer

Late-model cars are so complex that it takes a variety of different instruments to analyze engine problems efficiently. When you are thinking about the purchase of analyzing instruments, you have a choice. You can buy a number of separate instruments as you need them, or you can buy one unit that does the job of many different instruments. Karcheck Products' Model 2089 Electronic Engine Analyzer has the capability of performing almost all the tests that you will ever need to make on your car's ignition and charging systems. You can measure point resistance, voltage drops in all circuits and components as well as isolate defective battery cables, straps or starter solenoid. It features a 0 to 60-degree point dwell scale and separate low and high rpm scales for testing at idle and high speed. It also allows you to measure voltage available to the spark plugs during cranking and with the engine running, and lets you test the points, condenser, coil cap, rotor, and spark plug wires. An ohms-circuit resistance scale helps you locate broken wires, crossed or shorted circuits and allows you to check continuity of all electrical components. It has a 0 to 500 scale for measuring the starter draw and amps and a 0 to 100 scale for checking charging amps. In addition, the unit lets you isolate problems in the alternator, regulator and battery.

T HE IGNITION system, one of several electrical systems in your car, is primarily designed to ignite the air/fuel mixture that is drawn into the engine through the carburetor.

The ignition system of the car is separated into two circuits. These circuits are the primary or low voltage circuit and the secondary or high voltage circuit. However, they function together and are interdependent.

The primary circuit consists of the battery, ignition switch, the primary part of the ignition coil (the coil has a dual function), the primary side of the distributor (the distributor also has a dual function)—which includes the ignition breaker points and condenser—and, finally, the wires connecting each of these components to complete the electrical circuitry.

Components of the secondary circuit include the secondary part of the ignition coil, the secondary side of the distributor (distributor cap rotor and secondary wires) and, finally, the spark plugs.

The primary circuit depends on the battery for voltage to function when the car is being started. After the engine is running, the ignition system depends on the charging system for its voltage source.

When the ignition switch is turned on, the primary circuit (the low voltage or battery circuit) of the ignition system is activated. Voltage is applied to the primary side of the coil and to the ignition breaker points in the distributor. The

ignition coil has three wires connected to it. Two wires are small and connect to two small terminals on opposite sides of the coil. The third wire, heavier than the other two (about the size of an ordinary pencil), has a friction clip on one end and is fastened by simply pushing it into a receptacle, called the coil tower, in the center of one end of the coil.

Ignition coil location varies from one type of engine to another. On V-6 and V-8 engines, however, the coil will be mounted on top of the engine very close to the distributor. Four- and six-cylinder in-line engines will have the coil mounted on the side of the engine near the distributor, opposite the carburetor and intake manifold.

This is a good place in our description of the ignition system to explain the concept of any electrical circuit in an automobile. There is really nothing complicated about a circuit. It is simply a path for the flow of electric current (amperage) from a source (in this case, the battery or charg-

Here Is What You Will Need
Materials
● None
Tools
● Screwdriver

Tune-Up In A Can

Casite Engine Tune-Up, made by Hastings Manufacturing Co., works by adding it to the oil, the gas tank and through the carburetor's air intake. You can put it in your oil to flush away gum and sludge and clean your PCV valve. You would add it to the fuel in your gas tank or put it into the carburetor through the air intake to free sticky valves and rings, and to remove carbon, varnish and gum deposits. It also is designed to help clean plugs and carburetor jets.

The Runt

Every driver should always carry a few important tools for emergencies. You never know when a simple tool can make the difference between getting underway quickly and wasting hours waiting for a tow truck. Rubbermaid Specialty Products, Inc. makes a tool box called "The Runt" that is small enough to fit in the glove box of some cars. It is just the size to hold a small, well-selected quantity of tools.

Tune-Up Pays

American motorists could save 3.6 billion gallons of gasoline a year if they kept their cars in good operating condition. This is the high price that is paid for driving untuned cars. Every week, 70 million gallons of gas are wasted due to untuned engines.

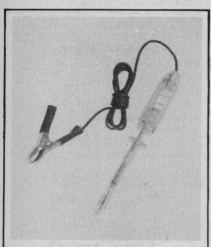

Hands-Free Circuit Tester

Circuit testers are great for solving electrical problems, but most require you to insert the testing needle into a wire and hold it there. Filko Automotive Products, a division of F & B Manufacturing Co., makes a tester, Model TE-560, that attaches to the wire and remains there by itself. You just retract the spring-loaded needle and slip the wire into the hooked retainer at the end of the tester. After you release the trigger on the instrument's shaft, the needle pierces the wire and is held to it by spring pressure. The unit also features a ground lead and clamp as well as current indicator in the handle.

Cal-Van's Combination Circuit Tester

If you are planning to buy a circuit tester, you might as well purchase one that you can use on both the auto circuits and the ignition system. Cal-Van Tools Division of Chemi-Trol Chemical Co. has a No. 145 high-low voltage combination tester that allows you to check low voltage (six to 12 volts)

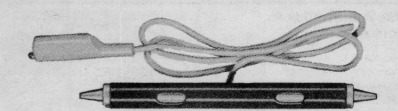

in auto circuits and also lets you check high voltage in the ignition system. You attach the ground lead to the body of the car and probe the wiring with the retractable needle. To switch from high to low voltage testing, you use the opposite end of the tester.

Elextron Ignition System Is Pretested

There is nothing more frustrating than installing an electronic ignition system and having it break down a few hours later. Sometimes this happens because transistors and other components are susceptible to failure in the first few hours of operation. Standard Plus Elextron electronic ignition modules, made by Standard Motor Products, Inc., receive an operation test called a "burn-in" before they are shipped to dealers. This helps prevent the possibility of early failure.

INTRODUCTION

ing system) to one or more electrically operated units or devices and back to the source.

If the current's path is interrupted by a switch or a break in the path continuity (a broken wire or a loose or poor connection), the circuit is said to be open and no current (amperage) will flow. In your car, one side of the battery (the source of power) is connected directly to the car frame, floor pan, body, or the engine.

For most electrical devices, the path of the circuit back to the battery is the car's frame, engine, or other metal part—since all of them are connected to one side of the battery. A wire from the other side of the electrical device is connected to the other side of the battery, completing the circuit.

For example, a test light is composed of two wires hooked to a filament or bulb. If you touch one wire to one terminal of the battery and the other wire to the other terminal, current will flow through the wires to light the bulb. The test light also will light when one wire is touched to the battery terminal that is not connected to the engine or other metal parts of the car and the other wire is touched to any metal part that is connected to the battery. The term for all of these metal parts hooked to one side of the battery is "ground." When we say that one side of a device is connected, or hooked, to the engine block, we mean that it is grounded.

The Primary Ignition Circuit

NOW THAT you have an idea of what a circuit is, let us get back to the primary ignition circuit. The two small wires connected to the ignition coil are the primary leads or wires. One of these wires is connected to the ignition switch, which, in turn, is connected by a wire to one terminal of the battery—the side not connected to the metal parts of the engine block. When the ignition switch is on, this completes a path from the battery, through the ignition switch and on to the ignition coil terminal on the ignition switch side of the coil.

Inside the ignition coil, there is a continuous series of wire loops or coils fastened between the primary coil terminals. The small wire connected to the other ignition coil terminal enters the distributor housing and is connected to one side of the ignition breaker points. The other side of the points is connected to the distributor

housing. The points are a simple switch that is opened and closed as a shaft in the distributor is turned.

The distributor housing is grounded to the engine block, which is connected to one side of the battery. When the ignition breaker points are closed by rotation of the distributor shaft, a circuit is completed and current flows through the primary circuit. When the rotation of the distributor shaft causes the ignition points to open, the flow of current is interrupted.

When the distributor is properly adjusted for engine timing, the distributor shaft rotates, opening and closing the ignition breaker points and timing the pulses of electrical energy that cause an arc at the electrodes of the spark plugs. The points, however, do not cause the arc at the spark plugs. They merely time the pulses from the secondary circuit. It is the secondary circuit that causes the arc.

The one remaining component in the primary circuit is the condenser, which is mounted in the distributor. It has two connections. One is connected to the ignition coil side of the ignition breaker points; the other is connected to the distributor's frame. The condenser has only one function—to act as an electrical "shock absorber" when the points open and close. It is designed to absorb a surge of high voltage and gradually feed it back into the ignition circuit at a rate that will not cause damage.

The ignition system will malfunction if the condenser is bad. If the points open and the condenser is unable to absorb some of the high voltage, the points will flash and burn.

Let us take one more look at the primary circuit before we describe the secondary or high voltage circuit.

As we explained, a circuit is established between the ungrounded battery terminal and the windings of the primary coil when the ignition switch is turned on. When the ignition breaker points close, the circuit is completed through the coil, the engine block and back to the battery. When the points are opened, the circuit is interrupted and current flow ceases. The condenser absorbs the voltage surge when the circuit is broken and gradually feeds it back into the circuit to prevent arcing or flash.

The Secondary Ignition Circuit

THE SECONDARY circuit begins at the distributor. This device has a plastic cap with a center crown or tower that holds the heavy sec-

Use A Slotted Screw Starter

Starting screws is much easier if you use a slotted screw starter like those offered by K-D Manufacturing Co. You merely twist the bit to firmly grip the screw. The tool releases and resets automatically. On the opposite end, there is a strong magnet to help you retrieve

dropped parts. It also has a convenient pocket clip and measures 5-5/8 inches. Two models are available: K-D 2282 is for straight-slotted screws; K-D 2283 is for Phillips head screws.

Clamp-On Power Timing Light

The biggest hassle in timing a car is hooking the timing light lead to the No. 1 cylinder. Usually, you have to disconnect the spark plug wire from the plug and insert an adapter between the two components. Hastings Manufacturing Co. makes a power timing light with an electronic pickup lead that lets you hook it up without disconnecting the spark plug wires. The Model 1922 works on American-made and imported cars and trucks, including those with solid-state, transistorized and high-energy ignition systems. All you do is connect one lead to the car's battery and attach the clamp on the other lead to the spark plug on the No. 1 cylinder. The clamp senses current by induction. The instrument has a high-impact resistant case.

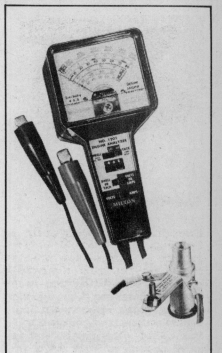

Engine Analyzer Includes Battery Post Adapter

Milton Industries, Inc. sells a deluxe engine analyzer, No. 1202, that includes a battery post adapter permitting one simple hookup for most basic tests. It is designed for all conventional and electronic six- or 12-volt ignition systems and features direct reading for four, six and eight cylinders, including rotary engines. The unit is factory calibrated and requires no batteries.

ondary ignition coil wire. The center tower is surrounded by as many other towers as your engine has cylinders. Each of these towers will have a wire leading to a spark plug. These wires and the wire connecting the ignition coil tower to the center tower of the distributor are the secondary wires. They carry the high voltage that causes the desired arc at the spark plugs.

Some distributors have a plastic cap held onto the distributor housing by two spring-steel bails or clips. Others may use two screws that require only 1/2 turn to release the cap from the housing.

If you know for sure that your car's ignition system uses breaker points in its distributor (many systems do not), examine the inside and outside of your car's distributor. It does not take a lot of time and the subject will mean more to you.

Release the distributor cap's hold-down fasteners. Spring-steel bails or clips can be pried from their grooves with a screwdriver. For screw-type caps, turn each of the two screws 1/2 turn with a screwdriver to release the cap. Carefully lift the cap and gently turn it over without disconnecting any wires in the top of the cap. When you look inside, you will see that each of the towers on top, including the center tower, has a large metal terminal that extends down inside the cap. Next, look inside the distributor housing (the area that is exposed when you remove the distributor cap). The first thing you should see is a piece of plastic mounted horizontally on the upper end of the distributor shaft. This plastic piece has a metal strip that extends from the center toward the round distributor housing. This is the rotor, which turns as the distributor shaft turns. Below the rotor, you should be able to see the ignition breaker points and condenser. These parts are mounted on a flat surface called the breaker plate.

Where the distributor shaft comes through the breaker plate, it is enlarged and shaped into a square, hexagon or octagon. This enlarged portion of the shaft is the cam. If you look at it closely, you should see that it has as many corners as there are cylinders in the engine. Look for a plastic or fiber part mounted on a section of the breaker points. This plastic or fiber part will be touching the cam. As the shaft turns, cam rotation causes the points to open and close. When this plastic or fiber part (usually called the rubbing block) touches one of the corners (high points) of the cam, the points open. When the rubbing block is in contact with one of the flats

(low points) on the cam, the points are closed.

Before you replace the cap, here is a simple check to prove that the primary circuit is operating. Turn the ignition switch to the On position. If the points are closed, you can push them open with a nonmetallic tool (a lead pencil or plastic pen will do) and a small blue spark should jump across the open circuit. This is one test that will be covered in detail later.

Place the distributor cap back into position and secure it with the hold-down fasteners. The cap can only seat one way on the housing because of a "guide key." Once the cap is on, look at the metal unit fastened to the side of the distributor housing. It has a small hose connected to it. This device, called the vacuum advance unit, automatically adjusts spark timing as the load on the engine varies.

Now, let us quickly review the process in which the electrical pulses that cause the spark plugs to fire are timed, generated and delivered. If you know how the spark occurs, it will be easy to learn how to check the ignition system for proper, efficient operation.

As we explained, the secondary ignition circuit begins at the coil, which serves both the primary and secondary circuit. In addition to the primary winding in the coil, there also is a secondary winding. There is no electrical wire connection between the two.

The secondary winding connects to the tower in the center of the ignition coil casing and extends to a connection on the end of the coil case. Since the coil is mounted on the engine, there is a complete return circuit to the battery. The secondary winding of the coil is so designed that every time the points open and interrupt the current flow in the primary winding, the secondary winding produces a sudden surge of high voltage (as much as 30,000 volts) and delivers it to the distributor tower in the center of the distributor cap. The metal strip in the rotor contacts the center tower. The turning rotor conducts this pulse of high voltage to the appropriate spark plug in the engine.

When the ignition system is operating properly, the voltage it produces in the secondary circuit will be high enough so that a hot spark will jump the small gap between the spark plug electrodes, igniting the compressed air/fuel mixture in the cylinder.

If your ignition system is not operating to your satisfaction, the service tips and procedure in this chapter should help you locate and make the needed repairs.

Seal Ignition System

If moisture is giving your ignition system problems, you might want to correct it with one of the sealants on the market, such as Ignition Sealer No. 156 from Gold Eagle Co. This product forms a plastic coating and protects the ignition against moisture, rust and corrosion. You also can use it to coat bumpers to protect them from salt and moisture. The sealer comes in six ounce aerosol cans.

IGNITION SYSTEM

Contact Dwell-Tach Makes Tune-Ups Easy

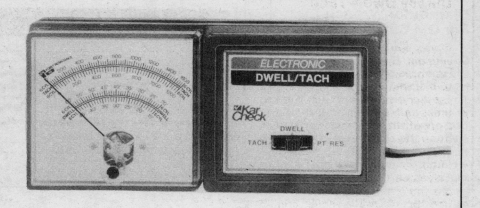

It is possible to set ignition points by gapping them with a gauge when the points are resting on a high point of the distributor cam lobe. But this is a time-consuming and often inaccurate way to perform a tune-up. An ignition tune-up requires a good quality dwell-tachometer, such as Kar-check Products' Model 2020. This instrument works on four-, six- and eight-cylinder engines that operate on a 12-volt system. It can be used on solid-state, transistorized and high-energy ignition systems. The unit features a points tester and a tachometer-dwell meter that measures from 15 to 45 degrees and 20 to 60 degrees. It also has a jeweled D'Arsonval meter movement and a high-impact plastic case.

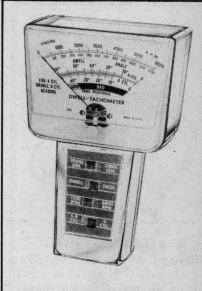

Dwell-Tach-Points Resistance Tester

The Sonco Model 2520 dwell-tach, made by Sonco Manufacturing Division of Mergo-Tronics Instrument Corp., is a hand-held unit that can help you quickly set your ignition points and engine rpm as well as check the point resistance. It has two engine rpm scales—0 to 1200 and 0 to 6000 rpm, and is calibrated for 0 to 60 dwell angle and point resistance. You also can use the instrument to check four-, six- and eight-cylinder engines that have six- or 12-volt systems. The dwell-tach features a chrome-plated, die cast housing. It comes with instructions and guarantee.

---

tion. **CAUTION:** This is important! Failure to do so can result in damage to the ignition switch grounding circuit.

8. Loosen the point adjusting screw or shift point bracket with a screwdriver. While cranking the engine, observe the dwell meter. Turn the point adjusting screw or shift point bracket to obtain specified degrees of dwell.
9. Retighten point lock or retaining screws with a screwdriver.
10. Turn the ignition switch to the Off position.
11. Reinstall the radio frequency interference shield or suppressor if one was attached.
12. Reinstall the distributor rotor.
13. Reinstall the distributor cap by closing the bails or spring clips.
14. Remove the jumper wire.
15. Reconnect the high voltage coil wire to the distributor.
16. Remove the remote starter switch, reversing step 2.
17. Start and idle the engine. Check the dwell setting.
18. Stop the engine and disconnect the dwell meter, reversing step 1. **NOTE:** Whenever points dwell is readjusted, the timing setting should also be checked and reset if necessary. Refer to the Ignition Timing section in this chapter.

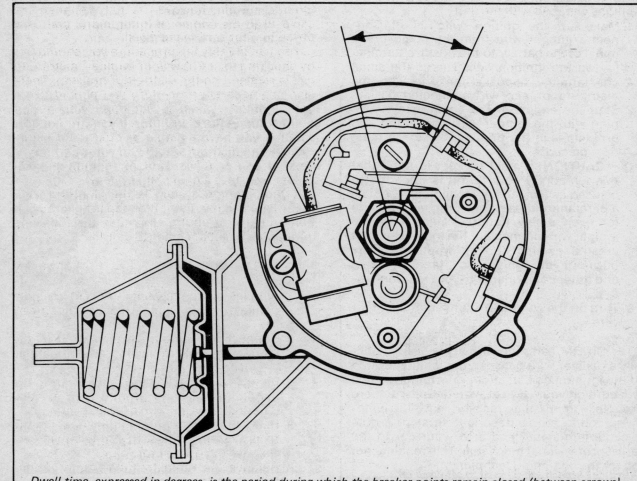

Dwell time, expressed in degrees, is the period during which the breaker points remain closed (between arrows).

Dwell-Tach Primary Analyzer

A dwell-tach that works on all vehicles with original equipment electronic and standard ignition systems is made by Peerless Instrument Co. You can use the Model 455 to test four-, six- and eight-cylinder engines with six-, 12- or 24-volt negative or positive ground electrical systems. Scales include a 0 to 1200 low tach scale, 0 to 6000 rpm high tach scale, 0 to 90 degree dwell angle, and an "ok/bad" static and dynamic point resistance scale. It also features a 5-1/2 inch D'Arsonval meter movement.

Starting Fluid Could Save You A Tow

If you live in a very cold climate or plan to travel in cold weather, it might be a good idea to keep a can of engine starting fluid spray, such as Prestone made by Union Carbide Corp., in your car. It comes in 15 ounce aerosol cans and is designed to help start engines in the coldest weather. It also includes an upper cylinder lubricant to protect your engine while you start it.

Tune-Up Chart

If your auto supply store sells Standard Motor Products, Inc.'s Hygrade tune-up parts, you may be able to obtain a free tune-up chart giving ignition and carburetor tune-up specifications for most late-model cars.

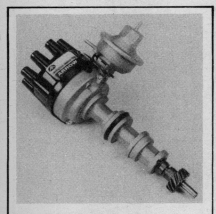

Remanufactured Distributors

When your distributor needs replacement, it may be more economical to consider a remanufactured unit rather than to purchase a new one. Arrow Automotive Industries markets a line of remanufactured distributors for most passenger cars and light trucks. The units have new distributor caps, springs, points, pins, condensers, screws, bushings and primary wires.

Distributor Wrench For GM Cars

Chevrolets, Buicks, Pontiacs and Oldsmobiles generally have a 9/16 inch distributor hold-down nut. To loosen this nut when you want to time your engine, you should use an offset 9/16 inch wrench such as the one made by Black-hawk Hand Tools. Their XT-1012 wrench makes ignition work much easier.

Tester For High-Energy Ignition Systems

Robinair Manufacturing makes an analyzer, Model 10456HEI, that provides a complete check for high-energy ignition distributors. The instrument includes all necessary adapters for the 1975 General Motors V-8, V-6, L-6 and L-4 high-energy ignition systems. Operating instructions are provided with the device.

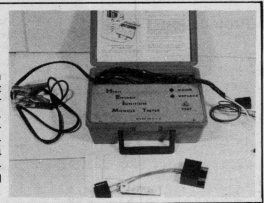

IGNITION PRIMARY RESISTOR

Here Is What You Will Need

Materials
- Jumper Wire
- Primary Resistor

Tools
- Screwdriver
- Wrench

IN MANY cars, the ignition system is designed to operate on less than full battery voltage when the engine is running. To accomplish this, a primary resistor is installed between the ignition switch and the ignition coil. This resistor lowers battery voltage (called charging voltage when the engine is running) by three volts. However, since full battery voltage is required for starting the engine, this primary resistor is bypassed when the engine is being started.

If your car's engine starts, but stops as soon as the ignition switch moves from the start to the run position, the primary resistor most likely is causing the problem.

The following procedure will verify that the resistor is inoperative:

1. Make sure the ignition switch is off. Connect a jumper wire from the positive terminal of the battery to the positive terminal (+) on the ignition coil. This is the small coil terminal opposite the one with the distributor primary wire connected to it.
2. Start the engine. If the engine stays running with the jumper wire connected, the problem is in the primary resistor. It must be replaced.
   CAUTION: It must be kept in mind that this temporary connection is intended to be used as a means of testing only — not as a permanent repair. If you run your engine for even a few hundred miles with the jumper wire connected, the increased heat created by this hookup would probably burn out your ignition coil, breaker points and other components of your ignition system.
3. Turn off the engine. Disconnect the jumper wire.

NOTE: On GM cars, the primary resistor is actually a resistor wire between the ignition switch and the ignition coil. If, after performing the test procedure on your GM car, you determine there is trouble in the primary resistor, leave the jumper wire connected as described in step 1, note the caution in step 2 and drive your car to the nearest professional mechanic. This repair is not a job for the beginning technician.

On most cars, the primary resistor is located on the fire wall of the engine compartment. It is simply a small coil of wire wrapped in a ceramic insulator. To replace it:

1. With a screwdriver, loosen the screws holding the wires on either end of the resistor assembly and disconnect the wires. Label them to make reinstallation easier.
2. With a wrench, remove the primary resistor mounting cap screw.
3. Remove the primary resistor from the fire wall.
4. Reverse steps 1 through 3 to install a new primary resistor.
   NOTE: Be sure to obtain the correct resistor for your car.
5. Start the engine. If it starts and continues to run, you have made a repair.

On most cars, the primary resistor is located on the fire wall of the engine compartment.

Protect Your Fenders

When performing ignition work, you often must lean over your car's fender. To prevent scratching it and to give you a spot to place your tools, you should use a fender protector such as Model 1043 from Hastings Manufacturing Co. It has soft padding that protects the car's finish from dropped tools, sharp-edged belt buckles or other metal objects. The surface is coated with neoprene, so you can clean it with solvent. The protector measures 27 by 40 inches.

Ignition Tester

If you plan to trouble-shoot your ignition system, you need a tester such as the No. 1295 from Hastings Manufacturing Company. This instrument, which lets you check the entire system, is easy to hook up and use. It is valuable for checking ignition voltage and current and for pinpointing problems.

Remote Starter Switch

The Model 175 remote starter switch, sold by Sonco Manufacturing Division of Mergo-Tronics Instrument Corp., enables you to start and stop the engine from outside the car. The product's long wire leads are gas and oil resistant and feature color-coded clips.

IGNITION SWITCH

A FEW years ago, an automobile's ignition switch had only one job—turning the primary circuit on and off. Now, it also actuates the starter motor, connects the alternator and accessories, locks the steering wheel and buzzes if you leave the key in it.

As the functions of the ignition switch became more complex, so too did its construction. On most ignition switches found in today's cars, you will find that there are five positions, each with a separate function: Accessories, Lock, Off, Run (or On) and Start. The first position, Accessories, allows you to operate various electrically operated units on the car without supplying voltage to the car's ignition circuit, which would not only drain the battery needlessly but could also "burn up" the ignition system. On most cars, power options such as windows and seats can only be operated when the switch is in the On position for reasons of safety.

When the switch is turned to the Lock position, all power that is supplied through the ignition switch is cut off. Power that does not go through the ignition switch, such as that for the lights and the cigarette lighter, is constantly supplied by the battery. In the Lock position, the ignition key can be removed. On older cars (pre-1966), the key could be removed in all but the Start position. On later models, there is a theft prevention device that locks the steering wheel and the gear shift lever against movement. On almost all cars with the locking steering wheel system, there is a position just to the right of Lock that allows the steering wheel and gear selector lever to be operated without draining the battery. This position is used when steering or suspension service is being performed or when adjusting the selector linkage. This is the Off position.

When the key is turned to the Run or On position, power is supplied to the circuits that would be used during normal operation of the automobile. These include the radio, blower motor, power accessories such as windows and seats, the windshield wipers, directional signals, back-up lights, cruise control and so on.

Another important function of the ignition switch is that it directs power to the primary ignition circuit through the primary ignition resistor. The resistor, as its name implies, limits the amount of voltage reaching the ignition coil.

Older cars use a resistor that cuts down the voltage to a specified amount regardless of engine operation. The modern component is called the ballast resistor. Due to its special construction, the ballast resistor can reduce the voltage available to the coil at lower engine speeds and, when needed, increase the voltage at higher engine speeds. If the resistor were not used, the ignition coil would be supplied with enough power to function efficiently at higher rpm, but the same amount of voltage would cause the coil to overheat and the ignition points to burn at lower speeds. The most common application of the primary resistor employs a specified length of resistance wire that lowers 12-volt battery voltage to about 9 to 10.5 volts during normal engine operation.

In the Start position, battery voltage is supplied to the starting motor through the starter solenoid. The solenoid has several functions, one of which is to act as a relay switch. When voltage is applied to the solenoid by the ignition switch, a circuit is completed, allowing power to be sent to the starting motor. The solenoid is mounted near the starter and eliminates the need for running the heavy battery cable all the way to the ignition switch. The starter solenoid is explained more fully in the chapter on Battery and Starting System.

An engine needs all the voltage it can get in order to start efficiently, especially on cold winter mornings when cranking speed is already hindered by thickened oil and higher electrical resistance due to lower temperatures. Because of this, the ignition switch incorporates a special by-pass circuit that allows full voltage to be supplied to the ignition coil during cranking.

If your automobile engine dies while running, then restarts easily only to die again at an odd moment, the ignition switch may be the problem. You should, however, have a trained mechanic check this condition thoroughly. If your key fits loosely in the switch and you get erratic operation of the ignition or accessories when you wiggle the key, then you know the switch needs replacement.

Cars with steering wheel locks require a special tool to remove the ignition switch. Home mechanics should not attempt to replace these switches due to the difficulty and potential damage involved without proper equipment.

On most cars, the ignition switch has five positions: Accessories, Lock, Off, On and Start.

Lightweight Lubricant Dries Out Your Ignition System

LPS Research Laboratories, Inc. makes a greaseless lubricant, LPS 1, that you can use as a penetrating oil, as a lubricant and, also, to dry out your ignition system. The product helps dry out coils, alternators, generators, magnetos, switches and relays quickly. You also can use it to lubricate locks, hinges, latches and seat slides. LPS 1 will not stain, and it is harmless to rubber, plastic, paint and fabric. Used as a penetrant, it helps loosen frozen parts such as nuts, bolts, automatic chokes, heat riser valves, mufflers and tailpipe clamps. Applied to chrome, it will prevent rust, corrosion and pitting. LPS 1 contains no chlorinated solvents or silicones.

Engine Starting Fluid

For a quick start in low temperatures, it is sometimes necessary to use a starting fluid such as Permatex Engine Starting Fluid No. 107 made by Woodhill/Permatex. The manufacturer formulated the fluid, which is sprayed into the carburetor, to insure quick starts at temperatures down to -55°F. The starting fluid is available in eight and 11 ounce aerosol cans.

Adapter For Ford Coils

When you bring your new dwell-tachometer home to try out on your car, you might be in for a surprise if the car is a Ford. This is because it is almost impossible to use an alligator clip on a Ford coil without using some sort of adapter. Filko Automotive Products Division of F & B Manufacturing Co. makes such an adapter. It is the Model TE-603.

Pagoda-Top Ignition Coil

An ignition coil sometimes fails due to moisture or accidental loosening of the high-tension cable in the coil socket. You also can experience problems if current jumps from the high-tension cable to the terminal. Standard Motor Products, Inc. manufactures Blue Streak ignition coils that feature a triple-length center terminal designed to reduce such problems. The coil also has Mylar insulation on the first three layers of high-voltage windings to prevent shorting and high-voltage breakdown. The windings also are balanced to provide high voltage for high speeds and continuous output power for sustained driving.

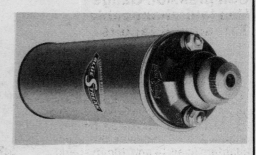

Replacement Ignition Coil

You cannot expect your ignition system to deliver a hot spark for burning fuel cleanly if the ignition coil is malfunctioning. Replacing a coil is simple and the component itself is inexpensive. Carol Cable Co. manufactures ignition coils for most automobiles. The vehicles that each coil will fit are listed on the front of the package to make selection easier.

One Coil Fits Most U.S. Cars

Ampco's heavy-duty, oil-filled ignition coil, Model C1819, will fit most American-made cars. The single model, made by Wells Manufacturing Corp., covers American Motors vehicles from 1957 to 1974, Chrysler Corp. cars from 1956 to 1976, Ford Motor Co. cars from 1956 to 1974, and General Motors cars from 1955 to 1974.

IGNITION COIL

Here Is What You Will Need

Materials
- Ignition Coil

Tools
- Open-End Wrenches

IN MOST cars, the ignition coil is a black, cylindrical unit about the size of a 12 ounce can of orange juice. Normally, it is located near the distributor. If you have a problem finding it, begin by tracing the heavy secondary ignition wire from the center of the distributor cap. The ignition coil will be at the other end of this wire.

A visual inspection is your first step in checking the ignition coil. Make certain that the coil is mounted tightly to assure a good ground and all its wire connections are clean and secure. Loose or dirty wire connections cause high resistance to flow in the wires. High resistance at these points could cause poor ignition system performance. Look for cracks at the top of the coil, a dented housing or oil leaking from inside the coil. If you find any of these conditions, the ignition coil must be replaced.

The ignition coil is actually a small transformer that boosts the 6- or 12-volt primary part of the ignition system up to 30,000-plus volts in the secondary system. High voltage is required to jump the spark plug gap to ignite the air/fuel mixture inside the engine.

Even though the ignition coil may appear, from the outside, to be in good condition, it could be defective electrically. Some signs of a defective ignition coil, or in some cases at least a weak one, include a loss of power at higher engine speeds, a hesitation of the engine during acceleration or, in extreme cases, a no-start condition.

If you experience any of these symptoms, it would be best to have your ignition coil checked by a service repairman who has the proper test equipment. If this is not convenient, you could purchase a new ignition coil and replace yours in an attempt to correct the problem. However, if the replacement coil does not solve the problem, do not expect to be able to return it to your auto supply store once you put it in your car. Most auto stores will not accept used electrical components for refunds once they have been installed. **NOTE:** Be sure to obtain the correct replacement ignition coil for your car. Many coils look similar but they may not be able to provide sufficient secondary voltage to operate your ignition system.

If you determine that your coil must be replaced, here is how to do it:

1. Disconnect the two primary wires connected to the terminals near the top of the coil. Some wires have press-on fittings that simply need to be pulled free. Others have nuts on the binding posts that can be removed with a small open-end wrench. The terminals are marked in various ways. Most often, the marks will be POS or (+), meaning positive, and NEG or (-), meaning negative. Tag the wires as you remove them for correct reconnection later.
2. Disconnect the secondary wire from the center tower of the ignition coil. This is the large wire that slips into the tower. The other end of this wire is connected to the distributor cap center tower connection.
3. With a wrench, loosen the ignition coil mounting bracket bolt. Generally, this bolt screws into the engine block.
4. Remove the old coil.
5. To install the new ignition coil, reverse steps 1 through 3.

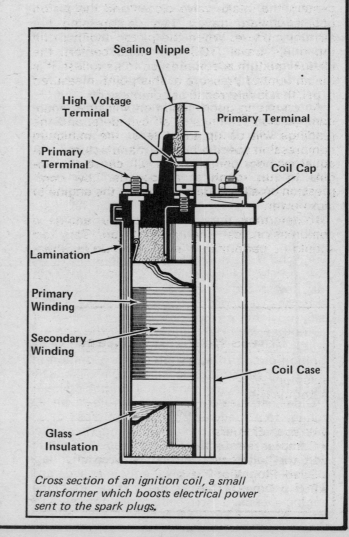

Cross section of an ignition coil, a small transformer which boosts electrical power sent to the spark plugs.

Compression Gauge Has Interchangeable Threaded Adapters

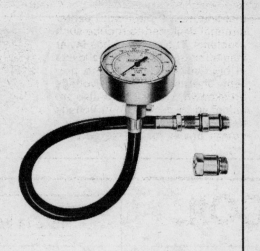

Fox Valley Instrument Company's Model C-19A2 compression gauge is a versatile device that can test the compression on any engine. Interchangeable threaded adapters fit all 14 and 18mm spark plug ports—conventional or tapered seat, long or short reach. A side vent valve permits repeating tests without disconnecting. The gauge is 2-1/2 inches in diameter and has a scale from 0 to 300 psi and 0 to 20 kilogram centimeters squared. Overall length is 20 inches.

Engine Compression Tester Kit With Attachments

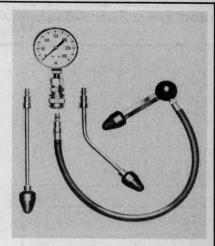

Before giving your car an ignition tune-up, you always should check the compression of each cylinder. It is impossible to tune up a car properly unless the cylinders are in good shape. Cal-Van Tools Division of Chemi-Trol Chemical Co. has a compression tester, Model 56, that fits all cars. It features a quick-release, air-tight covering for changing adapters and a gauge with an unbreakable dial that covers 0 to 300 pounds. The master stem has an 18 inch long, heavy-duty flexible hose with ball grip. Other adapters include a 7-1/2 inch straight stem and eight-inch, 45-degree offset stem.

COMPRESSION TESTING

A COMPRESSION test reveals the condition of an engine. No engine is able to operate as it is designed to unless each and every cylinder is operating at peak efficiency—that is, at specified compression. Specifications for compression are found in pounds per square inch (psi). For example, a particular engine may have a cranking compression pressure of 200 psi.

It may be helpful to understand how these compression specifications are determined. When the piston reaches the bottom limit of its travel on the intake stroke (BDC—before dead center), the intake valve closes and the piston begins upward travel, thus compressing the air/fuel mixture. When the piston reaches the top of its travel (TDC—top dead center), the air/fuel mixture is compressed to its fullest. It is the amount of pressure at this point, measured in psi, that is referred to as compression.

An engine in good condition will have equal compression readings in all cylinders, and the readings will be up to at least the minimum compression specified by the manufacturer. Unequal cylinder compression will cause the engine to run rough at all speeds. Low compression on all cylinders will cause the engine to lack power.

To determine the condition of your engine, a compression test should be taken. This test should be performed at every tune-up or when-ever your engine is running poorly.

Making The Compression Test

TO PERFORM a compression test, you first must gain access to each cylinder. Since the only possible access to the cylinders from outside the engine is through the spark plug holes, you must remove the spark plug from each cylinder. Depending on the type of engine you have, there will be either four, six, or eight spark plugs—one for each cylinder. These are located in the engine cylinder head or engine block.

On four- and six-cylinder in-line engines, the spark plugs will be readily visible since they will be lined up on one side of the engine. You will find a high voltage wire connected to each spark plug. This wire is inserted into the ignition's distributor cap at the other end. On V-8 and V-6 type engines, there will be either four or three spark plugs on both sides of the engine.

Here is how to perform the compression test:

1. Remove the air filter housing. You may need a wrench for this task. See the instructions in the Fuel System chapter in the section on Air Filter Service.
2. Disconnect the spark plug wires from each spark plug. This is done by grasping the boot on the end of each wire with your hand or a spark plug wire pliers and, with a twisting motion, pull the wire away from the spark plug. It is best to label each spark plug wire as you remove it to be sure you reconnect it to the proper spark plug.
3. Using a spark plug socket and ratchet wrench, loosen each spark plug about one-half turn. Do not remove the spark plug yet.
4. Disconnect the high voltage wire from the center tower of the distributor cap, which leads to the ignition coil, and connect it to a good ground on the engine with a jumper wire.
5. With the spark plugs slightly loose and the secondary (high voltage) ignition coil wire grounded, crank the engine for about five seconds by turning the ignition switch to the Start position. The reason for this cranking is to reduce the possibility of dirt or foreign material entering the compression chambers when the spark plugs are being removed. Engine compression will blow any debris away from the spark plugs while the engine is cranking.
6. Remove the spark plugs with the spark plug socket and ratchet wrench.

Here Is What You Will Need

Materials
- Jumper Wire
- Engine Oil

Tools
- Wrench or Pliers
- Compression Tester
- Spark Plug Socket and Ratchet Wrench
- Spark Plug Wire Pliers
- Pump-Type Oil Can

Remote Starter Switch

When performing compression tests and other automotive tests that require cranking the engine, a remote starter switch is sometimes better than having an assistant. After a simple hookup, you can crank or start the engine whenever necessary from outside the car. Karcheck Products' Model 2058 Remote Starter Switch consists of two heavy-duty clips and a spring-loaded thumb switch for easy operation.

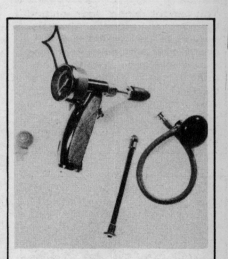

Pistol Grip Compression Tester

If you use a compression tester that has a rubber tip rather than a screw-in end, it is sometimes tough to keep the tip in the spark plug hole while you are cranking the engine. The Model 352 Pistol-Grip Compression Tester, made by Sonco Division of Mergo-Tronics Instrument Corp., makes this job easier because its grip allows you to hold the tip down firmly. It allows you to read the gauge to see the pressure buildup while the engine turns. The gauge reads to 300 pounds and holds the pressure until released. It comes with adapters—flexible and rigid—spare nose cone and valve. The instrument can help you indicate valve, piston and cylinder problems in your car. Complete instructions are included.

IGNITION SYSTEM

Sun Compression Tester

Diagnosing engine piston efficiency and condition is easy if you have a compression tester. You merely connect the tester to the cylinder spark plug hole and turn the engine over. By checking the specifications for your car's engine, you can tell whether or not the engine has ring or valve damage. If the pressure is low, you squirt some oil into the cylinder and make another check. If the pressure rises the second time —with the oil in the cylinder— you can be fairly certain the rings are at fault. No increase in pressure on the second test indicates valve trouble. Sun Electric Corporation makes a compression tester that screws directly into the spark plug hole (some are held in place by hand pressure). This instrument has a 2-1/2 inch dial face, chrome-plated steel housing and screw-on acrylic lens and bezel It provides readings up to 300 pounds per square inch on the standard scale and up to 21 kilograms per square centimeter on the metric scale. It also has 14mm and 18mm screw-in spark plug adapters, an 18 inch high-pressure hose, and a release valve for repeat testing without disconnecting the instrument.

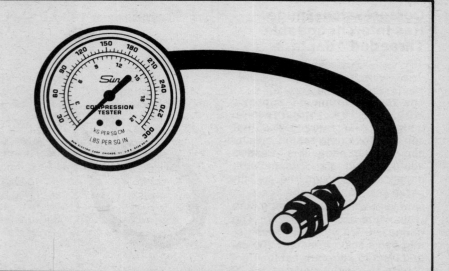

Remote Starter Switch Can Save You Time

When you are trying to test compression, locate timing marks or adjust the distributor point dwell, you need an assistant unless you have a remote starter switch. Otherwise, the job takes you a lot longer than it should. A remote starter switch from Fox Valley Instrument Co., Model PB-1, is one of many switches available. It has a lead length of five feet and weighs 13-1/2 ounces.

Standard Compression Gauge

Sonco Manufacturing Division of Mergo-Tronics Instruments Corp. makes a compression tester, Model 350, that is the standard one used by most home mechanics. It features a 2-1/2 inch universal dial with psi and kilogram/centimeters squared. The color-coded scales read from 0 to 300 pounds capacity. To help you reach spark plug cylinders, the stem of this instrument is offset 15 degrees. The fingertip valve retains the reading until it is released. You can use this compression gauge to pinpoint trouble in valves, pistons, rings and cylinder walls. The rubber cone and valve are replaceable. The unit is designed to fit all spark plug holes. Instructions are included.

COMPRESSION TESTING

7. Place the spark plugs on a bench or table in such a way so you will know from which cylinder they were removed. As pointed out in the section on Evaluating And Installing Spark Plugs in this chapter, the condition of a spark plug can aid you in diagnosing engine problems.
8. Open the carburetor throttle valve to the full open position and block it open, or have someone sit in the car and hold the accelerator pedal to the floor. This allows the greatest amount of air to enter the engine during the compression test.
9. Starting with the cylinder closest to the car's radiator, insert the compression tester into the spark plug hole and have your assistant crank the engine four or five revolutions by turning the ignition switch to the Start position. **NOTE:** It is best to have a compression tester that screws into the spark plug hole. Some gauges have a cone-shaped end on the tester, and it is virtually impossible to hold these in the cylinder of high compression engines.
10. As the engine is cranking, note the highest reading on the compression gauge. Most compression gauges have a valve in them that will retain the reading on the gauge until you release the pressure. Record the reading on a piece of paper or write it on the fender well in the engine compartment with chalk.
11. Repeat this procedure with each cylinder. On V-type engines, perform the test on one side of the engine at a time.
12. Compare your test results with the specifications given in the repair manual for your car. If all cylinder readings are within the

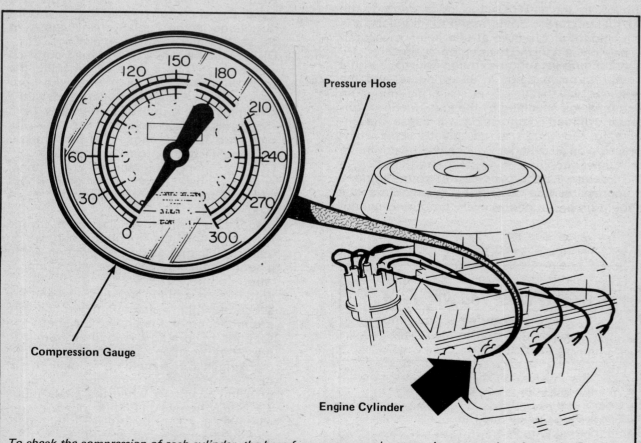

Compression Gauge

Pressure Hose

Engine Cylinder

To check the compression of each cylinder, the hose from a compression gauge is connected to the spark plug hole. The engine is cranked and the highest reading on the gauge is noted.

IGNITION SYSTEM

Advance Test Kit

If you are just starting out as a backyard mechanic, you may want to purchase a package of all the basic instruments you need for tuning a car. Karcheck Products sells a variety of tune-up kits, among them the Model 2084 Advance Test Kit that contains their Model 2009 DC power timing light, Model 2014 dwell-tach-points tester, Model 2512 vacuum and pressure gauge, and Model 2052 compression tester. These are all the basic instruments you need to tune your car and they are packed in a vinyl tote case.

Compression Tester

If your spark plug holes are not exceptionally difficult to reach, a compression tester such as the Cobra-GT Model 8701, made by Peerless Instrument Co., may be an economical choice. It can check the condition of rings, valves, head gasket and cylinders. It features a 0 to 300 psi scale and a metric 0 to 21 kilograms per square centimeter calibration. The unit has a 2-3/4 inch dial and Bourdon tube movement. It comes with illustrated instructions.

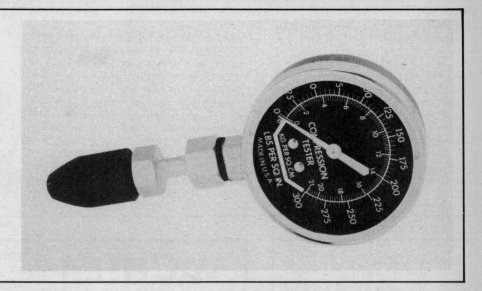

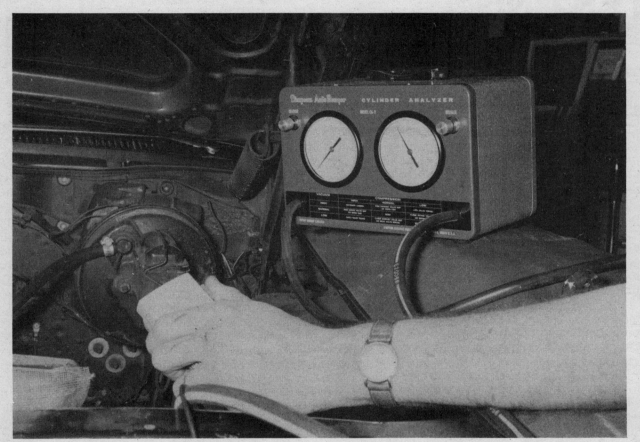

The compression test is performed separately for each cylinder. If cylinder readings are within specification and 5 or 10 psi of each other, compression is adequate.

specifications and each cylinder reading is within 5 or 10 psi of each other, your engine is in good condition as far as compression is concerned. If you find one (or more) cylinder has low compression, it may be because of bad valve or worn piston rings, allowing pressure to escape.

If the reading is low on a cylinder:

a. Using a pump-type oil can, squirt about a teaspoon of engine oil into the spark plug hole.

b. Repeat the compression test. If the compression test reading increases to almost normal, this indicates worn piston rings. (The oil you inserted into the cylinder has sealed the rings, causing compression pressure to increase.)

If the reading is still low, this most likely indicates a bad valve.

If two adjacent cylinders have low compression readings, chances are the engine head gasket is defective.

Compression readings that are higher than specifications indicate an engine with an excessive buildup of carbon in the cylinders.

Low, high or uneven compression readings indicate serious engine problems. Under these circumstances, no engine tune-up will make the engine perform satisfactorily until the compression problems are corrected. A professional mechanic should be consulted as to the correct repair procedure.

13. Turn off the engine.
14. Replace the spark plugs. Be sure you replace each spark plug in the cylinder from which it was removed.
15. Reconnect the secondary wire to the center tower of the ignition coil.
16. Reconnect the spark plug wires to each spark plug. Make sure you reconnect each wire to the proper plug.
17. Install the air filter housing.

Use A Compression Gauge Before You Tune Ignition System

It is impossible to tune your car's ignition system properly if the cylinders are not working efficiently. Using a compression gauge, such as Model CTR20 made by Proto Tool Division of Ingersoll-Rand, can help you check out the engine's condition before performing an ignition tune-up. The gauge's flexible hose helps you reach remote spark plug holes. The dual-reading gauge switch includes both psi and metric values, a convenient side-release valve and neoprene O-rings for a tight seal. Adapters fit regular 14mm and 18mm spark plugs and 14mm long-reach spark plugs.

Karcheck Model 2502 Compression Tester

Before you tune your car, you should check its overall mechanical condition to save yourself a lot of time and frustration. Trying to tune an engine that has burned valves, broken rings, scorched cylinders, worn pistons, leaking head gaskets, or broken valve springs is basically a waste of time. A compression tester such as Karcheck Products' Model 2502 can diagnose these problems easily. The instrument reads from 0 to 300 pounds per square inch and 0 to 30 kilograms per square centimeter. It also includes a thumb rest to help you hold the rubber insert in the spark plug opening during the test.

they are in a condition to be cleaned, gapped and reinstalled, or should be replaced. In addition, you can learn something about your engine's general health by examining them closely. Here are some of the conditions you may encounter:

1. NORMAL PLUG. This is what you would always like to see (see photo) when you remove your spark plugs from your car. Deposits have not had any detrimental affect on engine performance. The color of the plug's insulator nose will be a light brown-grayish color with a minimum amount of erosion at the center electrode. The conclusion is that you have a plug with the proper heat range and a sound engine.

2. OIL-FOULED PLUG. On such plugs, there are traces of oil on the center electrode (see photo). Somehow, oil is getting into the combustion chamber, either because of worn piston rings or engine valve guides. One of the contributors to an oil-fouled plug is a defective PCV valve. Whatever the cause, the problem is oil control, and replacing the spark plugs with plugs a step hotter is only a temporary solution. Sooner or later, the basic problem will have to be corrected.

3. CARBON-FOULED PLUG. If you find soft, sooty deposits on the tip of the spark plugs (see photo), you may have the wrong ones in your engine. Assuming the heat range of the plugs is correct, carbon-fouling usually can be blamed on an over-rich air/fuel mixture caused by a sticking choke or clogged air filter. It also can be caused by weak ignition, retarded timing or low compression. If you find this condition on only one or two plugs, check those plug wires for high resistance, corrosion, or poor insulation. You also may have a cracked distributor cap. Carbon-fouling also can be the result of stop-and-go, short-haul driving. If this is the case and if everything else is normal, a plug one step hotter in heat range may compensate for such driving conditions.

4. WORN-OUT PLUG. This is a plug that has served its useful life and should be replaced (see photo). The color of the insulator nose indicates that the heat range is correct; the deposits are normal but the electrodes are rounded and worn. The ground electrode could not be squared with the center electrode. The correction is simple: replace the plugs.

5. ASH-FOULED PLUGS. If you find excessive deposits on the tip of your plugs (see

Spark Plug Holding Socket

For installing or removing spark plugs, you need an extra-deep socket that accommodates the plug's insulator. Indestro Division of Duro Metal Products Co. sells a 3/8 inch, extra-deep, six-point socket designed for removing and installing 3/16 inch and 14mm spark plugs. It features an oil-resistant neoprene insert engineered to securely hold the plug at the insulator to prevent damage. Overall length of the Model 2748HS socket is 2-7/16 inches.

Universal Joint Spark Plug Socket

Indestro Division of Duro Metal Products Co. sells a universal joint spark plug socket in a 3/8 inch drive, Model 2748UV. A universal joint socket can be used in many areas where a regular socket cannot. Spring-loaded friction in this socket holds the driver at the required angle to position the plug. The extra-deep socket fits 3/16 inch and 14mm spark plugs and has a neoprene insert to hold the plug at the insulator. Overall length is 3-1/4 inches.

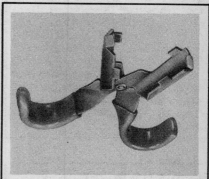

Spark Plug Wire Puller With A Difference

Thexton Manufacturing Company markets a spark plug wire puller designed like pliers so that the puller ends surround the spark plug boot. Most pullers only lift from one side of the spark plug boot but this tool's front tabs grip under the boot. The design makes it easier to work in confined spaces. The puller, which fits most standard boots, is made of steel and has vinyl grips.

Spark plugs look different as a result of different engine conditions: (1)normal plug, (2)oil-fouled plug, (3)carbon-fouled plug and (4)worn-out plug.

Plug Threading Aid

When installing spark plugs by hand in tight places, an old spark plug wire boot comes in handy. Fitted over the end of the plug, it lets your fingers do the threading much easier.

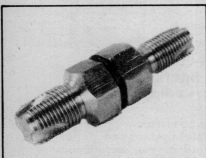

K-D Spark Plug Opening Thread Chaser

If you are having difficulty installing or removing spark plugs because the cylinder head threads are damaged or dirty, you can relieve the problem by using a spark plug thread chaser. K-D Manufacturing Co. has a combination 14mm and 18mm "chaser" that services virtually all makes and models of cars. It is designed to clean the threads of carbon and corrosion. The 13/16 inch hex on the tool, Model 730, has a neoprene band to hold the "chaser" firmly in a deep-wall spark plug socket wrench.

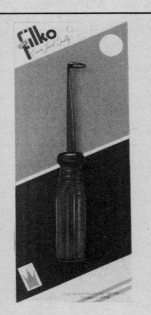

Spark Plug Cable Remover

Whenever removing spark plug wires from the plugs, you must be careful because it is easy to tear the spark plug boots. You also could damage wire terminals. The Model 7010 spark plug cable remover, made by Filko Automotive Products Division of F & B Manufacturing Co., allows easy removal of spark plug wires from the plugs. This tool is especially useful when working on a hot engine or one where the spark plugs are not easily accessible.

EVALUATING AND INSTALLING SPARK PLUGS

photo), you should give some thought to the type of gas you are burning or the oil you are using. It would be best to clean or replace the plugs and try the process of elimination. First, try changing your brand of gas to see if it helps. If not, you know you are faced with at least an oil and filter change with a different brand of oil and, most likely, some engine work.

6. SPLASH-FOULED PLUGS. This is a condition (see photo) you may find after a long-delayed tune-up. Deposits inside the combustion chamber suddenly loosen because normal combustion chamber temperature is restored after the engine is properly tuned. These are nothing but by-products of combustion that have collected not only on the spark plugs, but also on the pistons and valves. During hard acceleration, they may be shed from the piston and thrown against the hot insulator surface of the plug. These deposits can be removed by normal cleaning procedures and the plugs reinstalled to serve out their normal life.

7. INSULATOR GLAZING ON PLUG. This is a condition that can result from hard, fast acceleration on a car that has had normal combustion deposits on the firing tip (see photo). Instead of having the opportunity to burn off, they melt to form a conductive coating. Generally, glazing cannot be removed through normal cleaning procedures and it is better to replace the plugs. If the condition repeats itself, you may have to go to a plug that is one step colder to reduce the problem.

8. DETONATION. This is generally referred to as "knocking" or "pinging" (see photo). This phenomenon is caused by improper ignition timing; too low a gasoline octane; too lean an air/fuel mixture, possibly caused by poor carburetion and/or leaks in the intake manifold; an increase in compression ratio because of combustion chamber deposits or engine modification; excessive intake manifold temperatures; or lugging the engine.

When you hear your engine knocking, the condition is this: A portion of the air/fuel mixture has begun to burn spontaneously from heat and pressure imme-

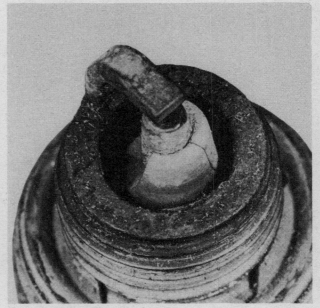

The way spark plugs look can help in diagnosing engine problems: (5)ash-fouled plug, (6)splash fouling, (7)plug with insulator and (8)detonation.

diately after ignition took place. The result is an explosion rather than an even burning inside the combustion chamber. Because of this, extreme pressure is exerted on internal engine components, including the spark plugs.

9. PRE-IGNITION. Pre-ignition is just what the term implies—ignition of the fuel charge prior to the timed spark (see photo). Hot spots within the combustion chamber are capable of initiating this combustion. It can be caused by combustion chamber deposits that become incandescent; hot spots in the combustion chamber due to poor control of engine heat; piston scuffing, caused by inadequate lubrication or improper clearance of engine parts; detonation; cross-firing (spark plug wires too close to one another and running parallel set up an electrical induction between one another); or spark plug heat range is too high for that particular engine. If you are lucky, the only damage is to the spark plug. But often, pre-ignition will damage the piston head as well.

10. OVERHEATED PLUG. High temperature shows on a spark plug as a clean white insulator core nose and/or excessive electrode erosion (see photo). The insulator may be blistered as well. It is probably a result of too hot a spark plug heat range, but also can come from over-advanced ignition timing, cooling system problems, lean air/fuel mixtures or a leaking intake manifold.

Cleaning The Spark Plugs

CONSIDERING the amount of time and effort

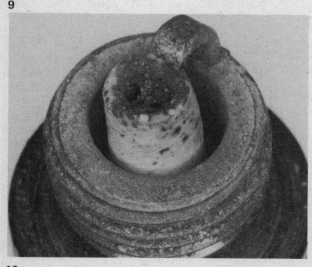
9

10

Plugs can also indicate (9)pre-ignition and (10)overheating.

involved in removing and reinstalling spark plugs, once you have them out you are generally better off to install new ones if the old plugs are approaching the end of their life expectancy. But if you have followed the conscientious 5000 to 6000 mile cleaning interval, they are probably in good condition and can be serviced as follows:

1. An abrasive cleaner, usually available from service stations, is the most thorough method of cleaning. Take your spark plugs to such a station and have the job done. If, however, this is not feasible, proceed to step 2.
2. Clean the plug with a solvent such as Gumout, Cyclo, or, when these are not available, lacquer thinner. **CAUTION:** Avoid using such products near an open flame or without adequate ventilation.
3. Clean the electrodes and insulator on each plug with a wire brush. Be careful if you use a motor-driven brush. You could wear down the metal on the spark plug.
4. After cleaning, file the plug's center and ground electrodes until they are square. Use an ignition point file if one is available.
5. The space between the center electrode and its L-shaped side electrode is the gap that, as mentioned, must be precisely adjusted for maximum performance. If the gap is too small, the spark will not ignite all of the fuel in the combustion chamber. If it is too wide. you may have no spark at all.

To find the correct spark plug gap for your car, check your owner's manual or the service manual and proceed as follows: Use the special spark plug gapping gauge, available at any auto supply store, to measure the gap on each plug. This will be a round wire gauge, not a flat one.

6. If the gap is too big or too small, the ground electrode must be adjusted with a bending tool, which is on the gauge.
NOTE: If you are installing new spark plugs, check the gaps before installing. Although they may have been pre-set at the factory, they can become changed during shipping or set to a specification that is wider than the one for your car.

Reinstalling The Spark Plugs

AFTER CLEANING and gapping, or buying and gapping your spark plugs, here is the procedure for installing them:

1. Place each new or cleaned spark plug into the engine, screwing them in finger tight. To avoid cross-threading, which chews up threads, go as far as you can by hand to be sure the threads are properly mated. **NOTE:** If you are having trouble getting the plug started into the hole, slip a short length of heater hose over the end of the plug to form a flexible "handle."
2. With the spark plug ratchet and socket, give the plug another 1/4 to 1/2 turn, making it snug—not too tight! If your car uses tapered-seat plugs, which do not have gaskets, you will have a metal-to-metal contact, so only about 1/4 turn is needed to establish a proper seal once the plugs are finger-tight.
3. Connect each wire to the proper plug. Push the rubber boot firmly over the tip of the plug with your hand.
4. Start the engine and test drive the car.

Spark Plug Boot Puller

Sometimes the simplest tune-up chores can cause you the most trouble. It would seem that removing the wires from the spark plugs would be one of the easier tasks, but that is not always the case. When spark plug boots are baked onto the plug insulators by thousands of miles of heat, removing them can be tough. And, conventional means may damage the boot or wire in the removal process. Owatonna Tool Company makes a spark plug boot puller, Model 7078, that makes this job easy. It is a small, spring-steel device that can relieve you of a lot of frustration during regular tune-ups.

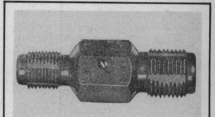

Spark Plug Hole Thread Chaser

If for some reason, the threads in your engine's spark plug holes become corroded or damaged, you can restore them with a thread chaser. Cal-Van Tools Division of Chemi-Trol Chemical Co. sells such a tool. Their Model 144 has 14mm and 18mm "chasers" on opposite ends. It also features a hexagonal section with a lock ball that permits use of any standard 13/16 inch open end wrench or deep socket. Each end of the chaser is slightly tapered for easier starting. You merely insert the tool in the hole and turn.

Round Wire Spark Plug Gauge

Many mechanics prefer a spark plug gapping tool that has the wire gauges mounted in a circular pattern. K-D Manufacturing Company's Model 166 spark plug gap wire-gauge is just such a tool. It has six hardened and plated electrode-adjusting gauges. Sizes range from 0.015 to 0.040 inch.

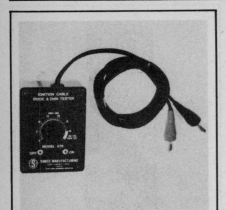

Ignition Wire, Diode And Ohm Tester

One instrument from Sonco Manufacturing, a Division of Mergo-Tronics Instrument Corp., checks ignition wires for continuity and proper resistance and checks diodes. The lightweight Model 576 tester features a solid-state design that provides accurate measurement of resistance up to 30,000 ohms. It is powered by two AA cells. Complete instructions are provided.

Crimping Tool Slices Bolts Too

Cal-Van Tools Division of Chemi-Trol Chemical Co. crimping tool with slicer, Model 1963, is designed for crimping both insulated and noninsulated terminals. It also has an end-position wire cutter and is able to strip wire and slice six sizes of bolts (10-32, 10-24, 8-32, 6-32, 5-40, and 4-40).

Ignition Cable Sets For Foreign Cars

Ignition cable sets for foreign-made automobiles sometimes may be hard to find. The Automotive Division of Robert Bosch Corp., however, has added ignition wire sets for foreign cars to its line. Sets are available for all Audi Foxes, including the Model 100; the Porsche 914/4; and many models of Volkswagens. The specific vehicle, model and year appear on each ignition cable set package.

Spark Plug Wire Gauge

A spark plug wire gauge is essential for ignition work. The most accurate way to measure the gap between spark plug electrodes is to use a rounded wire gauge such as the Model 28A sold by the Indestro Division of Duro Metal Products Co. This gauge provides the following measurements: 0.022, 0.025, 0.028, 0.030, 0.032, 0.035, 0.038 and 0.040 inch.

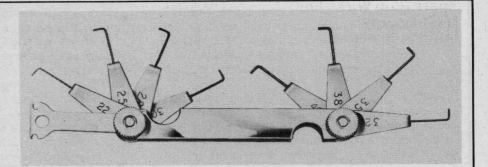

SPARK PLUG WIRES

WHETHER you are performing a complete engine tune-up, just replacing spark plugs or looking for the reason why your car's engine is not running properly, be sure to check the spark plug, or ignition, wires. If damage to one or more wires is not apparent, they are assumed—often incorrectly—to be in good shape. The spark plug wires often are only checked when everything else fails to produce a smoothly running engine.

If your car's engine is misfiring or if some of your spark plugs are carbon-fouled (see the section in this chapter on Evaluating And Installing Spark Plugs), the spark plug wires could be the cause.

Although a spark plug wire looks fine, it still could be defective. A professional mechanic using a special tester or a volt-ohmmeter can tell you if wires are defective by testing for high electrical resistance in the wire or checking to see if there are any gaps or breaks in the wire.

Spark plug wires like any other part, wear out with age, abuse or through the effects of the environment.

Three years or about 30,000 miles is a realistic lifespan to expect from a set of spark plug wires. When this period is reached, the spark plug wires should be replaced at the next engine tune-up.

Periodically, you should visually inspect the spark plug wires. Are there cracks or abrasions on the outside jacket? Are the wires oil-soaked? Have the boots at the spark plug end of the wire become hard and brittle? Have the rubber nipples at the distributor cap end of the wires become hard and brittle?

If any of these conditions are present, the spark plug wires must be replaced if you want your engine to run smoothly. Even if you determine that only one wire needs replacement, it is best to replace the entire set since they all have been working for the same amount of time. **NOTE:** American-made cars have used a carbon resistance wire for spark plugs wires since 1963. This often is referred to as TVRS wire, which means television and radio suppression. This wire is constructed with a 12-strand nylon center core impregnated with carbon. Since there is no metal core in this kind of wire, it is more easily damaged and likely to burn out. Resistance wire is heavily insulated with a silicone rubber material for high resistance to heat—one major enemy to this type of wire.

Spark plug wire replacement can be performed by any home mechanic on most any car engine. Some engines, however, have the spark plug wires run under parts of the engine, through tubes, looms or separators and through some unusual locations. Always visually inspect

the job before attempting replacement to be certain you can handle it.

When changing spark plug wires, make sure you have the correct wire set for your particular engine. Your best bet is to purchase a spark plug wire set that has the wires already tailored to the correct length for your car's engine with the nipples, connectors and boots in place.

To replace spark plug wires:

1. Let the engine cool. You will be working near the engine's exhaust manifold.
2. Remove the air filter housing. Refer to the section on Air Filter Service in the Fuel System chapter. This is necessary for access to all spark plug wires.
3. Starting at the spark plug farthest from the distributor (on V-8 engines, you may start on either side of the engine), pull the rubber boot from the spark plug with your hand. Use a twisting motion as you pull the boot. This will make it easier to remove the rubber boot.
4. Follow the wire you have removed at the spark plug up to the distributor.
5. Pull the other end of the wire out of the distributor cap with your hand. Once again, a slight twisting motion will make it easier to remove the wire.
6. Remove the spark plug wire from the engine. If the spark plug wire is threaded through any tubes or looms or held in place by separators, make a note of this to assist you in installing the new wire.
7. Select a spark plug wire from the new set you have purchased that is the same length as the wire you have just removed. Actually compare both wires to be sure.
8. Install this new spark plug wire by reversing steps 3 through 6. Be careful to route the new wire in the same manner as the one you removed.
9. At both the spark plug end of the wire as well as the distributor cap end, be sure to push the rubber boot and the nipple in as far as it will go to obtain a good connection.
10. Continue this same procedure, one spark plug wire at a time, until you have replaced the entire set.
11. Remove the secondary (high tension) wire from the ignition coil tower; this is the wire that is connected to the distributor at the other end. Pull it out of the tower with a slight twisting motion.
12. Remove the other end of this high tension wire from the center tower connection of the distributor cap. Once again, twist slightly as you pull the wire out.
13. Using the wire supplied in the wire set you purchased for your car's engine, replace the coil high tension wire by reversing steps 11 and 12. Once again, be sure to push the rubber nipples (there is one on each end of this wire) all the way down to assure a good connection.

IGNITION SYSTEM

Spark Plug Wires For High-Energy Ignition Systems

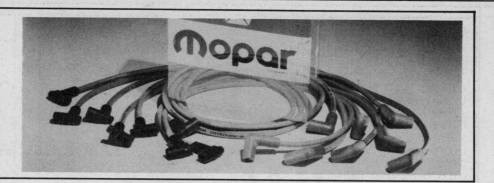

Mopar sells 8mm silicone ignition wires that can be used on 1974, 1975 and 1976 General Motors cars with high-energy ignition systems. The wires are available in custom sets or as individual spark plug leads.

Replacing Spark Plug Wires On High Energy Ignition Systems (General Motors)

IF YOU are working on a General Motors car equipped with a High Energy Ignition (HEI) system, the distributor cap and the way the wires attach to the distributor cap will be different from other systems. You will also note that the diameter of the spark plug wires is larger. Since the ignition coil is an integral part of the distributor cap assembly, there also will be no secondary wire at the coil.

To remove a spark plug wire on an HEI system:

1. Lift off the retaining ring from the distributor cap. This is done by moving the retaining clips (marked "latch") outward and lifting the ring up. All the spark plug wires will remain in the retaining ring.
2. Remove the nipple (distributor cap) end of the spark plug wire from the retaining ring by pressing down on the nipple with your thumb. The wire and nipple will come out of the ring.

3. Remove the opposite end of the wire from the spark plug.
4. Select a matching length of spark plug wire from the replacement set.
5. To install the new wire in the retaining ring, lubricate the nipple with a non-ammoniated soap or silicone spray and press the nipple into the retainer ring.
6. Repeat steps 2, 3, 4 and 5 for each spark plug wire until you have replaced the entire set. Remember, do one wire at a time to avoid confusion and time consuming mistakes.
7. When all spark plug wires have been replaced in the retainer ring, reinstall the retainer ring on the HEI distributor cap by reversing step 1.

Remember, all procedures for replacing spark plug wires on HEI systems are the same as for conventional systems except for those differences at the distributor cap as outlined above. If you have any doubts as to whether you can perform this task on the HEI system, it would be best to consult a professional mechanic.

Ignition Waterproofer

Even if your ignition system is in fine shape, it may still be susceptible to moisture. If you have trouble starting your car on damp days, you might try treating your ignition system with a waterproofer such as the Magnition ignition waterproofer made by Sorensen Manufacturing Co. You just spray it on the distributor, coil, ignition wires, and around spark plugs to repel water.

Fingers Were Not Meant To Remove Spark Plug Wires

If fingers were meant to remove spark plug wires, they would be shaped like a spark plug cable remover—which is designed to remove spark plug wires from spark plugs without tearing the plug boot or damaging the wires. Essex Automotive Parts, a subsidiary of United Technologies, markets a spark plug cable remover, Model 99-4, that can save you a great deal of time.

Keep Your Ignition System Dry

An ignition sealer is good insurance against difficult starting and engine misfiring due to moisture in your ignition system. The Maywood Company manufactures a sealer designed to protect against road spray, condensation and humidity. It comes in a 13 ounce aerosol can so you can just spray it on your spark plug wires, spark plug boots, distributor, coil, and other ignition wires.

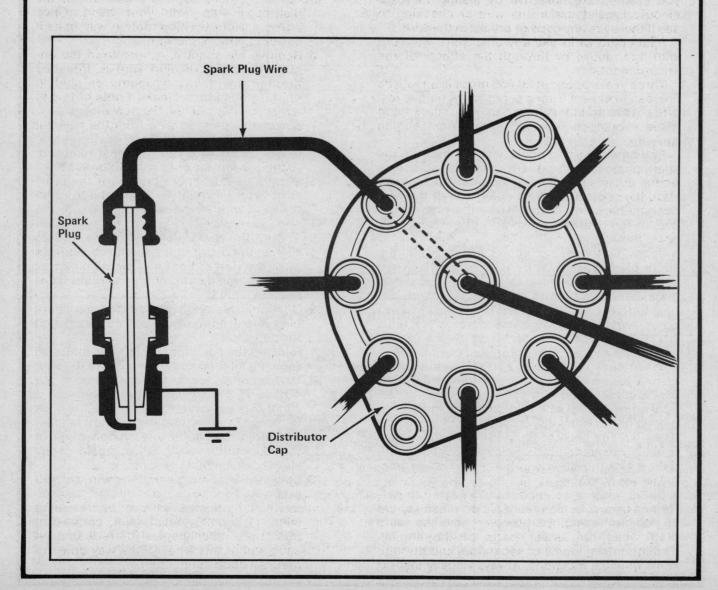

Spark Plug Wire

Spark Plug

Distributor Cap

IGNITION SYSTEM

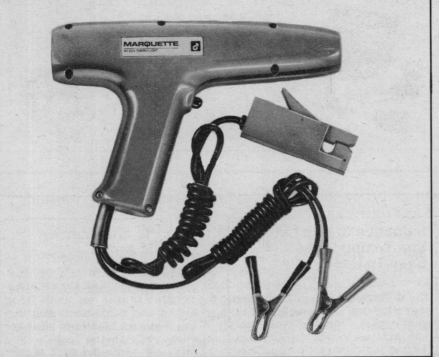

Timing Light Features Inductive Pick-Up

You should check the timing on your car each time you perform an ignition tune-up because the point setting directly affects the timing, and too much of an advance can cause your engine to knock and ping. Marquette, a Division of Applied Power, Inc., makes a timing light, Model 41220, that features a clamp-on inductive pick-up. This makes hooking up the timing light easy. The light has a xenon tube that will flash at speeds up to 8000 rpm and a voltage selector switch that offers excellent brightness on six or 12 volts. The light also has a high-impact shockproof case and a pushbutton trigger, which turns the light on only when you need it. Light circuits are protected against overload, improper hook-up and reversed polarity.

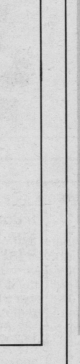

Starting Fluid Gives Your Engine A Boost

If you have ever had starting problems in winter and have called a service truck for assistance, you probably have seen starting fluid being used. Usually, this is the first thing the service attendant will use after trying to jump start the car. Phillips, a Division of James B. Carter, Inc., makes Zero Start starting fluid that works on both diesel and gasoline engines. It is available in two sizes, 8-1/4 ounces and 15 ounces. However, the product is not for use with preheated manifolds or glow plug installations.

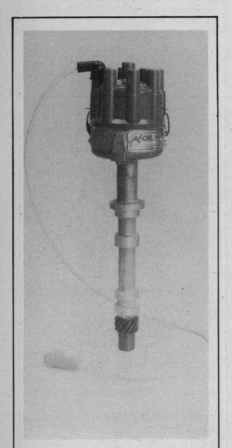

Spark Plug Cleaner Connects To Car Battery

Sometimes it is only necessary to clean your spark plugs at tune-up time rather than replace them. And, in between tune-ups, you should check your plugs periodically, cleaning them as needed. Cleaning plugs, however, can be a tough task if you try chipping the carbon and lead deposits with a screwdriver or try grinding them off with a small file. Automark, a Division of Wells Manufacturing Corp., makes a handy spark plug cleaner that is powered by your car's battery. It cleans spark plugs in the manner most manufacturers suggest—by sandblasting. To use the cleaner, you attach the unit's leads to the positive and negative battery posts and insert the bottom of the spark plug into the unit. A high-speed impeller reaches a surface velocity of 5000 surface feet per minute, impinging millions of abrasive particles to clean the plug thoroughly. Do not forget to regap plugs before replacing them in the engine!

Electronic Ignition Kit Includes Special Distributor

Most electronic ignition kits are designed to use your car's stock distributor. But Accel Eliminator Ignition's kit includes a special distributor that has an adjustable advance feature. It allows custom-tailoring of the distributor advance for optimum performance. Moving the stop pin to the desired position calibrates the advance in one-degree increments from 10 to 17 degrees. The complete kit includes a distributor cap, special distributor, an electronic power module, rotor, and wiring harness. The color-keyed wiring harness has quick-connect terminals. Complete instructions come with each kit.

Solid-State Electronic Ignition System For American-Made Cars From 1957 To 1974

Even if your car is a high-miler or getting on in years, you can provide it with an electronic ignition system. An electronic ignition setup reduces ignition system maintenance, makes starting easier in cold weather, and tends to keep spark plugs cleaner. Sorensen Manufacturing Co. makes an electronic ignition system called the Magnition that is a solid-state conversion kit requiring only a few basic tools to install. The kits cover most American-made cars from 1957 to 1974. There also are kits for trucks, farm vehicles, and for marine applications.

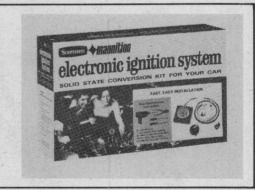

Spark Plug Hole Thread Chasers By Thexton

Spark plug hole thread chasers remove carbon and corrosion with just a few turns. The use of a chaser provides firm seating of plugs and assures a metal-to-metal contact for effective heat transfer. Thexton Manufacturing Company offers two spark plug hole thread chasers. Model 321 fits 18 to 14mm holes and has a 13/16 inch hex center. If your car uses the new small plugs, you might need Model 322, which fits 14 to 10mm holes and has a 5/8 inch hex center for turning.

7mm Ignition Cable Sets

There are two ways to replace your ignition wires. You can buy a set that is already tailored to your needs, or you can buy wires, nipples and terminals and fabricate your own set. Supronic 7mm ignition cable sets, sold by Whitaker Cable Corp., are available custom-tailored for your car. They save you a lot of work and look neater than homemade sets. These cables are suppression-type, all-metallic conductor wires with a built-in resistor. They are insulated to withstand increased voltages and engine operating temperatures. They also

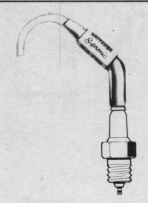

feature silicone and/or Hypalon-jacketed cable, plated steel Spring-Lok spark plug terminals and silicone boots. They meet or exceed FCCNSAE standards for radiation suppression.

IGNITION SYSTEM

Replacement Electronic Ignition Parts

Filko Automotive Products Division of F & B Manufacturing Co. makes replacement electronic ignition components for American Motors, Chrysler, Delco and Ford systems. You can choose from trigger wheels, power modules and other parts that will replace those in your present electronic ignition system perfectly.

ATP Nonmagnetic Electronic Ignition Conversion Kits

Even if you are the proud owner of a 1957 Rambler, you can still provide your car with the latest in electronic ignition systems. Automatic Transmission Parts, Inc. offers a wide range of electronic ignition conversion kits for cars from 1957 to 1974. There are three steps involved in making such a conversion. First, you remove the points and condenser from the distributor and replace them with a special (trigger) wheel assembly. Then, you mount a box-like control unit to the side of a fender or the firewall under the hood. Electrical connections are next. The three connections you have to make include bolting a ground wire to the coil bracket, attaching a wire to the negative side of the coil and a wire to the coil's positive terminal. This conversion eliminates point replacement at tune-up time.

Spark Plug Lead Pliers Also Remove Light Bulbs

When the engine is running, you can experience a shock while removing spark plug wires. In any case, it is often a tough job to remove spark plug wires that are stuck. A pair of spark plug lead pliers such as the shockproof Model 143 from Cal-Van Tools Division of Chemi-Trol Chemical Co. allows you to remove spark plug wires easily. This tool has its nose pieces covered with nylon, and the handles also are insulated to provide protection against shock. The angled, serrated jaws provide a solid grip. You also could use these pliers to remove light bulbs.

Inductive Clamp Makes Sun Timing Light Easy To Use

If you have ever been frustrated trying to hook up a timing light to your engine's No. 1 cylinder, you should take a look at the Inductive Timing Light made by Sun Electric Corporation. Usually, the hookup involves placing an adapter between the spark plug and the plug wire. Sometimes, this requires a bit of fumbling. With the Sun light, you just clamp an inductive unit to the plug wire—that is all there is to it. The timing light is powered by your car's battery. It features reverse polarity-protected circuitry, rubber nose cone and a one-year warranty.

Electric Analyzer For GM Autos

If you own a 1976 or 1977 Chevette, or a full-size 1977 General Motors car with an under-hood diagnostic connector, you can use a special electronic analyzer made by Owatonna Tool Co. You just plug it into the car's master diagnostic connector and it will pinpoint faults in the starter/charging systems. The handheld unit has ten lights, each of which corresponds to a specific problem. Designations include: low battery, fusible link, ignition/run position, ignition start position, neutral start switch, starter/solenoid, H.E.I./wiring, overcharge/regulator short, alternator bridge/stator and not charging/field or regulator open.

10-Piece Ignition Wrench Set

A 10-piece ignition wrench set, Model EW-40K, with open ends sold by Blackhawk Hand Tools gives you a choice of two angles and a wide range of size openings. The sizes range from 13/64 through 1/2 inch in graduations of 1/32 of an inch. Each size opening comes with a 15- and a 60-degree angle head.

Ignition Dryer And Protector

If you have been experiencing difficulty starting in damp weather, you may be able to use the Marvel Oil Company's Ignition Dryer and Protector. Sprayed on your ignition wires, distributor and coil, it removes moisture to eliminate shorting. It could save you a service call.

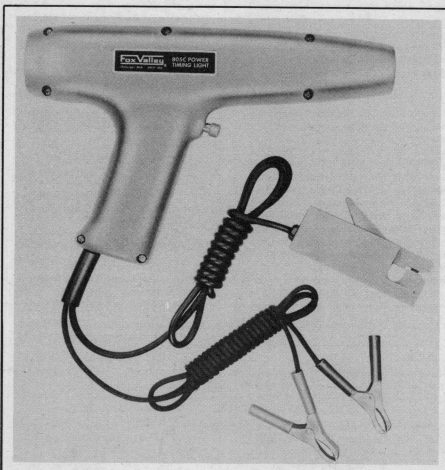

Power Timing Light

A power timing light from Fox Valley Instrument Co., Model 805C, features an induction pickup lead that eliminates the need for disconnecting spark plugs. Other features include a xenon flash tube that illuminates the timing mark at all engine speeds up to 8000 rpm. It also has a pistol grip design that allows you to get into close quarters and its pushbutton trigger turns the light on only when you need it. The device has a five foot lead and measures 7-3/8 by 10-3/4 by 2 inches.

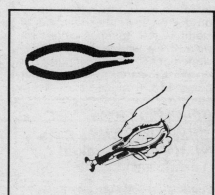

Nylon Spark Plug Wire Puller

Pulling spark plugs while the engine is running can be a shocking experience. You also run the risk of burning yourself on the hot manifold. Lisle Corporation's Model 51500 spark plug wire puller is made of nylon to help you pull spark plug wires quickly and safely without damage to the wire or the rubber protectors.

Custom And Universal Ignition Wire Sets

Standard Motor Products, Inc. sells both custom and universal ignition wire sets. They are available with Hypalon or silicone insulation in both 7mm and 8mm sizes. The wires are designed for high temperature engines. They come in many different styles.

IGNITION SYSTEM

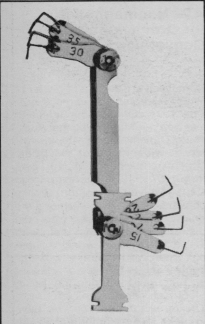

Spark Plug Gap Wire-Gauge Set

For gapping spark plugs, you should have a gauge with rounded wire ends. K-D Manufacturing Co. has a spark plug gap wire-gauge set, Model 165, that has eight wire gauges and an electrode adjusting tool. The wire sizes are: 0.015, 0.018, 0.020, 0.025, 0.028, 0.030, 0.035, and 0.040 inch. The wires also are marked to corresponding metric sizes.

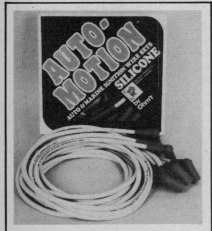

Ignition Wires Resist 500-Degree Heat

The high temperatures under the hood of modern automobiles put a strain on ignition wires. Ristance Products, Inc. manufactures Auto-Motion silicone-insulated ignition wires that are designed to perform under the high under-hood temperatures produced by today's vehicles. Auto-Motion ignition wire sets feature a carbon suppression core or stranded copper metallic core conductor, an inner rubber insulation for heat resistance and dielectric strength. There also is a fiberglass braid and a 500°F silicone outer insulation for heat, oil, chemical and moisture resistance. The wires also feature spring-lock plug terminals and silicone spark plug boots. Universal wire sets for six- and eight-cylinder cars, and tailored wire sets for most V8s are available.

Spark Plug Remover And Installer

The engine compartment of new cars is usually very cluttered and if you have air conditioning, it may be exceptionally difficult for you to change your spark plugs. You can make the job easier by getting a spark plug remover and installer such as the No. 309 from Thexton Manufacturing Co. This nine inch long tool has a flexible shaft to allow turning at any angle and to help prevent damaging the threads in the spark plug holes. A stepped, soft tip grips the procelain and the terminal so the plug will not drop to the floor.

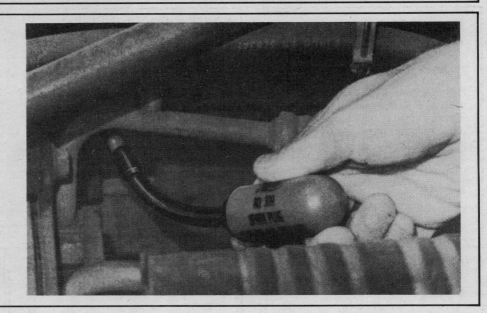

Grease Cutter Works Upside Down

A special valve on Permatex Grease Cutter, made by Woodhill/Permatex, allows you to use the aerosol can in any position — even upside down. To clean automotive parts, you simply spray on the grease cutter, allow it to stand a few minutes and then rinse it off with water. It is designed not to harm metal, rubber or plastic parts. Grease Cutter comes in a 20 ounce can.

Circuit Tester By Lisle

When a light flickers or an accessory fails to operate, it is sometimes caused by a short or break in your car's wiring system. Without an electrical tester, finding the problem is virtually impossible. Using a circuit tester such as one available from the Lisle Corporation, you can instantly determine if a wire is carrying power. The tester checks DC (and AC) current up to 20 volts. You merely clamp its lead to a ground source, turn the ignition to "accessory" if necessary, and probe the wire in question with the instrument's testing needle. The amount of current registers in the handle. You also can use this tester to check spark plug voltage by probing the plug cable while turning the engine over.

Motorola Electronic Ignition Systems For Do-It-Yourselfers

Motorola makes two breakerless electronic ignition system kits for do-it-yourself installation. The kits are available in two models. Motorola Model 6SK-2028 is designed for most American-made cars, while Model 6SK-2029 is made for many foreign-made cars. The kits contain an ignition amplifier, mounting hardware, magnet sensor to replace breaker points, distributor sensor plates, Allen wrench and feeler gauge. Complete instructions, a warranty card and decal are included in the kit.

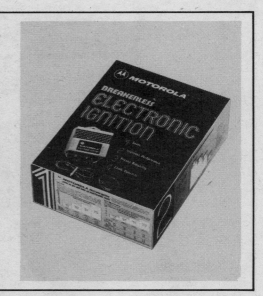

Spark Plug Cable Sets With Spring-Locked Terminals

A loose spark plug wire can reduce your fuel economy and performance drastically. Prestolite International Co. manufactures a line of distributed-resistance core and metallic conductor-type ignition cables with spring-lock terminals. These are 7mm wires insulated with Hypalon. The wires also are protected with a boot of Hypalon or silicone. The distributed-resistance core wire is used by most car and truck manufacturers and is recommended for replacement use to suppress radio and television interference on all vehicles. If you use a metallic conductor wire, you must include a system for suppressing radiated signals in your ignition system.

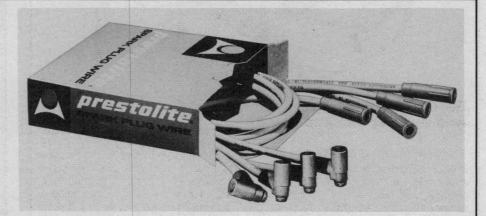

IGNITION SYSTEM

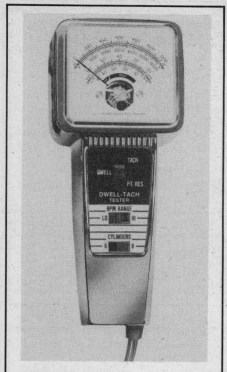

Easy-To-Hold Dwell-Tach Points Tester

If the hand-held type of dwell-tach is your preference, you might look into the Model R-11 made by the Kal-Equip Co. This instrument measures high and low rpm, cam angle, and point resistance. It has solid-state construction for maximum accuracy and reliability.

Spark Plug Boot Puller Saves Burns And Scraped Knuckles

When ignition wire boots are baked on by high temperatures, it is hard to get them off without breaking wires, burning fingers or scraping your knuckles. The best way to deal with this problem is to use a spark plug boot puller such as the Standard Plus Model PTC203 sold by Standard Motor Products, Inc. You can find this tool at auto supply stores.

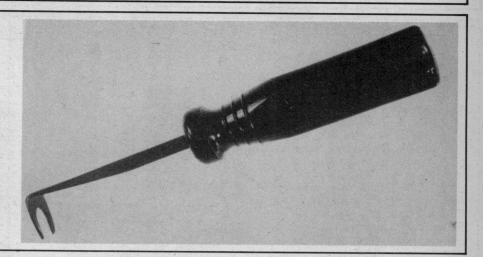

Combination Wiring Tool

If you plan on making your own spark plug and other ignition wires, you should have a cutting and stripping tool. Whitaker Cable Corporation's Model No. 2850-1 applies a "W" crimp to 7mm and 8mm straight or 90-degree spark plug and distributor terminals, either split or solid barrel. It also cuts and strips solid and stranded 22 through 10 gauge wire. In addition, this tool crimps uninsulated (1800 series) and insulated (2800 series) terminals, and disconnects or splices 22 through 10 gauge wire.

Ignition Sealer

Even a small amount of moisture can cause trouble in your ignition system. To prevent this, you might want to use an ignition sealer such as that offered by Siloo, Inc. The product, which comes in 14 ounce aerosol cans, provides a clear protective coating that is designed to keep rust, corrosion and moisture from attacking your ignition system.

Spark Plug Wire Tester And Ohmmeter

The only quick way to find out if your spark plug cables are working efficiently is to use a spark plug wire tester. Cal-Van Tools Division of Chemi-Trol Chemical Co. has a Model 1812 tester that checks the resistance of spark plug wires and makes continuity tests. The ohmmeter range is 0 to 100,000 ohms. The unit, powered by a single battery, comes with instructions. It measures 4-1/2 by 2-1/2 by 1-1/2 inches.

Vacuum Gauge Is Helpful In Ignition Work

A vacuum gauge such as the No. 1928 from Hastings Manufacturing Co. can help you locate a spark plug that is not operating properly. You just attach the gauge to the car's vacuum line and disconnect one spark plug at a time while the engine is running. Each time you disconnect a spark plug, the vacuum reading will drop. If it does not, you will know the spark plug is at fault. The vacuum and pressure tester has a 2-1/2 inch dial and measures to 30 inches and 700mm of vacuum. It also measures up to 10 pounds and 700 grams per square centimeter of pressure.

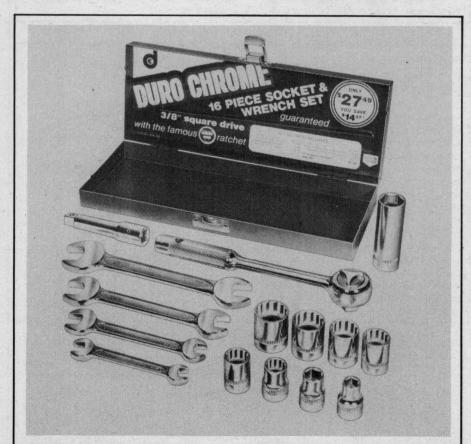

Set Combines Socket And Open End Wrenches

If your automotive needs include acquiring a 3/8 inch socket wrench set and a set of open wrenches, you can get both in a set sold by Duro Metal Products Co. The Duro-Chrome Model 84112 is a 16-piece, 3/8 inch square drive socket and wrench set. It includes four open end wrenches that are double-ended. Sizes range from 5/16 to 11/16 inch. Also included is a 5/16 inch six-point socket, and 12-point sockets (3/8, 7/16, 1/2, 9/16, 5/8, 11/16 and 3/4 inch). There also is a three-inch extension, a 5/8 inch spark plug holding socket and a reversible ratchet. The set is packed in a metal box.

Universal DC Timing Light For All Ignition Systems

Sonco Manufacturing Division of Mergo-Tronics Instrument Corp. sells a Model 2490 Universal "clamp-on" DC timing light that operates with ignition systems. The light, which features an induction-type clamp-on spark plug cable lead and all solid-state circuit design, will operate on any ignition system at any speed up to 10,000 rpm with full brilliance. It has a xenon bulb and prefocused lens for bright light output for timing outdoors. This chrome-plated, die cast timing light has long, gas and oil resistant leads. It comes with complete instructions.

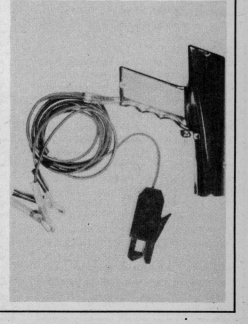

IGNITION SYSTEM

Remote Starter Switch

It would seem that automotive test procedures that involve such tasks as locating a timing mark would be fairly simple. But procedures such as these require cranking the engine, and if you do not have a remote starter switch that allows you to crank the engine from outside the car, the chore can be very frustrating. The Cobra-GT remote starter switch Model 8709, made by Peerless Instrument Co., can make that job much easier. It features heavy-duty, silver-plated contacts, molded high-impact case, and professional-quality clamps. An illustrated instruction booklet is included.

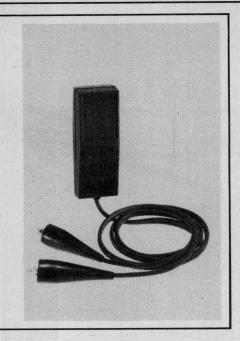

Electronic Ignition Installs Without Special Tools

Prestolite International Co. makes electronic ignition kits to fit a wide range of General Motors, Chrysler, Ford, American Motors, International Harvester, Toyota and Volkswagen cars. The kits consist of four basic parts: a trigger-wheel/sensor assembly that replaces the points, condenser and braker plate of the conventional ignition system; an electronic pack that takes over the job of the conventional system's contact set; a wiring harness; and a hardware package. Each kit comes with fully illustrated, step-by-step instructions showing how a simple distributor conversion replaces the points and condenser with a sensor/trigger wheel. After that procedure is accomplished, you install the electronic control on the firewall or over the fender well, and connect the wiring.

Eight-Piece Ignition Wrench Set

Proto Tool Division of Ingersoll-Rand offers an eight-piece ignition wrench set in its Challenger Line. Each wrench has a 15 and 75 degree angle head with the same size opening at each end. The sizes are: 13/64, 7/32, 15/64, 1/4, 9/32, 5/16, 11/32 and 3/8 inch.

Spark Plug Gap Gauge Set

Proto Tool Division of Ingersoll-Rand markets a spark plug electrode gap setter, Model 000K, that features an electrode bender and eight wire gauges in sizes 0.022, 0.025, 0.027, 0.028, 0.030, 0.032, 0.035, and 0.040 inch. The gauges also are marked with the metric equivalent.

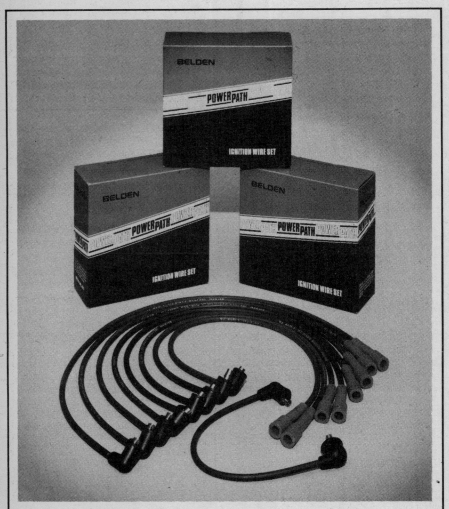

Ignition Wires For 1977 Fords

The Belden Corp. offers a complete line of ignition wire sets for 1977 Fords, which use 8mm ignition wire. Among the items in the Ford line are seven new custom wire sets for four cylinder, six cylinder (both V-6 and in-line), and eight cylinder cars and trucks. The firm also markets four-coil leads; bulk IRS/8mm wire in both blue and gray jackets; OE-type boots, nipples and terminals; a combination 7mm/8mm crimping tool; and an ignition lead make-up kit.

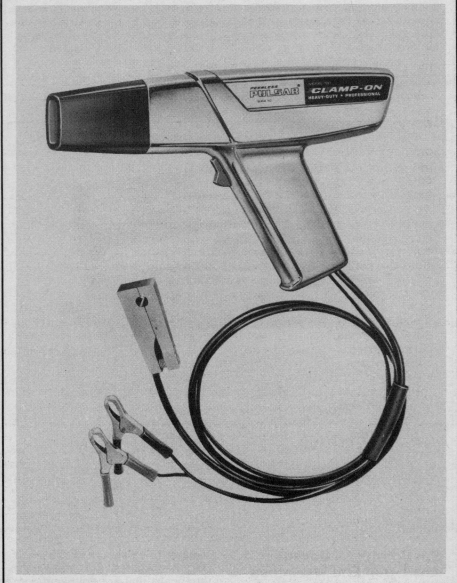

Penetrating Oil By Gold Eagle

When you are confronted with a nut, bolt or screw that is "frozen" by rust or corrosion, a good quality penetrating oil can save the day. Gold Eagle Company makes a penetrating oil, No. PO16, that can be used to free any part frozen by rust, corrosion, scale, paint, varnish, carbon or gum. It also cleans, lubricates and prevents parts from becoming frozen in the future. The product contains no harmful acids or alkalies and is noncorrosive. It comes in pint and gallon cans.

Clamp-On Inductive DC Timing Light

Peerless Instrument Company's Model 180 DC timing light features an inductive pickup that can save you time. With this light, you can set engine timing, centrifugal and vacuum advance, and check emission-control spark advance operation and distributor condition. It can be used on two- and four-cycle engines with single and multiple cylinders and 12-volt positive or negative ground systems. An illustrated instruction manual is included.

INTRODUCTION

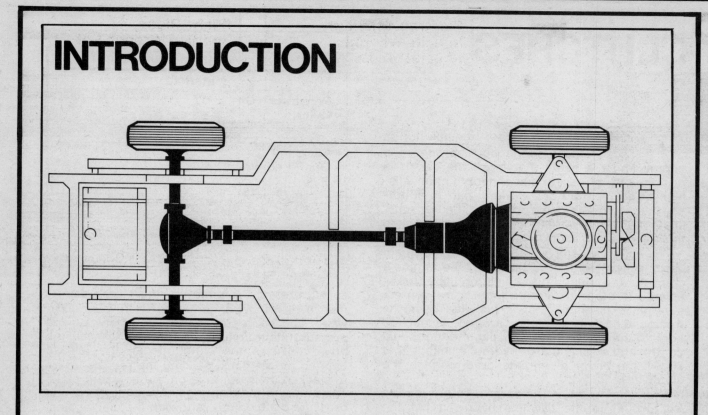

IN THIS chapter, we are introducing the technical term "driveline" that covers a lot of things. It includes all of the components it takes to transfer power from the end of the engine's rotating crankshaft to the drive wheels, the clutch (if the car is so equipped), transmission, universal joints, drive or propeller shaft, rear axle, rear axle shafts and, finally, the wheels and tires. **NOTE:** On most cars, the rear wheels are the drive wheels.

The transmission—manual or automatic— provides the driver with a selection of gears to permit the vehicle to operate under a variety of conditions and engine loads. The majority of passenger cars in use today are equipped with an automatic transmission that performs all clutching and gear-shifting operations with minimum assistance from the driver. However, a number of cars equipped with manual transmissions are sold each year. These cars must have a clutch, which is foot pedal-operated, and a transmission that is shifted from gear to gear by hand.

A clutch is merely a link or coupling between the engine and the rest of the driveline. The clutch permits a gradual application of engine power to begin moving the car. Once the clutch is engaged, all of the engine power is applied to the transmission and the rest of the driveline. In addition to aiding in the initial motion of the car, the clutch enables the driver to disengage the engine from the driveline so that the transmission may be shifted smoothly from one gear to another, or bring the car to a stop without stalling the engine.

You will only find two pedals, the accelerator pedal and brake pedal, on the floor of a car equipped with an automatic transmission. There is no need for a separate clutch pedal assembly as the torque converter (used instead of the clutch assembly), operating with other components in the transmission, automatically transfers engine power to the driveline.

Aside from using a lever to select the mode of operation desired—Park, Reverse, Neutral, Drive, Drive 1, or Drive 2—very little is required of the driver. As long as it is in good operating condition, the automatic transmission will automatically perform most of the functions that drivers of cars equipped with manual transmissions must do for themselves.

All that remains is to get engine power from the transmission to the drive wheels. The rear axle of your car is coupled to the output shaft of the transmission through the propeller shaft, which is merely a hollow steel tube. But since our roads and streets are not perfectly smooth and level, the propeller shaft must be coupled at both ends with flexible links called universal joints. Universal joints, or U-joints, are constructed so that they will flex and "give" as the car travels over rough and uneven roads. In this way, the propeller shaft can assume any angle required while continuing to transmit engine power from the transmission to the rear axle.

The function of the rear axle is to transmit the engine power it receives from the transmission to the rear wheels. It does this with the assistance of the differential, a specially built device that transfers the power received by the rear axle to the axle shafts that turn the rear wheels. Why is the differential necessary? Well, when you drive down a straight road, both rear wheels travel at the same speed. But what happens when you turn a corner? If you think for a moment, you will realize that during a right turn, for example, the wheels on the left side of the car travel further than the wheels on the right side of the car. Since the left side of the car and the right side have to complete the turn together, the wheels on the left side must travel faster than the wheels on the right. This is not a problem for the front wheels since they turn independently. The rear wheels, however, are another matter and this is where the differential is important. It is constructed so that regardless of which way you turn the car, the wheels on the outside of the turn will travel faster than the inside wheels, with power from the engine still applied.

The tires are the final component of the driveline. As the wheels turn, the tires move on the road and friction between the tires and the road moves the car. Traction, or the ability of the tires to grip the road, depends on tire condition and proper inflation. Tire and wheel service is covered elsewhere.

As you read the following sections of this chapter, you will find service tips as well as procedures for making adjustments to help you maintain the components of the driveline.

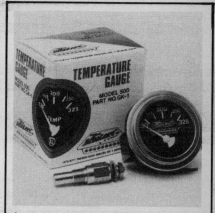

Temperature Gauge Kit

Integrity Transmission Koolers, Inc. offers a temperature gauge kit, No. GK-1, that includes a lighted gauge, sending unit, adapter and polished, stainless-steel, underdash mounting bracket. The kit is designed to be used with Integrity transmission coolers. Installation instructions are supplied.

All-Purpose Lubricant

Wolf's Head Oil Refining Co. markets HDX All-Purpose Lube designed for high performance applications. The lubricant is recommended for sports cars, racing cars, police cars and motorcycles. The SAE 90 oil is formulated to protect against unnecessary wear and tear caused by high torque, extreme temperatures and road shocks.

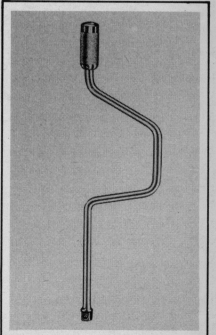

Speeder Handle For Transmission Work

Transmission work requires a tool with a long reach. One of the most popular tools for transmission removal and installation is a speeder handle such as the one sold by Indestro, a division of Duro Metal Products Co. This speeder handle, No. 2785, is 16-1/2 inches long and has a 3/8 inch square drive.

CLUTCHES

Here Is What You Will Need
Materials
● Penetrating Oil
● Ruler
Tools
● Pliers
● Open-End Wrenches
● Ruler
● Wheel Chocks
● Jack and Jack Stands

THE CLUTCH in a standard transmission is the mechanical connection between the engine and the gears that move the car. It is designed to connect or disconnect the transmission of power from one working part to another—in this case, from the engine to the transmission. The clutch, a friction-type device, is linked to a clutch pedal in the driver's compartment.

The clutch assembly is divided into four main parts: a flywheel that is bolted to the engine's crankshaft; a friction disc or clutch plate that is splined to the transmission input shaft; a pressure-plate assembly that is installed over the friction disc and is bolted around its outside edge to the flywheel; and, finally, the foot pedal control and mechanical or hydraulic linkage that allows the driver to engage or disengage the clutch as required.

The running engine imparts a rotary motion (or torque) to the flywheel by means of the crankshaft. To set the car in motion, this turning force (torque) must be transferred to the transmission shaft. This transfer is accomplished through the friction disc that is pressed and held against the turning flywheel until it turns with the flywheel. The turning disc, which is splined to the transmission input shaft, transfers the rotary motion (engine torque) of the flywheel through the clutch assembly and on to the transmission.

When the driver's foot is off the clutch pedal, the clutch is engaged and the clutch disc is tightly pressed between the flywheel and the pressure plate. The clutch disc is held against the turning flywheel by spring pressure in the pressure plate assembly. When the driver's foot depresses the clutch pedal, a release bearing (a part of the operating linkage) moves forward against clutch-release levers or "fingers" in the pressure plate. This movement retracts the pressure plate unit, compressing its springs. When spring pressure is removed, the clutch disc is free to turn independently of the revolving flywheel and soon coasts to a stop between the pressure-plate unit and the flywheel. When the driver releases the clutch pedal, the release bearing moves back, causing the release levers to slacken their leverage on the pressure plate. The pressure-plate springs once again force the pressure plate unit to sandwich the disc against the flywheel.

This system is simple but effective. With foot pressure, the driver can regulate the rate of engagement of the clutch slowly enough to apply the clutch smoothly and evenly.

Currently, there are two types of clutch pressure-plate assemblies used in automobiles. They are the coil-spring and the diaphragm-spring types. Their basic function, however, is the same.

The pressure plate assembly is composed of one or more springs, a pressure-plate unit, release fingers or levers, and a cover. The parts are assembled inside the cover, which is attached by bolts to the flywheel. The assembly rotates with the flywheel.

When the clutch is engaged, the pressure springs push the pressure-plate unit forward, forcing the clutch disc firmly against the flywheel. These springs must be strong enough to

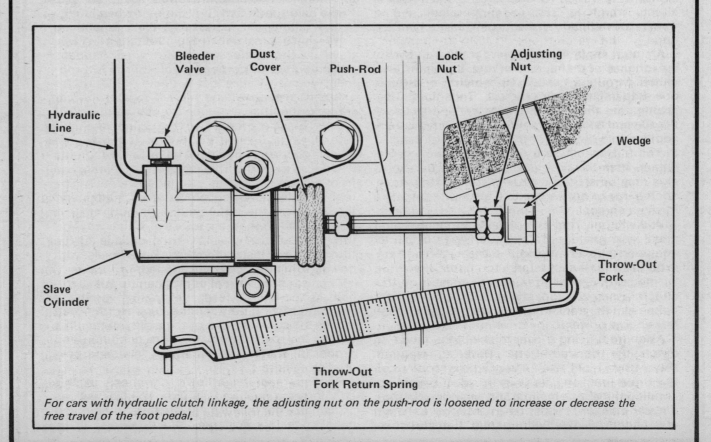

For cars with hydraulic clutch linkage, the adjusting nut on the push-rod is loosened to increase or decrease the free travel of the foot pedal.

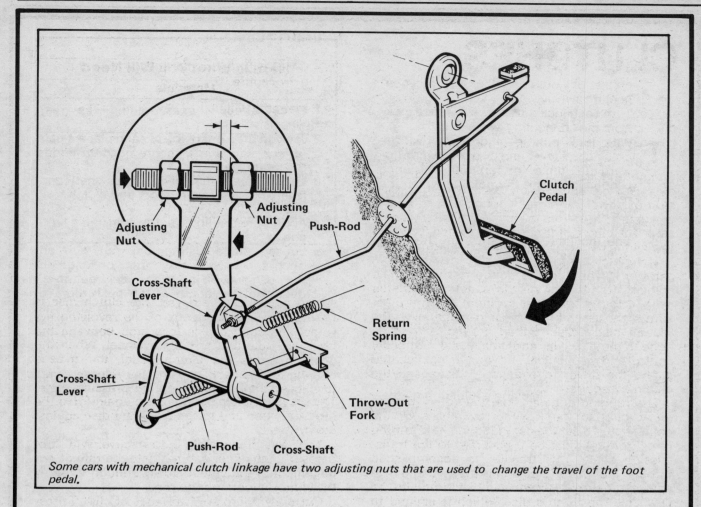

Some cars with mechanical clutch linkage have two adjusting nuts that are used to change the travel of the foot pedal.

Hydraulic Axle Jacks

If you own a truck or a recreation vehicle, a hydraulic axle jack provides easy lifting. Armstrong Beverly Engineering, Ltd. makes two models whose saddles are designed for maximum stability—the Strongarm 1-1/2 ton axle jack, Model A2, and the three-ton Model B2. Both feature all-welded construction for rigidity and protection against side load damage. Model A2 has a low height of 6-3/4 inches and a lift of 4-1/2 inches. The extension screw measures three inches; the handle length is 21-1/4 inches. This jack weighs about 7-1/2 pounds. Model B2 has a low height of 8-3/8 inches, a lift of 5-7/8 inches and an extension screw measuring 3-5/8 inches. Its handle length is 20-11/16 inches. The unit weighs 10 pounds. Each model comes with a two-piece handle.

hold the pressure disc against the flywheel and transmit the torque at all road speeds. The pressure plate requires more than 1000 pounds of spring pressure to hold the clutch disc against the flywheel.

Insufficient spring pressure causes loss of power, since all the engine torque will not be absorbed by the clutch disc. It would be carried to the transmission. This would cause the clutch disc to "slip." A slipping clutch disc will overheat and eventually result in clutch failure.

When the clutch is engaged, the clutch's friction disc is forced to revolve as a unit with the flywheel and the pressure-plate assembly. All torque developed by the engine is transmitted through the clutch friction disc to the transmission input shaft. The torque is picked up by the lined faces of the clutch friction disc and transmitted through its steel hub, which is splined to the transmission input shaft. The clutch-disc facings are made from sheets of long-fiber asbestos and copper wire thread. They are as thick and durable as brake lining.

The hub to which the linings or facings are attached includes a cushioning device and a torsional vibration-dampening unit. This cushioning device between the two facings permits a smooth engagement of the clutch and eliminates clutch chatter. The torsional device, located near the center of the hub, absorbs the torsional vibrations of the crankshaft, preventing them from reaching the transmission. The center of the hub is fitted with splines to transmit engine torque to the transmission input shaft.

The clutch pedal is connected through linkage to a release bearing so that pedal pressure moves the bearing against the release levers to disengage the clutch. The proper clutch-pedal free travel adjustment (at least 1/2 and no more than one inch) is necessary to compensate for wear on the clutch facings and to avoid slippage. Proper clearance must be maintained between the clutch-release bearing and the clutch-re-

lease levers. When wear of the facings has caused the release levers to move back against the release bearing, free play is eliminated and adjustment is necessary. An adjustment of one inch free play at the pedal is recommended.

Improper pedal adjustment causes erratic clutch action, excessive wear, overheating, and clutch failure. The purpose of adjusting the clutch pedal is twofold. It provides full release of the clutch and allows for full wear of the clutch-disc facings. These clearances are required for quick, easy gear shifting without gear clash. There are several methods of adjusting the free travel of the clutch pedal, depending on the make and model of your car and whether it has mechanical or hydraulic-actuated linkage.

Mechanical Linkage

FOR CARS with mechanical linkage, use the following procedure:

1. Raise the hood and locate the clutch pedal push-rod that extends from the fire wall. Follow the pedal rod down to where it connects with the clutch pedal cross-shaft lever.
2. Using pliers, disconnect the clutch pedal return spring at the cross-shaft lever and the frame, or fire wall.
3. Apply penetrating oil to the adjustable linkage.
4. While holding the push-rod, rotate the single, self-locking adjusting nut with an open-end wrench. Movement of the adjusting nut toward the rear of the car will decrease pedal free-travel. Movement toward the front of the car will increase travel. **NOTE:** On some cars, the vehicle will have to be raised to gain access to make the adjustment. Also, some cars will have two adjusting lock nuts. If this is the case, use the following procedure:
   a. Use two open-end wrenches to loos-

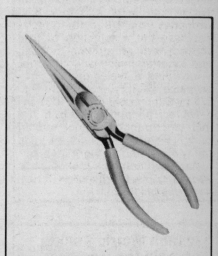

Needle-Nose Pliers Provide Long Reach Into Tight Places

You will need a couple of long, needle-nose pliers, particularly for electrical work. If the pliers have a cutter, so much the better. Vaco Products Company sells needle-nose pliers in a six inch length, No. 88102, and a seven inch length, No. 88103. The pliers feature milled jaws, hand-honed cutters, insulated yellow handles, and ground and polished heads. They also are available with a jaw-opening spring.

Double Cantilever Chest

Some mechanics prefer the cantilever chest over the gable-top type that has a lift-out tray. Rem Line, a division of Model Industries, Inc., makes a heavy-duty model, No. 522, that has trays that spread automatically when opened. This chest is ideal for small tools or parts. It also features a large bottom for bulky tools. The double cantilever chest measures 22 by 10-1/2 by 13 inches.

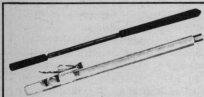

Retrieve Parts From Hard-To-Reach Places

If you drop a small part into the engine compartment or elsewhere, you could be in trouble. A magnetic pickup tool, however, can save the day. Lisle Corporation sells three types of magnetic pickup tools. All have magnets that are shielded to concentrate the magnetic field at the end of the tool. Model 31000 has a telescoping handle that extends the tool from 15 to 27-1/2 inches. An intermediate size, Model 31250, measures 9-1/2 inches. Model 31400 is designed for clipping in your pocket so it is ready for use at all times.

Jack Stands For Transmission Work

Working on transmissions means that you will be spending a lot of time underneath the car. The only safe way is to use jack stands that support the car solidly. It is extremely foolish to rely on a jack alone. The Watervliet Tool Company makes pin-type jack stands in two and three ton capacities that feature all-steel, tubular-welded construction and a lock-in position with heavy-duty steel pins. The two-ton model has four positions. The three-ton model has eight positions in height. The two-ton Model 2TP has a low height of 12 inches and a maximum height of 17 inches. Model 3TP, the three-ton unit, has a low height of 13 inches and a maximum height of 21-3/8 inches.

CLUTCHES

en the lock nuts on either side of a connecting swivel.

  b. Turn each lock nut at least 1/4 inch away from the connecting swivel.

  c. With lock nuts positioned, move the cross-shaft lever and swivel forward (toward the front of the car) until resistance is noticed. This is the point at which the release bearing in the clutch contacts the pressure-plate release levers.

  d. With the cross-shaft lever forward, rotate the lock nut nearest the fire wall until it just contacts the swivel. This should hold the clutch pedal up completely against the pedal stop located in the car.

  e. Back the lock nut off four turns.

  f. With the lock nut at this point, tighten the other lock nut securely against the swivel.

5. Connect the pedal return spring.
6. Using finger pressure only, depress the clutch pedal while using a ruler as a gauge. There should be about 3/4 inch—no less than 1/2 and no more than one inch—of free travel. If it is not within this range, repeat steps 2 through 5.
7. Start the engine.
8. Place the transmission in neutral and set the parking brake.
9. Engage and disengage the clutch several times with the engine running.
10. Recheck the adjustment.
11. Road test the car and make a final check of the adjustment.

CAUTION: If after repeated attempts at adjustment, you cannot bring free-travel within the specified range, it could indicate bent clutch linkage, a worn out disc, or other internal clutch problems. If this is the case, consult a qualified mechanic.

Hydraulic Linkage

FOR CARS with hydraulic linkage, use the following procedure:

1. Place wheel chocks behind the rear wheels.
2. Jack up the front of the car and place a pair of jack stands in a secure position under the frame.
3. Locate the clutch pedal cross-shaft and lever, clutch throw-out fork and clutch fork push-rod.
4. Apply penetrating oil to the adjustable linkage.
5. Loosen the adjusting lock nut with an open-end wrench to shorten or lengthen the push-rod. To increase pedal free travel, decrease the length of the push-rod. To decrease pedal free travel, increase the length of the push-rod.
6. After making the adjustment, retighten the lock nut, taking care not to change the length of the push-rod.
7. Using finger pressure only, depress the clutch pedal while using a ruler as a gauge. There should be about 3/4 inch—no less than 1/2 and no more than one inch—of free travel. If it is not within this range, repeat steps 5 through 7.
8. Lower the car, reversing steps 1 and 2.
9. Start the engine.
10. With the transmission in neutral and the parking brake set, engage and disengage the clutch several times.
11. Recheck the adjustment.
12. Road test the car and make a final check of the adjustment.

CAUTION: If after repeated attempts at adjustment, you cannot bring free-travel within the specified range, it could indicate bent clutch linkage, a worn out disc, or other internal clutch problems. If this is the case, consult a qualified mechanic.

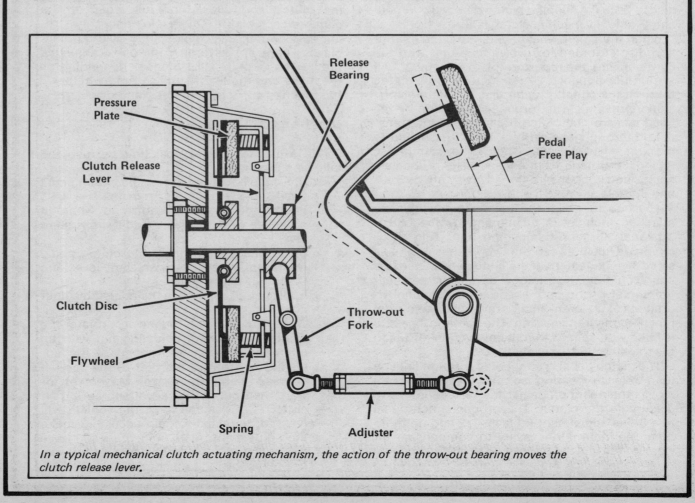

In a typical mechanical clutch actuating mechanism, the action of the throw-out bearing moves the clutch release lever.

STANDARD TRANSMISSION

Here Is What You Will Need

Materials
- Clean Wiping Cloths
- Lithium Grease

Tools
- Wheel Chocks
- Jack and Jack Stands
- 9/16 Inch Open-End Wrench
- 1/2 Inch Open-End Wrench

IN THE section on Clutches, we explained how the powerful rotating force of the engine is transmitted through the clutch assembly to the input shaft of the transmission. This force, called torque, has the power to turn one or more shafts to accomplish useful work. In your car, this useful work is, of course, the application of engine power to turn, or drive, the rear or drive wheels. In this and remaining sections to this chapter, any reference to torque means the application of engine power through shafts and gears to turn a car's drive wheels in a forward or reverse rotation.

Despite the engineering marvel represented by your engine, it must have help to supply the necessary torque to meet complex variations in speed and constant changes in road and load conditions.

The car's engine is helped in one way by units or assemblies that are capable of multiplying engine torque. One such unit is the standard transmission. By applying initial torque to a gear set or a combination of gears, the initial torque is multiplied. The driver is in control of this torque multiplication when gear ratios are activated by using the clutch and gear selector controls.

Most transmissions have at least three forward gear ratios and one reverse. Some sports or high-performance cars, as well as some with small engines, have four- or five-speed transmissions.

Transmissions are equipped with various devices to encourage longer life and quieter operation. One such device is the synchromesh which allows all forward gears to be of constant mesh design to provide smooth gear selection without clashing or grinding.

There are other provisions built into the standard transmission as well as the basic functions of gear selection:

NEUTRAL. The neutral gear position is the point at which the torque connection between the engaged clutch and the transmission is interrupted. This allows the engine to run with the clutch engaged and without moving the drive wheels.

LOW OR FIRST-SPEED GEAR. When low or first speed is required, the engine will run at a high rpm while the car moves very slowly. The rear wheels turn at a slower speed but with increased power. The torque multiplication at this time is approximately 3 to 1. This ratio means that three engine revolutions are required

Illuminated Tachometer

If you have a car with a standard transmission, a tachometer is a virtual necessity for efficient driving. It tells you the exact rpm of your engine so that you can shift to keep the engine in the most efficient range. It can also help you avoid costly engine damage that can be caused by running your engine at an rpm that is over its "red line." Stewart-Warner Corp. markets a Model 82607 tachometer that has a three inch, illuminated European face dial. It reads from 0 to 8000 rpm and has a 250-degree sweep. The black case blends with most automobile interiors.

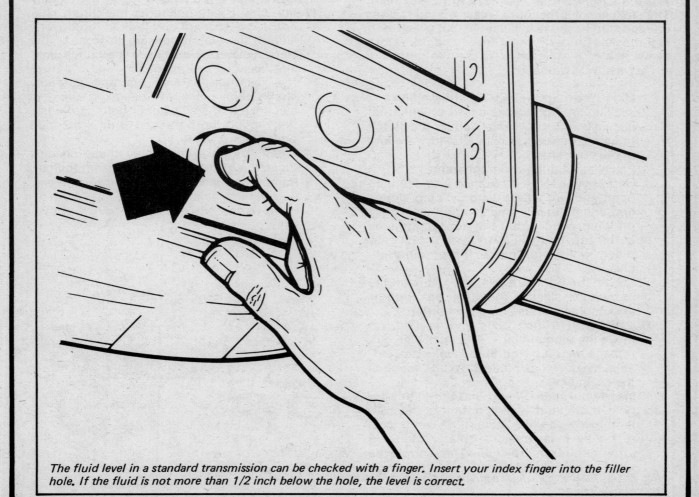

The fluid level in a standard transmission can be checked with a finger. Insert your index finger into the filler hole. If the fluid is not more than 1/2 inch below the hole, the level is correct.

Replacement Transmission Oil Pan Incorporates Cooler

While most transmission oil coolers are mounted on the radiator or air conditioning condenser at the front of the car, Integrity Transmission Koolers Inc.'s product is actually a replacement transmission oil pan with a built-in cooling feature. The bottom of the pan contains a series of aluminum tubes that are open at each side of the pan to allow a flow of air. Inside each cooling tube is a twisted steel strap that creates turbulence within the tube and allows the cool air to draw more heat from the fluid before escaping from the pan. Integrity oil coolers are available for most American-made cars and trucks.

Gear Oil Comes In Squeeze Bottle For Easy Application

When lubricating steering boxes, manual transmissions and differentials, it sometimes is difficult to add oil because the parts are in cramped places. Alemite CD-2 high performance gear oil made by Stewart-Warner Corp. comes in a package that makes it easy to use. The SAE 90 gear oil is available in a squeeze bottle with a nozzle. It also has a see-through "window," allowing you to measure accurately the amount of oil you are dispensing. Each bottle holds 32 ounces.

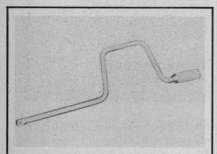

Speeder Handle From S-K Tools

When installing or removing a transmission, you will encounter situations where a regular wrench will not have enough clearance. A speeder handle by S-K Tools, a division of Dresser Industries, Inc., can be used to reach into small spaces for the removal or installation of bolts quickly. S-K Tools' Model 45181 is 16-1/2 inches long and 3/8 inch in diameter. It handles 3/8 inch drive sockets.

STANDARD TRANSMISSION

for each revolution of the transmission output shaft.

INTERMEDIATE GEAR. When the operator selects an intermediate gear position, torque multiplication is reduced to approximately 2 to 1.

HIGH GEAR. When the operator shifts to high gear, the speed of the output shaft of the transmission is the same as engine speed and there is no increase in torque. Therefore, the high gear ratio is 1 to 1 and is called direct drive.

REVERSE GEAR. When the operator shifts to reverse gear, the output shaft of the transmission reverses its rotation, which causes the drive wheels to turn in reverse. The approximate reverse gear ratio is 3 to 1.

You should now see how the gears in the transmission may be used to allow the engine to turn at higher speeds than the output and drive shafts and, at the same time, deliver more power. In this way, the vehicle may start smoothly and slowly without stalling the engine. Although transmissions vary in construction, most produce a gear ratio of approximately 3 to 1 for low gear and 1 to 1 for high gear.

The means of shifting the standard transmission are, for the most part, much the same. The shift pattern, however, is not always the same. Foreign-made vehicles often vary the shift pattern to suit the type of transmission used.

The standard transmission is very durable. If it is not mistreated, it should last as long as any other part of the drive mechanism.

Checking The Transmission

LET US now get acquainted with the underside of the transmission and learn where various points of preventive maintenance are located. There are so few that it is easy to forget them. The following procedure may sound rather unimportant because it is simple, but every road racer insists on performing these checks before every race.

This is how to proceed:

1. Block the rear wheels with wheel chocks.
2. Jack up the front of the car to a height that allows you to crawl safely under the clutch housing, transmission and the forward end of the drive shaft.
3. Place jack stands under the frame.
4. Gather your tools (9/16 inch and 1/2 inch open-end wrenches), some wiping cloths, and some lithium grease, and place them on the ground just at the door hinge area of the car. This will keep them within easy reach while you make these important checks.
5. Locate the lubricant filler plug. It is on the passenger side of the gear box and is about three inches above the bottom.
6. Using a 9/16 inch open end wrench, remove the plug. If fluid starts to dribble out, replace the plug; the fluid level is acceptable. If it does not, place the plug on one of the wiping rags.
7. Insert your index finger into the filler plug hole. If the fluid level is not more than 1/2 inch below the filler hole, the level is correct. Any measurement greater than 1/2 inch requires more fluid. This should be filled by a service station.
8. Replace the lubricant filler plug, reversing step 6.

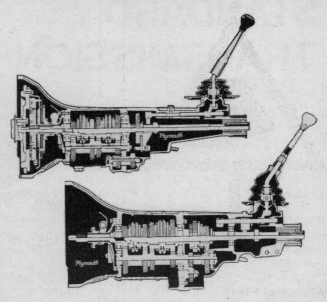

Diagrams show the difference in components of four-speed (top) and five-speed manual transmissions.

9. Look at the other side of the transmission. If it is a side shifter, the linkage arms will be located there. Take a wiping cloth and clean accumulated dirt off the shifter arms.
10. Apply a little lithium grease to each connection where linkage is fastened to the transmission.
11. Clean your hands and the underside of the transmission.
12. Move to the rear of the transmission. Reach up with both hands and grasp the shaft that extends from the transmission. Using reasonable pressure, try to move the shaft up and down. If you hear a metallic sound or if the shaft gives under pressure, the front universal joint must be replaced. Refer to the section on Drive Shaft And U-Joints in this chapter.
13. The final check concerns the clutch linkage. Move forward and look at the driver's side of the clutch housing in front of the transmission. You will see the clutch linkage fastened to the housing and a part of the car frame. Reach up and carefully shake each piece of linkage. If there is evidence that any fastener bolts are loose, they should be tightened with a 1/2 inch open-end wrench.
14. When you have completed these checks, move the tools out and away from the car.
15. Remove the jack stands and lower the car. Remove the jack.
16. Remove the wheel chocks from the rear wheels.
17. Test drive the car.

Manual five-speed transmission and engine from an imported sports car.

Warning Flares

At one time, the U.S. Department of Transportation approved the twin, round reflectors with red flags as the best type of road hazard warning for disabled vehicles. But that has changed since the introduction of the triangular reflector. One is the Model 7500 warning flare, made by Pathfinder Auto Lamp Co., that can provide a warning in excess of 1/2 mile. The unit folds compactly in a plastic case. Three are sold as a set.

Highway Emergency Kit

Having a breakdown on the highway can be dangerous, especially at night. Carter Hall, Inc. makes an illuminated highway emergency kit, No. 2000, that can help keep you out of trouble and even get you going again. It includes a Day-Glo orange-colored carrying case that completely lights up. Its flashing light has a bulb that lasts for 12,000 hours. The unit plugs in to your auto's cigarette lighter with a 25-foot cord. Inside the case, there also is a set of eight-foot-long jumper cables, a seven-by-10-inch SOS sign that attaches to the back of the case, a tire inflator that provides 25 pounds of pressure to a flat tire, and a gas siphon pump. It also contains a flashlight and first aid book with instructions.

Transmissions Can Overheat

When you become stuck in snow or mud, do not continually shift from drive to reverse for long periods of time. Transmissions can overheat very easily, and expensive damage will result. A tow truck service call is likely to be much cheaper than a transmission overhaul.

Protect Your Fender From Scratches

Whenever you are doing engine work, you should protect your fender from scratches by using a fender protective cover such as that sold by TRW, Inc. The fender protective cover, No. 671650, is 36 by 27 inches, vinyl-covered and has a rubber backing to prevent slipping and sliding. It gives body and fenders protection against dirt, oil, grease, grime, scratches from belt buckles and tools. It also has a tool-holder ridge.

PUSH-STARTING

IF YOUR standard transmission car will not start because of a weak battery and you do not have a pair of jumper cables, push-starting is an alternative. Keep in mind that an alternator-equipped car with a dead battery cannot be push-started since the alternator must have some power from the battery to create enough voltage to fire the spark plugs.

To determine whether your battery is completely dead or merely low, turn on the headlights. If the headlights do not light, you probably have a dead battery and push-starting will not work. You will have to have your battery jumped or call a service truck. If, on the other hand, the lights are bright, try cranking the engine. If the lights remain bright but the starter does not engage, there is something wrong that neither push-starting nor jump-starting will solve. If this is the case, do not hesitate to contact a reputable mechanic.

If you have determined, through this simple test, that your battery is not dead but very low, you can push-start the car. This procedure is not recommended because it can be a dangerous operation. If, however, you have no choice, here is how to push-start your car:

1. Before you begin, make sure that the rear bumper on your car and the front bumper

on the car that will be pushing yours line up. Getting the rear of your car or the front of the other car smashed could be the most expensive start you ever received. **NOTE:** Another way to keep damage to a minimum is to place a heavy pad or even an old tire between the two cars. A pad can be secured by placing one end in the trunk and then closing the trunk. A tire would have to be secured with rope or wire.
2. Once the two cars are lined up, shift the transmission into second gear and turn the ignition switch to the On position.
3. Depress the clutch and have the other person begin pushing your car with his or her car. While you are being pushed, keep an eye out for other cars and pedestrians. You can become so engrossed in attempting to start your car that you could run into another motorist or a pedestrian. **CAUTION:** If your car is equipped with power steering or power brakes, it will take considerable effort to operate these items until the engine has been started.
4. When you reach a speed of about 10 miles per hour, have the person pushing your car slow his or her car down and back off. Let out your car's clutch to engage the engine. When you do this, your car will slow down considerably due to the drag that the engine will cause. Your engine should have started. If not, you could repeat the operation. If it still does not start, it is best to call a service truck.

To avoid such problems, it would be wise to keep a set of jumper cables in your vehicle for such emergencies.

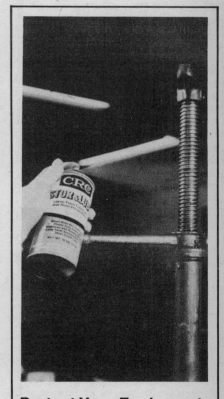

Protect Your Equipment

As you accumulate a quantity of automotive tools and equipment, you will find that there are certain items you use only once in a while. It is upsetting to take one of these items out of storage and find that it has become corroded or rusted. To protect your expensive equipment, you should coat it with a lubricant. Stor and Lube, a product made by CRC Chemicals, Inc., is a long-term lubricant and rust preventive. You can use it on brackets, cables, battery terminals, connectors, trailer hitches, stored engines, tools and other metal parts.

Automatic Transmission Fluids For Specific Vehicles

If you look at the automatic transmission dipstick on your General Motors car, you will notice that it says use Dexron Transmission Fluid. Wolf's Head Oil Refining Co. manufactures Dexron II, which is a new high-quality oil blended to provide an extremely high viscosity index, exceptional film strength and maximum resistance to oxidation and corrosion. It also contains a red dye to aid in detecting leaks. The product, approved by General Motors, is available in one and four quart cans. If your car is a Ford, Lincoln or Mercury, you will probably find that the automatic transmission fluid recommended is Type F. Wolf's Head also makes this transmission fluid, which meets Ford specification M2C33F. It also contains the red dye and is available in one and four quart cans.

Transmission Cooler Has Cross-Flow Design

If you travel in very hot climates or if you tow a trailer, you could save some wear and tear on your car's transmission by getting an auxiliary transmission oil cooler. Auxiliary coolers made by the Mesa Corporation feature four to six stacks of cooling plates in each unit. The number of plates varies according to cooler size. After hot oil enters the cooler's inlet tube, it must make four passes back and forth to each of the stack's cooling plates — 24 to 48 passes — before returning to the transmission. The coolers also feature wide, thin fins and aluminum construction. Each comes with mounting hardware, high-temperature hose, hose clamps and installation instructions.

AUTOMATIC TRANSMISSION

AN AUTOMATIC transmission works in conjunction with a torque converter to provide a faultless flow of power from a car's engine to its drive wheels. The automatic transmission, unlike the purely mechanical standard transmission, is driven by fluid power. The torque converter, a self-contained unit, replaces the clutch used with a standard transmission. It has the capability to multiply the torque developed by the engine, a feature not found in the conventional clutch. The torque converter couples and uncouples the force of the engine to the transmission and driveline. It does this by means of fluid or hydraulic pressure.

Because the automatic transmission reacts to accelerator pressure to increase or decrease the torque output of the engine, the need for the clutch pedal is eliminated. Once the transmission is placed in a gear position, the driver merely has to increase the engine speed to transmit variable force — through the operation of the converter — to the transmission. When the driver releases the accelerator pedal to slow the engine, the converter automatically will disconnect the power of the engine to the transmission.

With reasonable care, an automatic transmission will remain in sound condition for the useful life of a car. Since it is a hydraulically controlled unit, the maintenance required to keep the transmission in good working order is fairly simple. The fluid in the transmission is subject to contamination and must be changed at reasonable intervals.

Other maintenance chores include fluid level checks, the tightening of fittings that become loose due to normal vibration and road shock, and possibly a vacuum unit change due to diaphragm failure. The following procedures outline the steps to maintain an automatic transmission.

To check fluid level and condition, follow these steps:

1. Park the car on a level surface.
2. With the engine running at normal operating temperature (about 15 to 20 minutes), set the parking brake and place the selector lever in the park or neutral position.
3. Raise the hood and locate the transmission dipstick. It usually can be found at or near the rear of the engine on the passenger side of the vehicle.

Here Is What You Will Need

Materials
- Clean, Lint-Free Cloths
- Funnel
- Transmission Fluid
- Drain Pan
- Solvent such as Kerosene or Fuel Oil
- Transmission Filter and Gasket

Tools
- Wheel Chocks
- Jack and Jack Stands
- Socket Wrench and Short Extension
- 3/8 Inch Drive Ratchet Wrench
- Scraper
- Screwdriver
- Torque Wrench

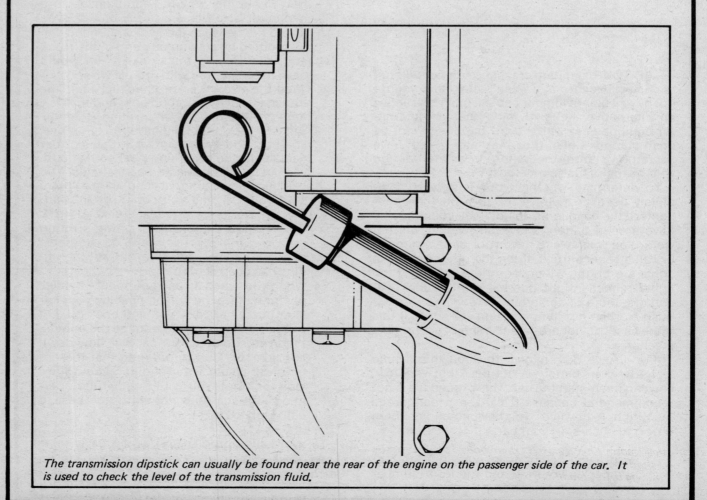

The transmission dipstick can usually be found near the rear of the engine on the passenger side of the car. It is used to check the level of the transmission fluid.

4. Remove the dipstick and wipe the end with a clean lint-free cloth.
5. Reinsert the dipstick completely and remove it a second time.
6. Check the fluid level on the dipstick markings. The correct fluid level should be between the Add One Pint or Low (L) and Full (F) marks on the dipstick. If it is not, use a funnel and refill the transmission with the correct type of fluid.
7. Reinsert the dipstick.
8. Close the hood and shut off the engine.

NOTE: When checking the transmission fluid, it also is important to observe its condition. If the fluid is discolored and has a strong "burned" odor, it could be an indication of internal damage or wear. If water has collected in the transmission, the fluid will have a milky appearance. If either of these conditions are present, consult a qualified mechanic immediately.

To change the transmission fluid and filter, follow these steps: **NOTE:** Transmission fluid should be at normal operating temperature to insure complete draining. This can be accomplished by driving the vehicle for 15 to 20 minutes after the engine is warmed up.

1. Place wheel chocks behind the rear wheels and engage the parking brake.
2. Jack up the front of the vehicle.
3. Place a pair of jack stands in a secure position under the frame.
4. Position a drain pan under the transmission and carefully loosen—do not remove—the transmission pan attaching bolts. You will need a socket wrench, a short extension and 3/8 inch drive ratchet wrench.

   CAUTION: Be extremely careful while draining transmission fluid. Hot transmission fluid can cause serious burns.
5. With one hand, hold up the transmission

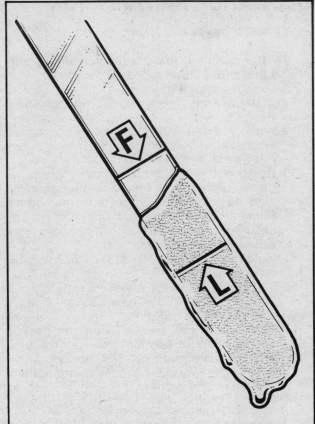

If the transmission fluid covers the portion of the dipstick between the L (Low) and F (Full) markings, the level is correct.

pan. With the other hand, carefully remove all of the transmission pan bolts except those holding the front of the pan to the transmission case.
6. Carefully lower the rear portion of the pan and allow the fluid to drain into the drain pan.

Automatic Transmission Oil Coolers For The Do-It-Yourselfer

Borg-Warner Corporation sells three sizes of automatic transmission oil coolers to fit all vehicles. The coolers feature a patented embossed-plate design engineered to make the oil passage and the cooling surface one and the same. The oil is spread across each plate and cooled by the air flow against the plate. This design eliminates the delicate fins crimped to a tube that many other oil coolers have. Each cooler comes with hose, clamps, mounting brackets and fasteners.

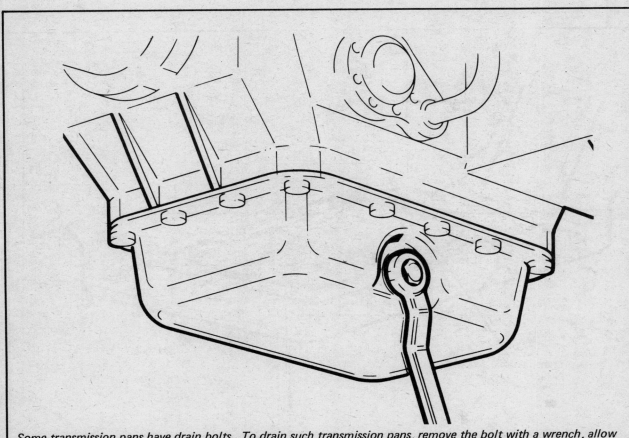

Some transmission pans have drain bolts. To drain such transmission pans, remove the bolt with a wrench, allow the fluid to run out, wipe the bolt clean and replace it. Most transmission pans are drained by removing the attaching bolts around the pan.

Automatic Transmission Cleaner

If you have an older automatic transmission, you may find it beneficial to use Trans Kleen. Made by Siloo, Inc., it is designed to smooth out automatic transmissions, eliminate creepage and between-speeds lurching. It is also formulated to prevent formation of gums, sludge or corrosion.

TRANSMISSION, DIFFERENTIAL AND REAR AXLE

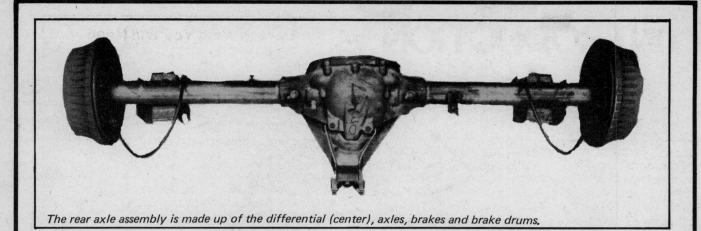

The rear axle assembly is made up of the differential (center), axles, brakes and brake drums.

suddenly swerve to one side, then the other. These maneuvers throw additional side loads on the wheel bearings and the howl should get louder. Or better yet, have someone ride in the rear seat to listen on both sides for the noise while you drive.

There is a possibility that the bad bearing could be one of the differential side bearings or the pinion bearing in the nose of the axle's center section. However, bearing trouble in the differential is much less likely than in the wheel bearings.

There are other possible axle troubles that are easy to determine. A broken axle shaft is one: the car will not move. A bad grease seal is another: there will be annoying oil spots everywhere you park the car. The grease seals are located at the wheel bearings on the outer ends of the axles. The wheel bearing seals are subjected to many stress forces under driving loads. Rear axle trouble will not be hidden for very long. It will get progressively worse and easier to locate.

With a few special tools, you can safely do some rear axle work. The simplest job is to pull an axle shaft and wheel bearing. To replace a broken shaft requires some patience and expertise. But you can pull the shafts, bearings and seals on most cars with a slide hammer axle puller and ordinary hand tools.

Rear Axle Removal

IF YOU have isolated the noise or other fault and have determined that the rear axle must be removed, follow this procedure:

1. Park the car on a clean, level surface.
2. Block the front wheels with wheel chocks to prevent the car from rolling.
3. Use a screwdriver or the pointed end of the jack handle to remove the wheel cover. Loosen the lug nuts of the wheel on the side of the axle you will be working on with a lug nut wrench.
4. Jack up the rear end of the car and support it under the rear axle housing with a pair of jack stands.
5. Remove the wheel lug nuts and the wheel.
6. Remove the brake drum. If resistance is encountered as you try to remove the drum, rotate the drum while pulling.
7. Using a ratchet, sockets and extension, remove the four axle retainer-to-brake-backing plate nuts from the bearing retainer. An access hole is provided in the axle flange for this purpose.
8. Separate the bearing retainer from the brake backing plate. This will prevent the backing plate and brake assembly from being disturbed during axle removal.
9. Attach a slide hammer axle puller to the

axle flange and, with a few sharp blows, the axle retainer, axle and bearing assembly should come free of the axle housing.
10. Remove the puller from the axle flange.
11. Carefully remove the axle assembly from the housing.
12. After the axle shaft and bearing have been removed, inspect them for wear, corrosion and cracks. You can tell a bad bearing very easily. It will feel rough—that is, the outer race will be loose on the balls. Sometimes, the balls are pitted and galled, or the central ball cage may be loose. If you have any doubts about the condition of the bearing, it should be replaced. It does, however, require a special tool and, sometimes, a press to remove the bearing from the axle shaft and replace it. You will probably have to have this job performed at an auto parts store that has a machine shop.
13. If you must merely replace an outer grease seal on the bearing, this can be done quite easily without removing the bearing from the shaft. There are different types and designs of seals, but their function is the same. Usually, seals can be pried off with a screwdriver or any sharp pointed tool. Most can be installed without special tools. **NOTE:** Use reasonable care and always install the seal with the open edge or flange facing the lubricant.
14. Clean and lightly lubricate the axle splines with chassis grease.

Rear Axle Installation

YOU ARE now ready to replace the axle shaft. Follow this procedure:

1. Carefully insert and rotate the axle shaft assembly into the axle housing until you feel the axle splines striking the differential side gear. Continue to carefully rotate and push the axle inward so that the axle splines engage the internal splines of the gear.
2. Once the axle is seated in the splines of the differential gear, continue to push inward until the axle bearing is seated firmly into the axle housing.
3. Reinstall the bearing retainer onto the brake backing plate at the axle housing.
4. Install the retainer nuts, reversing step 7 in the Rear Axle Removal procedure.
5. Install the brake drum.
6. Replace the wheel, and finger-tighten the lug nuts.
7. Remove the jack stands and lower the car, reversing steps 2 through 4 of the Rear Axle Removal procedure.
8. Road test the car.

Economy Hydraulic Service Jack

The home mechanic does not really need an expensive service jack since he will only give it limited use. The Watco Model MS-15 economy service jack made by Watervliet Tool Co. fits into the do-it-yourself category. It features all-welded, steel frame construction with a removable handle. The jack has a 1-1/2 ton capacity, a low saddle point of five inches and a high saddle point of 20 inches. Saddle diameter is 4-1/2 inches, and the unit is 12-1/2 inches wide at the widest point. The entire chassis is 28-5/8 inches long; handle length is 43 inches.

Safe Penetrating Fluid

Most types of penetrating oils are very effective for loosening stuck parts, but with some you may run the risk of damaging your car's finish. Unival Corp. sells Du-Ol, a product formulated to dissolve rust and corrosion but not to harm rubber or plastic. It is nonflammable, contains no Freon or petroleum distillates and is nontoxic. It comes in four and 13 ounce aerosol cans and a 16 ounce oiler-type can. A money-back guarantee is part of the deal.

INTRODUCTION

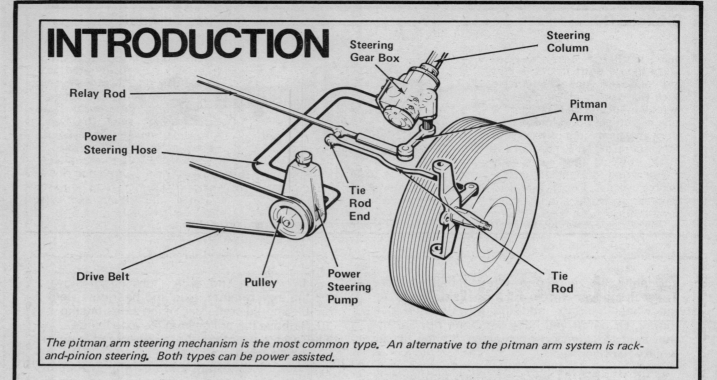

The pitman arm steering mechanism is the most common type. An alternative to the pitman arm system is rack-and-pinion steering. Both types can be power assisted.

THE DEVELOPMENT of the modern automobile embodies many engineering refinements. When the first automobile rolled out onto the road, it was little more than a horseless carriage. As speed capability increased, attention to steering and suspension became very important.

The steering characteristics of our cars can be traced back to the engineering efforts of men like Rudolph Ackerman. He proved that the inside wheel of a car will always follow a sharper angle than the outside wheel in a turn, with the result that each wheel follows the circumference of a correct circle. The inside wheel, then, by necessity, will always track a smaller circle than the outside wheel. This principle describes only one of many contributions to the steering and suspension geometry of cars.

It would seem that in more than 70 years of research and development, a standard would have been set so that at least the design of suspensions would have become the same on all cars. This, however, is not the case because there still is a difference of opinion on the best way to apply the principle.

There is a similarity, in that front wheels are suspended independently of each other, but the method may involve the use of either coil springs or torsion bars. There are, however, at least four ways in which rear wheels may be suspended, and the method may involve the use of either coil springs or leaf springs.

These suspension differences are necessary and important in their application because they affect the ride, comfort and ease of handling built into the car. To satisfy all the performance requirements we expect, suspension and steering must work together so that the car will handle easily, steer straight, turn corners without swaying, absorb road shock, use all the torque generated by the engine, and stand the stresses imposed by the brake system. All this must be accomplished smoothly, quietly and without imposing on the comfort of the driver and passengers.

When you suspect that your steering or suspension systems are performing at less than peak efficiency, it is time to look for telltale signs that indicate which components have become worn.

In this chapter, we will discuss methods and procedures that will allow you, in many cases, to diagnose and subsequently make repairs to restore all the ride and handling characteristics designed into your car.

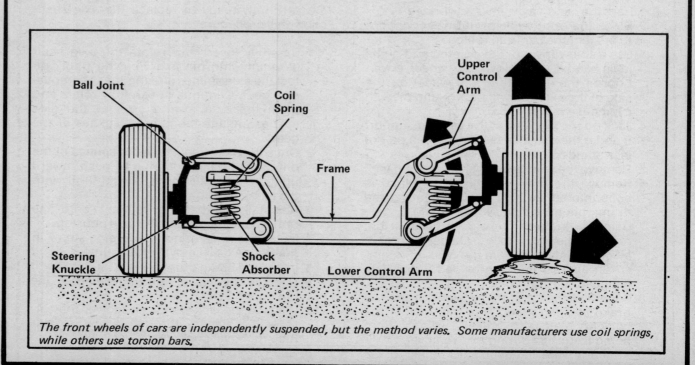

The front wheels of cars are independently suspended, but the method varies. Some manufacturers use coil springs, while others use torsion bars.

STEERING AND SUSPENSION

Dripless Oil

Oiling is often a messy task because the oil drips from the part you lubricate. American Grease Stick Co. has an all-purpose oil, called American Dripless Oil, that runs in but will not drip out. The product will not gum or harden at -20°F or drip at 200°F. You can use it to correct and seal body squeaks, and to lubricate hinges, flexible cables, door handles, generators, starters and stuck throttle controls. It also loosens

rusty parts and drys wet surfaces. The oil comes in 3.4 ounce squeeze cans and four ounce aerosol cans.

Gear Oil Additive

Bardahl Manufacturing Corporation offers a concentrated gear oil additive that is an extreme pressure lubricant for standard transmissions, differentials and power steering units. The manufacturer recommends that you use the gear oil additive in place of an equal amount of regular lubricant to help reduce differential noise, provide easier shifting, reduce power steering squeal and quiet transmission noise.

Ball Joint Separator

Rinck-McIlwaine, Inc. offers a ball joint separator, Model 35-B, that is designed to separate ball joints from steering knuckles. It features a tapered wedge with a jaw opening of 15/16 inch that slides between the ball joint and the steering knuckle. The tool is designed to separate the two members quickly with a few sharp hammer blows. Overall length is 11-7/8 inches.

BALL JOINTS

Here Is What You Will Need
Materials
- Wedge (Bar Stock Steel Approximately 1/4 by 2 by 5-1/2 Inches)
Tools
- Wheel Chocks
- Screw-Type or Scissors Jack
- Jack

THE STEERING knuckle at each front wheel is attached to two suspension components. The one at the top is the upper control arm. The one at the bottom is the lower control arm. Both the upper and the lower control arms are joined to the steering knuckle by ball joints.

Ball joints, which can be compared to a knee joint in a human and are often called ball-and-socket joints. The ball of the joint has a tapered shank that passes through a matching taper in the steering knuckle. The tapered shank is held firmly in the steering knuckle by a castle nut and cotter pin assembly that is threaded onto the portion of the tapered shank that sticks through the opening in the steering knuckle.

There are two basic types of ball joints. One is the load-carrying joint; the other is the "follower," or helper, type joint.

A load-carrying joint is a ball joint designed to support and carry more of the vehicle's weight. You can tell which is the load-carrying ball joint by examining the location of the coil spring. If the coil spring is installed between the upper and the lower control arms, the lower ball joint is the load-carrying one. If the coil spring is installed between the upper control arm and a frame member, the upper ball joint is the load-carrying ball joint. Generally, the load-carrying joint is subject to more wear than a follower ball joint.

A follower ball joint is a nonload-carrying joint. Usually, it will have a steel spring inside so the ball joint forms a snug connection between the steering knuckle and the control arm.

Hand Cleaner Has Guarantee

DL Skin Care Products, Inc. markets DL Blue Label Hand Cleaner with a 12-month shelf-life guarantee. The product can be used with or without water.

Fire Extinguisher In Deluxe Case

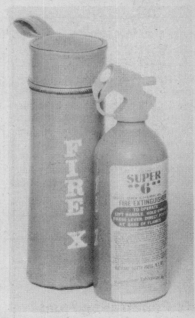

Carter Hall, Inc. sells a fire extinguisher that is stored in its own attractive case. The Model FCE-300 extinguisher has a case made of high-gloss red vinyl with a zipper top closure, making it easy to store in your vehicle. The UL-approved fire extinguisher can be used for grease, oil, gasoline and electrical fires. It has a classification of 2 B:C and weighs one pound, 11 ounces.

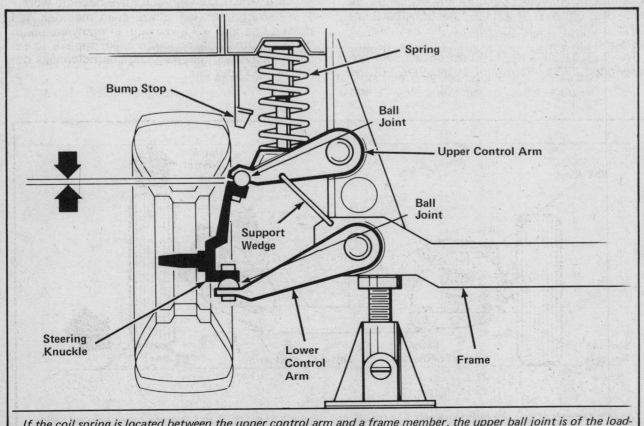

If the coil spring is located between the upper control arm and a frame member, the upper ball joint is of the load-carrying type. Tests for excessive play are made by wiggling the wheel to check for lateral movement.

Adjustable Pliers/Wrench

For sheer gripping strength, nothing beats an adjustable pliers/wrench. Sometimes called parallel jaw pliers, these heavy-duty pliers adjust for items of various sizes. The jaws lock firmly on the work when closed. A 10-inch model, such as the Automark Model 52209, made by the Automark Division of Wells Manufacturing Corporation, is good for heavy-duty work. Even though the jaws lock tightly on a part, they can be unlocked in an instant with a quick-release lever.

All-Purpose Vacuum Cleaner

Keeping your garage floor clean is easier if you have a vacuum cleaner designed for heavy-duty use. It eliminates all the airborne dust that is a result of sweeping, and you can use it to clean off shop benches as well. A five gallon size, such as Black and Decker Manufacturing Company's No. 6600, is ideal for the home mechanic. It features a 100 cubic feet per minute air flow, a one horsepower motor and a 2-1/2 inch hose connection. A 1-1/2 inch hose plus an assortment of accessories also can be used with this unit. The vacuum cleaner is only recommended for dry pickup chores.

Medium Weight Lubricant

LPS Research Laboratories, Inc. makes a medium weight lubricant, LPS 2, that you can use to loosen and lubricate steering and throttle linkages, protect rebuilt engines and dry out ignition systems. It also acts as a good penetrating fluid to free rusty and frozen parts. It is harmless to rubber, plastics, paint or finishes.

A Nut Buster Comes In Handy For Front End Work

Fasteners on a suspension system tend to be very difficult to loosen after many years of use. When a nut becomes stuck so tight that you cannot turn it with a wrench, you may have to cut it with a device such as the Model 1858 Nut Buster from Hastings Manufacturing Co. This tool can be used to remove corroded, frozen or rusted nuts up to 3/4 inch across flats. A few turns with any 3/4 inch hand wrench cut the nuts for easy removal. It splits frozen, rusted nuts up to 13/16 inch.

Telescopic Inspection Mirrors

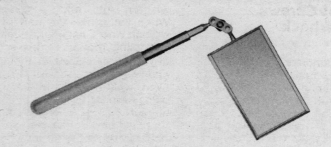

Inspection mirrors give you a fast and accurate visual inspection of hidden areas. K-D Manufacturing Co. offers telescopic, rectangular and round inspection mirrors. The mirrors feature double ball-joint links that swivel 360 degrees. The mirrors are replaceable. Nonrotating inner hex rods prevent mirrors from swinging out of alignment when in use. The Model 2108 rectangular inspection mirror measures 2-1/8 by 2-1/2 inches. Overall length is 11-1/4 inches, but it extends to 15-1/4 inches. Model 2109 is a round mirror, measuring 2-1/4 inches in diameter. Overall length is 10 inches, but it extends to 14 inches.

BALL JOINTS

Because it bears much of the vehicle weight, the load-carrying joint is designed to have no play. The follower joint, however, does have some visible play.

Checking Ball Joints

WHILE REPLACING ball joints is not a task for the do-it-yourselfer, it is possible for the home mechanic to inspect ball joints for wear and to determine if they need replacement. If the car swerves badly under braking or if clunking noises are heard in the front end of the car, the ball joints may need to be replaced.

Here is how to check lower load-carrying ball joints:

1. Place wheel chocks behind the rear wheels.
2. Place a screw-type or scissors jack under a lower control arm and jack up the car until the wheel is about two inches off the ground.
3. Have someone observe the lower load-carrying ball joint while you grasp the tire at the top and the bottom and wiggle it back and forth. Any side or lateral movement or play should be visible at the ball joint.
4. If there is play in the ball joint, consult a mechanic to determine if the ball joint requires replacement.
5. Lower the wheel to the ground and remove the jack.
6. Check the lower load-carrying ball joint on the other wheel by repeating steps 2 and 3.

7. Lower the wheel to the ground and remove the jack. Remove the wheel chocks.

To check the upper load-carrying ball joints for wear, use the following procedure:

1. Grasp the front bumper and, with a lifting motion, shift the weight of the car toward the rear. You will be able to raise the car approximately 1-1/2 inches in this manner. The car will remain in this position until downward pressure is exerted.
2. Place a wedge (bar stock steel approximately 1/4 x 2 by 5-1/2 inches) firmly between the upper control arm and the chassis on both sides of the car.
   CAUTION: Working around the springs can be dangerous, so be certain the wedges are properly positioned to avoid injury.
3. Block the back of the rear wheels with wheel chocks.
4. Jack up the front end of the car under the chassis — not under the lower control arms — until the wheels are two inches off the ground.
5. Shake each wheel vigorously at the top only to be certain that the wedge will not come loose.
6. Check the lateral play in each ball joint using the procedures in step 3 for checking lower load-carrying ball joints.
7. If there is play in the ball joint, consult a mechanic to determine if the ball joint requires replacement.
8. Lower the car and remove the jack. Remove the wheel chocks.
9. To remove the wedges, repeat step 1.

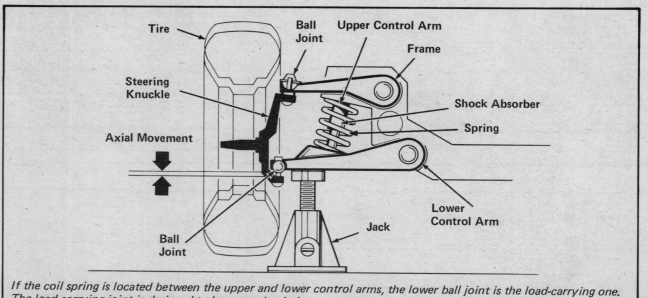

If the coil spring is located between the upper and lower control arms, the lower ball joint is the load-carrying one. The load-carrying joint is designed to have no play in it.

STEERING AND SUSPENSION

Loosens Screws With A Whack

Impact wrenches are great for tackling the really tough jobs. An impact wrench that is designed for use with a hammer is convenient and economical when compared to pneumatic and electric tools. Cal-Van Tools Division of Chemi-Trol Chemical Co. has a No. 650-S Impact Wrench Kit with a 3/8 inch square drive, which is representative of such impact wrench kits and accessories. When you strike the end of the wrench with a hammer, it imparts a twisting motion to the screwdriver bit or socket at the other end and loosens screws and bolts even when they are rusted or wedged tight. Cal-Van's impact wrench has a reversible action that also can tighten screws and bolts. Parts in the kit include the impact driver, 3/8 inch adapter, 3/8 inch straight bit, 1/2 inch straight bit, No. 2 and No. 4 Phillips screwdriver heads.

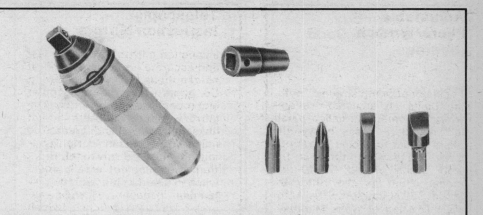

STABILIZERS

ANY CAR with independent front suspension will have a stabilizer bar, a heavy steel rod that extends across the car either in front of or behind the front lower control arm. Stabilizers range from 1/2 inch to slightly over one inch in diameter.

When you first look at a stabilizer, you might think that it is additional help for the main chassis spring. However, it does not help to sustain the weight of the vehicle. Rather, it is a torsion bar whose main purpose is to dampen the roll of the body and chassis of the car during turns. It accomplishes this by twisting as one side of the car leans over. The force generated helps to keep the rising side of the body level with the lowering side of the car body.

Each end of the stabilizer is connected to a lower control arm with a threaded fastener called a link. The link goes through a hole in the end of the stabilizer and through a hole in the lower control arm. It is secured with a series of washers and rubber grommets.

There is a supporting bracket at each end of the stabilizer. The brackets are mounted to the frame sections of the car.

Replacing Stabilizers And Links

STABILIZERS seldom break. If they do, you prob-

Here Is What You Will Need
Materials
● Penetrating Oil
● Stabilizer Bar, Link Assemblies, Mounting Brackets and Bushings
● White Lubricant
Tools
● Wheel Ramps
● Wheel Chocks
● Box-End Wrench
● Socket and Ratchet
● Hacksaw

A car with independent front suspension has a stabilizer bar, a heavy steel rod that runs from one end of the axle to the other. The stabilizer bar twists as the car turns to dampen the roll of the body and chassis.

Extra Large Tool Box

If you have long tools, you need a particularly long box. Waterloo Industries, Inc. makes a Model JL-52 Tradesman box that includes a deep, full-size tote tray with handle. Two draw bolts with hasp and staple for maximum security are other features. The box measures 19-3/4 by 7 by 8 inches. It weighs 10 pounds.

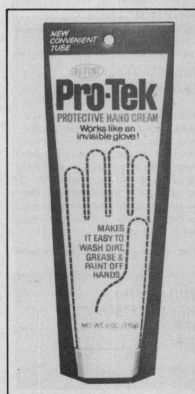

Hand Cream From DuPont

A product that gives your hand a soft, creamy coating to help protect them while you do dirty jobs around the garage is Pro-Tek, made by the DuPont Company. The cream prevents grease and dirt from adhering to your skin. Pro-Tek is available in six ounce tubes.

STEERING AND SUSPENSION

Long-Pattern Box Wrenches Give Good Leverage

Where clearance is not a problem, it is best to use box wrenches that are longer in length to give you good leverage. Six double-ended box wrenches, Model 360, in a long pattern are sold by S-K Tools, a division of Dresser Industries, Inc. The box ends range from 3/8 through 7/8 inch in increments of 1/16 inch. These sizes handle the bulk of automotive work. A tool roll is included.

1/2 Inch Drive Deep Socket Set A Welcome Addition

In most cases, you can use a box wrench to loosen nuts that have long protruding bolts. But sometimes, especially in close quarters, it is necessary to use a deep socket with a ratchet and extension. The nine-piece, 1/2 inch drive deep socket set, Model 5405, sold by Proto Tool Division of Ingersoll-Rand, should cover most of your needs. The deep sockets include: 1/2, 9/16, 5/8, 11/16, 3/4, 13/16, 7/8, 15/16 and 1 inch. They are all 12-point sockets that come packaged in a steel box.

1/4 Inch Socket Set Is Ideal For Dashboard Work

For general automotive repairs, you rarely use a 1/4 inch socket set. But they are very inexpensive and most useful when dealing with dashboard components or when working on your distributor, air conditioner, radio or other electronic components. A set such as the 12-piece No. 4700B, made by Proto Tool Division of Ingersoll-Rand, is adequate for most jobs. This set includes seven six-point sockets from 7/32 through 7/16 inch plus two eight-point sockets of 1/4 and 5/16 inch. It also gives you a screwdriver-type handle, a T-bar and reversible ratchet. The tools come in a metal box.

Workhorse Hand Box

One of the most popular types of mechanic's tool box is the kind that has a removable tray with a handle. Lumidor's No. 525R is such a box. The capped-end, hip-roof design provides extra strength and roominess. Two positive-catch draw bolts are included with a steel hasp and staple for padlocking. The tool box with tote tray has a red enamel finish and measures 19-3/4 by 7 by 8 inches.

Hacksaw Accepts Three Size Blades

Proto Tool Division of Ingersoll-Rand's No. 352 flat-frame, adjustable hacksaw has a heavy-duty adjustable frame that accepts eight, 10 or 12 inch blades. The blade can be set in four positions: with teeth up, down, left or right. The saw comes with a 10 inch blade. Overall saw length is 17 inches.

17-Piece, Half Inch Drive Tool Set Handles Variety Of Jobs

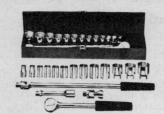

Wright Tool and Forge Company markets a 17-piece, 1/2 inch drive socket set, No. 422, that includes most of the size sockets you will need for normal automotive work. Thirteen 12-point sockets are included from 7/16 to 1-1/4 inches in 1/16 inch increments. You also get a ratchet, a flex handle, a five inch extension and a universal joint in a metal storage box. If you want to add a 13/16 inch spark plug socket to the set, the model to order is No. 423.

STABILIZERS

ably would notice that the car appears to roll much more than usual. Occasionally, the break will be visible.

What usually goes wrong with stabilizers is a loss of one or more of the rubber grommets in the links, or one of the links may break.

If your stabilizer is broken, you should replace everything that mounts or attaches to the stabilizer as well as the bar itself. **NOTE:** The links are likely to be rusted. Soaking the link assemblies with penetrating oil beforehand may ease removal.

To replace a stabilizer, follow this procedure:

1. Drive the car onto wheel ramps.
2. Set the parking brake.
3. Block the rear wheels of the car with wheel chocks.
4. Get under the car and remove the links that connect the stabilizer to the lower control arms at both sides of the car. Discard all the old pieces. You will need a box-end wrench and a socket and ratchet. **NOTE:** The links may be rusted to a point where it is not possible to remove them with the wrench. If this is the case, use a hacksaw to cut the stabilizer links in two in the middle of each link. Discard the pieces.
5. Loosen — but do not yet remove — the cap screws that hold the stabilizer support brackets to the frame sections.
6. Twist the loosened stabilizer bar so that its ends are pointing toward the ground to ease removal.
7. Remove the cap screws from one of the support brackets. Lower this end of the stabilizer bar.
8. Holding the bar with one hand, carefully remove the cap screws from the other bracket.
9. Lower the stabilizer and remove it from under the car.
10. Assemble the new mounting brackets and bushings according to instructions included with the new stabilizer. **NOTE:** Apply white lubricant to the surfaces of the rubber bushings before installing them around the stabilizer bar.
11. Reverse steps 5 through 9 to install the new stabilizer.
12. Install the stabilizer link assemblies according to the manufacturer's instructions.
13. Remove the blocks from the rear wheels.
14. Start the car, release the parking brake and back the car off the wheel ramps.

When problems with the stabilizer bar occur, they are usually the result of a broken link, or the loss of one or more rubber grommets.

Thread Repair Kits

Microdot Products Co. offers a product called Perma-Thread. These are thread replacement kits that permanently repair stripped, worn or damaged threads. They may eliminate the need to scrap or replace valuable automotive parts. Each kit contains what you need for thread repair, including the appropriate tap installation tool and a quantity of Perma-Thread stainless steel inserts for a designated thread size. In addition, you get an installation sheet with the proper drill size specifications. The kits are available in coarse and fine thread configurations in a large variety of sizes and lengths.

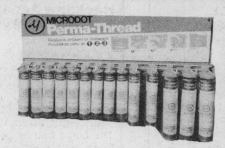

BUMP STOPS

BUMP STOPS, or bumpers, function like door stops. They are pieces of vulcanized rubber bonded to metal plates that are attached to the car's chassis or control arms. They limit the upward travel of the front or rear axle or control arms to prevent the suspension members from striking the frame.

On the front suspension, rubber bump stops are commonly mounted on the chassis below the upper control arm or below a frame section. On cars whose rear ends use leaf springs, you will find bump stops between the axle and chassis. These will be bolted to either the chassis or axle, depending on the make and model of car.

Replacing Bump Stops

RUBBER bump stops need replacement whenever they are missing or when it is apparent they are becoming unbonded from their metal plates. You can tell when the bonding is failing by pulling on the bump stop. If the rubber pulls away from the edge of the metal plate, they should be replaced.

Most bump stops are secured with a single stud on the back of the mounting plate. Some bump stops have ears on the plate and use two through-bolts.

The replacement procedure is different for front and rear bump stops.

For replacing rear bump stops, follow these steps:

Here Is What You Will Need
Materials
● Bump Stops
Tools
● Wheel Chocks
● Jack and Jack Stands
● Box-End Wrench

1. Block the front wheels of the car with wheel chocks.
2. Jack up the rear of the car and support it with a pair of jack stands under the frame.
3. Using the proper size box-end wrench, remove the stud nut or through-bolts securing the bump stop to its mounting plate on the chassis, rear axle housing or control arm.
4. Install the new bump stop, reversing step 3.
5. Lower the car, reversing steps 1 and 2.

To replace front bump stops, follow these steps:

1. Block the rear wheels with wheel chocks.
2. Jack up the front of the car and support it with a pair of jack stands under the frame.
3. Using the proper size box-end wrench, remove the stud nut or through-bolts securing the bump stop to the chassis or a control arm.
4. Install the new bump stop, reversing step 3.
5. Lower the car by reversing steps 1 and 2.

All-Purpose Tool Set By Proto

If you are going to use your tools for general-purpose repairs as well as auto repair, you might consider the Challenger Model 2654 58-piece, general-purpose set. Made by Proto Tool Division of Ingersoll-Rand, it provides a variety of sockets, handles and attachments in 1/4, 3/8 and 1/2 inch drives, and a range of socket sizes from 3/16 through 1-1/4 inches. A 5/8 inch spark plug socket and a 13/16 inch spark plug socket—both 3/8 inch drive—are included. It also gives you eight combination wrenches, 1/4 through 3/4 inch, and three screwdrivers—two standard and one Phillips. It comes in a hip-roof, utility tool chest with lift-out tote tray.

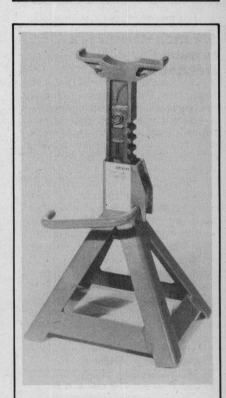

Car-Truck Stands

Two- and five-ton capacity jack stands featuring a ratchet design for easy raising and lowering are made by Watervliet Tool Co. Model 2T, the two-ton model, has a low height of seven inches and a high height of 17-3/4 inches. Model 5T, which supports five tons, has a low height of 14-3/4 inches and a high height of 25 inches. The heavy-gauge steel jack stands have a one-year warranty.

Bump stops made of vulcanized rubber are located between suspension members and the car chassis to prevent the components from striking each other.

BRAKES

Brake Tool Kit Services Lockheed Brakes

A brake tool kit for servicing Lockheed brakes is sold by K-D Manufacturing Co. The tool kit, Model 289, includes a high, offset brake wrench (1/4 and 3/8 inch), "C" washer pliers for Lockheed brakes, a brake piston-puller for Lockheed brakes, a brake adjusting tool for Corvair and Ford, and a brake shoe retaining spring tool for Comet, Falcon, Valiant and others using this particular type of spring.

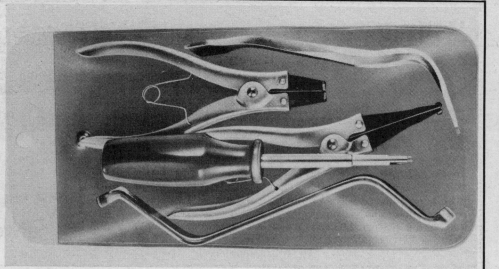

in the rather restricted area of the wheel recess. Airflow can be improved by ducting air into the wheel/drum cavity, finning the drums, and combining cast iron liners with aluminum drum housings. Usually, larger cars have one or more of these cooling devices.

Brake linings also assist in transferring some of the heat, but the necessity of a backing plate makes internal cooling without ducting difficult. In addition to holding the necessary shoe assembly, the backing plate is designed to reduce the chance of water and abrasive dirt getting into the critical space between the brake shoe and drum. While moderately effective in keeping small quantities of dust and water out, any that does get through is, unfortunately, trapped by this very same shield. The adverse effect of dust and water

on braking efficiency, however, has been virtually eliminated by the caliper disc brake system.

The disc brake system consists of a steel disc (rotor) that is connected to the wheel and a set of calipers (pads) that can grip the disc with padded jaws. When the brake cylinder has pressure applied to it in the form of hydraulic brake fluid, the calipers close on both sides of the disc, an action that generates friction and slows the car. The disc brake spreads the generated heat over a larger surface and therefore cools more rapidly than does the drum-type brake.

Disc brakes have superior fade-resistance and retain more stopping power than drum brakes when wet. However, disc brakes are more expensive, which is why they are used only on the front on most American-made cars.

Marvel's Brake Cleaner

If your brakes are dirty with accumulated soil, oil, grease, brake fluid and other grime, Marvel Oil Company's brake cleaner and degreaser may remove it. The product, which comes in 20 ounce aerosol cans, can be used to clean and degrease brake lining, drums, cylinders, springs, disc brake beds and other nonrubber parts. In most cases, there is no need to disassemble the brake unit.

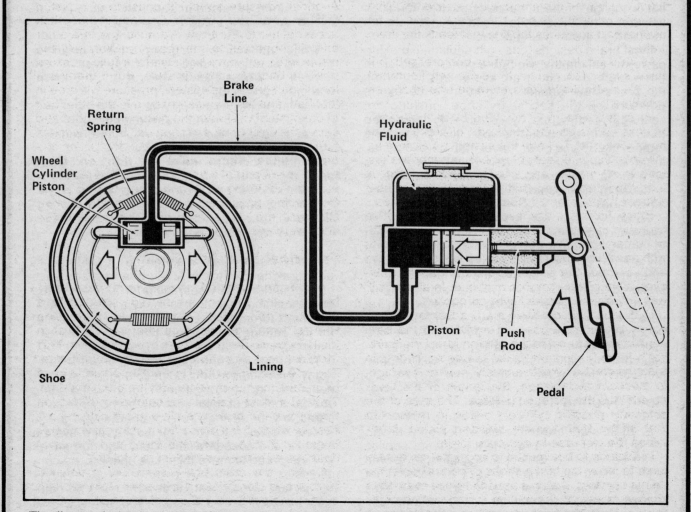

The diagram depicts how a hydraulic brake system operates. When the pedal is depressed, the action forces the fluid in the master cylinder, brake line and wheel cylinder to push the cylinder's pistons against the brake shoes.

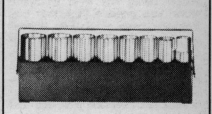

Deep Sockets Work Where Standard Ones Will Not

It is not an uncommon occurrence to find that a standard socket will not reach a nut because of a protruding bolt. This is when you need a deep socket. Wright Tool and Forge Company sells an eight-piece set of 12-point deep sockets, No. 409. Sizes are 1/2, 9/16, 5/8, 11/16, 3/4, 13/16, 7/8 and 15/16 inch. They are packaged in a metal storage tray.

Hand-Impact Wrench Kit

An impact wrench such as those used in service stations requires an air compressor of high output. This usually is out of reach of the home mechanic, who can either opt for an electrically operated model or a hand impact wrench. The hand impact type is the least expensive and is probably the best choice since an impact wrench is not used that often. K-D Manufacturing Company offers a hand impact wrench kit, No. 2060S, that has a 3/8 inch square drive and hex socket for bits. Giving the anvil end a sharp blow with a hammer loosens screws and bolts that are rusted or wedged tight. The reversible action also tightens screws and bolts. Instructions are on the tool. Kit components are contained in a snap-closing plastic pouch. Included is the impact driver, No. 2, No. 3 and No. 4 Phillips bit; a 5/16 inch wide slotted bit; 5/32 and 1/4 inch clutch head bits; 9/32 inch wide slotted bit; and 5/16 inch hex bit socket.

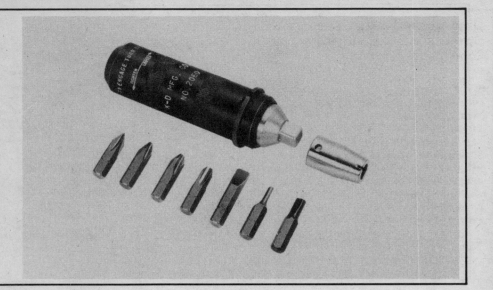

Adjustable Wrenches

The Challenger Line made by Proto Tool Division of Ingersoll-Rand includes four sizes of adjustable wrenches. The 1/2 inch, maximum jaw-opening model is four inches long, while the 3/4 inch, maximum jaw-opening model is six inches long. There also is an eight inch model with a one inch opening and a ten inch model that has an opening of 1-1/8 inches. The wrenches are chrome-plated.

Keep Your Brakes Clean

The brakes in your car are complex mechanisms that need to be clean to work properly. Every time you do take a look at your brakes, you should clean them with a brake parts cleaner like that offered by Siloo, Inc. It comes in 20 ounce aerosol cans. You also can use it to clean clutch parts. The product contains no carbon tetrachloride, silicones or petroleum solvents. It is nonflammable.

INTRODUCTION

The efficiency of a disc braking system depends on the condition of the friction surfaces of the rotor and the calipers.

The efficiency of a drum braking system depends on proper lining material of adequate thickness, internally smooth and round drums, maximum contact between lining area and drum surface, and cooling. In addition to the force exerted on the shoes by the mechanical and hydraulic leverage, additional pressure between shoes and drum is achieved by self-energizing brake shoe action. The actual contact of the shoe with the drum helps to apply additional force to the drum. As the brakes are applied, the friction between lining and drum attempts to force the shoes around in the direction of drum rotation. This slight movement accelerates brake application. The location of the brake shoe pivot point determines whether or not the shoe is forced against the drum to create self-energizing action.

Most brake designs today get additional braking power by linking the two brake shoes together. In this system, both shoes are self-energizing. When the brakes are applied, a primary shoe exerts pressure on the secondary shoe, pushing the secondary shoe into the drum with increased force. This is called duo-servo action. Despite the rather long up and down travel of the brake pedal, the wheel cylinders and brake shoes do not move very far to make contact with the drum. This is because of the mechanical and hydraulic leverage advantage.

To compensate for lining and drum wear, an automatic adjustment for setting the shoes closer to the drum is incorporated into the brake assembly. This self-adjusting feature has been standardized and eliminates the frequent need for brake adjustment service. The self-adjusting linkage uses the self-energizing shoe action in reverse to operate an adjustment lever. This lever uses ratchet action to move the star wheel adjuster nut when the brakes are applied and released. The adjustment, however, will happen only when the car moves in reverse.

Road Testing The Brakes

BEFORE starting a brake inspection on your car, try to determine by a road test just what service might be required. Select a dry, smooth, paved section of street or road free of traffic or other obstacles. At a speed of 20 mph, apply the brakes firmly for a rapid stop without skidding the wheels. If the pedal depresses to within two inches or less of the floorboard:

- The linings may be badly worn
- Brake fluid level may be low
- The shoes may need adjusting

A spongy feeling to the pedal indicates air in the system.

With the car stopped and the ignition off, press the brake pedal as hard as possible, holding it down firmly. Note whether it continues to move slowly downward. Any such movement indicates master cylinder problems or a leak somewhere in the hydraulic system.

If the car pulls or sways to one side or the other, or if one wheel grabs when the brakes are applied, it is an indication of several possible problems:

- Improper brake adjustment
- Grease or hydraulic fluid on the linings
- Loose brake backing plate
- Reversed primary and secondary shoes
- Brake shoes not properly fitted to the drum, resulting in partial contact
- An out-of-round drum

While conducting rolling brake tests, listen for grinding or rubbing noises with the brakes off and applied. Rubbing sounds without brake application may be due to:

- Improper initial adjustment
- Faulty or broken return spring
- Binding wheel cylinder or shoe guides

Grinding or squeaks when the brakes are applied can mean:

- Brake linings are worn out
- Improper lining material
- Oil or grease on the linings
- Warped backing plates

Faulty front wheel bearings can contribute to poor braking efficiency. A bad bearing can cause a lot of unnecessary searching for a defect in the brake assembly, when it is really a bearing fault.

Do not forget to check the mechanical linkage for the parking brake every time you do a brake inspection.

The sections contained in this chapter offer many procedures and guides to good maintenance of the brake system. You will need some special tools, but their cost will be nominal compared to your savings in labor charges.

Your decision to work on your brake system must include adequate time. Do not be hurried, as you are prone to make mistakes under those conditions.

The tasks you accomplish here must be complete in every respect, because your safety as well as that of others depends on your doing the work to the very best of your ability.

Disc Brake Pad Spreader For Use With Extension Wrench

Cal-Van Tools Division of Chemi-Trol Chemical Co. has a new product, No. 707, that you can use for installing brake pads. It spreads the pads and holds them in position when assembling the caliper over the rotor. You use it with a 3/8 inch drive extension wrench.

INSPECTING FRONT BRAKES

Here Is What You Will Need

Materials
- Paint Brush or Vacuum Cleaner
- Two Plastic Credit Cards
- Cotter Pins

Tools
- Lug Nut Wrench
- Wheel Chocks
- Jack and Jack Stands
- Channel-Lock Pliers
- Pliers
- 12 Inch Adjustable Wrench
- Soft-Faced Hammer or Mallet

A VERY THOROUGH brake inspection should include a visual examination of the friction surfaces, lining condition, and any components contained in the brake assembly at the wheels. This inspection is necessary not only to verify the wear condition of the brake surfaces, but also to examine any parts that may have failed and cannot be detected without a visual inspection.

The procedure for examining front drum brakes differs from that for examining rear drum brakes since there are many more components on the front drum brakes. In addition, the procedures for examining front drum brakes and front disc brakes differ. The only service you can perform on front wheel disc brakes is an inspection. Any removal of the pads, relining of the pads, or caliper service must be performed by a professional mechanic.

Inspecting Front Drum Brakes

TO INSPECT front drum brakes, proceed as follows:

1. Drive the car onto a level surface and engage the parking brake.

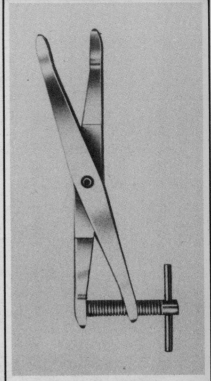

Disc Brake Pad Spreader From Owatonna

A disc brake pad spreader that can save you time when doing brake work is sold by Owatonna Tool Co. The tool, No. 7034, fits between the two new pads being installed and is then expanded to retract the piston. With the pads held firmly in place, you have both hands free to start the caliper over the rotor. After it is started, the spreader is removed and the caliper is slid over the rotor the rest of the way. The tool works on all standard and four-piston caliper disc brakes.

All-Purpose Tool Box

Although it does not keep your tools as organized as other types of tool boxes, the all-purpose box with a lift-out tray is popular with many mechanics. S-K Tools, a division of Dresser Industries, Inc., makes two versions—Nos. 2540 and 2539. Both feature cap-end construction, a full-length piano hinge, and positive-catch, draw bolt with padlock eye. A steel tote tray also is included. No. 2539 measures 19-1/8 by 6 by 6-1/2 inches. No. 2540 is 15 by 6 by 6-1/2 inches.

K-D Tools Disc Brake Pad Spreader

One of the tough jobs that requires a special tool is splitting the brake pads and holding them in position when assembling the caliper over the rotor on disc brakes. A special tool, Model 2145, from K-D Manufacturing Co. is specifically designed for this task.

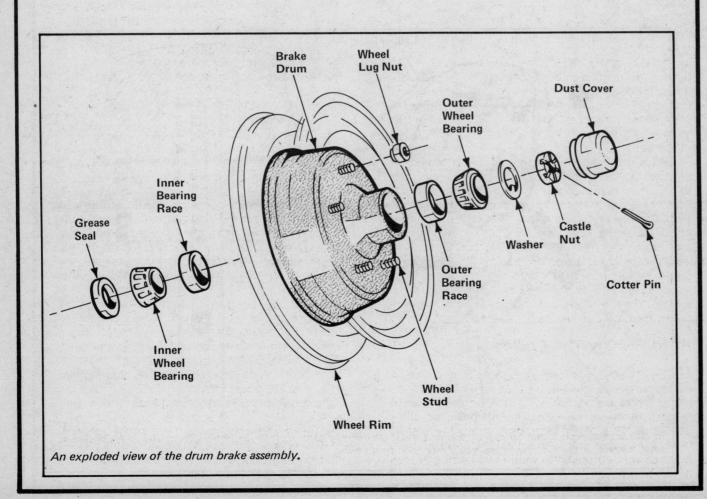

An exploded view of the drum brake assembly.

Grease Seal — Inner Bearing Race — Inner Wheel Bearing — Wheel Rim — Brake Drum — Wheel Lug Nut — Wheel Stud — Outer Wheel Bearing — Outer Bearing Race — Washer — Castle Nut — Dust Cover — Cotter Pin

Quieting New Disc Brakes

When brake pads are new, they will sometimes squeal because of vibrations at the caliper-brake pad interface. Disc Brake Quiet, No. 127, marketed by Woodhill/Permatex can be sprayed on the back of the new brake pad before reassembling to provide a thin, vibration-absorbing film between the caliper and pad. The product is available in a 12 ounce aerosol can.

Cordless Vacuum Cleaner

Black and Decker Manufacturing Co. makes a cordless vacuum cleaner that features a rechargeable energy pack. The vacuum cleaner is light yet strong, with an impact-resistant housing. It has a one quart capacity. The cleaner is 17 inches long and weighs 2-1/4 pounds. A 16-hour charger is included.

Larger Metric Open-End Wrench Set Gives Wider Selection

If you need metric open-end wrenches from 6mm to 26mm, Proto Tool Division of Ingersoll-Rand's Model 30000A metric open-end wrench set is for you. It includes 10 open-end wrenches in a range of 20 sizes. Each has a 15 degree angle head and is finished in nickel-chrome plate.

Extra Heavy-Duty Cutting Pliers

Smaller types of cutting pliers usually take little abuse because they are generally used only on small gauges of wire. But larger models used for tough cutting jobs need extra strength. Extra heavy-duty cutting pliers are made by Indestro, a division of Duro Metal Products Co. Model 2131 is seven inches long and is

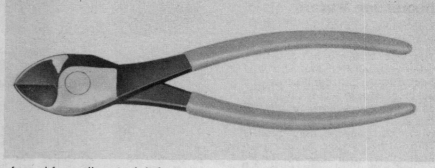

forged from alloy steel. It features hardened cutting edges. Handles have a bonded vinyl material coating.

INSPECTING FRONT BRAKES

2. Remove the wheel covers and loosen the lug nuts.
3. Place wheel chocks behind the rear wheels.
4. Jack up the front of the car and place a pair of jack stands under the frame.
5. Remove the lug nuts from the passenger side wheel first.
6. Remove this wheel.
7. Use channel-lock pliers to remove the dust cap from the hub.
8. Use pliers to remove the cotter pin from the axle spindle. Discard the pin.
9. Slide the nut lock off the axle spindle.
10. Use a 12 inch adjustable wrench to remove the adjusting nut. **NOTE:** Some cars will use a castle nut instead of the adjusting nut and nut lock.
11. Slide the washer off the axle spindle.
12. Wiggle the brake drum. This causes the outer bearing to move outward on the axle spindle. Grasp the outer bearing and remove it, being careful not to drop it. Place the bearing on a clean cloth. **NOTE:** If you have not inspected or lubricated your bearings within the interval recommended in the owner's manual, refer to the section on Repacking Front Wheel Bearings in the Lubrication chapter.
13. Grasp the brake drum, rotating it slightly forward, as you remove it, exposing the brake assembly.
14. Use an old paint brush to remove most of the dusty residue on the brake assembly and interior of the brake drum. **CAUTION:** Avoid breathing this dust. Another method of removing this residue would be to use a vacuum cleaner.
15. Inspect the interior of the brake drum's friction surfaces for scoring and visible cracks. Make sure the surface is smooth. If surfaces are worn, they should be resurfaced by an auto parts store that has a machine shop.
16. Examine the wheel cylinder on brake assembly for evidence of leakage.
17. Examine all springs in the brake assembly to see if they are secured and not broken.
18. Inspect the brake shoe lining. If the lining is riveted, see if any rivet heads are level with the lining surface. If linings are bonded, they should be no thinner than 1/16 inch — approximately the thickness of two plastic credit cards.
19. If shoe linings need replacement, refer to

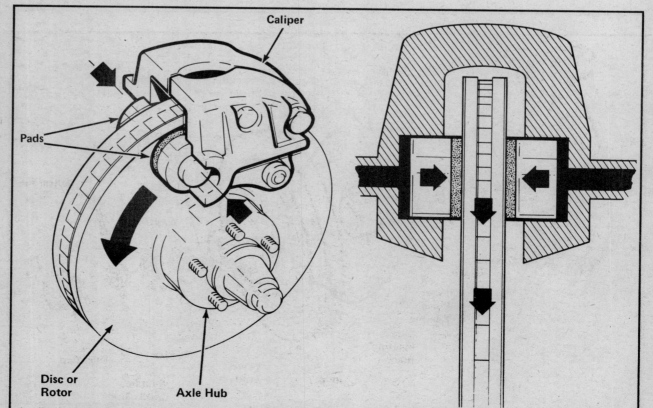

In disc brakes, pads in the caliper are forced against the turning rotor to stop its motion. Since the pads contact a small surface of the rotor, a larger area is left open for cooling.

BRAKES

Inspection Mirrors

The way cars are put together, often you will find that you suspect trouble, but cannot see the problem area to inspect it. In this case, you might have to first remove the obstructing part to work. You may be able to save yourself some time by using an inspection mirror, however. An inspection mirror such as Model 25 offered by Cal-Van Tools Division

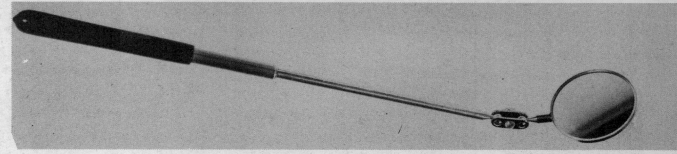

of Chemi-Trol Chemical Co. can let you see around obstructions easily. This device has a two inch round mirror and telescoping handle. In the closed position, the six inch handle makes the unit compact. The handle telescopes to 12 inches, giving the tool an overall length of 15 inches.

---

the section on Relining Drum Brakes in this chapter.

20. Replace the brake drum. You may have to rotate it slightly forward as you install it.
21. Replace the wheel bearing. You may have to wiggle the drum to seat the bearing properly.
22. Replace the washer over the axle spindle.
23. Replace the adjusting nut and tighten to 90 inch-pounds (7-1/2 foot-pounds) with a torque wrench and deep socket.
24. Back up the nut no more than 1/6 turn to align the openings for the cotter pin.
25. Slide the nut lock onto the axle spindle.
26. Replace the dust cap using a soft-faced hammer or mallet.
27. Replace wheel, reversing steps 5 and 6.
28. Repeat steps 5 through 27 for the wheel on the driver's side.
29. Lower the car, reversing steps 2 through 4.

Inspecting Front Disc Brakes

WHILE WE do not suggest that the do-it-yourselfer attempt any repairs on front disc brakes, we do recommend that a periodic inspection be performed. Follow these steps:

1. Drive the car onto a level surface and engage the parking brake.

2. Remove the wheel covers and loosen the lug nuts.
3. Place wheel chocks behind the rear wheels.
4. Jack up the front of the car and place a pair of jack stands under the frame.
5. Remove the lug nuts from the passenger side wheel first.
6. Remove the wheel.
7. Inspect the surfaces on each side of the rotor (disc) for scoring or visible breaks. **NOTE:** Some rotors have a groove machined on the face or friction surface of the rotor. (Otherwise, make sure the surface is smooth.) If the surfaces are worn, consult a qualified mechanic.
8. Inspect the brake pads on both sides of the rotor from the front. The pads should be no thinner than 1/16 inch — approximately the thickness of two plastic credit cards.
9. Turn the front wheel to the left and inspect the brake pads on both sides of the rotor from the rear. Again, the pads should be no thinner than 1/16 inch. **NOTE:** If there are appreciable differences in the wear pattern between the front and the rear of the rotor's brake pads, consult a qualified mechanic. The brake caliper may require realignment.
10. Replace the wheel, reversing steps 5 and 6.
11. Repeat steps 5 through 10 for the wheel on the driver's side.
12. Lower the car, reversing steps 2 through 4.

High-Temperature Pad Grease

A grease for lubricating brake backing-plate pads and star adjusters that has heat-resistant properties will last longer. One such high-temperature grease is available from Raybestos-Manhattan, Inc.

Clean Your Brakes When You Inspect Them

Whenever you inspect your brakes, you should take the time to clean them. A product such as Brākleen, made by CRC Chemicals, Inc., can make the job easier. The product, which comes in an aerosol can with an extension nozzle, can be used to clean brake linings, drums, cylinders, brake shoes, disc brake pads, discs, wedge brakes, springs, calipers and clutch discs. To use, you just spray it on and allow it to run off to remove brake fluid, grease, oil and other contaminants.

Caliper Mount

Hub Bore Diameter

Cotter Pin

Axle Spindle

Grease Seal

Inner Wheel Bearing

Inner Bearing Race

Outer Wheel Bearing

Washer

Dust Cap

Spindle Castle Nut

Disc or Rotor

An exploded view of the disc brake assembly.

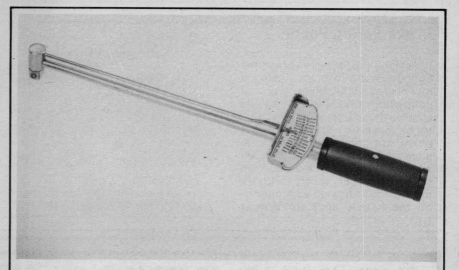

DB Wheel Bearing Grease

When you perform a brake job, it is an opportunity to repack wheel bearings. Valvoline DB Wheel Bearing Grease, No. 733, is an aluminum-complex soap base grease formulated for General Motors units equipped with disc brakes where a lubricant meeting GM Part No. 1051195 is specified. The grease has high-temperature, corrosion and rust protection properties. It is available only in NLGI No. 2 consistency in one pound containers. The grease should not be used in equipment manufactured by the Ford Motor Co.

Low-Capacity Inch/Pound Torque Wrench

If you work on automatic transmissions, you should have a torque wrench that has graduations in inch-pounds. Blackhawk Hand Tools has two such wrenches. Model 34830 has a 100 inch-pound capacity in five inch-pound graduations. The 10 inch tool has a 3/8 inch drive. The other wrench, Model 34840, also has a 3/8 inch drive, but it has a 200 inch-pound capacity in 10 inch-pound graduations. Both are designed for working in close quarters.

Combination Brake Lining/Tire Tread Depth Gauge

A combination instrument to quickly measure the amount of usable brake lining left above the rivet head and the depth of a tire tread is offered by K-D Manufacturing Company. The gauge, Model No. K-D 2045, is calibrated from 0 to 1/8 inch. Each scale division indicates 1/64 inch.

Waterless Hand Cleaner By Valvoline

Working on brake and wheel assemblies is certain to leave grease and oil on your hands and arms. A waterless hand cleaner, No. 933, with skin conditioners is made by Valvoline, a division of Ashland Oil, Inc. The product, which comes in a one pound container, removes grease, grime, tar, paint and other stains from hands. After application, simply wipe your hands with a cloth or rinse them with water.

INSPECTING REAR DRUM BRAKES

Here Is What You Will Need

Materials
- Paint Brush or Vacuum Cleaner
- Two Plastic Credit Cards

Tools
- Lug Nut Wrench
- Wheel Chocks
- Jack and Jack Stands
- Screwdriver

REAR DRUM brakes are a little easier to inspect than front drum brakes — there are fewer components to disassemble. The drum is free to be removed once the wheel assembly is off the car.

The rear drum brake assembly has a dual purpose. It contains both hydraulic and mechanical components. The hydraulic components perform an important function in the service brake system. The mechanical components are related directly to the parking brake.

Your inspection of the rear brake drums should include a thorough visual check of all component fasteners. Another important check is for fluid leaks, which can only be detected by removing the brake drum and examining the wheel cylinder. With the brake drum removed, you should also inspect the surfaces of the drum and the brake shoes for wear.

To inspect your rear drum brakes, follow this procedure:

1. Drive the car onto a level surface and engage the parking brake.
2. Remove the wheel covers and loosen the lug nuts.
3. Block the front wheels with wheel chocks.
4. Jack up the rear of the car and place jack stands under the frame.
5. Remove the lug nuts from the wheel on the passenger's side first.
6. Remove the wheel.
7. While pulling the drum free of the studs, rotate it slightly forward. **NOTE:** There may be a spring steel clip on one of the studs. Pry this free with a screwdriver and then remove the drum.
8. Use an old paint brush to remove most of the dusty residue on the brake assembly and the interior of the brake drum. **CAUTION:** Avoid breathing this dust. Another method of removing this residue would be to use a vacuum cleaner.
9. Inspect the interior of the brake drum's friction surfaces for scoring and visible cracks. Make sure the surface is smooth. If surfaces are worn, the drum should be resurfaced by an auto parts store that has a machine shop.
10. Examine the wheel cylinder on the brake assembly for evidence of leakage.
11. Examine all springs in the brake assembly to see if they are secured and not broken.
12. Inspect the brake shoe lining. If the lining is riveted, see if any rivet heads are level with the lining surface. If linings are bonded, they should be no thinner than 1/16 inch — approximately the thickness of two plastic credit cards.
13. If shoe linings need replacement, refer to the section on Relining Drum Brakes in this chapter.
14. Install the brake drum. You may have to rotate it slightly forward as you reinstall it over the studs.
15. Replace the wheel, reversing steps 5 and 6.
16. Repeat steps 5 through 15 for the wheel on the driver's side.
17. Lower the car, reversing steps 2 through 4.

Brake Spring Pliers

If you have ever tried to spread the springs on drum brakes using a tool like a screwdriver, you will appreciate brake spring pliers such as those offered by the Owatonna Tool Co. The Model 704 pliers can be used for removing and installing brake springs on nearly all makes of cars and light trucks. The tool, which is 13-1/2 inches long, has special fittings on the handle ends for various types of brakes.

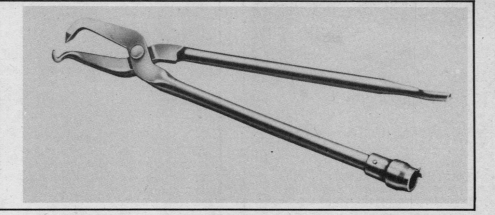

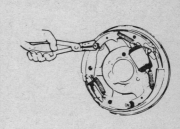

Brake Shoe Tool Has Pliers Action

It is easy to remove retaining spring washers from brake shoes if you have the right tool. Lisle Corporation's Model 10900 brake shoe retaining spring tool is designed for this job. It has a pliers action that holds the washer in nylon cups. The tool is designed to work with most washers, including those with "ears."

Replacement Brake Fluids

Prestone Brake Fluid, made by Union Carbide Corp., comes in 12 ounce, one quart, and one and five gallon cans. It is formulated for drum or disc brake systems and is designed to have a high boiling point to provide an extra margin of safety at all speeds. It complies with Federal Motor Vehicle Safety Standard No. 116 and DOT 3 motor vehicle brake fluid standard. It also surpasses SAE specification 11703 and federal specification VB-B-680 for heavy-duty brake fluid.

Pivot Head Jack Stands Are Versatile

When working under your car, you will find that a jack stand that has a pivoting head makes it easier. The pivot head allows you to position the jack stand saddle in just the right spot for proper car support. And, you can do this without moving the base. Hein-Werner Corp. makes a set of five-ton (capacity per pair) pivot head jacks, Model No. CS5.17. These jacks have a lifting range of 15 to 25-1/4 inches and a base size of 10 by 12 inches.

Use Torque Wrench To Tighten Lug Nuts

On disc brake systems, it is extremely important to tighten the lug nuts to the proper specifications. If one or two nuts are looser than the others, there is a possibility of warping the rotor and causing pedal pulsation. It is best to use a torque wrench for tightening lug nuts.

RELINING DRUM BRAKES

Here Is What You Will Need

Materials
- Paint Brush or Vacuum Cleaner
- Pencil and Paper
- White Lubricant
- Cotter Pins

Tools
- Lug Nut Wrench
- Wheel Chocks
- Jack and Jack Stands
- Channel-Lock Pliers
- Pliers
- 12 Inch Adjustable Wrench
- Wheel Cylinder Clamp
- Brake Spring Removal and Installation Tool
- Torque Wrench and Deep Socket
- Soft-Faced Hammer or Mallet
- Screwdriver

IN ORDER for the brake system to stop the wheels from turning with efficiency, the brake shoes must make contact with the brake drums. There are friction surfaces on both the brake shoes and on the brake drums of drum brake assemblies. When these surfaces wear, the efficiency of the brakes are affected. Periodic inspection of these surfaces is necessary to determine the condition of the brakes. For a complete discussion of how to inspect drum brakes, refer to the sections in this chapter on Inspecting Front Brakes and Inspecting Rear Drum Brakes.

When the brake shoes and drum come into contact in the stopping or braking process, heat is generated on the friction surfaces of the shoes and the drum. This heat must be dissipated. If it is not, the brake drums will warp and braking action will be reduced, which could be dangerous.

When brake drums become worn, they should be resurfaced by an auto parts store machine shop. This remachining assures a proper contact of the drum surface and brake shoe lining. If the wear on the brake drum is too great, the drum must be replaced. Shoes, too, wear and eventually need replacement.

The procedures for relining front and rear drum brakes differ, so they will be covered separately.

Relining Front Drum Brakes

FOLLOW THIS procedure for relining front drum brakes:

1. Drive the car onto a level surface and engage the parking brake.
2. Remove the wheel covers and loosen the lug nuts.
3. Place wheel chocks behind the rear wheels.
4. Jack up the front of the car and place a pair of jack stands under the frame.
5. Remove the lug nuts from the wheel on the passenger's side first.
6. Remove the wheel.
7. Use channel-lock pliers to remove the dust cap from the hub.
8. Use pliers to remove the cotter pin from the axle spindle. Discard the pin.
9. Slide the lock nut off the axle spindle.
10. Use a 12 inch adjustable wrench to remove the adjusting nut. **NOTE:** Some cars will use a castle nut instead of the adjusting nut and lock nut.
11. Slide the washer off the axle spindle.

12. Wiggle the brake drum. This causes the outer bearing to move outward on the axle spindle. Grasp the outer bearing and remove it, being careful not to drop it. Place it on a clean cloth. **NOTE:** If you have not inspected or lubricated your bearings within the interval recommended in the owner's manual, refer to the section on Repacking Front Wheel Bearings in the Lubrication chapter.
13. Grasp the brake drum, rotating it slightly forward as you remove the drum, exposing the brake assembly.
14. Use an old paint brush to remove most of the dusty residue on the brake assembly and the interior of the brake drum. **CAUTION:** Avoid breathing this dust. Another method of removing this residue would be to use a vacuum cleaner.
15. Inspect the interior of the brake drum's friction surface for scoring and visible cracks. Make sure the surface is smooth. If the surface is worn, the drum should be resurfaced by an auto parts store that has a machine shop.
16. Install a wheel cylinder clamp on the dust covers at each end of the wheel cylinder. This will prevent the cylinder parts from expanding out of the brake cylinder when the brake shoe return springs are removed.
17. Remove the two brake shoe return springs. Use a brake shoe spring removal and installation tool. **NOTE:** Make a simple sketch of the way the springs are hooked up to ease the installation of new springs. Note the differences in coil diameter of the springs.
18. Using pliers, remove the brake shoe hold-down springs by pressing in and turning the

PARKING BRAKE

A N AUTOMOBILE's parking brake is operated by mechanical cable linkage. When the car's parking brake lever is engaged, cables are pulled and a lever pivots on each rear drum brake. This lever pushes the brake shoes into the drums to hold the vehicle in place.

These cable-operated parking brakes need adjustment whenever the parking brake will not hold the car from rolling or when the rear brake shoes are worn. Here is how to adjust the parking brake:

1. Park the car on a level surface.
2. Block the front wheels with wheel chocks or wooden blocks so that the car will not roll.
3. Jack up the car so that both rear wheels are off the ground. Place jack stands under the rear axle.
4. Follow the steel cables from each rear wheel to where they meet, somewhere under the middle of the car. Use a creeper to move more easily under the vehicle.
5. Where the cables meet, there will be some type of adjusting device. The most common one is a long bolt with two lock nuts. As you tighten the nuts with an open-end wrench, the cables will tighten to engage the parking brake sooner. These adjusting devices are located in a position that is extremely vul-

nerable to rust and dirt, so it is advisable to apply some penetrating oil on the adjusting nuts before you attempt to work on the system.
6. Tighten the adjusting nuts by turning them in a clockwise direction until a slight drag is felt when you turn the rear wheels by hand. Then loosen the nuts just until the drag is eliminated.
7. Lock the adjusting nuts against each other using two open-end wrenches so that the cables cannot work themselves loose.
8. Be certain that there is absolutely no drag on the rear wheels. Any wheel drag can cause premature wear of brake shoes and create an unnecessary load on the engine.
9. Lower the car, reversing steps 2 and 3.
10. A proper adjustment will produce a definite slowing of the vehicle when only the parking brake is being applied.

Here Is What You Will Need

Materials
● Penetrating Oil

Tools
● Wheel Chocks or Wooden Blocks
● Jack and Jack Stands
● Creeper
● Open-End Wrenches

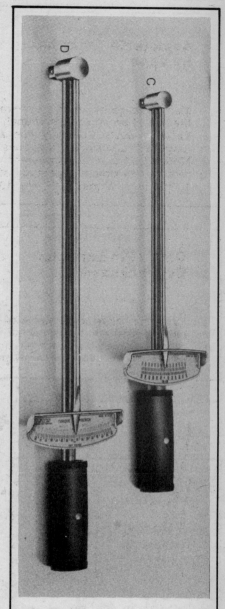

Deflecting Beam Torque Wrenches

Tightening wheel lug nuts and other nuts with an ordinary lug wrench or socket wrench does the job, but a torque wrench will do it better. Challenger deflecting beam torque wrenches, made by Proto Tool Division of Ingersoll-Rand, handle all normal torque requirements. They can be used for both right and left hand torquing applications. The wrenches feature a dual-reading English/metric scale and pivotal handle. Model 9710 has a torque range from 0 to 600 inch-pounds and is 16 inches long. Model 9709 has a range from 0 to 150 foot-pounds and is 19 inches long.

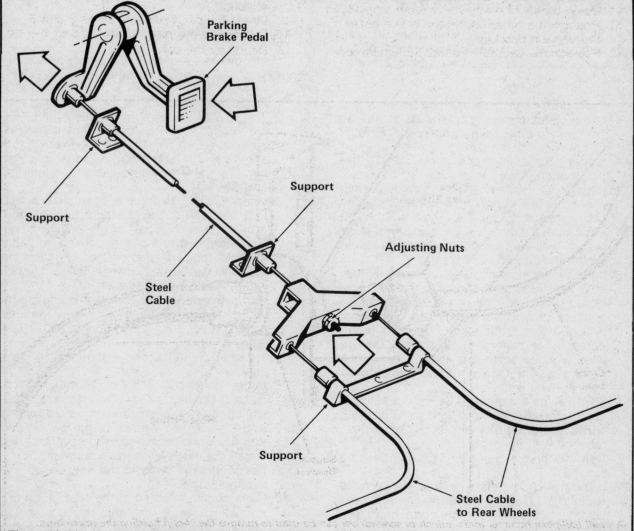

The parking brake is operated by mechanical cable linkage. Where the cables from each rear wheel meet there will be some type of adjusting device. A common one is a long bolt with two lock nuts.

Labels in figure: Parking Brake Pedal, Support, Support, Support, Steel Cable, Adjusting Nuts, Support, Steel Cable to Rear Wheels

Wheel Cylinder Clamp Eases Repairs

For passenger cars with double-end brake pistons, a wheel cylinder or piston clamp is sure to speed repairs. Such a tool is made by Cal-Van Tools, a division of Chemi-Trol Chemical Company. The device, Model No. 270, quickly applies pressure on the brake cylinder pistons. The spring steel tool, sold in sets of two clamps, adjusts to any size brake cylinder from 1-1/8 to 3-1/4 inches.

Impact Driver Kit

Hastings Manufacturing Co. sells an impact driver kit, No. 1149, that can help you remove the most stubborn screws and bolts. It comes with the following bits: Phillips No. 2, No. 3, No. 4; and 1/2 and 3-1/8 inch straight bits. Also included is a 3/8 inch adapter.

10 Inch Channel Locks Provide Five Adjustments

For gripping large fasteners, you need a pair of channel lock-type pliers in a fairly large size. Vaco Products Company's No. 88604 is this type of pliers. It has an overall size of 10 inches and provides five different adjustments with a maximum jaw opening of 1-1/2 inches.

Screw Starters End Fumbling

One of the trickiest jobs in repair work is starting small screws. Screw starters like those sold by Proto Tool Division of Ingersoll-Rand are the answer. These tools start screws quickly with a twist of the fingers. The screw-holding mechanism grips the screw. These screw starters come in three different models: No. 9851 (2-1/2 inches long), No. 9853 (5-1/2 inches), and No. 9855 (9-1/2 inches). All have a magnetic retrieving head on the other end of the tool.

1/2 Inch Drive Socket Set For The Beginner

When you are just starting out, you generally need only the basic automotive tools. Among these is a small 1/2 inch drive socket set from 7/16 through 1-1/4 inches. This is what Proto Tool Division of Ingersoll-Rand's Model 5402 16-piece, 1/2 inch drive socket set offers. You also get a reversible ratchet, a five inch extension, a 15 inch hinge handle and a steel storage box. You will probably need to add to this set in a short time, but for your initial attempts at auto repair, it will do just fine.

Screw Starters For Phillips And Straight-Slot Screws

Lisle Corporation sells three 5-1/2 inch long screw starters for Phillips and straight-slot screws. The tools feature a spring-loaded carbon-steel bit that grips the inside of the screw slot to hold the screw firmly on the screw starter. It releases and recocks automatically.

The Phillips screw starter also handles Reed and Prince-type screws. The straight-slot screw starter blade is 9/32 inch wide by 0.032 inch thick. Handles are insulated and magnets are set in the other end of the tool so you can use it for picking up small parts. Model 39200 handles Phillips screws; Model 39600 is for straight-slot screws. Model 39800 is a combination Phillips/straight-slot screw starter.

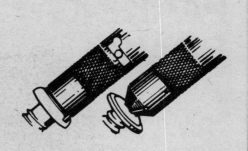

BRAKE LIGHT SWITCH

Here Is What You Will Need

Materials
- Brake Light Switch

Tools
- Test Light
- Screwdriver
- Box-End Wrench

WHEN ONE brake light on your car will not work when you depress the brake pedal, a burned out light bulb is the most common problem. When all of your brake lights do not operate, however, there are a few more parts of the brake system that could be at fault. The trouble could be in the light bulbs, light sockets, wiring, the turn signal switch or the brake light switch.

There are two types of brake light switches: mechanically and hydraulically operated switches. Check your owner's manual to determine which type your car has.

Servicing A Mechanical Switch

HERE IS how to find out if your mechanical brake light switch is at fault and how to change it if necessary. You will require a test light for this procedure:

1. Look under the car's dashboard near the brake pedal linkage. You should be able to see a push-button-type switch very near or touching the brake pedal linkange.
2. Inspect the switch and make certain the pushbutton moves in or out when the brake pedal is depressed. If it does not, the switch may have been bent and is not touching the brake linkage. Grasp the switch and bend it back into position. In addition, the push button itself may stick. If this is the case, the switch must be replaced.
3. If the switch appears to be functioning properly, use a test light to probe the electrical circuit. Clip one end of the test light to a suitable ground such as a door hinge or dashboard mounting bolt. Use the probe end of the test light to see if either of the two wires connected to the rear of the switch carries current. One of the two wires should light the test light.
4. Depress the brake pedal by hand and touch each wire with the test light's probe. Both wires should light the test light when touched with the probe.
5. Release the brake pedal and disconnect the test light.
6. If the switch is defective, you will have to replace it. Unplug the wire connections. Usually spade or slip-on connectors are used.
7. Using a screwdriver, loosen the screws holding the switch to its mounting bracket.
8. Remove the switch and replace it with one designed for your car.
9. Install the new switch, tightening the screws with a screwdriver.
10. Reconnect the two wires to the new switch. The order is not significant.
11. Have someone stand at the rear of the car and tell you when the lights come on as you depress the brake pedal. The brake lights should now be operable.

Servicing A Hydraulic Switch

IF YOUR car has a hydraulically operated brake light switch, follow this procedure:

1. Raise the car's hood.
2. The hydraulic brake light switch will be located on the front portion of the master cylinder or below it and on a junction block that contains a brake line from the master cylinder. This is a pressure-sensitive electrical switch.
3. Use a test light to prove the electrical circuit. Clip one end of the test light to a suitable ground such as a part of the engine block. Use the probe end of the test light to see if either of the two wires connected to the top of the switch carries current. One of the two wires should light the test light.
4. Have someone depress the brake pedal while you touch each wire with the test light's probe. Both wires should light the test light.
5. Release the pedal and disconnect the test light.
6. If the switch is defective, it must be replaced. Unplug the wire connections. Usually spade or slip-on connectors are used.
7. Apply a box-end wrench to the switch and turn it counterclockwise to remove it.
8. Install the new switch, reversing step 7.
9. Reconnect the wires to the new switch, reversing step 6.
10. Have someone stand at the rear of the car and tell you when the lights come on as you depress the brake pedal. The brake lights should now be operable.
11. Close the hood.

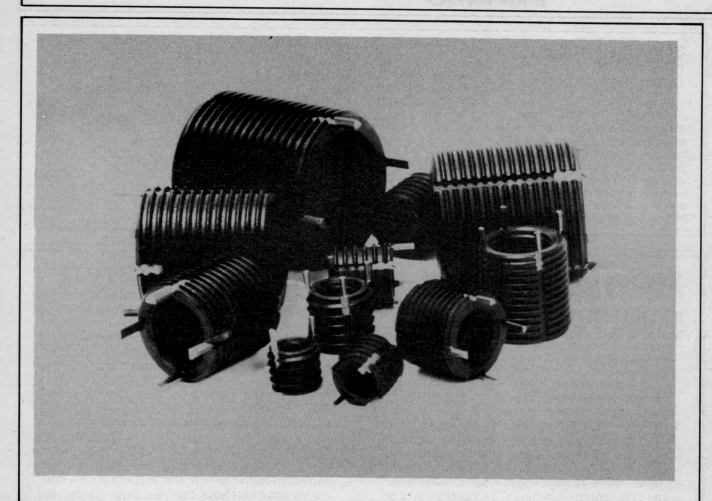

Repair Damaged Threads

If you damage the threads on an expensive automotive part, you need not always have to replace the entire part. There are inserts available that allow you to renew the threads. Kleenserts are metal thread inserts, sold by Tridair Industries, that are installed with standard drills and taps. And, they may be used in virtually any metal—aluminum, magnesium, cast iron, and cold-rolled steel. You drill out the old threads using a standard drill. Then you tap new threads using a standard tap. Next, you screw the insert until it is slightly below the surface. To finish, you drive the insert down with several light taps on the installation tool.

Nine-Piece Socket Set In "Flip-Lock" Tray

One of the best ways to assemble a socket wrench set is to buy a set of commonly used sockets and add to it as you need different sizes. If you have a 3/8 inch drive ratchet, a set made by S-K Tools, a division of Dresser Industries, Inc., may be just what you need. The set, No. 4509, includes nine standard sockets—both 6 and 12 point—packed in a handy "flip-lock" 8-1/4 inch long tray. The top of the tray flips over the sockets to hold them firmly in place, yet flips back to make them easily accessible.

11-Piece, 3/8 Inch Drive Socket Set

You can probably service your car for years without really needing a 3/8 inch drive socket set, but it does come in handy when there is not enough clearance for a large ratchet. Wright Tool and Forge Co. makes an 11-piece, 3/8 inch drive set that contains four six-point sockets: 3/8, 7/16, 1/2 and 9/16 inch, and three 12-point sockets of 5/8, 11/16 and 3/4 inch. Also included are a 13/16 inch spark plug socket, a three inch extension, a five inch extension, a ratchet and a storage box.

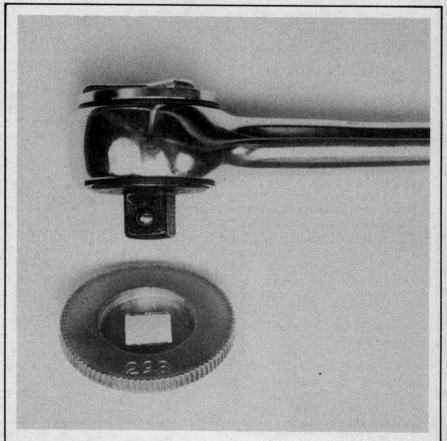

Ratchet Spinner

A ratchet spinner is an extremely handy tool for screwing nuts on or off when they are loose. This can certainly speed up your tune-up work by getting spark plugs in and out in a hurry. Cal-Van Tools Division of Chemi-Trol Chemical Co. sells a No. 298 ratchet spinner that fits 3/8 inch drive sockets without increasing the socket length.

Circuit Tester By Vaco

Tools and instruments that are designed to clip in your pocket are handy and can be ready for use whenever you need them. One such instrument is Vaco Products Company's circuit tester, Model 70130. The device can be used on 100 to 500 volt circuits AC or DC. The neon glow lamp indicates the hot side of the line. The 2-1/8 inch screwdriver-shaped probe easily fits into receptacles. The overall length of the tester is 5-1/2 inches.

Manual Impact Drivers Work Like Electric And Air Models

Sometimes a screw or bolt will not come loose even when it is soaked with penetrating oil. This is the time to turn to a reversible impact driver that can solve the problem of turning rusted, frozen or other stubborn screws. The driver is a hand-held unit that is hit with a hammer. Striking the end imparts a twisting motion to the screwdriver or socket head. Vaco Products Company sells a reversible impact driver set, No. 70220, that consists of an impact driver with a 3/8 inch square drive fitting, an adapter for 5/16 inch hex bits and four hex screwdriver bits (5/16 and 1/2 inch regular slotted, No. 2 and No. 4 Phillips).

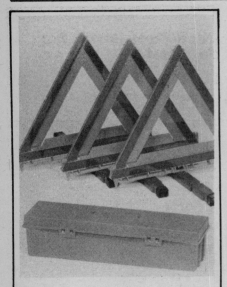

Safety Triangles

Carter Hall, Inc. sells a set of three heavy-duty safety triangles, Model ST-1000, that meets U.S. Department of Transportation specifications, including the 40 mph wind test. The triangles reflect in both directions and have nonslip rubber feet. They are easy to store since they collapse and fit into a heavy-duty plastic case. This type of road hazard warning device is one of the best and in Department of Transportation tests was found superior to any kind of flashing light, flag or flare.

Custom Tire Cleaner

White walls and raised white letters on tires add an attractive touch to a car, but they can be hard to keep clean. Le Vernier's Custom Tire Cleaner, from Le Vernier's Custom Crest Car Products, Inc., is made to keep your tires looking good. It comes in a 20 ounce can with a fingertip sprayer. To clean, you just spray it on the surface, wait two or three minutes, and then rub with a rag and hose off. You also can use this product for rubberette, vinyls and plastics, and convertible tops.

Heavy-Duty Tire Pressure Gauge

If you want your tires to give you the longest service possible, you should check their pressure often. To do this, you need an easy-to-read tire pressure gauge. The easiest to use is the type with a dial such as the Model 50125, made by the Automark Division of Wells Manufacturing Corp. It measures pressure from 20 psi to 150 psi. The instrument is silicone-lubricated and comes with a vinyl carrying case.

Check Tire Tread Depth Periodically

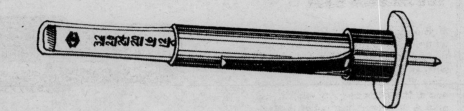

Every once in a while, you should check the depth of your tire treads to be certain that the tires are safe. Checking the tread depth periodically can also tip you off to front end alignment problems before they become so obvious that the tire is on the verge of being ruined. H. B. Egan Manufacturing Co. makes a pocket-type tire tread depth gauge, Camel Model 395, that can be used for measuring the depth of tread in 1/32 inch calibrations from 0 to one inch. It is small enough to fit into your pocket easily.

INTRODUCTION

YOUR CAR'S tires affect the safety, handling characteristics, performance, comfort and cost of operating your vehicle more than any other component. Because they are the part of the car that makes contact with the road, tires deserve much more than casual or occasional attention. Depending on the type of driving you do and the weight of your vehicle, tires—with proper care—should last at least 35,000 miles.

Anatomy Of A Tire

BEFORE discussing selection, maintenance and repair, you should know the various parts of a tire.

CORD BODY. The cord body consists of layers of rubber-impregnated fabric, or cords, called plies, that are bonded into a solid unit.

BEAD. The bead is the portion of the tire that helps keep the tire in contact with the rim of the wheel and provides the air seal on tubeless tires. The bead is constructed of a heavy band of steel wire wrapped into the inner circumference of the tire's ply structure.

TREAD. The tread, or crown, is the portion of the tire that comes in contact with the road surface. It is a pattern of grooves and ribs that provides traction. The grooves are designed to drain off water, while the ribs grip the road surface. Tread thickness varies with tire quality.

SIPES. On some tires, small cuts, called sipes, are molded into the ribs of the tread. These sipes open as the tire flexes on the road, offering additional gripping action, especially on wet road surfaces.

SIDEWALLS. These are the sides of the tire body. They are constructed of thinner material than the tread to offer greater flexibility.

WEAR BARS. New tires feature horizontal wear bars, bands or indicators in the tread pattern that become visible when the tread has worn to a level only 1/16 inch deep. After that level has been reached, they produce a thumping sound to remind the driver that the tire is ready for replacement.

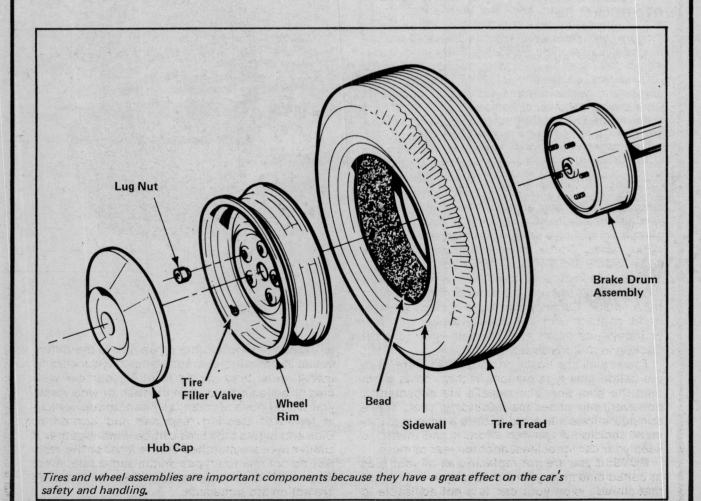

Lug Nut

Tire Filler Valve

Wheel Rim

Hub Cap

Bead

Sidewall

Tire Tread

Brake Drum Assembly

Tires and wheel assemblies are important components because they have a great effect on the car's safety and handling.

Valve Extensions Make Tire Inflation Easy

If your car is equipped with fancy wheel covers that extend out from the wheel, you may find it necessary to remove the wheel cover to gain access to the valve. You can avoid this unnecessary work if you use a tubeless tire valve extension, such as those sold by H. B. Egan Manufacturing Co. These extensions screw on to a standard 0.302 inch valve cap thread of the

stem to make the valve mouth accessible. Camel chrome-plated brass models are available in 3/4 and 1-1/4 inch lengths. Plastic models are available in 3/4, 1-1/4 and 1-1/2 inch lengths.

Types Of Tires

WHEN BUYING tires, good judgement can save you money. It also can save your life. A tire that is not up to the task of accepting additional load during emergency handling may fail just when you need that extra margin of safety. A tire that cannot withstand the impact of a curb or pothole when you have an extra-heavy load in your vehicle is giving you a false sense of security. Therefore, you should invest in tires that are at least as good as the original ones, or better if you think you will need them.

Basically, there are three types of tire construction: bias, belted bias and belted radial.

BIAS TIRE. Until the late 1960s, the bias tire was the standard for most cars made in the United States. It has two, four or more plies or layers of rubber-coated synthetic cords (rayon, nylon, polyester or other material) that cross from one bead to the other at an angle, or bias, of about 35 or 40 degrees. These plies alternate in direction with each ply to provide sidewall strength. Advantages of bias tires include low cost, good mileage and dependability.

BELTED BIAS TIRE. The construction of the belted bias tire is similar to the bias tire but it also features two or more broad belts of fabric between the tread and the bias plies. These belts, generally made of polyester, fiberglass or finely woven steel wire, are not connected to the tire beads as are the bias plies. They lend stability to the tire by reducing tread motion or "squirming" as the tire is rolling. And, the tread remains in better contact with the road surface. Belted bias tires are common replacement tires for most cars since they offer increased mileage, excellent traction and a resistance to punctures.

BELTED RADIAL TIRE. The belted radial tire is a major improvement in tire design. Instead of crossing at an angle or bias, the cords are placed radially (straight) across the face of the tire from bead to bead. Then, as with the belted bias tire, two or more belts of steel wire or fiberglass are placed on the bias under the tread and over the radial plies. These belts have relatively little "give" and keep the tread very stable, improving steering control and tread life. And, because flexing within the tire is reduced, the radial tire runs cooler. Other advantages include greater tread contact with the road surface and fuel economy—as much as 6 percent—due to a reduction in rolling resistance.

The radial tire costs considerably more than the belted bias type, which, in turn, costs more than the bias tire. The radial's life expectancy, however, can offset the additional cost. These considerations make radial tires a wise replacement decision if you can afford it and intend to keep your car for at least another year or more.

NOTE: If you are not replacing all of your bias or belted bias tires, you should stay with the type that already is on your car. It is not advisable to

The grooves in a tire are designed to drain off water; the ribs grip the road surface.

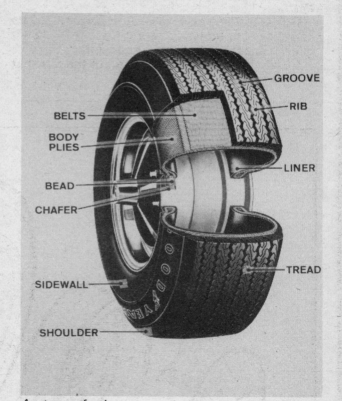

Anatomy of a tire

mix radial tires with other types due to the differences in handling characteristics. If you were to install radial tires on the front of your car with bias or belted bias tires on the rear, or vice versa, you would have a potentially dangerous vehicle in terms of steering response and cornering. Bias and belted bias tires can be used together if similar tires are matched on the front or the rear. But do not mix tire types on the same axle. Also, if you use two different sizes of tires, be sure they are not on the same axle.

Locks Protect Custom Wheels

If you own custom wheels, or even if you have priced them lately, you know that they are very expensive. They are also in great demand and prime targets for thieves. On-Guard Corporation of America sells custom wheel locks designed to protect mag and standard wheels against theft. These locks replace one lug nut on each wheel and cannot be removed unless you have the key that comes with the lock. They are sold in models to fit most American-made cars and Volkswagens. The wheel locks are chrome-plated.

Valve Stem Extensions

If your passenger car has ornamental wheel covers that make the valve stems hard to reach, you should purchase valve stem extensions like those sold by T.P.H. Division of Parker Hannifin. Two models cover applications in most passenger cars. Model 47-300 has a 3/4 inch effective length; the Model 47-304 has a 1-1/4 inch effective length.

Use Valve Extensions

If you cannot reach your tire valves without removing the wheel covers, install tire valve extensions. People tend to put off properly inflating their tires when they have to go to extra effort to do so, and underinflation accelerates tire wear.

TIRE SIZES

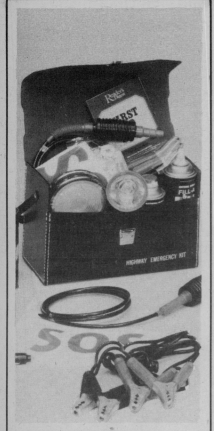

Deluxe Highway Emergency Kit

Many items that can help you whenever you encounter highway emergencies are contained in the Model 500 Deluxe Highway Emergency Kit made by Carter Hall, Inc. It includes a set of booster cables, a tire inflater, and a fire extinguisher in an aerosol can that is effective for all types of small fires. There also is an emergency blinker that operates on three standard D batteries, an auto spotlight that plugs into your cigarette lighter with a 10-foot cord, a gas siphon pump, a first aid pouch, an SOS flag, a first aid book, and instructions.

Wheel Chocks

Whenever you use wheel ramps, you also should use wheel chocks to prevent your vehicle from sliding or rolling. Steel wheel chocks such as those sold by TRW, Inc., Model No. 679104, can also be used when you have your car on a jack or parked on an incline.

Heavy-Duty Wheel Ramp

Primarily designed for the do-it-yourselfer, the heavy-duty wheel ramp, No. 679104, offered by TRW, Inc. can be stored vertically, horizontally or hung on hooks. It is made of heavy-duty structural steel with a red enamel finish. Capacity is 2-1/2 tons. The wheel ramp comes complete with wheel stops and skid-resistant rubber pads. Sold in pairs, each ramp is 10 by 11 by 42 inches.

ONCE, TIRE size was a rather simple matter. In the early 1920s, the sizes of tires were determined by the outside diameter of a tire and its greatest width. For example, a 30x3 tire would have been 30 inches in diameter and three inches wide.

Later, tire manufacturers began designating tire sizes using the width and the wheel rim diameter. If you saw 7.75x14 on the sidewall of a tire, it indicated the tire was 7-3/4 inches wide across the tread from sidewall to sidewall, and the 14 meant it was to be mounted on a wheel having a 14-inch diameter.

Today, the load-configuration-rim system is used. It is more complex but tells the consumer much more about the capability of the tire. This system was encouraged by the development of wide tread tires.

If you see a tire with F78-14 on its sidewall, the "F" is a letter code for the tire's load-carrying capacity. The "F" indicates that the tire is able to carry an amount of weight equal to any other "F" tire no matter what the other size factors are.

The number immediately following the letter code is the aspect ratio of the tire. The last number indicates the rim diameter.

In our specific example, "F" indicates the tire has a load-carrying capacity of 1280 pounds when inflated to 24 pounds per square inch (psi). The 78, the aspect ratio or series number, means the height of the tire from the bead to the tread is 78 percent of the tire's width. And, the 14 indicates the tire is designed for a 14-inch diameter wheel.

The following chart shows the maximum weight each tire size can carry when the tire is inflated to 24 psi:

CODE	CAPACITY
A	900 pounds
B	980 pounds
C	1050 pounds
D	1120 pounds
E	1190 pounds
F	1280 pounds
G	1380 pounds
H	1510 pounds
J	1580 pounds
K	1620 pounds
L	1680 pounds
M	1780 pounds
N	1880 pounds

In addition, another letter may appear with the load-configuration-rim designation. This is the letter "R," which simply indicates the tire is of radial construction. Sometimes, radial tires are measured using the metric system. For example, the radial size in metrics may be 195R-15. Under the load-configuration-rim system, this tire is known as FR78-15.

One thing to keep in mind is that the load-carrying figures for each letter designation are the maximum weights that each tire can carry when inflated to 24 psi. If you put more air pressure in the tire, it will carry more weight.

In addition, the sidewall of a tire has a load range designation. If an F78-14 tire (1280 pounds at 24 psi) is marked "Load Range B," it indicates a four-ply rating and the tire can be inflated to 32 psi when cold to increase its load-carrying capacity to 1500 pounds. A "Load Range C" (six-ply rating) tire can be inflated to 36 psi,

increasing its capacity to 1610 pounds. A "Load Range D" (eight-ply rating) tire can be inflated to 40 psi, increasing its capacity to 1700 pounds.

Other information on the sidewall of a tire includes whether it is a tube-type or tubeless tire. There also will be the letters "DOT" followed by a three-digit number. This indicates that the tire complies with the U.S. Department of Transportation safety standards, while the number is a code identifying the manufacturer and the tire plant location.

Finally, the sidewall will spell out the exact number of plies in the tire and sidewall and their composition.

Always replace tires with a size at least as large as the tires that came with the car originally. If load or driving requirements warrant it, you may wish to move up a step in tire size. If you decide to change tire size and type when replacing your car's tires, get the advice of a knowledgeable tire dealer before making your purchase.

Today's tires are marked with a wealth of information.

Collapsible or "compact" spare tires are being sold with some automobiles today. They occupy less room in the trunk, but cannot be used over long distances.

TIRE CARE

THE COST of keeping good quality tires on your car could as much as double if you fail to give them the attention they deserve. The main causes of rapid tire wear are improper inflation, incorrect wheel alignment, incorrect wheel balance, wrong size for car and load, defective shock absorbers and poor driving habits.

Inflation

AIR is one of the few things you can still get for free, even in compressed form at your local service station. But because modern tires give us so little trouble, we often forget about them until the damage is done. A good practice is to check tire pressure every week or two, prior to a long trip, and if you are driving from a relatively hot climate to a cold climate or vice versa. Tires should always be checked when they are cool. Properly inflated tires at one temperature could suddenly become overinflated or underinflated as temperature changes.

A good investment is an accurate tire pressure gauge, which can be purchased for a few dollars. Do not rely on the accuracy of the gauge that is mounted on the hose at your service station. They often are mistreated—run over and dropped—and are known to be inaccurate. To check your tire pressure:

1. Examine the side of your tire. The maximum cold inflation pressure for a full load will be marked. For example, on a tire marked "Load Range B," this will probably be 32 psi. This indicates that the tires should be inflated to 32 pounds when they are cool and when your car is loaded. When the tires are not required to carry a maximum load, run them at two or three pounds less of pressure. **NOTE:** Never deflate tires when they are hot just because they indicate an overinflated condition. When they cool, they will return to their normal inflation pressure.
2. Locate the tire air valve on the wheel.
3. Unscrew the cap on the air valve by hand.
4. Press the end of the tire pressure gauge that fits over the tire air valve down on the valve.
5. Read the tire air pressure indicated on the gauge.
6. If the pressure is correct, reinstall the tire air valve cap.

   NOTE: The correct tire inflation for your car will be provided in the owner's manual or on an information decal or sticker

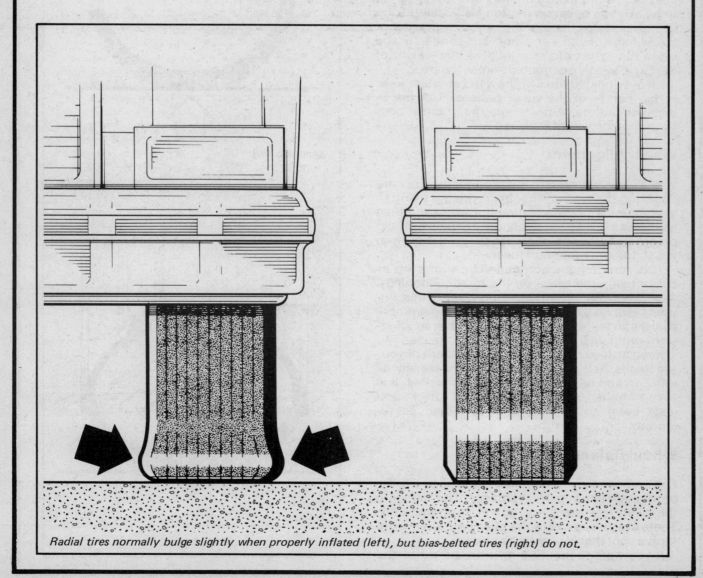

Radial tires normally bulge slightly when properly inflated (left), but bias-belted tires (right) do not.

Whitewall Tire Brushes

It is a lot easier cleaning your whitewall tires if you have a brush that is designed for the task. Rittenbaum Brothers, Inc. makes three whitewall tire brushes. Their Nun-Better Model 4-34 has nylon fiber bristles and a large block. The Model 4-35 is a brass wire brush with the same size block. They also produce Model 4-37, which is a small block brush with brass wire bristles for tough jobs.

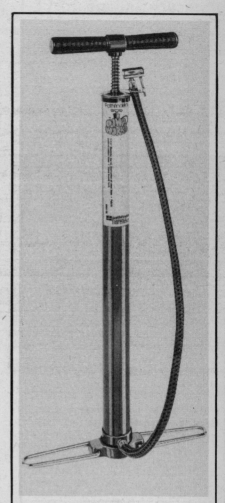

Heavy-Duty Air Pump

It is always a good idea to have an air pump in your garage for those occasions when you find that your tires are low on air. Pathfinder Auto Lamp Company sells a heavy-duty air pump, Model PW42, that features an extra-large 1-1/2 inch diameter barrel and provides 25 cubic inches of displacement. It is rated at 60 pounds per square inch (psi). Fittings are brass and aluminum, and the hose is fabric-covered rubber with a quick-disconnect thumb lock.

Deluxe Tire Brush

After washing your car, did you ever notice that the nooks and crannies of your custom wheels are still dirty? This often happens because it is hard to reach the parts of the wheel with a regular sponge. Mastermotive, Inc. sells a hub and tire tool, No. 800, that hooks up to a garden hose. It features a brush head with nylon bristles.

Passenger Car Pressure Gauges

At least once a month and always before you take a long trip, you should check your tire pressure. A passenger car-type pressure gauge such as the Camel Model 400 made by H.B. Egan Manufacturing Co. is a pocket-type gauge with a nylon stick calibrated to 50 pounds in one pound units. It has a chrome-plated barrel and a fountain pen-type clip.

White Sidewall Cleaner Saves Elbow Grease

A spray-on White Sidewall Cleaner to clean dirt, scuffs and grime from white wall tires with a minimum of effort is made by Johnson Wax. You can also use the J-Wax cleaner on all other colored sidewalls. It is available in a 16 ounce can.

Four-Way Lug Nut Wrenches Ease Tire Changing

The four-way type of lug wrench is superior to the kind that comes with your jack when you buy your car. It gives you better leverage and allows you to spin the lug off with the wrench. This offers faster wheel changing. Four-way lug wrenches are sold by Proto Tool Division of Ingersoll-Rand. No. 9414 has the following sizes: 11/16, 3/4, 13/16 inch and 19mm. It measures 14 inches. Another 14-inch model, the No. 9414M gives you 17mm, 19mm, 22mm, and 13/16 inch openings. The No. 9416 provides openings of 3/4, 13/16, 7/8 inch and 19mm. A 20-inch model, the No. 9420, gives you the same size openings except that a 15/16 inch opening is substituted for the 19mm one.

Tire Brushes

Cleaning white wall tires can be a tough job if you do not have the right brush. TRW, Inc. makes a line of short-handled tire brushes measuring 8-3/4 by 2-1/2 inches. The brushes are available with brass wire, steel wire and nylon bristles.

TIRE CARE

somewhere in your car. Usually, this can be found inside the glove compartment door.

7. If the pressure of a tire is not correct, place the end of the air supply hose over the tire's air valve. If the air supply hose is equipped with its own air pressure gauge, keep the hose on the air filler valve until the gauge indicates the approximate amount of air pressure you require, but use your own gauge to read the exact pressure. If no gauge is on the air supply hose, check the pressure from time to time with your own air pressure gauge as you fill the tire.

   NOTE: If you are carrying a heavy load or are pulling a trailer, you should put in two to four pounds more pressure than normal.

8. Once the proper air pressure is achieved, reinstall the air valve cap.

Whenever checking the tire pressure, you also should take time to check as best you can for bruises, cuts or unusual wear patterns. The best time to do this task thoroughly, however, is when your car is elevated during lubrication. Do not just examine the tread and outside sidewall. Check the inside sidewall too. Remove nails, small stones or other objects imbedded in and between the tread. Do not forget to examine the tire air valve. Keep all air valves equipped with extensions and caps to keep out dirt and moisture.

You can identify probable inflation problems by visually checking your tires. An underinflated tire wears more rapidly on the outer edges of the tread. This is because the too-soft body of the tire tends to flex more at the center, with most of the weight of the car being supported by the sidewalls. When properly inflated, the weight of the car is evenly distributed across the tread.

An overinflated tire will show the greatest wear at the center of the tread pattern. The tire is distended at the center where the greatest concentration of weight is placed.

Wheel Alignment

WHEN your wheels are misaligned, the tires are "bucking the system." In effect, you are trying to make the car go in one direction while the tires are pulling in another direction. Therefore, in the process of forcing them back on track, you are scrubbing rubber off the tread.

This scrubbing action generally shows up as cut or feathered areas on the tread. Eventually, such tires will begin to thump due to this unevenness. An experienced wheel alignment specialist can tell whether or not you have an alignment problem by studying your tires' treads.

Keep a close check on the wear pattern of your tire treads. At the first sign of unevenness, check inflation and have the alignment rechecked. It is wise to have your wheel alignment checked at least every six months and corrected as required.

Wheel Balancing

IT IS extremely rare when a tire comes off the production line in perfect balance. The rubber in the plies just does not go on that smoothly. There are places where the plies butt together to form a spot that is slightly heavier.

If you were to mount a new tire on a rim and

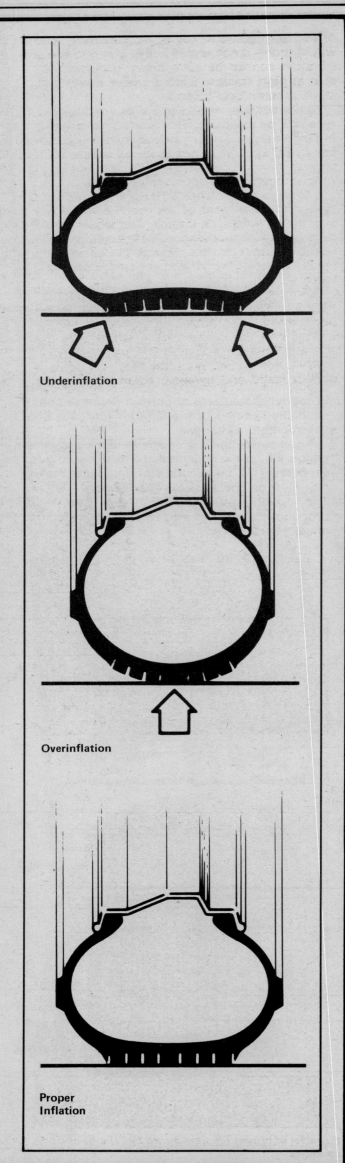

Underinflation

Overinflation

Proper Inflation

drive away without having it balanced, you would soon—if not immediately—begin to feel a vibration caused by such heavy spots as they spin at high speeds. Such a wheel would lack static or centrifugal balance.

To correct this, wheels and tires are balanced as a unit or assembly. This is accomplished by adding an equal amount of lead weight opposite the heavy spot. It is not quite as simple as it sounds, however, since weights are added at various locations for optimum balancing.

If there is a difference in weight between the inner and outer faces of the tire, the wheel will shimmy or wobble as it turns. The wheel would then lack dynamic balance. Both static and dynamic imbalances are solved by positioning small lead weights on the wheel rim opposite any heavy areas.

One method of balancing uses a "bubble" machine. The wheel and tire assembly is set horizontally on a balancing device. A bubble indicator at the center of the wheel tells the operator when the assembly is in static balance.

While some specialists say they can achieve perfect static and dynamic balance using the bubble device, your best investment is to have the assembly checked by the dynamic method described below.

The most common and generally accepted system of wheel balancing is dynamic balancing, which means spinning the tire and wheel assembly at high speeds with the wheels either on the car or dismounted and placed on a special machine. Actually, spin-balancing covers both dynamic and static conditions and is the surest way of knowing your wheel/tire assembly will be in balance when you are traveling at highway speeds.

Poor Driving Habits

THE ONLY one who can correct poor driving habits is the driver. Tire life can be increased—sometimes significantly—by avoiding jack rabbit starts, panic-like stops, and hard, fast cornering that scrubs off tread from your tires. Other factors that contribute to shortening the lifespan of your tires are impacts against curbs and potholes and high speed driving.

1

2

3

4

Examples of uneven tire wear caused by (1) over-inflation, (2) underinflation, (3) misalignment and (4) improper balancing.

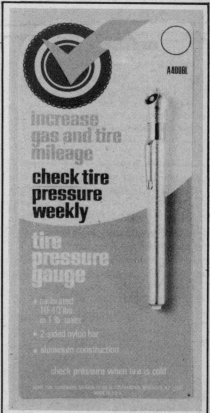

Basic 16-Piece Socket Set

The beginning mechanic needs a basic 1/2 inch square drive socket set. This size set is best for all-around automotive repair and should be the first socket set that the beginner buys. Indestro, a division of Duro Metal Products Co., sells a 16-piece socket set that includes 13, 12-point, 1/2 inch drive sockets in sizes that are most normally used: 7/16, 1/2, 9/16, 5/8, 11/16, 3/4, 13/16, 7/8, 15/16, 1, 1-1/16, 1-1/8 and 1-1/4 inch. There also is a 5-1/2 inch extension and a 15-1/2 inch swing-head handle and reversible ratchet. All tools are in a metal box measuring 15-3/4 by 4-1/8 by 1-13/16 inches.

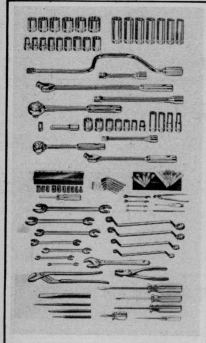

62-Piece Socket Wrench And Tool Set

The complexity of the modern automobile means you will be using many different types of tools in your repair work. Right from the beginning, you will find a large, basic tool set very useful. Indestro, a division of Duro Metal Products Co., sells a 62-piece socket wrench and tool set that includes most of the basic tools you will need. The kit, No. 7834, includes 1/4, 3/8, and 1/2 inch square drive socket sets, a selection of box wrenches, open-end wrenches, screwdrivers and an array of miscellaneous tools. They come in a utility-type metal tool box measuring 19-3/4 by 7 by 8 inches.

TIRE ROTATION

THERE ARE two schools of thought regarding tire rotation. One says rotate tires periodically. The other says do not bother unless the wear pattern indicates a need.

The principle of tire rotation is that tires be changed periodically from position to position on the car to level out any unevenness that may develop due to driving conditions and load factors. Rotation has the benefit of extending tire life because tread wear is more even during the life of all four (or five, including the spare) tires. The tires all tend to wear out at the same time.

A negative factor is that once your tires are balanced on a wheel, rotation could conceal alignment problems. However, you will probably have satisfactory performance by letting your tires stay where they are, providing inflation is maintained and wheels are kept in alignment. If you move a tire from left front to right rear, for example, you may have to have the tires rebalanced.

Those in favor of rotation say we also should take the spare tire into consideration. Why have a brand new spare in the trunk while wearing out the rest of the tires? But, on the other hand, why not keep the spare brand new until such time as you need two new tires? This way, you already have one to match up with the new one you just purchased. However, tires do deteriorate with age.

If you should decide to do your own tire rotation, do it once a year and proceed as follows:

1. Place the car into parking gear.
2. Remove all four wheel covers, using a large screwdriver or the pointed end of your car's jack handle.
3. Using the wrench end of the jack handle or a socket wrench of proper size, loosen all wheel lug nuts about one turn.
4. Place a wheel chock at the front and rear of each rear wheel.
5. Using the car jack, raise up the front of the car until the wheels are off the ground.
6. Place jack stands under the front of the car to support it.
7. Jack up the rear of the car until the rear wheels are off the ground.
8. Place jack stands under the rear of the car to support it.
9. Remove the wheel lug nuts of each wheel, placing the nuts for each wheel into their respective wheel covers for safe keeping. Most lug nuts can be removed by turning them counterclockwise. Some cars, however, will have a left-hand thread on the lug nuts. In such a case, the lugs may be marked with the letter "L." If your car has left-handed threaded lugs, turn the nuts clockwise to loosen them.

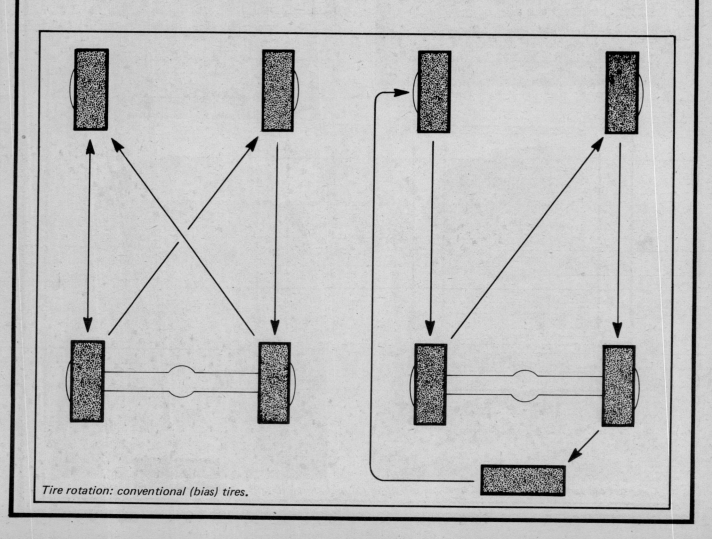

Tire rotation: conventional (bias) tires.

NOTE: On some cars, it is difficult to remove the rear wheels unless the car body is jacked up above the rear wheels. If you encounter this situation, carefully jack up the rear bumper of the car while it is still on the jack stands to slide the tire off the lugs. Be careful not to raise the car off the jack stands!

If your car is equipped with full rear wheel fender skirts, they must be removed before you can remove the rear wheels. There is a locking bar on the inside of the fender skirt. Lift it upward with your hand to remove the fender skirt.

10. Relocate the tires as shown in the accompanying diagrams, depending upon the type of tires you have. **NOTE:** Radial and bias belted tires should not be switched across the car—only from front to rear and rear to front on the same side of the car. If you include your spare radial or bias belted tire in the rotation process, be sure that you mark the tire that goes into the trunk to indicate which side of the car it came from. It should always be used on that side when needed again, except in an emergency situation.
11. Remount all the wheels in their new positions.
12. Firmly tighten the lug nuts by hand on each wheel. **NOTE:** Tighten the uppermost lug nut first and then tighten the opposite one on the bottom. Then tighten opposing pairs. When all nuts on a wheel have been tightened firmly but not completely, spin the wheel and check to make sure all the lug nuts have been seated properly.
13. Raise the rear of the car with the jack and remove the jack stands.
14. Lower the car until the wheels are firmly on the ground.
15. Place a wheel chock in the front and the rear of each rear wheel.

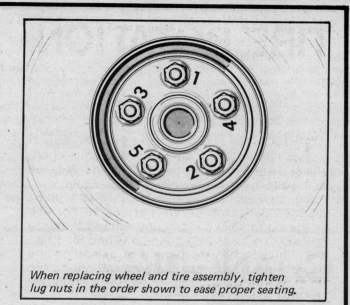

When replacing wheel and tire assembly, tighten lug nuts in the order shown to ease proper seating.

16. Raise the front of the car and remove the jack stands.
17. Lower the car until the wheels are firmly on the ground.
18. With the car's wheels on the ground, tighten all the lug nuts snugly with the jack wrench or socket wrench. **NOTE:** As you tighten the lug nuts, tighten them in the manner described in step 12.
19. Reinstall the wheel covers. You may need a rubber mallet or hammer for this task.
20. Remove the wheel chocks.

NOTE: It may be necessary to have your wheels rebalanced after tire rotation. This is generally the case if your wheels were originally balanced by an on-the-car method. If you detect any wheel shimmy or vibration while driving, have the wheel balance checked by a professional mechanic.

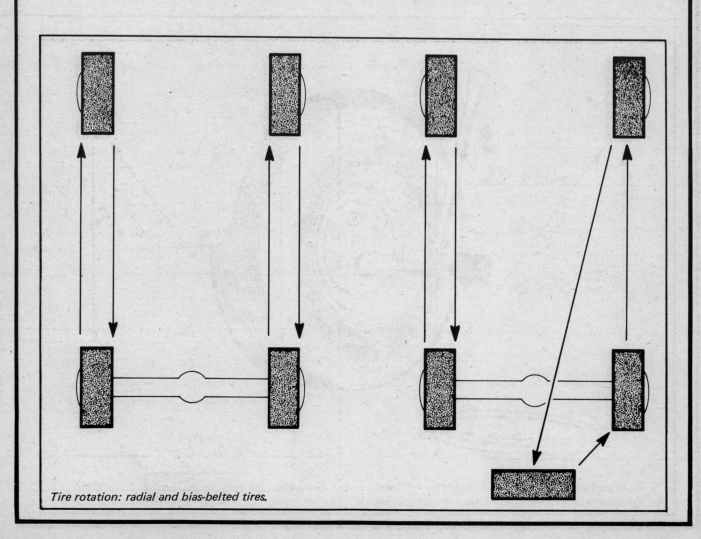

Tire rotation: radial and bias-belted tires.

84-Piece Assortment Of Tools

If you can afford the initial investment, you might make your first tool purchase a large set, such as the 84-piece tool set by Blackhawk Hand Tools, Model 604-B. This set includes 1/2, 3/8, and 1/4 inch drive socket sets. The 1/2 and 3/8 inch drive sets include regular and extra deep sockets. In addition, you get rib-lock pliers, six-inch slip-joint pliers, 6-1/2 inch side-cutting pliers, four inch shank screwdriver, six inch shank screwdriver, three inch Phillips screwdriver, four inch Phillips screwdriver, and all-purpose feeler gauge.

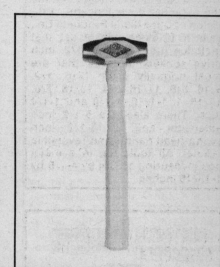

Bronze Hammer Reduces Spark Hazard

Cal-Van Tools Division of Chemi-Trol Chemical Co. has a soft bronze hammer, No. 126, that is designed to drive easily damaged parts in areas where sparks could be hazardous. The two-pound bronze hammer has a polished and lacquered head of cast bronze. It also has a straight-grain hickory handle with a hex design for positive gripping.

Mechanic's Starter Set

Eighty-eight of the most useful everyday tools for auto service and repair are included in a mechanic's starter set from Proto Tool Division of Ingersoll-Rand. The 88-piece set is ideal for the starting mechanic. It includes gauges, punches, cold chisels, a variety of pliers and a hacksaw. Also included are a wide variety of combination wrenches (open-end and box), a ball-peen hammer, a plastic tip hammer, an ignition point file, a carbon scraper, and a set of screwdrivers. Most important, it has a selection of 3/8 and 1/2 inch drive socket sets with ratchets, extensions, hinge handles and speed handles. The Model 9912 tool set comes in a metal chest with a lift-out tote tray. If you already have a box, you may purchase the tools separately as Model 9911.

Easiest Way To Fix A Flat

Sometimes changing a flat tire is very inconvenient. You may have on good clothes, or it may be snowing or raining. In such an emergency, you can use an aerosol tire sealant and inflator such as Seal-N-Flate, sold by Unival Corp. It is designed to seal most punctures in the tread and inflate the tire at the same time. Removal of the cause of the puncture is unnecessary. The product is formulated not to affect wheel balance. It comes in a 12 ounce aerosol can.

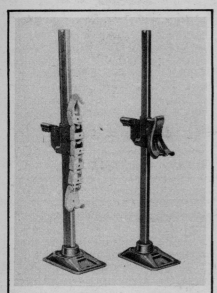

Replacement Emergency Jack

A jack is the most important type of emergency equipment you can carry in your car. If you use a bumper jack often, it usually will need replacement. The Blackhawk portable jack, No. 67207, made by Applied Power, Inc. is designed for late-model cars that have jacking slots in their bumpers. This jack, with a capacity of 2000 pounds, has a flexible, vinyl-coated lifting hook that adjusts to the contour of the bumper. The jack base measures six by eight inches. The lifting range is from 6-1/2 to 34-1/8 inches. It weighs 14 pounds.

Four-Way Lug Wrenches

The lug wrench you get with your jack as original equipment is not always the easiest type to use. You will find that a four-way lug wrench will remove lugs easier and faster because it gives you better leverage and allows you to spin the lug off. S-K Tools Division of Dresser Industries, Inc. offers them in 14, 16-1/2, 20, and 22 inch sizes. The lug wrenches are available with standard-size sockets.

Emergency Tire Pump

H. B. Egan Manufacturing Co. sells a convenient tire pump apparatus that requires almost no effort on your part. You can use this pump for inflating tires anywhere. It is composed of a 16 inch flexible braid, covered, heavy-duty rubber hose; a built-in pressure gauge that indicates pressure while pumping; and a universal pumping kit to fit all spark plug openings. To use, you remove a spark plug and attach the hose in its fitting by screwing it into the spark plug hole. You attach the other end of the hose to the tire you want to inflate. As you run the engine, air enters the cylinder through the intake ports. This outside air is then pumped into the tire. The Camel Spark Plug Tire Pump, No. 488, is designed to provide up to 130 psi and to inflate an auto tire in less than two minutes. All parts are plated steel to resist rust.

CHANGING A TIRE

Tires worn from overinflation (left) and underinflation (right).

TIRES HAVE come a long, long way. Once, an outing in the family's motor car was delayed by at least one or two flats, and in those days, every car carried two or more spare tires for such routine emergencies.

Although flat tires are nowhere near as common as they once were, everyone who drives an automobile should know how to change a tire. Trouble could occur when no one else is around to lend a hand.

Changing a tire is relatively simple if you follow a few directions and are aware of a few safety precautions. One thing to remember if you have tire trouble is: Always drive your car well off the road and as far away from traffic as possible.

If you do not, you are endangering your own life as well as the lives of others should an accident happen. If you are in a position where you cannot quickly pull off the road to a safe site, such

To avoid accidents, wheel lug nuts should be loosened one full turn before the car is jacked up. With the wheel off the ground, the loose nuts can then be removed safely. Most nuts come off with a counterclockwise turn.

A Spare Tire In A Can

A tire inflator and sealant called Air and Repair is marketed by Gold Eagle Co. The product is designed to quickly inflate and seal tires damaged by a normal puncture. One can contains enough for one tube or tubeless tire. The product is designed not to affect tire balance or wear alignment and, depending upon the tire size, will give the tire 15 to 25 pounds of pressure. Air and Repair contains an antifreeze additive.

Four-Way Lug Wrenches With Standard Sockets

TRW, Inc. markets two, four-way, heat-treated lug wrenches for tires. You can select a 17 or 22 inch wrench with socket sizes of 3/4, 13/16, 7/8, and 15/16 inch. You should be careful when choosing the length of a lug wrench. A longer model will give you better leverage, but it may not allow you to spin the lug on and off the wheel if its length causes it to contact the ground.

Safety Wheel Chocks

When you are jacking up your car to change a flat tire, there is always a danger that the weight of the car might shift and the car may fall off the jack. You can prevent this by stopping the car from rolling. The way to do this properly is to place a wheel chock in front and behind the tire diagonally across from the tire you are working on. Pathfinder Auto Lamp Company sells a pair of inexpensive chocks, Model 7420, that are made of extra-strength red plastic. They are tested for load resistance and store handily in your trunk.

Here Is What You Will Need

Materials
- Spare Tire
- Emergency Markers

Tools
- Wheel Chocks or Rocks
- Jack and Jack Handle

---

as on an interstate highway or a bridge, it is better to risk damaging your tire than to risk lives. Drive on the flat until you can find a safe site to pull over.

If you have tire trouble, the spare tire in your car becomes part of the repair. For this reason, it is good practice to periodically check the air pressure of the spare tire. You never know when you will need it. To change a flat tire, follow these steps:

1. Drive the car onto a level surface safely out of the way of traffic.
2. Put on your car's emergency flashers and turn off the engine.
3. Place emergency markers on the roadway behind your vehicle. A well-equipped motorist will have an emergency kit that contains marker flags and emergency flares.
4. Place wheel chocks under the front and rear of the wheel at the opposite corner from the flat tire. You may use rocks found in the area if you do not have wheel chocks of some type available.
5. Open the car trunk and remove the spare tire, jack and jack handle. Usually these items are removed by unscrewing by hand the wing nut that secures the spare tire. Place the spare tire on the ground.
6. According to the jacking instructions for your car (these are usually found on the underside of the trunk lid), place the jack at the corner of the car where the flat tire is located. Jack up the car only high enough to put tension on the jack.
7. Using the pointed end of the jack handle, remove the wheel cover of the flat tire wheel. **NOTE:** If you are working on a rear wheel, there may be a fender skirt that must be removed before the tire can be removed from the wheel. There is a locking bar on the inside of the fender skirt. Lift the bar upward with your hand to remove the fender skirt.
8. Using the lug nut wrench end of the jack handle, loosen the wheel's lug nuts one full turn by turning them counterclockwise. **NOTE:** Some cars will have a left-hand thread on the lug nuts. In such a case, the lugs may be marked with the letter "L." If your car has left-hand threaded lugs, turn the nuts clockwise to loosen them.
9. With the lug nuts loosened one full turn, jack up the car until the tire is off the ground.
10. Remove the lug nuts with the wrench and remove the flat tire.
11. Place the spare tire in position on the lugs and reinstall the lug nuts by hand. Begin with the uppermost nut. Then tighten the opposite nut on the bottom. Continue to tighten opposite pairs until all nuts have been tightened firmly by hand. Spin the tire and check to see if the wheel is on properly and all nuts have been seated correctly.
12. With the jack, lower the car until it is touching the ground.
13. Tighten the lug nuts snugly with the lug wrench end of the jack handle.
14. Lower the car the rest of the way to the ground and remove the jack from the car.
15. Replace the wheel cover and fender skirt if applicable.
16. Place the flat tire, jack, jack handle, emergency flags and wheel chocks in the trunk.
17. Turn off the emergency flashers.
18. Have the flat tire repaired.

Fix A Flat In A Minute

Radiator Specialty Co. manufactures a product that is designed to fix a flat tire in less than a minute. Solderseal Puncture Seal No. M11-12 comes in a 12 ounce aerosol can. To fix a flat tire, you merely insert the nozzle over the tire valve and push. It inflates the tire and seals the puncture.

Heavy-Duty Tire Pump

A hand-type tire pump is an inexpensive but convenient piece of equipment to have in your garage. It comes in handy when you find that one of your tires has a slow leak. A tire pump can reinflate the tire so you can quickly drive to a service station to have the tire fixed. You also can use a tire pump to keep the pressure correct for best tire wear and handling. TRW sells a heavy-duty tire pump, No. 671600, that has a 1-1/2 by 21 inch barrel, ball-check valve and a die-cast threaded cap with oil hole. Its 24 inch reinforced hose is made of braided nylon.

TIRE REPAIR

PROPER REPAIR of a puncture on tubeless tires should be performed with the tire dismounted from the rim. Any on-the-wheel repair should be considered only an emergency measure and should be corrected properly as soon as possible. If the tire casing is not patched on the inside, air—under pressure—can make its way inside the plies, causing ply or belt separation. Eventually, this can ruin your tire.

Because your safety and the safety of others is at stake, think twice about using a tire that has been repaired, even when the work was performed by a capable professional. Your best bet is to use the tire as a spare. Mark it in some manner to make it easily identifiable.

We recommend that tire repairs, even temporary on-the-wheel repairs, be left to the experienced and well-equipped professional.

INTRODUCTION

THERE ARE TWO ways to care for your automobile: preventive maintenance and corrective maintenance. One is designed to prevent trouble, the other to correct it.

A great deal of what you do to maintain your vehicle will determine whether or not you will be preventing or correcting trouble. If, for example, you tend to ignore tire inflation until you notice steering or handling problems, the corrective measure will probably be to replace the tire since it soon will be worn out.

If you fail to have your car's brake pads or shoes checked and replaced as a preventive measure, they may wear into the rotors or drums. The corrective measure can be expensive because you may have worn the brakes to the point where metal is contacting metal. The rotors or drums will then have to be resurfaced or replaced.

Periodic maintenance is the way to avoid many expensive corrective measures. The accompanying maintenance and lubrication chart serves as a guide to preventive maintenance. Keep in mind that maintenance schedules vary from car to car, but the major systems on most vehicles are so similar that the main difference will probably be the recommended interval before servicing.

Weatherstrip Adhesive

If your car's trunk or windows are leaking, it is probably the fault of the weatherstripping. Sometimes rubber weatherstripping works loose or goes out of shape, creating a leak. Woodhill/Permatex sells a Super Weatherstrip Adhesive that is available in two and five ounce tubes. It bonds rubber and vinyl to metal.

Heavy-Duty Bug Screens

At certain times of the year, you may find that the front of your car and radiator have been splattered with bugs. A bug screen such as that made by Rittenbaum Brothers, Inc. under the Nun-Better tradename may be just what you need. These heavy-duty bug screens have reinforced metal eyelets, elastic straps and S-hooks. They come in three sizes: Model 21-56 measures 24 by 56 inches, Model 21-72 is 24 by 72 inches, and Model 21-84 is 24 by 84 inches.

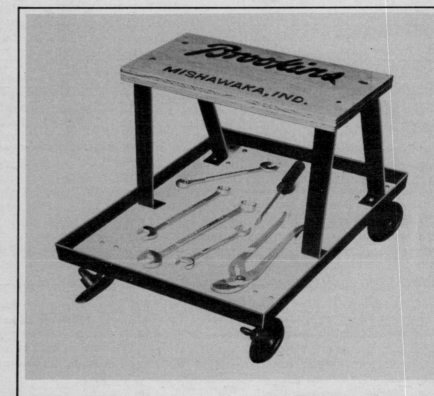

Clean And Polish Vinyl Top At One Time

Just as a cleaner and polish saves time when working on your car's paint finish, a combination cleaner and polish is also a timesaver for vinyl top maintenance. Dupli-Color Products, a division of American Home Products Corp., offers a vinyl cleaner and dressing that is formulated for one-step cleaning and polishing. You can use it on any color vinyl top as well as interior trim.

Mechanics Seat And Tool Tray

If you are tired of kneeling on cold hard cement floors when servicing brakes, adjusting wheels or making body repairs, you should consider purchasing a mechanic's seat of the proper height. Brookins Model 273, made by Balcrank Products Division of Wheelabrator-Frye, Inc., measures 14 by 18 by 12 inches, just about the right dimensions for comfortable working. The seat rolls on sturdy, three inch metal casters and features a handy tool tray beneath the seat.

Let Your Vinyl Shine

Next time you are in your automobile, take a look around and see how much of the interior is vinyl. Vinyl looks good and can reduce the weight of a car, but if it is dull, it is unattractive. If there is much vinyl in your car, you should get a special product to clean it. Pizazz made by Woodhill/Permatex is such an item. It is made to shine and protect leather, vinyl, rubber, acrylic, and even wood. It comes in an eight ounce spray bottle.

Vinyl Dressing Offers Guaranteed Protection

A vinyl dressing offered by Le Vernier's Custom Crest Car Products, Inc. is guaranteed to protect your car's vinyl top for at least 12 months after the original application. The Custom Vinyl Dressing is applied by scrubbing the top clean and making sure all detergent is rinsed off. Then, you dry the top and in a warm, but not hot, location, and liberally apply one coat of the dressing with a small, cloth pad. It dries in about 15 minutes. If you notice any uneven spots, apply another coat. The product also can be used on your tires to make them look newer.

Cleaner For Electrical Contacts

Electrical components on a car often become dirty and gummed with oil and other residue. For efficient operation, they should be cleaned from time to time. CRC Chemicals, Inc. sells Electra-Motive Cleaner for electrical systems and equipment. It is non-flammable, making it an ideal replacement for carbon tetrachloride. No rinsing is required since it leaves no residue. It is available in six and 20 ounce aerosol cans. This cleaner should be tested on a small area before use because it may be harmful to some plastics, such as Lexan, a polycarbonate.

AUTO CARE

QUICK-REFERENCE MAINTENANCE AND LUBRICATION GUIDE

Service at Indicated Time and/or Mileage Intervals		2 Months		6 Months		12 Months		24 Months	36 Months
	Fuel Stop	2000 Miles	4000 Miles	5000 Miles	6000 Miles	10000 Miles	12000 Miles	24000 Miles	36000 Miles
Check Engine Oil Level	●								
Check Radiator Coolant Level	●								
Check Battery Liquid Level	●								
Check Windshield Washer Reservoir Level	●								
Lubricate Generator Cup(s) (if so equipped)		●							
Lubricate Distributor Cup		●							
Lubricate Water Pump (if equipped with grease fittings)		●							
Change Engine Oil and Filter (Capacity)			●						
Check Tire Air Pressure (Front Rear)			●						
Lubricate Front Suspension (# of points)			●						
Lubricate Exhaust Manifold Valve			●						
Check Brake Master Cylinder Fluid Level			●						
Check Hydraulic Clutch Master Cylinder Fluid Level			●						
Check Automatic Transmission Fluid Level			●						
Check Power Steering Fluid Reservoir			●						
Check Steering Gear Lubricant Level			●						
Clean & Lubricate Oil Wetted Wire Mesh Air Cleaner*			●						
Clean & Lubricate Oil Filler Cap*			●						
Perform Minor Engine Tune-Up				●					
Check and Clean Crankcase Ventilation System					●				
Check Manual Transmission Lubricant Level (early type)					●				
Check Manual Transmission Lubricant Level (full syncro type)							●		
Check Rear Axle Lubricant Level (early)					●				
Check Rear Axle Lubricant Level (late)								●	
Lubricate Transmission, Brake & Clutch Linkage					●				
Adjust Clutch Pedal Travel					●				
Lubricate Universal Joints W/Grease Fittings					●				
Lubricate Universal Joints W/o Grease Fittings								●	
Perform Brake Adjustment**					●				
Clean Body & Door Drain Holes					●				
Rotate Tires					●				
Clean Dry-Type Air Cleaner*					●				
Replace Dry-Type Air Cleaner*							●		
Clean Polyurethane-Type Air Cleaner*					●				
Perform Body Lubrication (hinges, striker plates, etc.)					●				
Inspect Brake Hoses					●				
Check Accessory Drive Belt Tension					●				
Perform Major Engine Tune-Up						●			
Clean & Refill Oil Bath Type Air Cleaner*						●			
Clean & Lubricate Accelerator Linkage						●	●		
Clean & Repack Front Wheel Bearings							●		
Lubricate Dash Controls & Seat Tracks							●		
Major Brake Adjustment (remove drums, clean dust, lube pivots, etc.)							●		
Check Headlight Adjustment							●		
Check Front End Alignment**							●		
Clean Battery Terminals**							●		
Check Air-Conditioning System (bolts, hose connections, sight glass)							●		
Replace PCV Valves & Clean Hoses							●		
Inspect Cooling System**							●		
Lubricate Slip Yoke (automatic transmission models)							●		
Change Automatic Transmission Fluid								●	
Check Shock Absorbers & Bushings								●	
Replace Leaf Spring Inserts (small pads between leaves)								●	
Check Convertible Top Operation								●	
Lubricate Speedometer Cable								●	
Lubricate Long-Life Front Suspension									●

* Perform This Service More Frequently In Dusty Areas

** More Frequently If Necessary

Make a note of when each service was last performed and keep an accurate list to avoid future problems.

USE THIS SPACE TO RECORD SPECIFICATIONS FOR YOUR CAR:

PLUG TYPE_____ DWELL_____ DEG. TIMING_____ OIL FILTER_____

Replacement Windshield Washer Pumps

TRW sells a line of heavy-duty, original equipment replacement windshield washer pumps. They are designed to replace worn-out pumps or those damaged by wear on rubber seals, cam and gear; electromagnet failures; and dirt or contamination. Models are available for most American-made cars.

Antiwind-Lift Wiper Blades

When traveling at high speed in rain, some windshield wipers tend to lose contact with the windshield. The Anderson Company, which markets Anco windshield wiper parts, has a solution. It markets an antiwind-lift blade that uses the flow of the air on the windshield to keep the blade firmly against the glass. Anco's special blade comes in 13, 15, 16, 18 and 19 inch lengths and fits virtually any American-made car, pickup truck or recreational vehicle plus many imported cars. If you have a car that has hidden wipers, however, you will have to pass this item up. It will not function with hidden wiper systems.

Windshield Wiper Arm Puller Tool

Trico Products Corp., a major manufacturer of windshield wiper blades and refills, also makes a tool that simplifies the job of removing old wiper arms. The Trico Arm Puller tool, No. AT-2, has a hex wrench designed to loosen bolts on screw-type wiper shafts.

WINDSHIELD WIPERS AND WASHERS

JUST AS you can count on your tires eventually wearing out and your gas tank going dry if you do not refill it, so can you count on your windshield wiper blades wearing out and your windshield washer reservoir running out of solvent if they are not maintained. Unfortunately, we often discover this during a rainstorm or when a passing truck has splashed mud on the windshield. Keeping a close check on the wiper-washer system is as important to safety as knowing the lights are working properly.

Replacing Wiper Blades

FREQUENTLY, the only thing you will need to renew your wiper blades is a pair of refills. Wiper blades are the rubber parts that slip into the metal blade assembly. But if the metal blade frame or wiper arm has been damaged, you will have an extra investment to make. A thoughtful motorist carries at least a spare set of wiper blade refills in the car and thinks about checking and replacing his car's blades when the weather is dry.

There are two types of wiper blade refills, which differ somewhat on the method of replacement. One features a release button (usually a black or red plastic button) about one-third of the way up the blade frame. When you push the button down by hand, it releases a lock, allowing the rubber blade to slide out of the metal frame. A new blade refill will slide back in the same way, locking securely in place.

The other type of blade refill unlocks at the end of the rubber portion of the blade where there are two small metal tabs. By squeezing these tabs together, the rubber blade is released and can be slid out of the frame. A new refill is replaced in the same way. **NOTE:** Be careful to engage all frame tabs as the blade refill slips into place. When the blade is slid into position, the tabs should click, locking the blade into place. Check for proper operation, making sure no part of the blade holder contacts the windshield. This is especially important if you have metal blade holders, which can scratch your windshield glass.

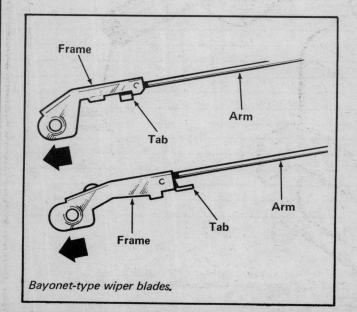

Frame

Arm

Tab

Arm

Tab

Frame

Bayonet-type wiper blades.

Here Is What You Will Need
Materials

- Wiper Blade Refills
- Wiper Blade Frame
- Wiper Blade Arms
- Windshield Washer Fluid
- Fuse
- Clean Rag

Tools

- Screwdriver
- Wrench
- Thin Wire

Now available are refillable blade holders made of nonmetallic polycarbonate. They fit most types of wiper arms.

NOTE: Some types of windshield wipers feature an airfoil design. The purpose is to prevent the blade from lifting off the windshield at high speeds. An airfoil is mounted on top of the wiper blade and responds to wind pressures, pressing the blade against the glass.

If your windshield wipers are the type that are hidden below the cowl in front of the windshield, you can bring them into an accessible position for checking or replacement by turning on the ignition switch, turning the wiper switch on, and turning the ignition switch off as soon as the blades have reached a convenient position on the windshield.

Replacing Wiper Arms

WIPER ARMS do not last forever. They are designed to press the wiper blade against the windshield at a specific tension. But when age and the elements have taken their toll of the arm spring and pivots, it may be necessary to install new arms. Your service station or auto supply store can supply you with the proper wiper arm designed for your car.

Most wiper arms are simply pressed onto a knurled shaft. The arm can be removed by pulling it off the base of the shaft by hand. Occasionally, it is necessary to use a special puller tool to remove a stuck arm. In this case, your best bet is to go to a mechanic who has the equipment. But before tugging on the wiper arm, make sure that it is not secured at the base with a screw or nut. You may have to loosen or remove the screw or nut first, using a screwdriver or a wrench.

Windshield Washers

WINDSHIELD WASHERS are standard equipment on new cars today and require very little maintenance. But, if you have ever been caught in a situation where your windshield was streaked by mud and your washers were not working properly, you know how important it is to keep your washers in good condition.

The most a home mechanic need do for windshield washers is keep the fluid in the washer reservoir filled to the proper level. Most cars have the washer fluid reservoir under the hood in the engine compartment. Usually, the reservoir bottle is glass or plastic, with level marks indicated. Simply fill the bottle with windshield washer fluid to the level recommended.

Windshield washer fluid either comes ready-mixed or in a concentrate form. The ready-mix is more convenient. This special fluid is used for several reasons. In the winter, it acts

AUTO CARE

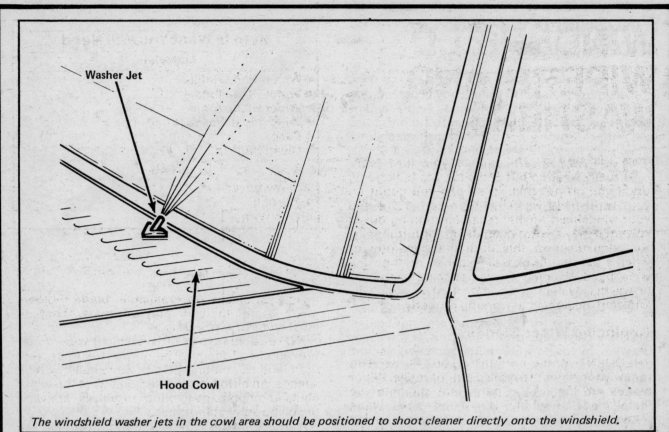

The windshield washer jets in the cowl area should be positioned to shoot cleaner directly onto the windshield.

Washer Jet

Hood Cowl

as an antifreeze. A frozen washer system can take a long time to thaw out. The special fluid also is a solvent. It will clean the windshield much better than plain water.

Your windshield washer system is relatively troublefree, but if the system fails to work, you can do the following:

1. Check the water jets for obstruction. These jets (there usually are two of them located in front of the windshield by the cowl) can sometimes be clogged with dirt. Pushing a thin piece of wire into the jet will usually clear any obstruction.
2. Check the fluid reservoir for fluid level. Refill as necessary.

3. Check the rubber hoses of the system. Starting from the fluid reservoir, look for any kinks, breaks or loose connections in the rubber hoses that may obstruct the flow of fluid.
4. Check the filter screen in the reservoir for sediment or foreign particles. To do this, you will have to remove the reservoir filler cap. Most caps snap on and off. The filter screen will be on the end of the hose connected to the filler cap. Wipe it clean.
5. Check the fuse in the washer system and any electrical connections to the switch on the dashboard or at the washer pump. Usually, the fuse is located in the fuse block under the dashboard.

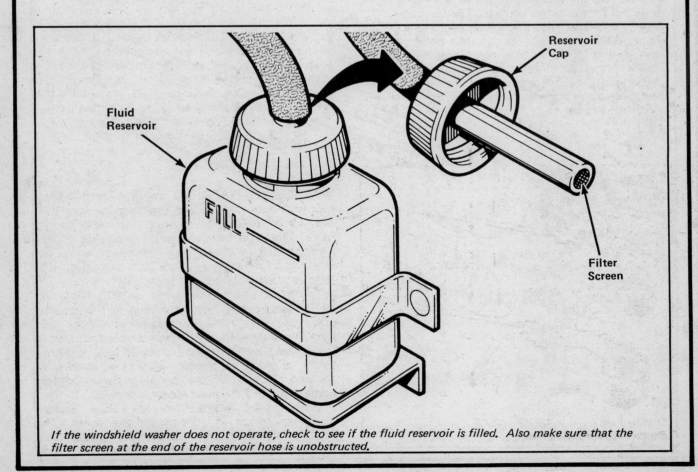

Fluid Reservoir

FILL

Reservoir Cap

Filter Screen

If the windshield washer does not operate, check to see if the fluid reservoir is filled. Also make sure that the filter screen at the end of the reservoir hose is unobstructed.

AUTO CARE

Cleaner Makes Vinyl Shine

Most late-model cars have a great deal of vinyl, which needs to be cleaned often for a good appearance. There are many products on the market for this purpose. Among them is Vinyl Cleaner No. UC12 made by Gold Eagle Co. The product, which is available in a 12 ounce bottle with sprayer, cleans vinyl tops, interiors, leather, plastic or vinyl furniture, and luggage. The product is nonflammable.

Make Mag Wheels Shine

If you use a wheel cleaner especially designed for magnesium wheels, upkeep can be much easier. The Maywood Company's mag wheel cleaner can be used on magnesium, aluminum, chromium, nickel, brass and stainless steel.

Premixed Windshield Washer Solvent

Premixed windshield washer solutions are convenient because you do not have to mix them with water before pouring into your washer's reservoir. Trico Products Corp. sells Anti-Smear Redi-Mix Solvent, WA-32, in a 32 ounce bottle. It is formulated for year-round use to remove road film and grime. In the winter, it will keep the washer system in working condition to 25° below zero. It comes in one quart bottles.

NET WT. 4.5 OZ.

Chrome Cleaner And Polish

Rusted chrome can make a new car look old fast. Loctite Chrome Cleaner and Polish, made by Woodhill/Permatex, is designed to polish and protect chrome and metal surfaces and to remove rust, leaving a protective film to help prevent further rusting and tarnishing. The product, No. 78191, comes in 4.5 ounce tubes.

Liquid Polish Concentrate

A cream polish in concentrated form for automobiles is offered by Le Vernier's Custom Crest Car Products, Inc. The polish, designed to provide a high gloss, has a chemical cleaner that cleans and polishes a car in one step. It also contains a rust inhibitor and chemicals that shield the car's finish from ultraviolet rays. Custom Gloss Cream Auto Polish comes in pint and gallon cans.

Oblong Car Washing Brush

Most car washing brushes that hook up to your garden hose have a round head. But the one offered by TRW, No. 659701, has a large oblong head that is seven by 2-1/2 inches. The bristles are soft horsehair and palmyra. A 29 inch handle gives you a long reach. A soap chamber is built into the cap. Detergent cartridges are available from the manufacturer.

Paint Does Get Old

After a number of years, car paint can become dull due to oxidation. Wax alone will not bring back the luster. So before waxing, you should apply a cleaner or use a one-step cleaner and polish such as Car Groom No. 26 Cleaner & Polish from M & H Laboratories, Inc. It is made to remove scratches and oxidation, and to shine the finish in one step. The product contains no harsh abrasives, wax or silicone. The cleaner comes in a one pint or one gallon can.

Concentrate For Windshield Washers

There are some advantages in buying a concentrated windshield washer compound that you mix with water yourself. For one thing, it is easier to store because it takes up less space. You also may be able to save money. You can do this by varying the amount of concentrate used, depending on the season. Union Carbide Corp. makes Prestone Concentrated Windshield Washer Antifreeze and Cleaner that can give you protection to -30°F. Of course, in the summer you can use a less-concentrated solution to make the 16 ounce can last longer.

Engine Enamel Withstands Temperatures To 250°F

For a really clean machine, you need a new looking engine. Many car owners spark up the look of their engine by first cleaning it with a degreaser and then painting it with special heat-resistant engine enamel. Dupli-Color Products Division of American Home Products Corp. makes Bright Beauty Engine Enamel that comes in 19 colors to match almost any original engine color. The enamel, which comes in a 13 ounce spray can, seals out moisture and drys fast. It is formulated not to blister, flake or crack when applied on a clean surface.

Rubber Utility Mats

Low-cost rubber mats, called Rubber Squares, are made by Rubbermaid Specialty Products, Inc. The mats, No. 1408, measure 18-1/4 by 16-1/2 inches and come in black, blue, brown and green.

Install A Windshield Washer System In Your Car

If your car is not equipped for a windshield washer system, you can easily install one. TRW sells a universal windshield washer pump, No. 620265, with a reservoir that fits cars and trucks with 12 volt systems. It is adaptable to imported cars not equipped with a washer pump. The kit contains a two quart plastic reservoir; plastic lid with check valve, filter and tube; mounting bracket and all tubing clamps and screws. Instructions are included.

Avoid Water Spots After Washing

The best way to avoid water spots after washing your car is to dry it with a piece of chamois. This is more expensive than other materials you might use to dry your car, but it does a good job and chamois lasts a long time. TRW sells a heavy-duty chamois that is 100 percent oil-tanned. It is about 3-1/2 feet square.

Finishing Sander For Body Repairs

If you plan to tackle any major body repairs, you should have a finishing sander. Robert Bosch Corp. has a Model 1286-034 finishing sander that includes a rubber pad material for wet sanding—important for automotive repair work. A counterbalance drive mechanism in this sander reduces vibration. The tool produces a 10,000 orbits per minute pad speed. The orbit diameter is 3/32 of an inch. The sander is 9-1/2 by 4-5/8 by 7 inches. It uses a standard 4-1/2 by 11 inch, half-sheet sandpaper.

Body Repair Kit For Big And Small Jobs

Easy White auto body repair kits are available in three sizes for different sized jobs. The kit, made by U.S. Chemical & Plastics, comes in quart, pint and 1/2 pint sizes. You can use it to make repairs on metal or wood. Each kit contains filler, hardener, fiberglass screen, spreader, sandpaper and instructions.

Fiberglass Repair Kit

If you have "customized" your car by striking some immovable object, you can use Dynatron/Bondo Corporation's fiberglass repair kit to make your car look like new again. The kit, No. 422, contains a quart of polyester resin, 1/2 ounce of liquid hardener, and eight square feet of fiberglass mat. It is available at auto supply stores.

Adhesive Fixes Broken Plastic Grilles

Woodhill/Permatex makes Loctite Neat Epoxy Kits for repairing broken plastic grille work as well as loose trim and door glass channels. The clear adhesive sets in about five minutes. Kits come in three sizes. You can buy one containing three four-gram mixer cups, 15 four-gram mixer cups, or 10 one-ounce mixer cups. The mixer-cup packaging permits the epoxy to be premeasured to assure consistent results and little waste or mess.

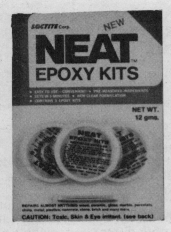 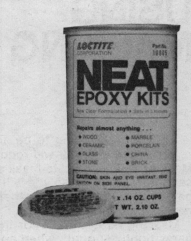

INTRODUCTION

IF YOU have owned your car for six months or more, chances are it already needs some body repair. In fact, most new cars need some minor body repair the minute they leave the dealer's showroom. Many unsuspecting new car buyers drive away with chipped paint, small scratches and other minor imperfections that can be the breeding ground for major corrosion later.

To prevent corrosion, always give any new car a meticulous inspection before you buy it. Open all the doors, the trunk, the hood and check their metal edges (do not forget the bottom edges of the doors) for chipped paint, scratches and beginning rust. These are areas often ignored by the new car buyer. If left unrepaired, they can cause major problems later. Once rust starts, it just keeps spreading until it is stopped. And, it is much easier and cheaper to stop a small rust spot than to stop and repair a large one.

When purchasing a new car, you are perfectly within your rights to request the dealer to repair those minor chips and scratches before he delivers the vehicle to you. Any reputable dealer will fix them.

If your new car is some months old and you neglected to give it a close inspection before you bought it, do it now—or even if you did, do it again. By now, you probably have some minor body repairs to make. Make them now and continue to inspect your car at least once every six months.

Inspection is simple. Pay particular attention to edges—any edges—including door edges and edges and folds in the metal where other items attach, such as headlight rims, rocker panel trim, etc. What you will usually find are a few areas with small chips of paint missing, perhaps a scratch or two and, possibly, small spots of rust here and there.

This chapter will tell you everything you need to know about making body repairs on your car with materials available from auto supply stores. It must be pointed out, however, that the average person cannot always make repairs that look as good as quality professional work. One reason is that the average individual does not have the experience of a body repair specialist. Another is that the average person does not have access to expensive equipment, and it would not be economical to purchase it. Despite these reasons, you can still make satisfactory repairs to scratches, dents, rust spots and rust holes; restore luster to faded paint; and do a number of other things to restore your car's appearance. In fact, some of your work may come out virtually indistinguishable from that performed by a professional body man.

Your biggest problem will be paint. It is virtually impossible to buy a spray can of paint to match the original color of your car. Even professionals have problems obtaining perfect matches despite the fact that they mix their own paint and are able to control other factors in the painting process that you will be unable to do.

So, you have two choices—either settle for a slightly off-shade paint job, or prepare the metal to the point where it is ready for painting and let a professional apply the paint. You will save some money either way.

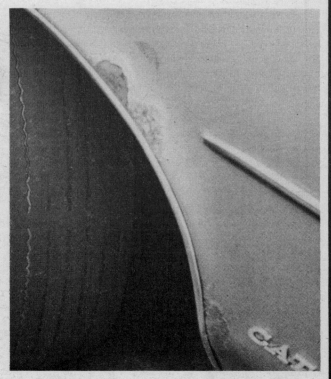

Once rust starts, it spreads until it is stopped. It is much easier and cheaper to stop a small rust spot than to repair a large one.

USING MASKING TAPE

Here Is What You Will Need
Materials
• 1/2 Inch Masking Tape
• Old Newspapers
Tools
• Single-Edge Razor Blade

IF YOU are going to be doing any painting on your car, you will require masking tape. Masking tape is used to mask off portions of the car's body and trim so you will not get primer or paint on chrome, glass or other parts that do not require painting.

Masking tape is made for this purpose. It adheres tightly enough, when applied properly, to keep paint from seeping into other areas, yet it is easy to remove once the painted surface is dry. And, unlike some other types of tape, it does not leave any adhesive behind when it is removed. Although it is available in a variety of widths, 1/2 inch masking tape is recommended for most repair purposes.

To mask off an area of your car's body for priming or painting, follow this procedure:

1. Align masking tape along one edge of a sheet of old newspaper so that about 1/4 inch of the 1/2 inch tape is left exposed.
2. The newspaper with the exposed tape should be positioned along one side of the area to be repaired. Apply the exposed tape to the metal surface of the car.
3. Repeat step 2, completely surrounding the area to be primed or painted. Tack the other sides of the newspaper to the car.
4. Double-check the masking tape seal by pressing it firmly against the metal with your fingers to make certain that it is firmly sticking to the car's metal surface and that there are no "ripples" or openings that could allow paint to seep through. **NOTE:** You may find a single-edge razor blade

handy for cutting and butting pieces of tape.

A careful masking job is the mark of a good paint job. If you do a careless masking job, the resulting paint job will be sloppy too, so take your time.

Often, people mask too much of an area. In general, sufficient protection is provided by masking no more than four feet beyond the area to be painted.

For areas that have chrome trim, you should be particularly careful about how you apply the tape. The masking tape should completely cover the chrome, but it should not come in contact with adjoining metal surfaces to be painted or you will leave a thin, often noticeable, edge between the paint and the masking tape.

Applying masking tape to chrome areas is not as difficult as it may sound. Use the following procedure:

1. Place one edge of the tape carefully against the edge of the chrome—be careful not to touch the metal surface being painted—pressing only the edge of the tape—not the full width—against one edge of the chrome. Do this slowly until you have masked off the length of chrome.
2. After you have the edge of tape perfectly aligned with one edge of the chrome, press the rest of the tape against the chrome to complete the masking operation.

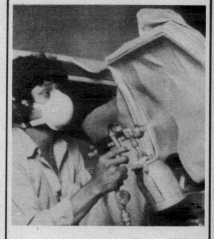

Protect Your Health With A Paint Spray Respirator

When you do any automotive spray painting in a confined area, you should provide yourself with some type of respiratory protection from paint vapors and particles. This is especially true when you use the fast-curing coatings used today. The 3M Company offers a spray paint respirator, No. 6984, that fits over your mouth and nose to filter out harmful, airborne particles and vapors. It offers protection against vapor and paint particulates from enamels, lacquers, epoxies, acrylic enamel and polyurethanes. The respirator is designed to be disposable after a certain period of time; but if you use it with acrylic enamels, polyurethanes or other materials containing isocyanate hardeners, it must be disposed of after five days of use.

After masking the site to be primed or painted, double-check the masking tape seal by pressing it firmly against the metal with your fingers to make certain that it is firmly sticking to the car's metal surface.

Patch Kits Designed For Do-It-Yourselfer

Swiss Snowite Patch Kits, made by Go-Jo Industries, Inc., are designed for the do-it-yourselfer. Each includes an amount of Snowite flexible mender, color-guide orange cream hardener, plastic applicator, coarse and fine sandpaper, fiberglass screen and instructions. The kits come in quart, pint and 1/2 pint sizes.

File Blade For Forming Body Contours

The tougher parts of doing a good auto body repair at home are preparing the surface properly, shaping the body filler and finishing it. To make the shaping part easier, you should use a file that is specifically designed for this job. Dynatron/Bondo Corp. offers a 10-inch, half-round blade, No. 122, that fits a variety of file holders.

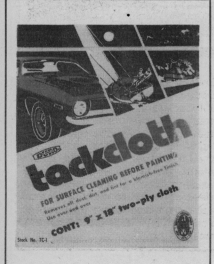

Tack Cloth For A Smooth Finish

If you have ever walked into a professional body repair shop, you may have noticed that professionals use a tack cloth to clean metal surfaces before painting them. A tack cloth is made to remove particles of dust, dirt and sand, eliminating any blemishes or defects on the final coat of paint. Woodhill/Permatex, Co. sells a 9 by 18 inch, two-ply tack cloth, No. TC-1, that is perfect for surface cleaning.

Rivet Tool

When working on auto bodies, you will find that some parts—such as mirror mounting brackets—are mounted with rivets. To replace items like this, you need a rivet tool, such as the Richline Pro 404 rivet tool from Townsend Division of Textron, Inc. This tool is made of cast aluminum and chrome-plated steel. It sets 3/32, 1/8, 5/32 inch steel and 3/16 inch aluminum alloy Snapo blind rivets without adjustments. Features include a spring-loaded handle for automatic ejection of mandrel and one-handed operation. It is small enough to fit in your pocket.

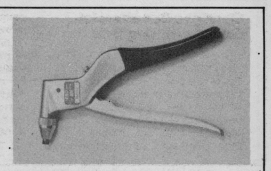

PREPARING METAL FOR PAINTING

Here Is What You Will Need

Materials

- No. 50 or 80 Grit Sandpaper or Sandpaper Disc
- Spray Can of Primer
- Masking Tape
- Newspaper
- No. 320 or 400 Grit Wet or Dry Sandpaper
- Solvent-Type Cleaner such as Naphtha or Benzene
- Tack Cloth

Tools

- Sanding Block
- Electric Drill and Sanding Attachment or Electric Grinder

ONE OF the differences between a good paint job and a poor one is the preparation of the metal surface to be painted. In performing minor body work on your car, you will be doing one of two types of painting—painting on a bare metal surface where all the layers of paint and primer have been removed, or painting over a surface that has layers of primer and/or paint on it.

Sanding To Bare Metal

IF THE job requires you to get down to the car's bare metal surface, there are two ways to do this: hand or power sanding (or grinding as it is sometimes called). With hand sanding, you will need a sanding block, which is nothing more than a rubber or plastic block designed to hold a sheet of sandpaper.

Here is how to sand an area down to bare metal:

1. Fasten a sheet of No. 50 or 80 grit sandpaper to the sanding block and sand the area in a back and forth motion until the bare sheet metal is exposed. Hand sanding is time-consuming and requires

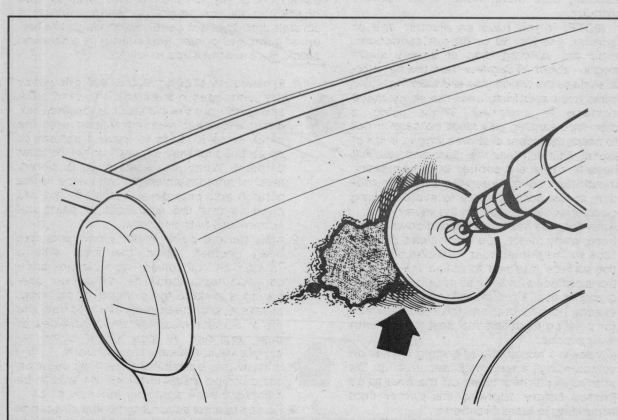

An electric drill and sanding disc with No. 50 or 80 grit sandpaper will speed sanding down to bare metal. Always keep the sander in motion at the proper angle to avoid making gouges or depressions in the repair area.

BODY REPAIRS

Cordless Commercial-Duty Reversing Drill

There are plenty of cordless electric drills on the market, but most of them are not designed for heavy-duty use. Black and Decker Manufacturing Co. makes a 3/8 inch cordless, commercial-duty reversing drill, No. 9081, that will drive a 1/8 inch screw through 0.050 aluminum up to 350 times without recharging. The drill operates at 750 rpm and is reversible for backing out screws and jammed drill bits. The energy pack is removable and can be recharged up to 500 times before replacing. A 16-hour cup charger is included. The unit weighs 3-1/8 pounds.

Fiberglass Repair Kit For Small Jobs

TRW offers a small fiberglass repair kit, No. 640510, that provides everything needed for minor fiberglass, steel or wood repair jobs. The kit includes 1/2 pint of liquid resin, hardener, applicator, fiberglass cloth and instructions. If you are just starting out, this is a good kit for tackling a small project.

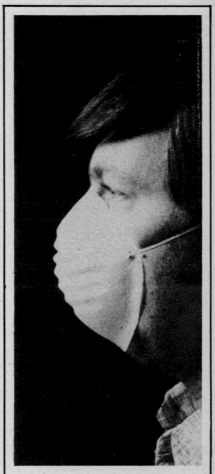

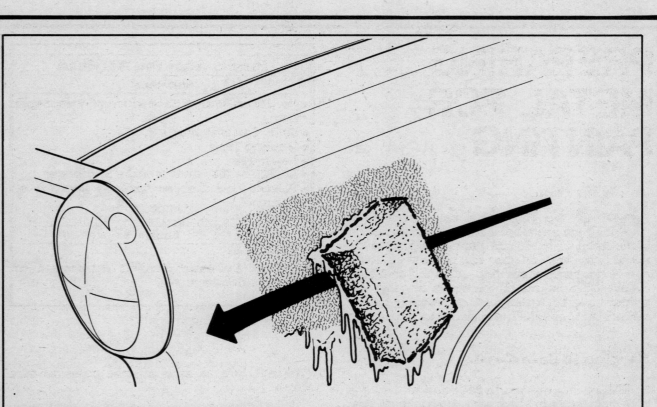

Before applying paint to a primed area, wash any dust or dirt from the site, clean the area with a solvent-type cleaner and then rub it down with a clean tack cloth.

considerable effort, especially if the area to be sanded is large. It can be much easier and faster to use an electric drill with a sanding disc attachment or an electric grinder.

NOTE: If you have an electric drill or grinder, use No. 50 or 80 grit sandpaper. Hold the sanding disc at a very slight angle—about 10 degrees from the flat metal surface on which you are working—and sand back and forth until the shiny metal surface is exposed. When using a disc-type sander, you must be careful not to catch the paper disc on a jagged edge of metal. This will tear the disc, and you will have to replace it sooner than necessary. In addition, always keep the sander in motion at the proper angle to avoid making gouges or depressions in the repair area.

2. After the area has been sanded down to the bare, shiny metal, you must clean the surface so the primer coat will adhere well to the surface. It is best to follow the instructions provided on the can of primer you are going to use. Most manufacturers will tell exactly how to prepare the metal surface for priming to obtain the best results with their product.
3. If there is a possibility of getting primer on surrounding areas that are not to be primed or painted, mask off the area to be primed before applying the primer coat according to label directions.
4. Prime the area. Refer to the Using Primer and Paint section in this chapter.

Sanding Primer or Paint

WHEN YOU are preparing a surface for painting but are not going down to the bare metal surface of the car, as you might do when painting a scratch that does not penetrate through the layers of paint and primer, you need only a sanding block. Here are the steps to follow:

1. Fasten a sheet of No. 320 or 400 grit wet or dry sandpaper in the block and sand back and forth until the old paint is roughed up. Avoid a circular sanding motion with the block since it tends to leave a pattern of scratches that may show through the coat of paint. What you want to do is simply level or smooth down the area around the scratch and provide a "tooth" to the old paint so that the new coat of paint will adhere well to the surface.
2. After the old paint in the repair area has been scuffed, clean the area with a "prep-coat" or solvent-type cleaner such as naphtha or benzene. Whenever preparing a surface for priming or painting, always use a clean tack cloth to rub the metal surface clean of small particles of dust and lint. A tack cloth is an inexpensive, chemically treated cloth.
3. If there is a possibility of getting paint on surrounding areas, mask off the area to be painted before applying the new paint.
4. Paint the area according to the directions found on the paint can. Refer to the Using Primer and Paint section in this chapter.

Disposable Dust Mask

Dust masks for do-it-yourself auto body refinishers are made by the 3M Company. The No. 3180, dust mask, is designed to protect against nontoxic dusts and particles in concentrations of less than 15mm per cubic meter of air where no toxic impurities are present. This is the same type mask used by sanders, grinders, packagers and other tradesmen. You can buy it in packs of five masks each.

Fix Vinyl And Leather Upholstery

Not only are tears in your car's upholstery unsightly, but if they are not repaired quickly, they will become larger. You can fix these rips with Loctite Vinyl and Leather Adhesive No. 45285 made by Woodhill/Permatex. The clear-drying product is also useful for mending vinyl tops, dashboards, and even leather garments, handbags, luggage and furniture. It comes in 1.5 ounce tubes.

USING PRIMER AND PAINT

Here Is What You Will Need
Materials
● Spray Can of Primer
● Newspaper
● Masking Tape
● Turpentine or Paint Thinner
● No. 400 Grit Sandpaper
● Tack Cloth
● Solvent-Type Cleaner such as Naphtha or Benzene
● Spray Can of Paint
● Rubbing Compound
● Soft, Clean Cloth
Tools
● None

WHY IS it necessary to use a primer coat before applying paint? Why not just spray paint on the bare metal surface? The primer coat serves two purposes. It acts as a filler to help smooth out a rough metal surface and as a bonding agent. If you would apply paint directly onto bare metal, it would not adhere well. The primer coat bonds to metal much better than paint, and paint adheres well to the primer coat. Whenever you must paint a bare metal surface, it is a two-step process. You must first prime the metal and then apply paint to the primer.

Applying Primer

HERE IS how to apply primer to bare metal using cans of spray paint:

1. Shake the can of primer coat well. The spray can will have a metal ball inside that will mix the primer as you shake the can. Follow the directions on the can.
2. Tape a sheet of newspaper to a wall or other vertical surface with masking tape and depress the button on the spray can while aiming the nozzle at the newspaper. Hold the can approximately 12 inches away from the paper. This is to make certain that the can will emit a fine, even spray. If there is a buildup of primer on the nozzle clogging it, pull the nozzle off the can and soak it in turpentine or paint thinner to clear the passage. When the nozzle is clean again, replace it on the can.
3. If you have never applied primer before, practice on an old board or piece of metal. Hold the can about 12 inches away, depress the nozzle and move the can in smooth, even side-to-side strokes across the board or metal. Your stroke should always remain the same distance away from the object you are spraying. Often, people use a semicircular motion as they spray, with the middle of their stroke closer to the object than the ends of their stroke. This results in an uneven amount of primer on the surface of the object being sprayed.

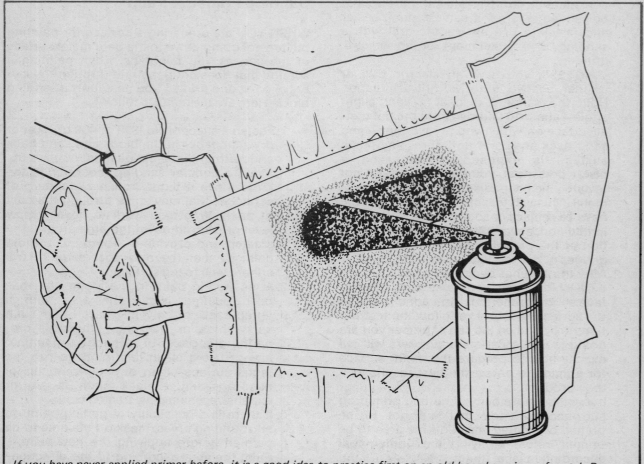

If you have never applied primer before, it is a good idea to practice first on an old board or piece of metal. Do not try to cover a repair with a heavy coat. Best results are obtained with several fine, misty coats.

BODY REPAIRS

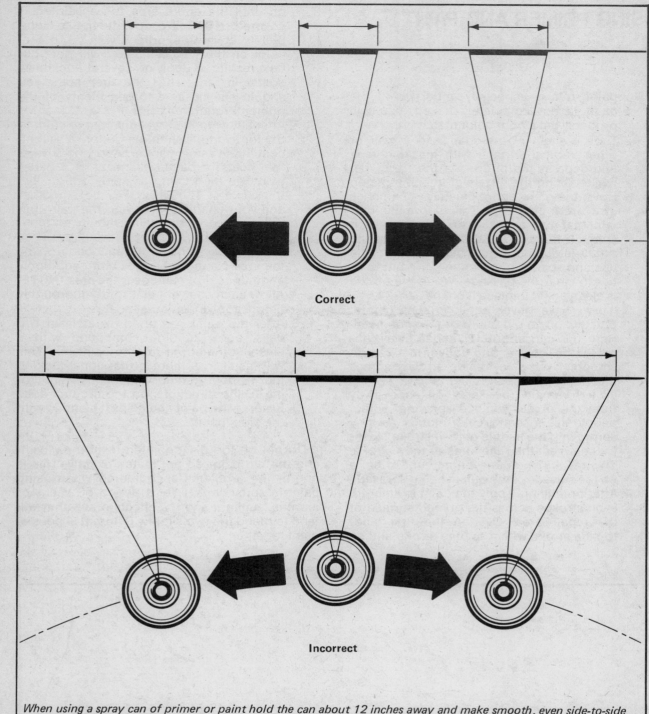

Correct

Incorrect

When using a spray can of primer or paint hold the can about 12 inches away and make smooth, even side-to-side strokes. Always stay the same distance away from the object being sprayed. An arc-like stroke will result in an uneven paint job.

Sandable Primers

When doing auto body repairs, you must cover the bare metal or plastic filler with a primer before you paint it. Dynatron/Bondo Corporation makes three sandable primers that come in aerosol cans. Colors available are light gray, hot rod black and red oxide. They all can be sanded to a glass-smooth finish before applying a final coat of paint.

Enamel Paint For Touch-Ups

When you touch up your car's body paint, you should use the exact color. Sometimes, this is impossible, so you try to come as close as you can. Spray Products Corporation offers a quick-drying, rust-resistant enamel paint in 32 colors. You are likely to find one that matches your original paint exactly or come close to it. The paint is available in 16 ounce cans.

Primer Sealer By Duro

A primer sealer enables you to sand smooth uneven surfaces before you apply a coat of paint. Duro Metal Products Co. markets a sandable primer sealer in 13 ounce aerosol cans. The quick-drying sealer is available in gray, red and black.

4. After practicing, apply the primer in smooth, even strokes across the bare metal surface of the repair area. Overlap the first side-to-side stroke with a second stroke and so on until the entire area to be primed is covered. **NOTE:** Do not attempt to completely cover the area with a heavy coat of primer. You will get your best results by applying several fine, misty coats.
5. After allowing the first, thin coat of primer to dry for two to five minutes, apply a second light coat. **NOTE:** If the primer coat accidentally begins to run, allow it to dry thoroughly. Then sand the run with No. 400 grit sandpaper. Wipe the area clean with a tack cloth and apply another coat of primer over the area.
6. Allow the final primer coat to dry.

When applying primer from a spray can, never hold the nozzle closer than 12 inches to the object being sprayed. If you hold it too close, you are likely to get runs. Also, after each coat has

been sprayed, turn the spray can upside down and aim it at some old newspaper, depressing the nozzle for a few seconds until the primer stops coming out of the can. This will clear the nozzle and prevent it from clogging.

Before applying paint to the primer, you must sand and clean the primer coat. Refer to the section on Preparing Metal For Painting in this chapter.

Applying Paint

AFTER THE primer coat has been sanded and cleaned with a solvent-type cleaner such as naphtha or benzene and a tack cloth, you are ready to apply paint to the repair area. Here is the procedure:

1. Shake the can of spray paint well. The spray can will have a metal ball inside that will mix the paint as you shake the can. Follow the directions on the can. With

Handy Auto Sprayer

The best way to apply touch-up paint is to spray it on. But this is not always possible because you may not be able to purchase the correct color in a spray can. There is an alternative, however. Precision Valve Corporation makes an inexpensive auto sprayer that you can use with an acrylic, lacquer, enamel, vinyl, primer, or custom color paint. The device consists of a glass jar to hold the paint and an aerosol can that you fit to the jar's top. The aerosol can is replaceable and sprays up to 16 ounces of paint. It features a built-in strainer that screens out solid particles. It also is self cleaning—a few short bursts of the solvent or cleaner cleans the unit. You also can use the Preval Pre-Valve Auto Sprayer for all small paint jobs.

Avoid A Tacky Paint Job

If the sheet metal surface on your car is not absolutely free of dust and dirt, you will end up with a disappointing paint job. The best way to remove debris from sheet metal is to use a tack cloth. This type of cloth is designed to wipe a surface clean, leaving no lint. Swiss tack cloths, No. 6723, are sealed in a plastic bag ready for use.

USING PRIMER AND PAINT

paint, this is especially important. If the paint is not completely mixed, you will probably get a poor color match.

2. Tape a sheet of newspaper to a wall or other vertical surface with masking tape and depress the button on the spray can while aiming the nozzle at the newspaper. Hold the can approximately 12 inches away from the paper. This is to make certain that the can will emit a fine, even spray. If there is a buildup of paint in the nozzle clogging it, pull the nozzle off the can and soak it in turpentine or paint thinner to clear the passage. When the nozzle is clean again, replace it on the can.

3. If you have never applied paint before, practice on an old board or piece of metal. Hold the can about 12 inches away, depress the nozzle and move the can in smooth, even side-to-side strokes across the board or metal. Your stroke should always remain the same distance away from the object you are spraying. Often, people use a semicircular motion as they spray, with the middle of their stroke closer to the object than the ends of their stroke. This results in an uneven amount of paint on the surface of the object being sprayed.

4. After practicing, apply the paint in smooth, even strokes across the primed surface of the repair area. Overlap the first side-to-side stroke with a second stroke and so on until the entire area to be painted is covered. **NOTE:** Do not attempt to completely cover the primer with a coat of paint on the first coat. You will get your best results by applying several fine, misty coats. In fact, after the first coat, you should still be able to see plenty of the primer through the paint.

5. After allowing the first light coat of paint to dry for two to five minutes, apply a second coat in the same manner. Applying several thin coats of paint will result in a better paint job than trying to apply one or two thick coats. The finish will be smoother and your chances of having the paint run are reduced. If the paint should accidentally run, allow it to dry thoroughly. Then sand the run with No. 400 sandpaper. Wipe the area clean with a tack cloth and apply another coat of paint over the area. **NOTE:** Allow each coat of paint to dry thoroughly before applying another coat.

6. After the paint has dried for at least two days, apply rubbing compound with a clean, soft cloth to rub the paint out. This will result in a more professional-looking job. Rubbing compound applied according to the directions on the product adds luster to the paint and helps it blend in with the older paint.

Do not be too disappointed if the new paint and the old paint do not match exactly. This is one of the problems encountered when using paint in spray cans. Over a period of weeks or months, sunlight and the effects of weather will tend to blend the two slightly different shades of paint together.

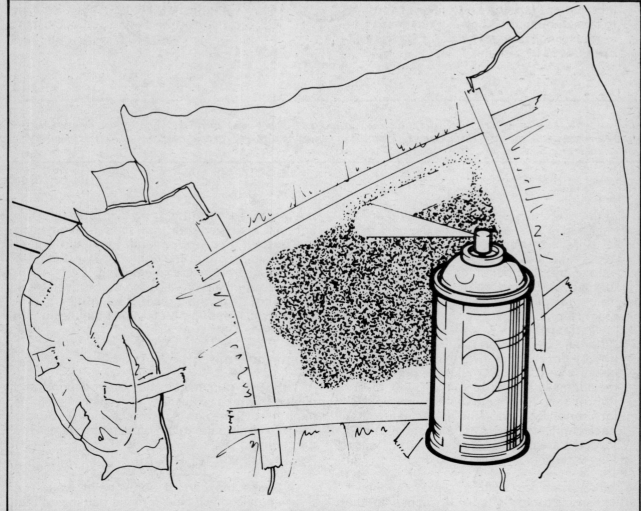

If you apply several thin coats of paint, the finish will be smoother and your chances of having the paint run are reduced.

REPAIRING RUST SPOTS AND HOLES

RUST ON your car's body will spread if it is not stopped. All rust begins as a tiny rust spot, generally because some bare metal was exposed to moisture or other corrosive element. This can even occur during the manufacturing process before the sheet metal is painted. Despite the cause, a rust spot should be repaired before it becomes a rust hole. They are much easier to repair.

Here Is What You Will Need

Materials

- No. 50 Grit Sandpaper Disc and Sandpaper
- Body Filler
- No. 80 Grit Sandpaper and Sandpaper Disc
- Spot Putty
- Solvent-type Cleaner such as Naphtha or Benzene
- Tack Cloth
- Body Repair Kit

Tools

- Electric Drill with Sanding Attachment
- Sanding Block
- Plastic Spreader
- Ball-peen Hammer
- Knife

Repairing Rust Spots

TO REPAIR a rust spot on your car, follow these steps:

1. Use an electric drill with a sanding disc attachment. Attach a No. 50 grit sandpaper disc. You could use a sanding block, but the drill and disc sander is the easiest way to repair a rust spot.
2. Sand the rust spot until bare metal is exposed and all traces of rust have been removed. At this point, you will have to decide whether body filler will be needed to level any indentation in the body's sheet metal. If no indentation is left, proceed to step 6. Otherwise, proceed to step 3.
3. To fill an indentation in the sheet metal, mix enough body filler material to fill the indentation. Mix the body filler according to label directions. Apply slightly more filler than is necessary. The slight excess will be removed by sanding.

4. Allow the body filler to dry thoroughly according to the directions on the product you use.
5. Sand the repair by hand with No. 80 grit sandpaper until the area is smooth and blends in with the surrounding sheet metal.
6. If, after sanding, there are any minor imperfections in the body filler, they may be filled in with spot putty. Rub a very thin layer of spot putty over the imperfections with a plastic spreader (provided with many auto body repair kits).
7. Allow the spot putty to dry.
8. Sand the repair smooth by hand using No. 80 grit sandpaper. **NOTE:** When sanding by hand, the four fingers of your hand should apply even pressure for the best results.

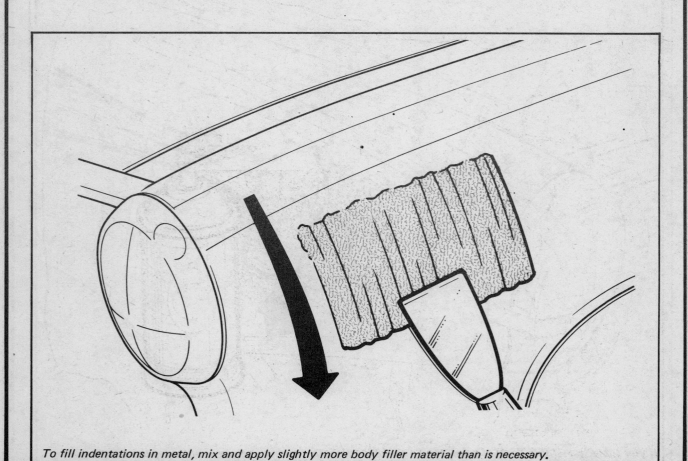

To fill indentations in metal, mix and apply slightly more body filler material than is necessary.

Electric Spray Gun

Most body shops use spray guns that work on air pressure from an air compressor. But if you do not want to buy an expensive air compressor, you can use an electric spray gun. Kastar, Inc. offers a "Spray-All" electric spray gun, No. 5000, that features a five-position spray volume control lever and a 110/120 volt, 60 cycle AC electromagnetic vibrator motor. The gun's nylon pump is designed to be choke free. The unit includes a sealed electric switch.

1/4 Inch Electric Drill

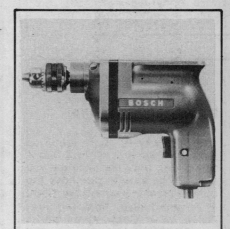

Many mechanics prefer a 1/4 inch capacity electric drill for light-duty drilling jobs. Robert Bosch Corp. offers a Model 1106, 1/4 inch electric drill with a maximum of 1700 rpm. Capacity in wood is 5/8 inch, 15/16 inch in aluminum, and 1/4 inch in steel. It works on 115 volt AC current, weighs 2-1/2 pounds and measures 9-3/8 inches long.

Support Yourself While Working On Your Car

With all the stretching and reaching you have to go through while working on a complex late-model car, you should take it easy when you can. A mechanic's work seat such as the Model 302 made by J-Mark Quality Products, Inc. lets you do just that. It has a plywood seat and rolls on three swivel steel rollers. The seat measures 14 by 18 by 12 inches.

Repair Kit Contains Everything You Need

Fibre Glass-Evercoat Co., Inc. sells a trio of fiberglass repair kits containing all that is needed for fiberglass repairs and restyling. Kit No. 641 contains eight ounces of resin and a 20 by 25 inch fiberglass cloth. Kit No. 370 contains one quart of automotive resin and nine square feet of fiberglass mat. For really big jobs, you will need Kit No. 369. It contains two quarts of resin, nine square feet of fiberglass mat and 11 feet of fiberglass cloth. Each kit includes mixing cups, applicator, mixing stick and the repair materials.

Body Blade And Body File For Smoothing Contours

When you need to trim a small amount of body filler, sandpaper is just fine. But for big jobs, you need a trimming blade and a body file such as those offered by Go-Jo Industries, Inc. The Swiss body blade, No. 4935, and the Swiss body file, No. 4931, are available at auto supply stores.

Finishing Sander With Integral Vacuum Pump

Sometimes, a sander creates a lot of dust that can affect a car's finish as well as your health. Robert Bosch Corp. markets a finishing sander, No. 1286-934, featuring an integral vacuum pump that pulls sandy debris into a dust bag attached to the sander. Other features include a rubber pad material for wet sanding; a positive, quick-change clamping system, and a pad speed of 10,000 orbits per minute. Orbit diameter is 3/32 of an inch. Dimensions are 9-1/2 by 4-5/8 by 7 inches high. The tool weighs five pounds. It comes with a dust bag; 4-1/2 by 11 inch, half-sheet sandpaper (60, 80, 120, 180 and 240 grit); and an auxiliary handle.

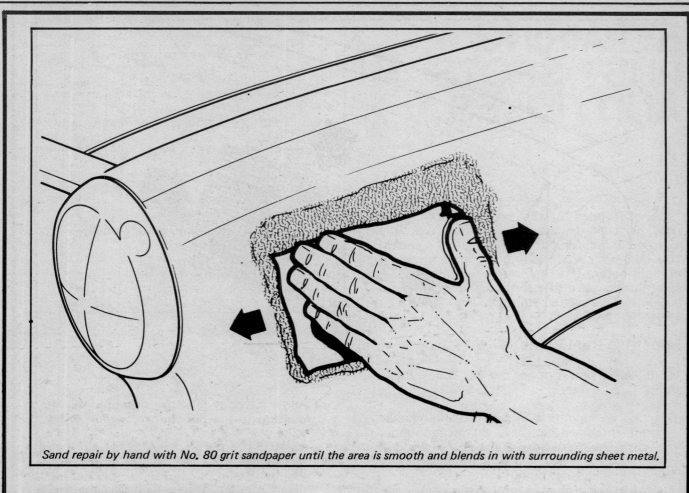

Sand repair by hand with No. 80 grit sandpaper until the area is smooth and blends in with surrounding sheet metal.

REPAIRING RUST SPOTS AND HOLES

9. After sanding, clean the repair with a solvent-type cleaner and tack cloth.

Once the repaired rust spot has been cleaned, it is ready for priming and painting. Refer to the section on using Primer and Paint in this chapter.

Repairing Rust Holes

IF YOU ignore a rust spot on your car, it is likely to become a hole before too long. Assuming the rust hole is still small enough for the do-it-

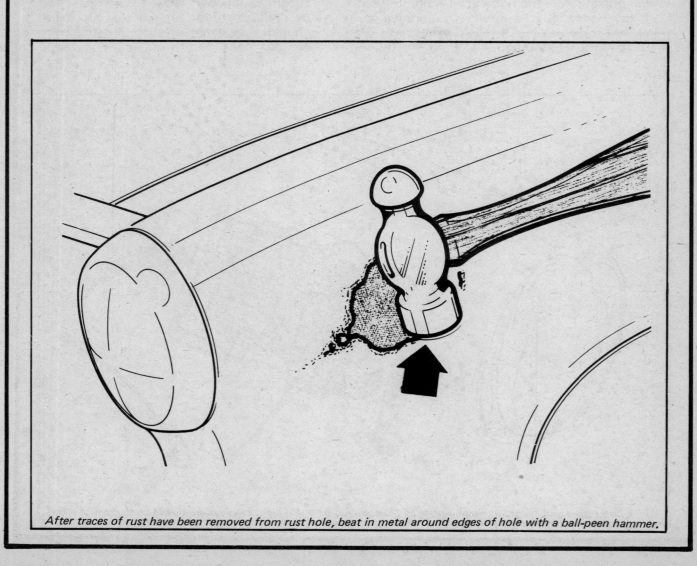

After traces of rust have been removed from rust hole, beat in metal around edges of hole with a ball-peen hammer.

BODY REPAIRS

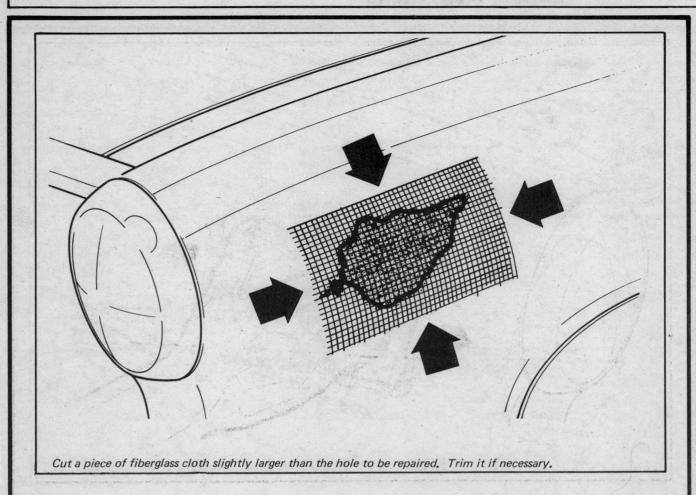

Cut a piece of fiberglass cloth slightly larger than the hole to be repaired. Trim it if necessary.

yourselfer to repair, follow this procedure:

1. Purchase a body repair kit from an auto supply store. The contents of various kits may vary but most contain body filler, hardener to make the filler harden, fiberglass cloth and a plastic scraper.
2. Attach a No. 50 grit sandpaper disc to an electric drill's sanding attachment.
3. Sand the area around the rust hole down to bare sheet metal, removing all traces of rust. When finished, you should have an area of bare metal around the hole that is about two to four inches wide. **NOTE:** Do not stop sanding until all traces of rust have been removed. If you leave a small

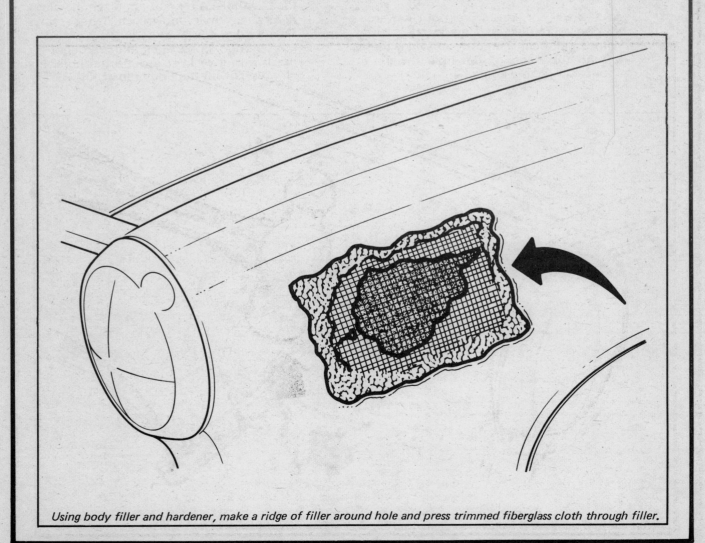

Using body filler and hardener, make a ridge of filler around hole and press trimmed fiberglass cloth through filler.

Penetrating Oil Loosens Stubborn Nuts, Screws

When loosening nuts, bolts and screws that have been on an automobile for many years, you can save yourself a lot of work by first applying a penetrating oil. Woodhill/Permatex makes Solvo-Rust No. 68, which is a blend of strong, quick-acting solvents. A molybdenum disulfide formula lubricates and speeds release of parts frozen due to rust, corrosion, scale, paint, varnish, carbon and gum. The liquid comes in one pint spout-top cans and five and 14 ounce aerosol cans.

Filler Spreaders Clean Themselves

Dynatron/Bondo Corporation makes spreaders in three by four inch and three by five inch sizes. They also make a 12 by 12 inch mixing board. The spreaders are available singly or in a three-pack. They feature high-polish polyethelyene that can be used over and over again. Hardened plastic or fiberglass resin pops right off.

x

269

BODY REPAIRS

Hammers For Body And Fender Work

A line of soft-face hammers for body and fender work are manufactured by Blackhawk Hand Tools. The hammers have a rough, molded plastic, replaceable head. Three sizes are available: Model HT-1450 has a six ounce head, a 7/8 inch diameter tip and weighs seven ounces. Model HT-1451 has an eight ounce head, a one inch diameter tip and weighs eight ounces. Model HT-1452 has a 12 ounce head, a 1-3/16 inch diameter tip and weighs 15 ounces.

Zinc Offers Good Rust Protection

Zinc is recognized as one of the best rustproofing agents available. CRC Chemicals, Inc. has a product called Zinc-It that is 95 percent pure zinc to provide a cold galvanized coating. You can use it to undercoat your car or as a primer before painting. It leaves a smooth matte finish that dries to the touch in about 15 minutes. Zinc-It comes in a 16 ounce aerosol container.

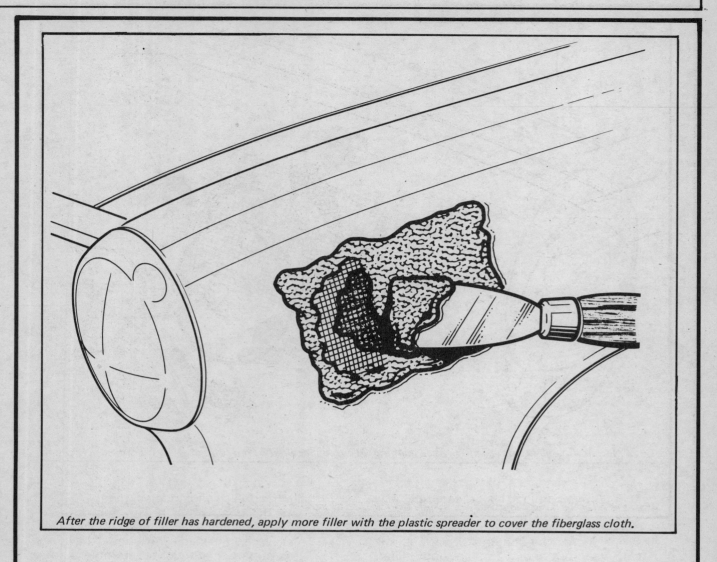

After the ridge of filler has hardened, apply more filler with the plastic spreader to cover the fiberglass cloth.

REPAIRING RUST SPOTS AND HOLES

spot, it will continue to rust out the area, making your repair only temporary.

4. With a ball-peen hammer, beat the metal around the edge of the hole inward to about a 45-degree angle.

5. Taking the fiberglass cloth from the body repair kit, cut a piece that is slightly larger than the hole. After cutting, place the cloth against the hole and trim it if necessary. Set it aside.

6. Mix enough body filler and hardener to make a ring of filler around the hole. Instructions with the body repair kit will ex-

Before the filler completely hardens, carefully trim any excess filler material away with a sharp knife.

TOOLS

Heavy-Duty Oil Filter Wrench

When you run into a stubborn oil filter, you need a heavy-duty oil filter wrench to loosen it. Not only does it have to be a model with a long handle for good leverage, but the band should be wide enough to help prevent crushing the spin-off type of oil filter. Brookins Service Station Equipment Division of Balcrank Products makes one called Model 1152. It has a big, 1-1/4 inch wide clamp and an eight inch handle that provides a good grip.

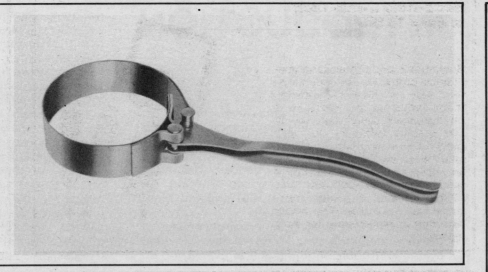

16-Piece Metric 3/8 Inch Drive Socket Set

If you own a foreign car that is built on the metric system, Proto Tool Division of Ingersoll-Rand's Challenger 16-piece metric socket set can be what you need to begin doing your own auto repairs. The set includes three six-point sockets in 12mm, 13mm and 14mm sizes. There also are eight 12-point sockets from 15mm to 22mm. Other components are a 13/16 inch spark plug socket, reversible ratchet, a three and six inch extension, and a flex handle. The tools come in a steel storage box.

lems or piston ring trouble. A compression test is important, especially on older cars.

A vacuum gauge is a valuable and inexpensive gauge that should be a part of any tune-up kit. Properly installed and used, it can tip you off about your ignition timing, manifold leaks, carburetor, valve or head gasket problems, and even a clogged muffler.

There are two types of feeler gauges, both of which may be included in a single tool. The wire type is used for checking and adjusting the spark plug gap. The flat type is for ignition breaker points spacing and for adjusting valves on cars that have adjustable valve tappets.

TIRE GAUGE. Here is a gauge that can save its price in a short time. Because improperly inflated tires wear out fast, it is a good idea to carry a tire gauge in your car's glove compartment and check the inflation pressure at least once a month and before every long trip.

LUG WRENCH. The lug wrench that came in the car, like the bumper jack, is an emergency tool. If you are going to be doing considerable wheel removal, buy a cross-shaft wrench, which has four different socket sizes and provides you with much more leverage than you get with the standard lug wrench. It also provides a straighter, more even twist to prevent possible damage to the wheel nuts.

GREASE GUN. Whether or not you should invest in a grease gun depends upon the age of your car and how many other pieces of equipment with lube fittings you own. A small grease gun is inexpensive, and it is certainly easy enough to pump a little extra grease into the fittings when you are doing chores under your car.

MISCELLANEOUS ITEMS. On some jobs, when you are handling a number of small parts, it is a good idea to have a couple of egg cartons in which to keep everything clean and orderly.

Start out right by having a professional-type hand cleaner (available from auto supply stores) and plenty of rags. You also may want to get some protective paste, which is applied to the hands before work is started. It acts like a chemical "glove" and rinses off easily with water.

You can save yourself a lot of time and trouble by including a selection of the popular-size nuts, bolts, washers and lock washers, plus sheet metal screws, plastic and electrical tape, penetrating oil, sealers and other such commonly used materials in your "shop" inventory.

Assuming you will be buying tools for the car you now own, you probably will be investing in standard rather than metric sizes. However, with the advent of metric fasteners becoming more common, you should consider phasing metric sizes into your tool collection. Keep in mind, foreign-made cars demand metric tools.

A good way to buy tools if you are starting from scratch is to look for sales of complete sets. For example, you can buy a basic set that includes most common sockets, open-end wrenches, hex keys (for those hex head bolts) and miscellaneous other necessities for about $50. Usually, a set like this will save you about 30 to 40 percent as compared to buying individual pieces.

Power Tools Need Care Too

THERE IS pride and satisfaction in owning and using good power tools. They will help you do your job more quickly. But, like your car and other equipment, power tool dependability is in direct relationship to the care you give them. To get the most from your tools, use them properly and take care of them.

Here are a few tips from the experts:

1. Be sure you are operating your tools with adequate electric current. A long extension cord with insufficient capacity can burn out a motor. Too much load on the circuit can have the same effect. Use good quality extension cords of adequate gauge.
2. Do not overload your tools. Putting an oversized drill with a reduced sized shaft into the chuck is asking for trouble. Loading a motor until it stalls out will shorten the motor life, too. If you have a heavy job to do, save your equipment by renting or borrowing the proper size equipment for the job. For example, a large sanding disc with coarse paper in a lightweight 1/4 inch drill will get your drill hot in a hurry and probably burn out the motor. That is why the professionals use heavy-duty equipment for that kind of work.
3. Keep the motor cool. Clean out accumulated dirt and dust from air passages on your power tool housing to allow the free flow of air around the motor.
4. Learn how to service power tools. For example, it is a good idea to check the motor brushes every few hundred hours of use. If they are worn down to less than one-third of their original length, replace them. If you are unfamiliar with this kind of electrical work, take your power tool to an electrical repair shop so the job can be done before the tool fails you.

And, if the instructions that came with your equipment recommend occasional lubrication, be sure to do it.

Nut Driver Stand Keeps Tools Organized

One of the trademarks of a good mechanic is organization. You can waste a lot of time looking for tools. Vaco Products Company offers 10 solid-shaft metric nut drivers from 4mm to 11mm in a white enameled metal stand, No. 70200, that makes selection of the right tool easy. The stand also includes a label for easier selection. With the drivers in place, the unit is 7 by 3-1/2 by 7-1/8 inches. Included are sizes for the following hex nuts—4mm, 4.5mm, 5mm, 5.5mm, 6mm, 7mm, 8mm, 9mm, 10mm, and 11mm. Shaft sizes are three inches; overall lengths are 6-3/4 inches except for the two largest drivers, which measure seven inches.

Reversible Drill Can Be Used On Fasteners

A 3/8 inch drill is a helpful work companion for the home mechanic, especially if it reverses and has a variable-speed feature. Ingersoll-Rand manufactures a 3/8 inch standard-duty, variable-speed reversible electric drill, Model 7732. It can operate at speeds up to 1000 rpm but can be slowed down with a fingertip control to self-start holes at slow speeds without center punching. It also reverses to remove jammed drill bits, screws, nuts and bolts. And, it is a real work-saver when you have to fasten a large number of screws. The drill weighs three pounds, measures 8-3/4 inches in length and uses 2.5 amps of 115-125 volt AC current.

INTRODUCTION

AS A do-it-yourselfer, one of your most gratifying experiences can be diagnosing your own car troubles, especially if you also can correct the problem. But diagnosis can be quite difficult, even for the experienced mechanic. This is particularly true when working on late-model cars with more sophisticated electrical, ignition and fuel systems.

To help you determine the probable causes of the most common symptoms, we have provided a series of trouble-shooting charts. Even if you do not plan to tackle the corrective measures yourself, these charts will help you deal more confidently with your mechanic.

Because there may be several areas of the car in which to search for the source of your difficulties (starting trouble, for example, can be related to ignition, fuel, electrical or emission control systems—or a combination of these), we have provided a guide to assist you to begin pinpointing your specific trouble.

Most troubles, such as brake, steering, or lighting malfunctions, fit into obvious categories. Drive train trouble, however, can be more difficult to diagnose because there are so many interrelated components.

Take some time to study the charts and you may be ahead of the game when, if ever, you find it necessary to become your own diagnostician.

IF YOU NOTICE THESE SYMPTOMS:	REFER TO THESE TROUBLE-SHOOTING CHARTS:
Car performs poorly, runs rough or uses too much gas	A, C, G, H or I
Engine stalls	C, H, or I
Engine is hard to start	A, C or I
Engine uses excessive oil	A or H
Engine overheats	E or G
Car smokes	A, C or H
Car shifts erratically	D
Car makes unusual noises	A, B, C, D, G, H, I or J
Car handles poorly, vibrates or steers hard	J
Abnormal braking action	B
Lights, turn signals or windshield wipers malfunctioning	F
Heater or air conditioner not working properly	E

(A) The Engine

Symptoms / Causes	Burned or worn valves	Worn piston rings	Worn valve guides	Oil leaks	Valves need adjustment	Faulty valve lifters	Valve sticking	Valve spring broken	Broken timing gear or chain	Broken distributor drive	Broken engine mounts	Damaged main bearing	Damaged connecting rod bearing	Worn piston pins
Engine lacks power	●	●												
Poor fuel mileage	●	●												
Excessive oil use		●	●	●										
Fumes from engine		●												
Light clicking noise					●	●	●	●						
Rough operation						●	●	●						
Engine will not run									●	●				
Engine shakes											●			
Heavy thudding												●		
Sharp metallic knock													●	●

Ignition Work Takes Special Tools

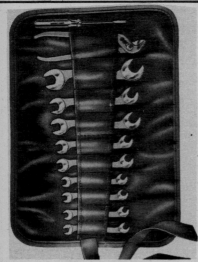

When working on ignition systems, you will find that there are certain practically indispensable tools. A 12-piece ignition set, No. 300B, sold by Proto Tool Division of Ingersoll-Rand in their Challenger line contains an ignition point file, screw starter and ignition pliers. There also is a 10-blade ignition gauge that measures thicknesses from 0.013 to 0.040 inch. An eight-piece ignition wrench set included in the kit provides tools with openings from 13/64 through 3/8 inch. The wrenches have the same size opening on each end, but one end has a 15-degree head while the other has a 75-degree angle head. They come in a compartmented, vinyl roll-up kit.

S-K Sells Starter Socket Set

Why struggle with stubborn nuts in cramped working areas? You can get the job done easily with a ratchet set such as the one made by S-K Tools, a division of Dresser Industries, Inc. S-K has several combination socket sets—some with the ratchet, some with just sockets. The starter set, No. 4512, consists of 12 pieces: eight sockets, a 1-1/2 inch ratchet extension, six inch ratchet extension, the ratchet itself, and a spark plug socket with neoprene insert. All are 3/8 inch drive and come in a metal carrying case.

Engine Friction-Proofing

Wynn's Friction-Proofing, made by Wynn's Friction Proofing Supply, Inc., was developed on the premise than an automobile engine needs a chemical barrier on its moving parts to protect them from corrosion damage caused by acid and water; the acid is a natural by-product of combustion. This additive is designed to provide that chemical barrier. It is available in 15 ounce cans at local auto parts stores.

TROUBLE—SHOOTING CHART

(B) Braking System

Symptoms \ Causes	Low fluid level	Air in hydraulic system	Brakes need adjustment	Brake fade due to overheating	Grease or fluid on linings	Linings glazed	Wet brakes	Faulty vacuum booster	Linkage binding	Weak flexible hoses	Loose or worn wheel bearings	Loose or worn front end parts	Front wheels out of alignment	Loose disc brake caliper	Warped brake disc	Eccentric brake drum	Faulty wheel cylinder	Faulty master cylinder	Weak or broken retracting springs	Scored brake drums	Dirt in brake mechanism	Clogged or kinked brake lines
Play in pedal	●	●	●						●								●	●				
Hard pedal				●	●	●	●	●	●								●	●				●
Spongy pedal	●	●							●													
Pedal sinks to floor	●																●	●				
Pedal vibrates											●				●	●						
Brakes grab					●															●		
Brakes drag			●						●										●	●		●
Brakes pull			●		●						●	●	●							●		●
Erratic braking			●		●						●	●		●	●					●		
Squeal or chatter			●			●									●	●					●	

(C) The Fuel System

Symptoms \ Causes	Faulty automatic choke	Low fuel pump pressure	Faulty carburetor adjustment	Fuel line hot — vapor lock	Dirt or water in fuel	Clogged fuel filter	Dirty carburetor	Clogged air cleaner	Faulty accelerating pump	Binding accelerator linkage	High fuel pump pressure	Sticking needle valve
Hard starting when cold	●											
Hard starting when hot	●			●								
Engine stalls	●		●		●		●					
Smoky exhaust	●		●				●	●			●	●
Poor gasoline mileage	●		●				●	●			●	●
Engine 'starves' at high speed		●	●		●	●						
Rough idle	●		●				●				●	●
Engine stumbles on acceleration			●				●		●	●		
Flooded carburetor	●		●				●				●	●
Engine backfires		●	●		●	●						

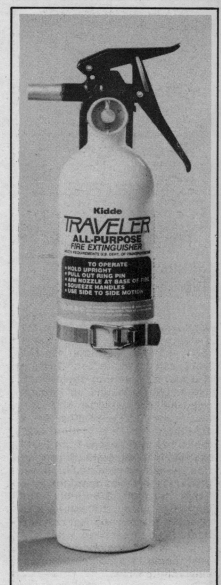

All-Purpose Fire Extinguisher

Walter Kidde & Co., Inc. has an all-purpose fire extinguisher, Model T-110. The Traveler All-Purpose Fire Extinguisher is designed for Class B and C fires.

Triple-Use Gear Lubricant

Manual transmissions, standard and limited-slip differentials and steering boxes usually call for an oil that is in the SAE range. The William Penn Company, Inc. manufactures a gear oil called the Super MP Gearlube-90 that is recommended for limited-slip differentials. It is formulated to prevent chattering, reduce wear, resist oxidation, protect against rust and resist foaming. It is not recommended for use in Fuller Road Ranger Transmissions.

Filter Wrench Gripper

If you find that your oil filter must be removed from directly underneath the car or directly above, the Filter Wrench Gripper, Model 51501, sold by Automark Division of Wells Manufacturing Corp. will fill the bill. It has a rugged tubular steel body and a steel slide bar. The filter is gripped by a polypropylene web strap that is designed not to slip.

Ignition Tool Set Includes Midget Pliers

Indestro, a division of Duro Metal Products Co., sells a five-piece tool set, No. 885, designed for ignition work that includes four wrenches with eight open-end sizes. Wrench sizes are 7/32 by 1/4 inch, 13/64 by 15/64 inch, 5/16 by 9/32 inch and 11/32 by 3/8 inch. Midget utility pliers are included. It looks like a miniature version of channel locks and is the standard tool used on ignition systems.

Flare-Nut Wrenches For Fuel Line Work

If you intend to do any type of fuel line work on your car, you should invest in a set of flare-nut wrenches. Their design prevents rounding off corners and damaging soft metal fittings. Vaco Products Company sells a set of three double-ended flare-nut wrenches packed in a vinyl pouch, No. 70275. The milled openings of these wrenches allow the wrench to slip over tubing. Included are wrench size openings of 3/8, 7/16, 1/2, 9/16, 5/8 and 11/16 inch.

Intermediate 1/4 Inch Drive Socket Set

S-K Tools, a division of Dresser Industries, Inc., has put together an intermediate 1/4 inch drive socket set, No. 4915, that is suitable for the home mechanic. The 15-piece set includes 11 standard sockets, a ratchet and three accessories. The sockets are six-point models and come in 3/16, 7/32, 1/4, 9/32, 5/16, 11/32, 3/8, 7/16 and 1/2 inch. The set also includes two eight-point sockets, 1/4 and 5/16 inch sockets. Accessories include a spinner handle, a two inch extension and a six inch extension.

(D) Transmission and Drive Line System

Symptoms \ Causes	Clutch needs adjustment	Clutch disc worn	Transmission low on lubricant	Incorrect grade of lubricant	Shift linkage out of adjustment	Low fluid level	Bands need adjustment	Control valve sticking	Throttle linkage needs adjustment	Leaking seals or gaskets	Worn universal joints	Unbalanced drive shaft	Unbalanced tires	Worn rear axle gears	Worn rear axle bearings	Tire noise
Clutch slips	●	●														
Hard shifting	●		●	●	●											
Gears clash	●		●	●	●											
Automatic transmission slips						●	●	●								
Automatic does not shift properly							●	●	●							
Transmission low on fluid										●						
Rough engagement of Drive or Reverse								●								
Heavy 'clunk' at low speed											●					
Whine from rear end														●	●	●

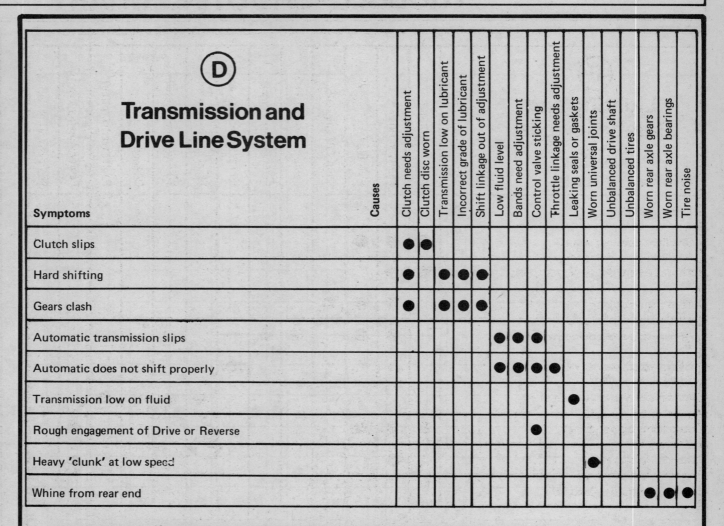

Many transmission and drivetrain problems are first indicated by noises coming from beneath the car.

(E) The Cooling System

Symptoms \ Causes	Low coolant level	Cooling system clogged	Loose or broken fan belt	Thermostat stuck closed	Thermostat stuck open	Debris on radiator	Faulty water pump	Collapsed water hose	Leaking cylinder head gasket	Late ignition timing	Heater core clogged	Faulty temperature control	Low refrigerant charge	Loose or broken drive belt	Faulty compressor clutch	Debris on condenser
Engine overheats	●	●	●	●		●	●	●	●	●						
Engine warms up slowly					●											
Insufficient heat					●						●	●				
Insufficient air conditioning												●	●	●		●
No air conditioning													●	●	●	

TROUBLE–SHOOTING CHART

(F) Lighting and Safety Devices

Symptoms \ Causes	Battery discharged	Bulb burned out	Faulty wiring	Fuse blown	Faulty flasher unit	Faulty wiper motor	Faulty wiper linkage	Faulty wiper park switch	Fluid low in reservoir	Tubing disconnected	Clogged nozzle	Faulty washer pump	Faulty stop light switch	Short circuit in wiring
Lights very dim	●													
One light does not work		●	●	●										
Turn signals flash on only one side		●	●											
Turn signals do not flash			●	●	●									
Windshield wipers do not work			●	●		●	●							
Windshield wipers do not park								●						
Windshield washers do not work									●	●	●	●		
Stop lights do not work		●	●	●									●	
Stop lights stay on			●										●	
Headlights flash on and off														●

(G) The Exhaust System

Symptoms \ Causes	Hole in muffler	Tailpipe bent or clogged	Exhaust pipe or muffler clogged	Leaking tailpipe	Loose pipe or muffler	Pipe touching frame or body	Loose tubes inside muffler
Loud exhaust	●						
Hissing exhaust		●					
Fumes under car	●			●			
Rattles					●		●
Vibration						●	
Engine lacks power		●	●				
Engine overheats		●	●				

(H) Emission Control System

Symptoms \ Causes	Clogged or sticking PCV valve	Clogged PCV hoses	Leaking PCV hoses	Faulty air injection pump	Air pump belt slipping	Faulty transmission spark control
Rough idle	●	●	●			
Oil fumes from engine	●	●	●			
Oil on outside of engine	●	●	●			
Squeal or knock				●	●	
Stalling	●	●	●			
Engine lacks power	●	●	●			●
Poor gasoline mileage	●	●	●			●

A dirty carburetor is the cause of many engine disorders. Cleaning can be a simple matter if performed regularly.

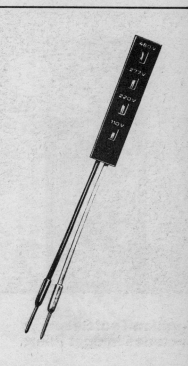

Multi-Volt Twin Lead Tester

A car has a number of electrical circuits and a do-it-yourselfer will have many occasions to check its circuits. Vaco Products Company makes a multi-volt twin lead tester, No. 70307, that checks and indicates voltage. It can be used on circuits up to 460 volts AC or DC. A combination of glow lamps indicate the voltage being tested: 110 volts, 220 volts, 277 volts or 460 volts. The instrument, which weighs 12 ounces, comes with red and black test leads that are furnished with probes.

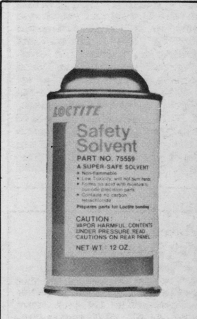

Safety Solvent

Before you apply any type of adhesive or gasket, you should make certain that the parts to be joined are completely clean. Loctite Safety Solvent, No. 75559, made by Woodhill/Permatex comes in a 12 ounce spray can. It dissolves grease, dirt and oil from parts, providing a good mating surface because it leaves no film.

Ⓘ Electrical System

Symptoms	Battery discharged	Loose or broken cables	Faulty starter or solenoid	Faulty ignition switch	Faulty distributor points	Faulty neutral switch	Spark plugs fouled	Improper spark plug gap	Faulty coil	Faulty condenser	Damaged distributor cap or rotor	Damaged ignition cables	Incorrect spark timing	Alternator belt slipping	Faulty voltage regulator	Low regulator setting	Faulty alternator	Battery worn out
Starter will not operate	●	●	●	●	●	●												
Starter turns, engine will not start					●		●	●	●	●	●	●	●					
Engine stalls					●				●	●		●						
Engine misfires					●			●	●	●	●	●						
Engine cuts out at high speed					●			●	●		●	●						
Engine knocks, or 'pings'													●					
Engine lacks power					●			●	●	●	●	●	●					
Engine idles roughly					●			●	●			●						
Battery frequently discharged														●	●	●	●	●
Alternator does not charge														●	●		●	

Fire Extinguisher Fits In Glove Compartment

Every vehicle should have a fire extinguisher for emergencies. But it is not always easy to store one because they usually are rather large. Unival Corporation sells an F. D. fire extinguisher spray no larger than an ordinary 12 ounce aerosol can. The fire extinguisher is designed not to stain fabrics, leave a mess, penetrate upholstery cushions or mattresses. Directions appear on the can.

Extension Tube Helps Remedy Stuck Door Locks

Mechanics Helper, made by CRC Chemicals, Inc., has a special extension tube for unsticking door locks. The nozzle fits into the key slot so you can spray the CRC 5-56 lubricant directly into the mechanism. There also are many other uses, such as loosening and lubricating nuts and bolts; mufflers; manifolds and even windshield wiper linkage; box and latches; electric switches; aerials; and electric motors. It can be used to remove moisture from distributor ignition wires, starter motor, spark plug wires, generator/ alternator, solenoid, and electrical contacts.

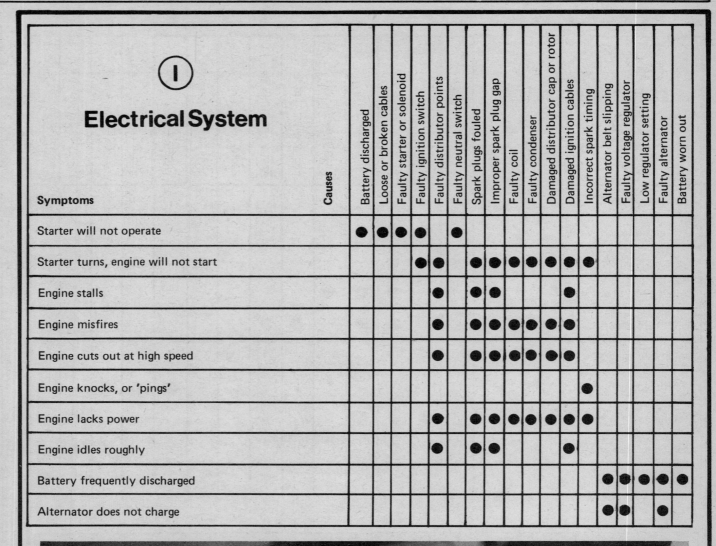

Stalling, misfiring, lack of engine power, and a rough idle often can be traced to distributor trouble.

TROUBLE–SHOOTING CHART

Steering and suspension components which are ignored can lead to serious problems, especially on older cars.

Thaw Frozen Locks

Special products are on the market to unfreeze locks and keep them from freezing. One such product is Lock-Thaw from Gold Eagle Co. It does not contain graphite and is designed not to gum up or harden in severe sub-zero temperatures. It also is formulated not to harm auto finishes. A special slot-shaped cap fits right into the lock and allows you to apply the fluid easily. Lock-Thaw comes in a one ounce bottle.

Impact Hammer From Steck

Steck Manufacturing Company, Inc. makes a Model 2500 impact hammer kit with attachments. This unit has a three pound slide hammer and a shaft collar that is guaranteed not to break away from the shaft for the life of the tool. With this type of tool, you drill a hole and insert an L-shaped or pick-type metal rod. Then you pull on the tool and use the slide hammer to pull the dent out. To finish, you fill in the hole, sand, prime and paint.

10-Piece Drill Bit Set

Black and Decker Manufacturing Co. makes a 10-piece drill bit set, No. 71-010, that is a good choice for the home mechanic. The set includes 1/16, 5/64, 3/32, 7/64, 1/8, 9/64, 5/32, 3/16, 7/32, and 1/4 inch bits. They come in a folding plastic case with the sizes marked.

(J) Steering and Suspension System

Symptoms \ Causes	Low or uneven tire pressure	Steering linkage dry	Front end out of alignment	Suspension arms damaged	Ball joints binding	Sagging springs	Power steering belt slipping	Power steering fluid low	Loose front wheel bearings	Worn ball joints	Loose steering linkage	Maladjusted steering gear	Worn shock absorbers	Wheels and tires out of balance
Hard steering	•	•	•	•	•	•	•	•				•		
Car pulls to one side	•		•	•		•			•	•	•	•		
Car wanders from side to side	•		•			•			•	•	•	•	•	
Uneven tire wear	•		•	•					•	•	•		•	•
Front wheel shimmy									•	•	•			
High-speed vibration													•	•
Car not level				•		•								
Heavy thumps on rough roads				•	•					•			•	
Play or looseness in steering									•	•	•	•		
Rattle in steering gear												•		
Thump from front end				•						•				

289

DIRECTORY OF MANUFACTURERS

On-Guard Corporation of America
350 Gotham Parkway
Carlstadt, New Jersey 07072

The Orelube Corporation
126-06 18th Avenue
College Point, New York 11356

OTC
Division of Owatonna Tool Company
122 Eisenhower Drive
Owatonna, Minnesota 55060

P

Panef Manufacturing Company,
  Incorporated
5700 West Douglas Avenue
Milwaukee, Wisconsin 53218

Pathfinder Auto Lamp Company
6201 West Howard Street
Niles, Illinois 60648

P&D Automotive Division
Facet Enterprises, Inc.
P.O. Box 1767
74 Conalco Drive
Jackson, Tennessee 38301

Peerless Instrument Company
6101 Gross Point Road
Chicago, Illinois 60648

Wm. Penn
Division BP Oil, Incorporated
1882 Guildhall Building
Cleveland, Ohio 44115

Pennwalt Automotive Products
Special Chemicals Department
Pennwalt Corporation
Pennwalt Building
Three Parkway
Philadelphia, Pennsylvania 19102

Pennzoil Company
Gumout Division
2686 Lisbon Road
Cleveland, Ohio 44104

Perfect Parts, Incorporated
33 Commerce Road
Carlstadt, New Jersey 07072

Per-Lux, Incorporated
804 East Edna Place
Covina, California 91723

Petersen Manufacturing Company,
  Incorporated
DeWitt, Nebraska 68341

Petroleum Chemicals Company
1444 South 20th
Omaha, Nebraska 68108

Phillips
Division of James B. Carter, Incorporated
A Budd Company
8200 Grand Avenue South
Minneapolis, Minnesota 55420

Plews Division Parker Automotive
3033 Excelsior Boulevard
Minneapolis, Minnesota 55416

Poly-Oleum Corporation
16135 Harper
Detroit, Michigan 48224

PPG Industries, Incorporated
Chemical Division
One Gateway Center
Pittsburgh, Pennsylvania 15222

Prestolite Electrical Division
An Eltra Company
Toledo, Ohio 43694

Preval Sprayer Division
Precision Valve Corporation
P.O. Box 309
Yonkers, New York 10702

Progressive Armature
1643 West Broad Street
Richmond, Virginia 23220

Proto Tool Division Ingersoll-Rand
2600 East Nutwood Avenue
Fullerton, California 92631

Pyroil Company
A Division of Champion Laboratories,
  Incorporated
P.O. Box 207
Albion, Illinois 62806

R

Radiator Specialty Company
1400 West Independence Boulevard
Charlotte, North Carolina 28237

Raybestos Division
RM Friction Materials Company
A Division of Raybestos-Manhattan,
  Incorporated
Trumbull, Connecticut, 06611

Rem Line
A Division of Model Industries, Incorporated
Highway 47 at Cannonball Trail
Yorkville, Illinois 60560

Rimac Tools
Rinck-McIlwaine, Incorporated
69 Armour Place
Dumont, New Jersey 07628

Ristance Products, Incorporated
Industrial Park
Argos, Indiana 46501

Rite Autotronics Corporation
3485 South La Cienega Boulevard
Los Angeles, California 90016

Rittenbaum Brothers, Incorporated
P.O. Box 1264
691 Houston Street, Northeast
Atlanta, Georgia 30312

Robinair Manufacturing
1224 South East Avenue
Montpelier, Ohio 43543

Rubbermaid Specialty Products,
  Incorporated
Callaway Industrial Park
LaGrange, Georgia 30240

S

Schrader Automotive Products Division
Schoville Automotive Products Group
2000 Richard Jones Road
Nashville, Tennessee 37215

Sem Products, Incorporated
Sem Lane & Shoreway Road
Belmont, California 94002

The Shaler Company
21 East Jefferson Street
Waupun, Wisconsin 53963

Signal-Stat Corporation
1200 Commerce Avenue
Union, New Jersey 07083

Siloo Incorporated
393 Seventh Avenue
New York, New York 10001

Silvatrim Corporation of America
140 South Avenue
South Plainfield, New Jersey 07080

Silver Seal Products Company, Incorporated
19280 Allen Road
Trenton, Michigan 48183

S-K Tool Group Marketing Division
Dresser Industries, Incorporated
3201 North Wolf Road
Franklin Park, Illinois 60131

Sonco Manufacturing
Division of Merc-O-Tronic Instrument
  Corporation
1402 Sabal Palm Drive
Bonita Springs, Florida 33923

Sorensen Manufacturing Company,
  Incorporated
1115 Cleveland Avenue
Glasgow, Kentucky 42141

Spartan Plastics, Incorporated
P.O. Box 67
Holt, Michigan 48842

Spray Products Corporation
P.O. Box 737
Norristown, Pennsylvania 19404

Standard Motor Products, Incorporated
37-18 Northern Boulevard
Long Island City, New York 11101

Stant Manufacturing Company, Incorporated
A Purolator Products Company
Connersville, Indiana 47331

Steck Manufacturing Company,
  Incorporated
1319-25 West Steward Street
Dayton, Ohio 45408

DIRECTORY OF MANUFACTURERS

Stewart-Warner
1826 Diversey
Chicago, Illinois 60614

Stimsonite Automotive Products
Amerace Brands Division
Amerace Corporation
Ace Road
Butler, New Jersey

Sun Electric Corporation
Consumer Products Division
3011 East Route 176
Crystal Lake, Illinois 60014

Superior/Ideal Incorporated
A Subsidiary of Superior Industries
    International, Incorporated
14721 Keswick Street
Van Nuys, California 91405

Superior Industries International,
    Incorporated
14721 Keswick Street
Van Nuys, California 91405

T

Talsol Corporation
4677 Devitt Drive
Cincinnati, Ohio 45246

Taylor Cable Products, Incorporated
301 Highgrove Road
Grandview, Missouri 64030

Teledyne AWD
8190 Byron Road
Whittier, California 90606

Tempo Products Company
An Alco Standard Company
6200 Cochran Road
Cleveland, Ohio 44139

Thexton Manufacturing Company
P.O. Box 35008
7685 Parklawn Avenue
Minneapolis, Minnesota 55435

3M Company
Public Relations Department
3M Center
St. Paul, Minnesota 55101

Townsend/Richline
Townsend Division of Textron, Incorporated
P.O. Box 3518
2515 Pilot Knob Road
St. Paul, Minnesota 55165

T.P.H. Division
Parker Hannifin
3033 Excelsior Boulevard
Minneapolis, Minnesota 55416

Trico Products Corporation
817 Washington Street
Buffalo, New York 14203

Tridair Industries
Specialty Fasteners/A Rexnord Company
3000 West Lomita Boulevard
Torrance, California 90505

Triple-A Specialty Company
5750 West 51st Street
Chicago, Illinois 60638

TRW, Incorporated
TRW Replacement Division
8001 East Pleasant Valley Road
Cleveland, Ohio 44131

U

Union Carbide Corporation
270 Park Avenue
New York, New York 10017

United States Aviex Company
1056 Huntly Road
Niles, Michigan 49120

United States Chemical & Plastics
An Alco Standard Corporate Partner
P.O. Box 6208
1446 West Tuscarawas Street
Canton, Ohio 44706

Unival Corporation
157 Summerfield Street
Scarsdale, New York 10583

V

Vaco Products Company
510 North Dearborn Street
Chicago, Illinois 60610

Valvoline Oil Company
Division of Ashland Oil, Incorporated
Box 391
Ashland, Kentucky 41101

Very Important Products, Incorporated
Department CW-6
3901 Westerly Place, Suite 101
Newport Beach, California 92660

Virginia Chemicals, Incorporated
3340 West Norfolk Road
Portsmouth, Virginia 23703

W

Walker Manufacturing
A Tenneco Company
1201 Michigan Boulevard
Racine, Wisconsin 53402

Waterloo Industries, Incorporated
P.O. Box 209
300 Ansborough Avenue
Waterloo, Iowa 50704

Watervliet Tool Company
413 North Pearl Street
Albany, New York 12207

WD-40 Company
1061 Cudahy Place
San Diego, California 92110

Wells Manufacturing Corporation
26 South Brooke Street
Fond Du Lac, Wisconsin 54935

Westinghouse Electric Corporation
Lamp Divisions
One Westinghouse Plaza
Bloomfield, New Jersey 07003

Whitaker Cable Corporation
2801 Rockcreek Parkway
North Kansas City, Missouri 64116

Wix Corporation
P.O. Box 1967
Gastonia, North Carolina 28052

Wolf's Head Oil Refining Company
P.O. Box 38
21 Seneca Street
Oil City, Pennsylvania 16301

Woodhill/Permatex Company, Incorporated
18731 Cranwood Parkway
Cleveland, Ohio 44128

Wright Tool & Forge Company
42 East State Street
Barberton, Ohio 44203

Wynn's Friction Proofing Supply,
    Incorporated
P.O. Box 4370
2600 East Nutwood Avenue
Fullerton, California 92631

X

X-I-M Products, Incorporated
1169 Bassett Road
Westlake, Ohio 44145

Z

Zecol, Incorporated
Lubaid Company
3270 South Third Street
Milwaukee, Wisconsin 53207

Zenith Division
Gulf+Western Manufacturing Company
Seneca Falls, New York 13148

Zim Manufacturing Company
2850-56 West Fulton Street
Chicago, Illinois 60612

GLOSSARY

A

ACCELERATOR: The floor pedal used to control, through linkage, the throttle valve in the carburetor.

ACKERMAN PRINCIPLE: Bending the outer ends of the steering arms slightly inward so that when the car is making a turn, the inside wheel will turn more sharply than the outer wheel. This principle produces toe-out on turns.

ADDITIVE: Some solution, powder, etc., that is added to gasoline, oil, grease, etc., in an endeavor to improve the characteristics of the original product.

ADVANCE (Ignition timing): To set the ignition timing so that a spark occurs earlier or more degrees before Top Dead Center (TDC).

AIR GAP: The space between the spark plug electrodes; the space between rotating and stationary assemblies in a motor or generator; the space between contact points of a relay.

AIR LOCK: A bubble of air trapped in a fluid circuit that interferes with normal circulation of the fluid.

ALTERNATOR: An AC generator that produces alternating current that is internally rectified to DC current before being released.

ALTERNATING CURRENT (AC): An electrical current that moves first in one direction and then in the other (positive to negative, then negative to positive).

AMMETER: An instrument used to measure the rate of current flow (in amperes).

AMPERAGE: The total amount of current (amperes) flowing in a circuit.

ANTIFREEZE: A chemical added to the cooling system to prevent the coolant from freezing in cold weather.

ANTIFRICTION BEARING: A bearing containing rollers or balls plus an inner and outer race. The bearing is designed to roll, thus minimizing friction.

ARC: Flow of electricity through the air between two electrodes that produces a flash and releases a lot of heat.

AUTOMATIC CHOKE: A carburetor choke device that automatically positions itself in accordance with carburetor needs.

AXIAL: Having the same direction or being parallel to the axis of rotation.

AXLE: A crossbar supporting a vehicle on which wheels turn.

AXLE (Full-floating): An axle used to drive the rear wheels. It does not hold the wheels on or support them.

AXLE (Semi or one-quarter floating): An axle used to drive the wheels, hold them on and support them.

B

AXLE (Three-quarter floating): An axle used to drive the rear wheels as well as hold them on. It does not support them.

BACK PRESSURE: Refers to the resistance to the flow of exhaust gases through the exhaust system.

BALL JOINT: Commonly used as suspension and steering linkage connectors on independent front suspension, it has a hardened steel stud threaded on one end, is tapered in the middle, and formed into a ball on the other end.

BALL JOINT STEERING KNUCKLE: A steering knuckle that pivots on ball joints.

BATTERY: A device used to store electrical energy in a chemical form.

BATTERY CHARGING: The process of renewing the battery by passing an electric current through the battery in a reverse direction.

BDC: Bottom dead center.

BEARING: The area or unit in which the contacting surface of a revolving part rests.

BEARING CLEARANCE: The amount of space left between a shaft and the bearing surface. This space is for lubricating oil to enter.

BLEEDING THE BRAKES: This refers to the removal of air from the hydraulic system. Bleeder screws are loosened at each wheel cylinder (one at a time), and brake fluid is forced from the master cylinder through the lines until all air is expelled.

BLOCK: That part of the engine containing the cylinders.

BLOW-BY: Refers to the escape of exhaust gases past the piston rings.

BODY PUTTY: A material designed to smooth out dented body areas. Upon hardening, the putty is dressed down and the area painted.

BONDED BRAKE LINING: Brake lining that is attached to the brake shoe by an adhesive.

BORE DIAMETER: The diameter of the engine cylinders.

BOURDON TUBE: A circular, hollow piece of metal that is used in some instruments. Pressure on the hollow section causes it to attempt to straighten. The free end then moves a needle on the gauge face.

BRAKE BACKING PLATE: A rigid steel plate upon which the brake shoes are attached. The braking force applied to the shoes is absorbed by the backing plate.

BRAKE - DISC TYPE: A braking system that uses a steel disc with a caliper and pads. When the brakes are applied, the pad on each side of the spinning disc is forced against the disc, thus imparting a braking force. This type of brake is very resistant to brake fade.

BRAKE DISC (Rotor): A disc that is machined on both sides to allow for brake pads that will push or clamp against the disc to stop the car.

BRAKE DRUM: A cast metal cylinder attached to the wheel, used to house the brake shoes and provide a friction surface for stopping the vehicle.

BRAKE FADE: The loss of braking power due to overheating of the brake lining.

BRAKE FLUID: A mixture of hydraulic fluids with a high boiling point and a low freezing point, plus other characteristics needed for good brake action.

BRAKE LINING: A molded material with a suitable coefficient of friction to stop the car. It is either riveted or bonded to the brake shoe.

BRAKE - PARKING: A brake used to hold the car in position while parked. One type applies the rear brake shoes by mechanical means and the other type applies a brake band to a brake drum installed in the drive train.

BRAKE - POWER: A conventional hydraulic brake system that utilizes engine vacuum to operate a vacuum power piston. The power piston applies pressure to the brake pedal or, in some cases, directly to the master cylinder piston. This reduces the amount of pedal pressure that the driver must exert to stop the car.

BRAKE PULL: The result of a difference in friction between brakes on the two sides of the automobile.

BRAKE SHOES: That part of the brake system, located at the wheels, upon which the brake lining is attached. When the wheel cylinders are actuated by hydraulic pressure, they force the brake shoes apart and bring the lining into contact with the drum.

BRAKE WHEEL CYLINDER: A cylinder containing a movable piston that is activated by hydraulic pressure, which, in turn, pushes the brake shoes against the brake drum.

BREAKER ARM: The movable part of a pair of contact points in a distributor.

BREAKER POINTS: Two points (one movable) in the distributor that, when moved apart, interrupt current flow in the primary circuit.

BRUSH: A piece made of conducting material, that when bearing against a commutator, slip ring, etc., will provide a passage for electric current.

BUTTERFLY VALVE: A valve in the carburetor that is so named due to its resemblance to the insect of the same name.

BYPASS VALVE: A valve that can open and allow a fluid to pass through in other than its normal channel.

C

CALIPERS (Inside and outside): An adjustable measuring tool that is placed around, or within, an object and adjusted until it just contacts. It is then withdrawn and the distance measured between the contacting points.

CAM ANGLE or DWELL (Ignition): The number of degrees the breaker cam rotates from the time the breaker points close until they open again.

CAMBER: Tipping the top of the wheel centerline outward produces 'positive' camber. Tipping the wheel centerline inward at the top produces 'negative' camber. When the camber is positive, the tops of the tires are further apart than the bottom.

CAMSHAFT: A shaft with cam lobes (bumps) used to operate the valves.

CAMSHAFT GEAR: A gear that is used to drive the camshaft.

CAPACITOR (Condenser): A device used to store an electrical charge.

CARBON: Used to describe the hard, or soft, black deposits found in the combustion chamber, on the plugs, under the rings, on and under the valve heads.

CARBURETOR: A device used to mix gasoline and air in the correct proportions.

CARBURETOR ICING: The formation of ice on the throttle plate or valve. As the fuel nozzles feed fuel into the air horn, it turns to a vapor. This robs heat from the air, and when weather conditions are just right (fairly cold and quite humid), ice may form.

CASTLE OR CASTELLATED NUT: A nut having a series of slots cut into one end into which a cotter pin may be passed to secure the nut.

CELL: A compartment that contains one set of positive and one set of negative plates that, with electrolyte, will produce electricity when the circuit is closed.

CENTER STEERING LINKAGE: A steering system utilizing two tie rods connected to the steering arms and to a central idler arm. The idler arm is operated by a drag link that connects the idler arm to the pitman arm.

CENTRIFUGAL ADVANCE (Distributor): A unit designed to advance and retard the ignition timing through the action of centrifugal force.

CENTRIFUGAL CLUTCH: A clutch that utilizes centrifugal force to expand a friction device on the driving shaft until it is locked to a drum on the driven shaft.

CENTRIFUGAL FORCE: That force that tends to keep moving objects traveling in a straight line. When a moving car is forced to make a turn, centrifugal force attempts to keep it moving in a straight line. If the car is turning at too high a speed, centrifugal force will be greater than the frictional force between the tires and the road, and the car will slide off the road.

CHARGE (Recharge): To restore the active materials in a battery cell by electrically reversing the chemical action.

CHASSIS: The vehicle frame, suspension, and running gear; everything except the car body.

CHOKE: A butterfly valve located in the carburetor that is used to enrich the mixture for starting the engine when cold.

CID: Cubic inch displacement.

CIRCUIT: The path of electron flow from the source through components and connections and back to its source.

CIRCUIT (Parallel): An electrical system in which all positive terminals are joined through one wire, and all negative terminals through another wire.

CIRCUIT (Series): An electrical system in which separate parts are connected end to end, using one wire to form a single path for current to flow.

CIRCUIT (Closed): An electrical circuit in which there is no interruption of current flow.

CIRCUIT (Open): Any break or lack of contact in an electrical circuit, either intentional (switch) or unintentional (bad connection).

CIRCUIT BREAKER: A device, other than a fuse, for interrupting a circuit under high load conditions.

CLEARANCE: A given amount of space between two parts—between piston and cylinder, bearing and journal, etc.

CLOCKWISE: Rotation to the right, as that of clock hands.

CLUSTER OR COUNTER GEAR: The 'cluster' of gears that are all cut on one long gear blank. The cluster gears ride in the bottom of the transmission. The cluster provides a connection between the transmission input shaft and the output shaft.

CLUTCH: A device used to connect or disconnect the flow of power from one unit to another.

CLUTCH DIAPHRAGM SPRING: A round dish-shaped piece of flat spring steel. It is used to force the pressure plate against the clutch disc in some clutches.

CLUTCH DISC: Part of a clutch assembly that is splined to the transmission clutch or input shaft. It is faced with friction material. When the clutch is engaged, the disc is squeezed between the flywheel and the clutch pressure plate.

CLUTCH HOUSING OR BELL HOUSING: A cast iron or aluminum housing that surrounds the flywheel and clutch mechanism.

CLUTCH PEDAL FREE TRAVEL: The specified distance that the clutch pedal may be depressed before the throw-out bearing actually contacts the clutch release fingers.

CLUTCH PILOT BEARING: A small bronze bushing, or in some cases a ball bearing, placed in the end of the crankshaft or in the center of the flywheel depending on the car, that is used to support the outboard end of the transmission input shaft.

CLUTCH PRESSURE PLATE: Part of a clutch assembly that, through spring pressure, squeezes the clutch disc against the flywheel thereby transmitting a driving force through the assembly. To disengage the clutch, the pressure plate is drawn away from the flywheel via linkage.

CLUTCH SEMI-CENTRIFUGAL RELEASE FINGERS: Clutch release fingers that have a weight attached to them so at high rpm, the release fingers place additional pressure on the clutch pressure plate.

CLUTCH THROW-OUT BEARING: The bearing that is forced against the pressure plate throw-out fingers to disengage the clutch.

CLUTCH THROW-OUT FORK: The device or fork that straddles the throw-out bearing and is used to force the throw-out bearing against the clutch release fingers.

COEFFICIENT OF FRICTION: A measurement of the amount of friction developed between two objects in physical contact when one of the objects is drawn across the other. If a book were placed on a table and a measuring scale used to pull the book, the amount of weight or pull registered on the scale would be the coefficient of friction.

COIL: A spiral made of wire; a device used in automobiles to increase the voltage to the spark plug, or to provide the electromagnetic force in a solenoid.

COIL SPRING: A section of spring steel rod wound in a spiral pattern or shape. Widely used in both front and rear suspension systems.

COMBUSTION: The process involved during burning.

COMBUSTION CHAMBER: The area above the piston with the piston on TDC. The head of the piston, the engine cylinder and the head form the chamber.

COMMUTATOR: A device to provide a current path between the armature coil and the brushes of an electric motor or generator.

COMPRESSION: Applying pressure to a spring, or any springy substance, thus causing it to reduce its length in the direction of the compressing force.
  Applying pressure to a gas, thus causing a reduction in volume.

COMPRESSION CHECK: Testing the compression in all the cylinders at cranking speed. All plugs are removed, the compression gauge placed in one plug hole, the throttle opened wide and the engine cranked until the gauge no longer climbs. The compression check is a way to determine the condition of the valves, rings and cylinders.

COMPRESSION GAUGE: A gauge used to test the compression in the cylinders.

COMPRESSION RATIO: Relationship between the cylinder volume (clearance volume) when the piston is on TDC and the cylinder volume when the piston is on BDC.

CONCENTRIC: Two or more circles so placed as to share a common center.

CONDENSE: Turning a vapor back into a liquid.

CONDENSER (Ignition): A unit installed between the breaker points and coil to prevent arcing at the breaker points. A condenser has the ability to absorb and retain surges of electricity.

CONDENSER (Refrigeration): The unit in an air conditioning system that cools hot compressed Freon-12 and turns it from a vapor into a liquid.

CONDENSATION: Moisture, from the air, deposited on a cool surface.

CONDUCTION: The transfer of heat from one object to another by having the objects in physical contact.

CONNECTING ROD: The connecting link between the piston and the crankshaft.

CONSTANT MESH GEARS: Gears that are always in mesh with each other—driving or not.

CONSTANT VELOCITY UNIVERSAL JOINT: A universal joint so designed as to effect a smooth transfer of torque from the drive shaft to the driving shaft without any fluctuations in the speed of the drive shaft.

CONTACT POINTS (Breaker points): Two movable points or areas that, when pressed together, complete a circuit. These points are usually made of tungsten, platinum or silver.

COOLANT: Solution of antifreeze and water in the cooling system.

COUNTER-BALANCE: A weight attached to some moving part so that the part will be in balance.

COUNTERCLOCKWISE: Rotation to the left as opposed to that of clock hands.

CRANKCASE: Part of the engine that surrounds the crankshaft. This is not to be confused with the pan which is a thin steel cover that is bolted to the crankcase.

CRANKSHAFT: A shaft running the length of the engine. Portions of the shaft are offset to form 'throws' to which the connecting rods are attached. The crankshaft is supported by main bearings.

CRANKSHAFT GEAR: A gear mounted on the front of the crankshaft. It is used to drive the camshaft gear.

CROSS SHAFT (Steering): The shaft in the steering gear box that engages the steering shaft worm. The cross shaft is splined to the pitman arm.

CYLINDER: The hole, or holes, in the engine cylinder block that contain the pistons.

CYLINDER HEAD: The metal section that is bolted on top of the block. It is used to cover the tops of the cylinders. In many cases, the cylinder head contains the valves. It also forms part of the combustion chamber.

D

DEAD AXLE: An axle that does not rotate but merely forms a base upon which to attach the wheels.

DEGREE (Circle): 1/360 part of a circle.

DETONATION: The fuel charge firing or burning too violently, almost exploding.

DIAPHRAGM: A flexible cloth-rubber sheet that is stretched across an area, thereby separating two different compartments.

DIESEL ENGINE: An internal combustion engine that uses diesel oil for fuel. The true diesel does not use an ignition system but injects diesel oil into the cylinders when the piston has compressed the air so tightly that it is hot enough to ignite the diesel without a spark.

DIFFERENTIAL: A unit that will drive both rear axles at the same time but will allow them to turn at different speeds when negotiating turns.

DIFFERENTIAL CASE: The steel unit to which the ring gear is attached. The case drives the

'spider' gears and forms an inner bearing surface for the axle and gears.

DIPSTICK: The metal rod that passes into the oil sump. It is used to determine the quantity of oil in the engine.

DIRECT CURRENT (DC): An electric current that flows in one direction only.

DIRECT DRIVE: Such as high gear when the crankshaft and drive shaft revolve at the same speed.

DIRECTIONAL STABILITY (Steering): Ability of a car to move forward in a straight line with a minimum of driver control. A car with good directional stability will not be unduly affected by side wind or road irregularities.

DISCHARGE (Battery): Drawing electric current from the battery.

DISPLACEMENT: The total volume of air displaced by the piston in traveling from BDC to TDC.

DISTRIBUTOR (Ignition): A unit designed to make and break the ignition primary circuit and to distribute the resultant high voltage to the proper cylinder at the correct time.

DISTRIBUTOR CAP (Ignition): An insulated cap containing a central terminal with a series (one per cylinder) of terminals that are evenly spaced in a circular pattern around the central terminal. The secondary voltage travels to the central terminal where it is then channeled to one of the outer terminals by the rotor.

DRAW (Amperage): The amount of current required to operate an electrical device.

DRIVE SHAFT: The shaft connecting the transmission output shaft to the differential pinion shaft.

DROP (Voltage): The net difference in electrical pressure when measured on both sides of a resistance.

DUAL BREAKER POINTS (Ignition): A distributor using two sets of breaker points to increase the cam angle so that at high engine speeds, sufficient spark will be produced to fire the plugs.

DUALS: Two sets of exhaust pipes and mufflers — one for each bank of cylinders.

DYNAMIC BALANCE: When the centerline of the weight mass of a revolving object is in the same plane as the centerline of the object, that object would be in dynamic balance. For example, the weight mass of the tire must be in the same plane as the centerline of the wheel.

E

ECONOMIZER VALVE: A fuel flow control device within the carburetor.

ELECTRICITY: Positive or negative charges in motion or at rest.

ELECTROCHEMICAL: Chemical (battery) production of electricity.

ELECTRODE (Spark plug): The center rod passing through the insulator forms one electrode. The rod welded to the shell forms another. They are referred to as the center and side electrodes.

ELECTROLYTE: A solution of sulphuric acid and water used in the cells of a battery to react chemically with the differing materials in the electrodes and produce an electrical current.

ELECTROMAGNET: A magnet produced by placing a coil of wire around a steel or iron bar. When current flows through the coil, the bar becomes magnetized and will remain so as long as the current continues to flow.

ELEMENT (Battery): A group of plates. Three elements for a six volt and six elements for the twelve volt battery. The elements are connected in series.

EMF: Electro-motive force (voltage).

ENGINE DISPLACEMENT: The volume of the space through which the head of the piston moves in the full length of its stroke — multiplied by the number of cylinders in the engine. The result is given in cubic inches.

ETHYLENE GLYCOL: A chemical solution added to the cooling system to protect against freezing.

EVAPORATOR: The unit in an air conditioning system used to transform Freon-12 from a liquid to a gas. It is at this point that cooling takes place.

EXHAUST GAS ANALYZER: An instrument used to check the exhaust gases to determine combustion efficiency.

EXHAUST MANIFOLD: Connecting pipes between the exhaust ports and the exhaust pipe.

EXTREME PRESSURE LUBRICANTS (E.P.): A term used to designate a lubricant to which an ingredient has been added to increase the lubricant's ability to withstand high pressure, as between gear teeth.

F

FATIGUE: A breakdown of material through a large amount of flexing or bending. The first signs are cracks, followed shortly by breaks.

FEELER GAUGE: A thin strip of hardened steel ground to an exact thickness that is used to check clearance between parts.

FIELD (Magnetic field): The area in which magnetic lines of force occur.

FILAMENT: A resistance in a light bulb that glows and produces light when a current is forced through it.

FIRE WALL: The metal partition between the driver's compartment and the engine compartment.

FIRING ORDER: The order in which cylinders must be fired—1, 5, 3, 6, 2, 4, etc.

FLARING TOOL: A tool used to form flare connections on tubing.

FLASH POINT: The point in the temperature range at which a given oil will ignite and flash into flame.

FLOODING: A condition where the fuel mixture is overly rich or an excessive amount has reached the cylinders. Starting will be difficult and sometimes impossible until the condition is corrected.

FLYWHEEL: A relatively large wheel that is attached to the crankshaft to smooth out the firing impulses. It provides inertia to keep the crankshaft turning smoothly during the periods when no power is being applied.

It also forms a base for the starter ring gear and, in many instances, for the clutch assembly.

FLYWHEEL RING GEAR: A gear on the outer circumference of the flywheel. The starter drive gear engages the ring gear and cranks the engine.

FOOT-POUND: A measurement of the work involved in lifting one pound one foot.

Also, a one pound pull one foot from the center of an object.

FRAME: The assembly of metal structural parts and channel sections that support the engine and the body, and that is supported by the wheels and suspension system.

FREE PLAY: Looseness in a linkage between the start of application and the actual movement of the device, such as the movement in the steering wheel before the wheels start to turn.

FREEZING: When two parts that are rubbing together heat up and force the lubricant out of the area, they will gall and finally 'freeze' or stick together.

FREON-12: A gas used as the cooling medium in air conditioning and refrigeration systems.

FRICTION: Resistance to slipping or skidding.

FRICTION BEARING: A bearing made of Babbit, bronze, etc. There are no moving parts and the shaft that rests in the bearing merely rubs against the friction material in the bearing.

FUEL INJECTION: A fuel system that uses no carburetor but sprays fuel either directly into the cylinders or into the intake manifold just ahead of the cylinders.

FUEL MIXTURE: A mixture of gasoline and air. An average mixture, by weight, would contain 16 parts of air to one part of gasoline.

FUEL PUMP: A vacuum device, operated either mechanically or electrically, that is used to draw gasoline from the tank and force it into the carburetor.

FUSE: A device consisting of a piece of wire with a low melting point inserted in a circuit. It will melt and open the circuit when the system is overloaded.

FUSION: Two metals reaching the melting point and flowing or welding themselves together.

G

GAP: The space or "break" in the continuity of a circuit, such as between ignition contact points.

GAS: A non-solid material. It can be compressed. When heated, it will expand and when cooled, it will contract.

GASKET: A material placed between two parts to insure proper sealing.

GASOLINE: A hydrocarbon fuel used in the internal combustion engine.

GEAR RATIO: The relationship between the number of turns made by a driving gear to complete one full turn of the driven gear. If the driving gear turns four times to turn the driven gear once, the gear ratio would be 4 to 1.

GENERATOR: A device that changes mechanical energy into electrical energy.

GROUND: A condition where the electrical circuit is connected to the unit frame by means of a strap or rod.

GUM (Fuel system): Oxidized portions of the fuel that form deposits in the fuel system or engine parts.

H

HEAT RANGE (Spark plugs): Refers to the operating temperature of a given style plug. Plugs are made to operate at different temperatures, depending upon the thickness and length of the porcelain insulator as measured from the sealing ring down to the tip.

HEAT RISER: An area surrounding a portion of the intake manifold through which exhaust gases pass to heat the fuel mixture during warm-up.

HELICAL GEAR: A gear that has the teeth cut at an angle to the centerline of the gear.

HIGH COMPRESSION HEADS: A cylinder head with a smaller combustion chamber area, thereby raising the compression. The head can be custom built or can be a stock head milled (cut) down.

HORSEPOWER: A measurement of the engine's ability to perform work. One horsepower is defined as the ability to lift 33,000 pounds one foot in one minute. To find horsepower, the total rate of work in foot pounds accomplished is divided by 33,000. If a machine was lifting 100 pounds 660 feet per minute, its total rate of work would be 66,000 foot pounds. Dividing this by 33,000 foot pounds (1 horsepower) you find that the machine is rated as 2 horsepower (hp).

HORSEPOWER—WEIGHT FACTOR: The relationship between the total weight of the car and the horsepower available. By dividing the weight by the horsepower, the number of pounds to be moved by one horsepower is determined. This factor has a great effect on acceleration, gas mileage and all-around performance.

HOT WIRE: A wire connected to the battery or to some part of the electrical system in which a direct connection to the battery is present.

HUB (Wheel): The unit to which the wheel is bolted.

HYDRAULIC: Refers to fluid in motion.

HYDRAULIC BRAKES: Brakes that are operated by hydraulic pressure. A master cylinder provides operating pressure that is transmitted via steel tubing to wheel cylinders, which in turn apply the brake shoes to the brake drums.

HYDRAULIC LIFTER: A valve lifter that utilizes hydraulic pressure from the engine's oiling system to keep it in constant contact with both the camshaft and the valve stem. They automatically adjust to any variation in valve stem length.

HYDRAULICS: The science of liquid in motion.

HYDROCARBON: A mixture of hydrogen and carbon.

HYDROMETER: An instrument with a float housed in a glass tube that measures specific gravity of a liquid.

I

IMPACT WRENCH: An air or electrical driven wrench that tightens or loosens nuts, cap screws, etc., with a series of sharp, rapid blows.

IMPELLER: A wheel-like device upon which fins are attached. It is whirled to pump water, move and slightly compress air, etc.

INDEPENDENT SUSPENSION: A suspension system that allows each wheel to move up and down without undue influence on the other wheels.

INDICATED HORSEPOWER (ihp): Indicated horsepower is a measure of the power developed by the burning fuel within the cylinders.

INDUCTION: The imparting of electricity from one object to another not connected to it by the influence of magnetic fields.

IN-LINE ENGINE: An engine in which all the cylinders are arranged in a straight row.

INSULATION: A substance through which electrons do not readily pass. A protective covering on wires or electrical parts to prevent short circuits or grounds.

INSULATOR: A nonconducting substance or body, such as porcelain, glass or Bakelite used for insulating wires in electrical circuits to prevent the leakage of electricity.

INTAKE MANIFOLD: Connecting tubes between the base of the carburetor and the port openings to the intake valves.

INTERMEDIATE GEAR: Any gear in the auto transmission between first and high.

INTERNAL COMBUSTION ENGINE: An engine that burns fuel within itself as a means of developing power.

J

JET: A small hole or orifice used to control the flow of gasoline in the various parts of the carburetor.

K

KICK-DOWN SWITCH: An electrical switch that will cause a transmission, or overdrive unit, to shift down to a lower gear. Often used to secure fast acceleration.

KNOCKING (Fuel): A condition, accompanied by an audible noise, that occurs when the gasoline in the cylinders burns too quickly. This is also referred to as detonation.

KNURL: A roughened surface caused by a sharp wheel that displaces metal outward as its sharp edges push into the metal surface.

L

LAMINATED: Something made up of many layers.

LAP or LAPPING: To fit two surfaces together by coating them with abrasive and then rubbing them together.

LEAF SPRING: A suspension spring made up of several pieces of flat spring steel. Varying numbers of leaves (individual pieces) are used, depending on the intended use.

LEVER: A rigid bar or beam capable of turning about one point called a fulcrum.

LIMITED-SLIP DIFFERENTIAL: A differential unit designed to provide superior traction by transferring driving torque, when one wheel is spinning, to the wheel that is not slipping.

LINKAGE: A system of links and levers connected together to transmit motion or force.

LIVE AXLE: An axle upon which the wheels are firmly affixed. The axle drives the wheels.

LIVE WIRE: Same as hot wire.

LONG AND SHORT ARM SUSPENSION: A suspension system utilizing an upper and lower control arm. The upper arm is shorter than the lower. This is done so as to allow the wheel to deflect in a vertical direction with a minimum change in camber.

LONGITUDINAL LEAF SPRING: A leaf spring that is mounted so that it is parallel to the length of the car.

LOW BRAKE PEDAL: A condition where the brake pedal approaches too close to the floorboard before actuating the brakes.

LOW PIVOT SWING AXLE: A rear axle setup that attaches the differential housing to the frame via a pivot mount. A conventional type of housing and axle extend from the differential to one wheel. The other side of the differential is connected to the other driving wheel by a housing and axle that is pivoted at a point in line with the differential to frame pivot point.

LPG: Liquified petroleum gas.

LUBRICANT: Any material, usually of a petroleum nature such as grease or oil, that is placed between two moving parts in an effort to reduce friction.

M

MAGNET (Permanent): A piece of magnetized steel that will attract all ferrous material. The permanent magnet does not need electricity to function and will retain its magnetism over a period of years.

MAGNETO: An engine driven unit that generates high voltage to fire the spark plugs. It needs no outside source of power.

MANIFOLD HEAT CONTROL VALVE: A valve placed in the exhaust manifold, or in the exhaust pipe, that deflects a certain amount of hot gas around the base of the carburetor to aid in warm-up.

MASTER CYLINDER: That part of the hydraulic brake system in which pressure is generated.

MECHANICAL BRAKES: Service brakes that are actuated by a mechanical linkage connecting the brakes to the brake pedal.

MECHANICAL EFFICIENCY: An engine's rating as to how much of the potential horsepower is wasted through friction within the moving parts of the engine.

METERING ROD: A moveable rod used to vary the opening area through a carburetor jet.

METRIC SIZE: Units made to metric system measurements.

MICROMETER: A precision measuring tool that will give readings accurate to within a fraction of one thousandth of an inch.

MILLIMETER: A metric measurement equivalent to 0.039370 of an inch.

MOTOR: An electromagnetic device used to convert electrical energy into mechanical energy.

MPH: Miles per hour.

MUFFLER: A unit through which the exhaust gases are passed to quiet the sounds of the running engine.

MULTIPLE DISC CLUTCH: A clutch utilizing several clutch discs in its construction.

MULTI-VISCOSITY OILS: Oils meeting S.A.E. requirements for both low temperature requirements of a light oil and the high temperature requirements of a heavy oil. Example: (S.A.E. 10W-30).

N

NEGATIVE: Condition at a pole from which electrons leave a generator or battery.

NEGATIVE TERMINAL: That terminal (such as that on the battery) from which the current flows on its path to the positive terminal.

NEOPRENE: A synthetic rubber that is highly resistant to petroleum products.

NONFERROUS METALS: All metals containing no iron.

O

OCTANE RATING: A rating that indicates a specific gasoline's ability to resist detonation.

ODOMETER: A device used to measure and register the number of miles traveled by the car.

OHM: A unit of measurement of electrical resistance.

OHMMETER: An instrument used to measure the amount of resistance in a given unit or circuit.

OHM'S LAW: A law of electricity that states the relationship between voltage, amperes and resistance. It takes a pressure of one volt to force one ampere of current through one ohm of resistance. Equation: Volts = amperes x ohms ($E = I \times R$).

OIL BATH AIR CLEANER: An air cleaner that utilizes a pool of oil to insure the removal of impurities from air entering the carburetor.

OIL BURNER: An engine that consumes an excessive quantity of oil.

OIL FILTER: A device used to strain the oil in the engine, thus removing abrasive particles.

OIL - 'ML' (Motor Light): Engine oil designed for light-duty service under favorable conditions.

OIL - 'MM' (Motor Medium): Engine oil designed for moderate-duty service with occasional high speeds.

OIL - 'MS' (Motor Severe): Engine oil designed for high-speed, heavy-duty operation. Also for a great deal of stop-and-go driving.

OIL PUMP: The device used to force oil, under pressure, to various parts of the engine. It is driven by a gear on the camshaft.

OIL PUMPING: A condition wherein an excessive quantity of oil passes the piston rings and is consumed in the combustion chamber.

OIL SEAL: A device used to prevent oil leakage past a certain area.

OSCILLATION: A rapid back and forth movement of a gauge.

OVERDRIVE: A unit utilizing a planetary gear set so actuated as to turn the drive shaft about one third faster than the transmission output shaft.

OVERRUNNING CLUTCH: A clutch mechanism that will drive in one direction only. If driving torque is removed or reversed, the clutch slips.

OVERRUNNING CLUTCH STARTER DRIVE: A starter drive that is mechanically engaged. When the engine starts, the overrunning clutch operates until the drive is mechanically disengaged.

OVERSTEER: The tendency for a car, when negotiating a corner, to turn more sharply than the driver intends.

P

PARALLEL: Straight lines that are the same distance apart from end to end.

PARALLEL CIRCUIT: An electrical circuit with two or more resistance units so wired as to permit current to flow through both units at the same time. Unlike the series circuit, the current in the parallel circuit does not have to pass through one unit to reach the other.

PARALLELOGRAM STEERING LINKAGE: A steering system utilizing two short tie rods connected to the steering arms and to a long center link. The link is supported on one end on an idler arm and the other end is attached directly to the pitman arm. The arrangement forms a parallelogram shape.

PAWL: A stud or pin that can be moved or pivoted into engagement with teeth cut on another part - such as the parking pawl on the automatic transmission that can be slid into contact with teeth on another part to lock the rear wheels.

PEEN: To flatten out the end of a rivet, etc., by pounding with the round end of a hammer head.

PENETRATING OIL: A special oil that is used to free rusted parts so that they can be removed.

PHILLIPS HEAD SCREW: A screw having a fairly deep cross slot instead of the single slot as used in conventional screws.

PINGING: A metallic rattling sound produced by the engine during heavy acceleration when the ignition timing is too far advanced for the grade of fuel being burned.

PINION CARRIER: That part of the rear axle assembly that supports and contains the pinion gear shaft.

PIPES: Exhaust system pipes.

PISTON: A round plug, open at one end, that slides up and down in the cylinder. It is attached to the connecting rod and when the fuel charge is fired, the piston will transfer the force of the explosion to the connecting rod and then on to the crankshaft.

PISTON HEAD: That portion of the piston above the top ring.

PISTON PIN or WRIST PIN: A steel pin that is passed through the piston. It is used as a base upon which to fasten the upper end of the connecting rod. It is round and is usually hollow.

PISTON RING: A split ring installed in a groove in the piston. The ring contacts the sides of the ring groove and also rubs against the cylinder wall, thus sealing the space between the piston and the wall.

Also, a ring designed to seal the burning fuel charge above the piston. Generally, there are two compression rings per piston and they are located in the two top ring grooves.

Also, a piston ring designed to scrape oil from the cylinder wall. The ring is of such a design as to allow the oil to pass through the ring and then through holes or slots in the groove. In this way, the oil is returned to the pan. There are many shapes and special designs used on oil control rings.

PISTON RING SIDE CLEARANCE: The space between the sides of the ring and the ring lands.

PITMAN ARM: A short lever arm splined to the steering gear cross shaft. The pitman arm transmits the steering force from the cross shaft to the steering linkage system.

PLATES (Battery): Thin sections of lead peroxide or porous lead. There are two kinds of plates - positive and negative. The plates are arranged in groups called elements in an alternate fashion. They are completely submerged in the electrolyte.

PLAY: Movement between two parts.

PLUG GAPPING: Adjusting the side electrode on a spark plug to provide the proper air gap between it and the center electrode.

POLARITY: The quality or condition inherent in a body that exhibits opposite properties or powers in opposite parts or directions.

POLARIZING (Generator): The process of sending a quick surge of current through the field windings of the generator in a direction that will cause the pole shoes to assume the correct polarity. This will insure that the generator will cause current to flow in the same direction as normal.

POLES: The positive and negative terminals in a cell or battery; the ends of a magnet (north and south).

POSITIVE TERMINAL: The terminal at which electrons enter a battery or a generator.

POWER STEERING: A steering system utilizing hydraulic pressure to increase the driver's turning effort. The pressure is utilized either in the gear box itself or in a hydraulic cylinder attached to the steering linkage.

PREHEATING: The application of some heat prior to the later application of more heat.

PRELOAD: The amount of load imposed on a bearing before actual loads are imposed. It is accomplished with an adjusting nut such as the spindle nut on front wheel bearings.

PRESSURE BLEEDER: A device that forces brake fluid, under pressure, into the master cylinder so that by opening the bleeder screws at the wheel cylinders, all air will be removed from the brake system.

PRESSURE CAP: A special cap for the radiator. It holds a predetermined amount of pressure on the water in the cooling system. This enables the water to run hotter without boiling.

PRESSURE RELIEF VALVE: A valve designed to open at a specific pressure. This will prevent pressures in the system from exceeding certain limits.

PRIMARY: The inducing current to the coil windings or capacitor that is the source of the high tension secondary voltage in an ignition system.

PRIMARY, FORWARD or LEADING BRAKE SHOE: The brake shoe that is installed facing the front of the car. It will be a self-energizing shoe.

PROGRESSIVE LINKAGE: Carburetor linkage designed to open the throttle valves of multiple carburetors. It opens one to start with and when a certain opening point is reached, it will start to open the others.

PROPELLER SHAFT: The shaft connecting the transmission output shaft to the differential pinion shaft.

PULL: The tendency of a vehicle to pull to the right or left.

PULSATION DAMPER: A device used to smooth out the pulsations or surges of fuel from the fuel pump to the carburetor.

PUMPING THE GAS PEDAL: Forcing the accelerator up and down in an endeavor to provide extra gasoline to the cylinders. This is often the cause of flooding.

PUSH ROD: The rod that connects the valve lifter to one end of the rocker arm. Used on valve-in-head installations.

R

RACK AND PINION GEAR BOX (Steering): A type of steering gear utilizing a pinion gear on the end of the steering shaft. The pinion engages a long rack (bar with a row of teeth cut along one edge). The rack is connected directly to the steering arms via rods.

RADIAL: Moving straight out from the center.

RADIUS: The distance from the center of rotation to the arc, or circumference of the circle made by the rotation.

REAR AXLE: The drive element or shaft between the differential side gear and the wheel.

REBOUND: An expansion of a suspension spring after it has been compressed as the result of jounce.

RED LINE: Top recommended engine rpm. If a tachometer is used, it will have a mark (red line) indicating maximum rpm.

REFRIGERANT: The liquid (Freon-12) used in refrigeration systems to remove heat from the evaporator coils and carry it to the condenser.

REGULATOR (Gas or liquid): A device to reduce and control pressure.

RELAY: An electromagnetic switching device using low current to open or close a high current circuit.

RESISTANCE: That property of an electrical circuit that tends to prevent or reduce the flow of current.

RESISTOR: A device installed in an electrical circuit to permit a predetermined current to flow with a given voltage applied.

RESISTOR SPARK PLUG: A spark plug containing a resistor designed to shorten both the capacitive and inductive phases of the spark. This will suppress radio interference and lengthen electrode life.

RESONATOR: A small muffler-like device that is placed into the exhaust system near the end of the tailpipe. It is used to provide additional silencing of the exhaust.

RETAINER: A device to hold parts together.

RETARD (Ignition timing): To set the ignition timing so that a spark occurs later or less degrees before TDC.

REVERSE FLUSH: Cleaning the cooling system by pumping a powerful cleaning agent through the system in a direction opposite to that of normal flow.

REVERSE IDLER GEAR: A gear used in the transmission to produce a reverse rotation of the transmission output shaft.

RIDING THE CLUTCH: Riding the clutch refers to the driver resting his foot on the clutch pedal while the car is being driven.

RING GEAR: The large gear that is attached to the differential carrier.

RING GROOVES: The grooves cut into the piston to accept the rings.

RING JOB: Reconditioning the cylinders and installing new rings.

RIVET: A metal pin used to hold two objects together. One end of the pin has a head and the other end must be 'set' or peened over.

ROCKER ARM: An arm used to direct the upward motion of the push rod into a downward or opening motion of the valve stem. Used in overhead valve installations.

ROCKER ARM SHAFT: The shaft upon which the rocker arms are mounted.

ROCKER PANEL: That section of the car body between the front and rear fenders and beneath the doors.

ROLLER CLUTCH: A clutch utilizing a series of rollers placed in ramps that will provide drive power in one direction but will slip or 'free-wheel' in the other direction.

ROLLER TAPPETS or LIFTERS: Valve lifters that have a roller placed on the end contacting the camshaft. This is done to reduce friction between the lobe and lifter. They are generally used when special camshafts and high tension valve springs have been installed.

ROTOR (Distributor): A cap-like unit placed on the end of the distributor shaft. It is in constant contact with the distributor cap central terminal and as it turns, it will conduct the secondary voltage to one of the outer terminals.

RUN-OUT (Radial): Out of roundness of a wheel or other circular part.

S

SAFETY FACTOR: Providing strength beyond that needed, as an extra margin of insurance against part failure.

SAFETY HUB: A device that is installed on the rear axle to prevent the wheels leaving the car in the event of a broken axle.

SAFETY VALVE: A valve designed to open and relieve the pressure within a container when container pressure exceeds a predetermined level.

SCALE (Cooling system): The accumulation of rust and minerals within the cooling system.

SCORE: A scratch or groove on a finished surface.

SCREW EXTRACTOR: A device used to remove broken bolts and screws from holes.

SCUFFING: Sliding a tire on the road surface.

SEALED BEAM HEADLIGHT: A headlight lamp in which the lens, reflector and filament are fused together to form a single unit.

SEALED BEARING: A bearing that has been lubricated at the factory and then sealed. It cannot be lubricated during service.

SECONDARY CIRCUIT (Ignition system): The high voltage part of the ignition system.

SECONDARY, REVERSE, or TRAILING BRAKE SHOE: The brake shoe that is installed facing the rear of the car.

SELF-ENERGIZING BRAKE SHOE: A brake shoe (sometimes both shoes) that when applied develops a wedging action that actually assists or boosts the braking force applied by the wheel cylinder.

SERIES CIRCUIT: A circuit with two or more resistance units so wired that the current must pass through one unit before reaching the other.

SERVO ACTION: Brakes so constructed as to have one end of the primary shoe bearing against the end of the secondary shoe. When the brakes are applied, the primary shoe attempts to move in the direction of the rotating drum and in so doing applies force to the secondary shoe. This servo action makes less brake pedal pressure necessary and is widely used in brake construction.

SHACKLE: A swinging support by which one end of a leaf spring is attached to the car frame.

SHIFT POINT: This refers to the point, either in engine rpm or road speed, at which the transmission should be shifted to the next gear.

SHIM: A spacer to adjust and maintain the distance between two parts.

SHOCK ABSORBER: A hydraulic device to dampen or stabilize the up and down movement of the car frame by controlling the compression and rebound of the springs.

SHORT CIRCUIT: A direct grounding of a circuit.

SHUNT WINDING: A wire coil forming an alternate or bypass circuit through which the current may flow.

SIDE SWAY: A force causing a lean one way and then the other.

SINGLE BARREL, DOUBLE BARREL AND FOUR BARREL CARBURETORS: This refers to the number of throttle openings or barrels from the carburetor to the intake manifold.

SKID: A tire sliding on the road surface.

SKIRTS: A cover for the rear fender cutout.

SLIP JOINT: A joint that will transfer driving torque from one shaft to another while allowing longitudinal movement between the two shafts.

SLUDGE: Black, mushy deposits throughout the interior of the engine. Caused by a mixture of dust, oil and water being whipped together by the moving parts.

SOLDERING: Joining two pieces of metal together with a lead-tin mixture. Both pieces of metal must be heated to insure proper adhesion of the melted solder.

SOLENOID: A tubular coil containing a magnetic core that moves when the coil is energized.

SPARK: The bridging or 'jumping' of a gap between two electrodes by a current of electricity.

SPARK ADVANCE: Causing the spark plug to fire earlier by altering the position of the distributor breaker points in relation to the distributor shaft.

SPARK PLUG: A device containing two electrodes across which electricity jumps to produce a spark to fire the fuel charge.

SPECIFIC GRAVITY: The ratio of the weight of any volume of a liquid compared to an equal volume of water.

SPIDER GEARS: Small gears mounted on a shaft pinned to the differential case. They mesh with and drive the axle and gears.

SPINDLE: A shaft or pin around which another part rotates.

SPIRAL BEVEL GEAR: A ring and pinion setup widely used in automobile differentials. The teeth of both the ring and the pinion are tapered and are cut on a spiral so that they are at an angle to the centerline of the pinion shaft.

SPLINED: Sized grooves on a shaft and in a hole that match to prevent torque slippage.

SPLIT MANIFOLD: An exhaust manifold that has a baffle placed near its center. An exhaust pipe leads out of each half.

SPRING: An elastic device that yields under stress or pressure but returns to its original state or position when the stress or pressure is removed.

SPRING BOOSTER: A device used to 'beef' up sagged springs or to increase the load capacity of standard springs.

SPRING LOADED: A device held in place or under pressure by a spring or springs.

SPRING STEEL: A heat-treated steel having the ability to stand a great amount of deflection and yet return to its original shape or position.

SPRING WINDUP: The curved shape assumed by the rear leaf springs during acceleration or braking.

SPRUNG WEIGHT: This refers to the weight of all the parts of the car that are supported by the suspension system.

SPUR GEAR: A gear on which the teeth are cut parallel to the shaft.

STABILIZER BAR: A torsional bar and linkage used to eliminate sway and decrease the side rolling tendency of the car frame and body, often called an anti-sway bar.

STATIC BALANCE: Balance at rest, or still balance. It is the equal distribution of weight of the wheel and tire around the axis of rotation such that the wheel assembly has no tendency to rotate by itself regardless of its position.

STATIC PRESSURE (Brakes): A certain amount of pressure that always exists in the brakes lines - even with the brake pedal released. Static pressure is maintained by a check valve.

STATOR: The stationary winding of the alternator. An armature in a DC generator.

STEERING ARMS: Arms that are either bolted to or forged as an integral part of the steering knuckles. They transmit the steering force from the tie rods to the knuckles, thus causing the wheels to pivot.

STEERING GEAR: A device consisting of a worm and gear sector or cross shaft and roller that transmits the driver's effort with increased leverage to the steering linkage to guide the car on its course.

STEERING GEOMETRY: A term sometimes used to describe the various angles assumed by the components making up the front wheel turning arrangement, camber, caster, toe-in, etc.

Also used to describe the related angles assumed by the front wheels when the car is negotiating a curve.

STEERING KNUCKLE: The inner portion of the spindle that is affixed to and pivots on upper and lower ball joints.

STEERING LINKAGE: That system of links, rods or tubes and arms or levers connected together to transmit the force or motion of the steering gear to the front wheels.

STICK SHIFT: This refers to a transmission that is shifted manually through the use of various forms of linkage. Often refers to the upright gear shift stick that protrudes through the floor.

STROKE: The distance the piston moves when traveling from TDC to BDC.

STUD: A metal rod with threads on both ends.

SWING AXLE: An independent rear suspension system in which each driving wheel can move up or down independently of the other. The differential unit is bolted to the frame and various forms of linkage are used to mount the wheels. Drive axles utilizing one or more universal joints connect the differential to the drive wheels.

SWITCH: A device used to open, close or redirect the current in an electrical circuit.

SYNCHRO-MESH TRANSMISSION: A transmission using a device (synchro-mesh) that synchronizes the speeds of gears that are being shifted together. This prevents "gear grinding." Some transmissions use a synchro-mesh on all shifts, while others synchronize second and high gear shifts.

SYNCHRONIZE: To bring about a timing that will cause two or more events to occur simultaneously—for example, plug firing when the piston is in the correct position, the speed of two shafts being the same, a valve opening when the piston is in the correct position, etc.

T

TACHOMETER: A device used to indicate the speed of the engine in rpm.

TANDEM: One directly in front of the other and working together.

TAP: To cut threads in a hole or can be used to indicate the fluted tool used to cut the threads.

TAPERED ROLLER BEARING (Antifriction): A bearing utilizing a series of tapered, hardened steel rollers operating between an outer and inner hardened steel race.

TDC: Top dead center.

TERMINAL: A connecting point in an electric circuit. When referring to the battery, it would indicate the two battery posts.

TERMINAL VOLTAGE: Voltage that is given off at the battery terminal.

THERMAL EFFICIENCY: The percentage of the heat developed in the burning fuel charge that is actually used to develop power determines thermal efficiency. Efficiency will vary according to engine design and use. If an engine utilizes a great deal of the heat to produce power, its thermal efficiency would be high.

THERMOSTAT: A temperature sensitive device used in the cooling system to control the flow of coolant in relation to the temperature.

THROTTLE VALVE: A valve in the carburetor that is used to control the amount of fuel mixture that reaches the cylinders.

THROWING A ROD: When an engine has thrown a connecting rod from the crankshaft. Major damage is usually incurred.

THRUST BEARING: A bearing designed to resist side pressure.

THRUST WASHER: A bronze or a hardened steel washer placed between two moving parts. The washer prevents longitudinal movement and provides a bearing surface for the thrust surfaces of the parts.

TIE RODS: In the steering system, the rods that link the center link to the steering arms.

TIMING CHAIN: A drive chain that operates the camshaft by engaging sprockets on the camshaft and crankshaft.

TIMING GEARS: Both the gear attached to the camshaft and the gear on the crankshaft. They provide a means of driving the camshaft.

TIMING LIGHT: A stroboscope unit that is connected to the secondary circuit to produce flashes of light in unison with the firing of a specific spark plug. By directing these flashes of light on the whirling timing marks, the marks appear to stand still. By adjusting the distributor, the timing marks may be properly aligned, thus setting the timing.

TIMING MARKS (Ignition): Marks, usually located on the vibration damper, used to synchronize the ignition system so that the plugs will fire at the precise time.

TIRE: The casing and tube assembled on a car wheel to provide pneumatically cushioned contact and traction with the road.

TIRE BEAD: That portion of the tire that bears against the rim flange. The bead has a number of turns of steel wire in it to provide great strength.

TIRE CASING: The main body of the tire exclusive of the tread.

TIRE PLIES: The layers of nylon, rayon, etc., that are used to form the casing. Most car tires are four ply. Four ply indicates four layers of cloth or plies.

TIRE ROTATION: Moving the front tires to the rear and the rear to the front to equalize any wear irregularities.

TIRE SIDEWALL: That portion of the tire between the tread and the bead.

TIRE TREAD: That part of the tire that contacts the road.

TOE-IN: The turning in of the front wheels; wheels are closer together at the front than at the back of the wheels.

TOE-OUT ON TURNS: When the car negotiates a curve, the inner wheel turns more sharply; while the wheels remain in this position a condition of toe-out exists.

TORQUE: Turning or twisting effort measured in foot-pounds or inch-pounds.

TORQUE MULTIPLICATION (Automatic transmission): Increasing engine torque through the use of a converter.

TORQUE WRENCH: A special wrench that indicates the amount of torque being applied to a nut or bolt.

TORSIONAL VIBRATION: A twisting and untwisting action developed in a shaft caused by intermittent applications of power or load.

TORSION BAR: A long spring steel rod attached in such a way that one end is anchored while the other is free to twist. If an arm is attached at right angles to the free end, any movement of the arm will cause the torsion bar to twist. The bar's resistance to twisting provides a spring action. The torsion bar replaces both coil and leaf springs in some suspension systems.

TORSION BAR SPRING: A long, straight bar fastened to the frame at one end and to a control arm at the other. Spring action is produced by the twisting of the bar.

TORSION BAR SUSPENSION: A suspension system that uses torsion bars in place of the leaf or coil springs.

TRACK: The distance between the front wheels or the distance between the rear wheels. They are not always the same.

TRACKING: The following of the rear wheels directly behind or in the tracks of the front wheels.

TRANSISTOR IGNITION: Form of ignition system that utilizes transistors and a special coil. The conventional distributor and point setup is used. With the transistor unit, the voltage remains constant, thus permitting high engine rpm without the resultant engine "miss." Point life is greatly extended as the transistor system passes a very small amount of current through the points.

TRANSMISSION: A device that uses gearing or torque conversion to effect a change in the ratio between engine rpm and driving wheel rpm. When engine rpm goes up in relation to wheel rpm, more torque but less speed is produced. A reduction in engine rpm in relation to wheel rpm produces a higher road speed but delivers less torque to the driving wheels.

TRANSMISSION - Automatic: A transmission that automatically effects gear changes to meet varying road and load conditions. Gear changing is done through a series of oil-operated clutches and bands.

TRANSMISSION - Standard or Manual: A transmission that must be shifted manually to effect a change in gearing.

TRANSVERSE LEAF SPRING: A leaf spring that is mounted so that it is at right angles to the length of the car.

TUBE CUTTER: A tool used to cut tubing by passing a sharp wheel around and around the tube.

TUNE-UP: The process of checking, repairing and adjusting the carburetor, spark plugs, points, belts and timing to obtain the maximum performance from the engine.

TURBINE: A wheel upon which a series of angled vanes are affixed so that a moving column of air or liquid will impart a turning motion to the wheel.

TURBINE ENGINE: An engine that utilizes burning gases to spin a turbine, or series of turbines, as a means of propelling the car.

TURNING RADIUS: Difference in angles between the two front wheels and the car frame during turns. The inner wheel turns out or toes-out more.

TWIST DRILL: A metal cutting drill with spiral flutes (grooves) to permit the exit of chips while cutting.

U

UNDERCOATING: The soft deadening material sprayed on the underside of the car, under the hood, trunk lid, etc.

UNDERSTEER: The tendency of a moving vehicle to maintain a straight-ahead line while the front wheels are being turned in either direction. Commonly known as pushing or plowing.

UNIT BODY: A car body in which the body itself acts as the frame.

UNIVERSAL JOINT: A flexible joint that will permit changes in the driving angle between the driving and the driven shaft.

V

VACUUM: An enclosed area in which the air pressure is below that of the surrounding atmospheric pressure.

VACUUM ADVANCE (Distributor): A unit designed to advance and retard the ignition timing through the action of engine vacuum working on a diaphragm.

VACUUM GAUGE: A gauge used to determine the amount of vacuum existing in a chamber.

VACUUM PUMP: A diaphragm type of pump used to produce a vacuum.

VACUUM RESERVOIR: A tank in which a vacuum exists. It is generally used to provide vacuum to a power brake installation in the event engine vacuum cannot be obtained. The tank will supply several brake applications before the vacuum is exhausted.

VACUUM RUN-OUT POINT: This refers to the point reached when a vacuum brake power piston has built up all the braking force it is capable of with the vacuum available.

VALVE: A device used to either open or close an opening. There are many different types.

VALVE FACE: The outer lower edge of the valve head. The face contacts the valve seat when the valve is closed.

VALVE GUIDE: The hole through which the stem of the poppet valve passes. It is designed to keep the valve in proper alignment. Some

guides are pressed into place; others are merely drilled in the block or in the head metal.

VALVE LIFTER or CAM FOLLOWER: The unit that contacts the end of the valve stem and the camshaft. The follower rides on the camshaft and when the cam lobes move it upward, it opens the valve.

VALVE OIL SEAL: A neoprene rubber ring that is placed in a groove in the valve stem to prevent excess oil entering the area between the stem and the guide.

VALVE SEAT: The area onto which the face of the poppet seats when closed. The two common angles for this seat are forty-five and thirty degrees.

VALVE SEAT INSERT: A hardened steel valve seat that may be removed and replaced.

VALVE SPRING: The coil spring used to keep the valves closed.

VALVE TAPPET: An adjusting screw to obtain the specified clearance at the end of the valve stem (tappet clearance). The screw may be in the top of the lifter or in the rocker arm. In the case of the ball joint rocker arm, the nut on the mounting stud acts in place of a tappet screw.

VALVE TIMING: Adjusting the position of the camshaft to the crankshaft so that the valves will open and close at the proper time.

VALVE TRAIN: The various parts making up the valve and its operating mechanism.

VANE: A thin plate that is affixed to a rotatable unit to either throw off air or liquid, or to receive the thrust imparted by moving air or liquid striking the vane. In the first case, it would be acting as a pump, and in the second case as a turbine.

VAPOR: The gaseous form of a liquid.

VAPORIZATION: Breaking the gasoline into fine particles and mixing it with the incoming air.

VAPOR LOCK: Boiling or vaporizing of the fuel in the lines from excess heat. The boiling will interfere with the movement of the fuel and in some cases will completely stop the flow.

VAPOR SEPARATOR: A device used on cars equipped with air conditioning to prevent vapor lock by feeding vapors back to the gas tank via a separate line.

VARIABLE PITCH STATOR: A stator that has vanes that may be adjusted to various angles, depending on load conditions. The vane adjustment will increase or decrease the efficiency of the stator.

VENTURI: That part of a tube, channel or pipe that is tapered to form a smaller or constricted area. A liquid or a gas moving through this constricted area will speed up and as it passes the narrowest point, a partial vacuum will be formed. The taper facing the flow of air is much steeper than the taper facing away from the flow of air. The venturi principle is used in the carburetor.

VIBRATION DAMPER: A round weighted device attached to the front of the crankshaft to minimize the torsional vibration.

VISCOMETER: A device used to determine the viscosity of a given sample of oil. The oil is heated to a specific temperature and then allowed to flow through a set orifice. The length of time required for a certain amount to flow determines the oil's viscosity.

VISCOSITY: A measure of an oil's ability to pour.

VISCOSITY INDEX: A measure of an oil's ability to resist changes in viscosity when heated.

VOLT: A unit of measurement of electrical pressure.

VOLTAGE: The electrical pressure that causes current flow in a circuit.

VOLTAGE DROP: The loss of electrical pressure that is caused by resistance in a circuit.

VOLTMETER: An instrument used to measure the voltage in a given circuit (in volts).

VOLUME: The measurement—in cubic inches, cubic feet, etc.—of the amount of space within a certain object or area.

VOLUMETRIC EFFICIENCY: A comparison between the actual volume of fuel mixture drawn in on the intake stroke and what would be drawn in if the cylinder were to be completely filled.

W

WATER JACKET: The area around the cylinder and valves that is left hollow so that water may be admitted for cooling.

WATT: The unit for measuring electrical power or "work." One watt is the product of one ampere multiplied by one volt. (W = A x V)

WHEEL ALIGNER: A device used to check camber, caster and toe-in.

WHEEL ALIGNMENT: The mechanics of properly adjusting all the factors of the front and rear wheels so that the car will steer a true course with the least effort, reducing tire wear to a minimum.

WHEEL BALANCER: A machine used to check the wheel and tire assembly for static and dynamic balance.

WHEELBASE: The distance between the center of the front wheels and the center of the rear wheels.

WHEEL CYLINDER: That part of the hydraulic brake system that receives pressure from the master cylinder and, in turn, applies the brake shoes to the drums.

WHEEL LUG or LUG BOLT: The bolts used to fasten the wheel to the hub.

WHEEL SPINDLE: The shaft extending from the front steering knuckle about which the front wheel rotates.

WHEEL TRAMP: Tendency for the wheel to move up and down so it repeatedly bears hard, or tramps, on the pavement. Sometimes called high-speed shimmy.

WORM GEAR: Type of gear on the lower end of the steering shaft.